THE 21ST CENTURY JOURNALISM HANDBOOK

Tim Holmes
Sara Hadwin
Glyn Mottershead

THE 21ST CENTURY JOURNALISM HANDBOOK

ESSENTIAL SKILLS FOR THE MODERN JOURNALIST

PEARSON

Harlow, England • London • New York • Boston • San Francisco • Toronto • Sydney • Auckland • Singapore • Hong Kong
Tokyo • Seoul • Taipei • New Delhi • Cape Town • São Paulo • Mexico City • Madrid • Amsterdam • Munich • Paris • Milan

Pearson Education Limited
Edinburgh Gate
Harlow
Essex CM20 2JE
England

and Associated Companies throughout the world

Visit us on the World Wide Web at:
www.pearson.com/uk

First published 2013

ISBN 978-1-4058-4632-5

British Library Cataloguing-in-Publication Data
A catalogue record for this book is available from the British Library

Library of Congress Cataloguing-in-Publication Data
A catalog record for this book is available from the Library of Congress

10 9 8 7 6 5 4 3 2 1
16 15 14 13 12

Typeset in 10/12.5pt Minion by 35
Printed in Malaysia (CTP-VVP)

CONTENTS

Companion Website

For open-access **student resources** specifically written
to complement this textbook and support your learning,
please visit **www.pearsoned.co.uk/holmesetal**

ON THE
WEBSITE

INTRODUCTION

21st Century Journalism – read all about it!

Marie Colvin, Remi Ochlik, Rami al-Sayed, Anas al-Tarsha . . .

You may recognise these as the names of journalists who died in pursuit of a story to share across the globe. The four were all killed in Syria – the most deadly country in the world for journalists in early 2012, followed by Brazil, Indonesia and Somalia.[1]

No-one wants any journalist to have to make that ultimate sacrifice. We all want a world where journalists – and civilians – are safe from wars, narco gangs and corrupt political and business regimes. We all need to work harder to assess carefully and reduce the risks journalists face not just in war zones but in day-to-day reporting.

But even the most timid of us should have some sense of what drives a journalist to court danger if that's what it takes. The most humble fellow journalist will understand why, when everyone else flees from disaster, we run – or at least edge cautiously – towards it.

The best journalists want to know what is going on – and are desperate to share it with the world. That combination of finding and imparting information is at the heart of what we do.

For journalists the world is infinitely fascinating, filled with intriguing people and places. Some pursue their thirst for information gathering and storytelling on the barricades of the Arab Spring; others inspire an audience to share a passion for a football team or hobby.

We are all driven by the power of sharing information. The exercise of freedom of expression is central to all human development but it is particularly important in a democracy.

Journalism collectively provides one of the essential checks and balances on the powers-that-be. Pushing the boundaries of what the public has a right to know is key to the legitimacy of a representative democracy.

Journalists help people to function as citizens by making sense of the world they live in from what's happening down their street to the machinations of global warming.

Dealing with the unexpected is part of the thrill of journalism – yet journalists themselves can be remarkably averse to change. The dynamism in society that we relish reporting can be unnervingly challenging within our own industry.

Text-based media has been through many transitions – as you will see in Chapter One, but the pace and scope of the changes in the 21st century are particularly daunting. There will be winners and losers in such transformation. The dinosaurs will become extinct but going with the flow of every new technical development is not necessarily the answer either. When so much is in flux, we need to judge carefully how to preserve the essentials of our role within a shifting world. How do we combine the best of the past, present and future to help journalism thrive?

That is the challenge we rise to in this text. One of the first tasks is for you as the reader to appreciate just how radical the changes of the 21st century are proving. We need you to use this text as a platform from which you can track the dynamics of journalism; update and build on your knowledge and understanding. The connections you make will be the first step on your way to becoming a 21st century networked journalist.

---

[1] International News Safety Institute, **http://www.newssafety.org/casualties.php**

Throughout the chapters you will confront a whole raft of 21st century developments mainly driven by the spread of digital, and particularly mobile, media but also by broader social and economic change. Journalists face:

- new ways of information gathering
- new ways of reaching an audience
- new expectations of what readers want and need
- new legislation and regulation
- new relationships with readers
- new ways of making it pay

That's a long list – especially for anyone who has to make the leap from 20th century to 21st century journalism. Those just starting out should find it easier to see the opportunities rather than the threats emerging from the new. Exploiting the potential of social media, data-driven journalism and mobile platforms should come naturally. How audiences access news and other journalism is changing rapidly with a surge in the 140-character microblog alongside a continuing appetite for long-form journalism

As we go to press, major developments are pending in the legal and regulatory framework in which 21st century journalists must operate. More journalists and media executives are to be prosecuted in the wake of the News of the World phone hacking scandal. Mainstream print media are set to face stricter regulation as an outcome of the ensuing Leveson inquiry, which also examines the broader relationship between police, politicians and the media. Much will depend on his ultimate recommendations, expected late 2012.

A new Defamation Bill is also in play which may make our libel laws marginally less draconian. The 2012 revised version puts new responsibilities on website owners, as media law attempts to cope with the digital free-for-all of bloggers and Tweeters. Technically the law applies to all material put into the public domain but the 'one-size-fits-all' approach is proving difficult to sustain.

Similarly, the explosion of digital communication is testing our laws of copyright, privacy and general limits of decency. Check out the controversies around the collapse of Bolton footballer Fabrice Muamba, the prosecution of a racist Tweeter and the contrast between the coverage by mainstream and informal media.

The business models of journalism are in massive flux between print and digital. Audiences are switching platform faster than revenues which are being diverted to transmission mechanisms and platform devices away from content providers. The expectation of 'free' content has undermined cover-price revenues for legacy media organisations struggling to generate sufficient new revenue streams.

Much has changed – and is still changing all about us – but some fundamentals remain.

As we see in the chapters to follow, journalists still have a job to do. The specific challenges change over time but our task has never been easy.

Audience remains at the forefront of what we do. We must bear witness but also dig beneath the surface and verify information. We must engage our audience with what they want and need to know. We must endeavour, in the words of the Committee for Concerned Journalists, to make the significant interesting.

So, as journalists and the authors of this textbook, we are driven by the wants and needs of an audience of would-be journalists. We share what we know – helping you to learn from our expertise and study but also from our past mistakes. We hope to inspire you to develop your skills and conjure with the issues of the day, both those directly affecting journalists and the challenges facing the wider world.

The aim of much vocationally-based education is the development of a reflective practitioner – what we might call a 'thinking' journalist. A 21st Century journalist needs to develop the skills for the job but also an understanding of the potential contribution of journalism to individual readers, to a democratic society and to freedom of speech.

Regular features in each chapter are designed to support your learning and take you beyond the confines of our single text.

Putting it into practice

Scenarios set up an activity through which you can apply your learning to real-world challenges facing journalists

A Closer Look

Each chapter opens with a case study but we also take time out within the text to examine particular aspects of an issue in specific detail.

Section and chapter summaries

Chapter summaries are provided but we also offer pit-stop 'remember' lists along the way to help consolidate your learning.

Thinking it Through

Towards the end of each chapter we examine some of the key issues and controversies arising within the relevant area of practice. We explore the debate but leave you to conjure with some of the dilemmas faced by individual journalists and by the industry. As in life, you have to come up with some of the answers for yourself.

Recommended reading

Annotated lists are designed to help you explore the wider literature on our topics, much of it by practitioners.

Recommended weblinks

Crucial sites are chosen to help you to track changes and challenges across the industry. These include popular blogs hosting debates on journalism and more formal sites linking you to the wider world of law, statistics and other specialist areas. These are a must in such a dynamic environment to help you keep up-to-date.

21st Century Journalism Handbook – digital support

We are also offering readers a back-up website (**www.pearsoned.co.uk/holmesetal**) to accompany the publication focussed on updates and links. This will help you to follow advice given throughout the book to keep abreast of the industry you hope to join. The three authors will point you in the direction of key developments we feel you most need to know about.

Information is power so please be empowered by this book. Get out there and be a journalist. Your audience awaits.

ACKNOWLEDGEMENTS

Tim Holmes

My sincere thanks to all those who have helped shape my thinking about the hows and whys of journalism in the 21st century. Of the many who have contributed, from the publishing industry I must pick out Nick Brett, MD of the BBC Magazines unit, Mel Nichols, former Editorial Director of Haymarket, and Loraine Davies, Director of the PTC; among the colleagues who provide daily food for thought, Jane Bentley has made sure the course we run never rests on its laurels; and above all, the many, many students whom I have taught – and learned from – over my 17 years at Cardiff University's School of Journalism, Media and Cultural Studies.

Sara Hadwin

I would like to thank all my students for inspiring me to articulate notions of what it means to be the best journalist you can be, and to develop my thinking and practice for a new generation. Many colleagues, editors, media lawyers and even proprietors have contributed too over the years. The greatest influence has to be my late father Arnold who counted me among the umpteen 'wet behind the ears' youngsters he 'knocked into shape' as reporters. Through word and deed he demonstrated the enduring significance of good journalism.

Glyn Mottershead

I would like to thank my colleagues and former students from both Highbury College, Portsmouth, and Cardiff University for their advice, guidance and questions over the years – and obviously Tim Holmes and Sara Hadwin.

An 'I couldn't have done it without you' to the teams at the newspaper groups I've worked at over the years and to every journalist who has ever shared a story over a coffee or beer.

A big 'thank you' to those who offered help, support and advice on key issues, some of whom became interviewees: Neil McDonald, Alison Gow, Tim Hart, Paul Bradshaw, Garrett Goodman, Ciaran Jones, Chris Broom, Sarah Hartley, Joanna Geary, Lee Swettenham, Rory Cellan-Jones, Phil Trippenbach, Ed Walker, Hannah Waldram, Dr Kelly Page, Andy Dickinson, Adam Tinworth, Kevin Anderson, Suw Charman-Anderson, Murray Dick, Tony Hirst, Nicola Hughes, Dan Kerins, Aron Pilhofer, David Donald and Tony O'Shaughnessy.

It would be remiss of me not to say 'thanks' to the many people who share with me on social networks – you are too many to name but you inspire me to question my practice every day, and for that you have my heartfelt respect.

And, of course, my family for giving me the space to write, support, encouragement and countless cups of tea.

PUBLISHER'S ACKNOWLEDGEMENTS

The publishers would like to thank the anonymous panel of reviewers for their support with the development of the manuscript.

The publishers would further like to thank the authors for the dedication, effort and skill they demonstrated in producing this book.

We are grateful to the following for permission to reproduce copyright material:

Figures

Page 87 from Infographic by Anthony Huggins (**http://www.thebeautifulgame.org.uk**), created for Delayed Gratification magazine (**www.dgquarterly.com**); Figure 4.2 from Carbon emissions, **http://www.ft.com/cms/s/0/d0940004-c7d5-11de-8ba8-00144feab49a.html#axzz1VNNH6Mnh**, © The Financial Times Limited. All Rights Reserved.

Screenshots

Screenshot 6.1 from Google.com, Google; Screenshot 8.3 from **twitter.com**, Dan Roberts

Text

Chapter 3 extract from Are reporters reporters doomed: Citizen journalism is here to stay. But in the rush to embrace new media we risk destroying the soul of traditional reporting. David Leigh, 12 November 2007, The Guardian: Copyright Guardian News & Media Ltd 2007.

Chapter 6 extract from Wandsworth Council report p4 of 8 **http://www.wandsworth.gov.uk/download/3752/fairer_charging_consultation**.

In some instances we have been unable to trace the owners of copyright material, and we would appreciate any information that would enable us to do so.

The publisher would like to thank the following for their kind permission to reproduce their photographs:

(Key: b-bottom; c-centre; l-left; r-right; t-top)

Alamy Images: CJG Technology 47, David T Green 41, Neil Fraser 34, Oleksiy Maksymenko 27, Robert Daly 50, Uk Stock Images Ltd 43; **Crack Magazine/www.youlovecrack.com/UK Arts & Music Magazine:** James Stopforth 278; **Fotolia.com:** WaveBreakMediaMicro 36; **Getty Images:** 57, 177; **John Frost Historical Newspapers:** 172; **Portsmouth News:** 27b; **Press Association Images:** Steven Day 215; **Western Mail:** 160, 161t, 161bl, 161br

All other images © Pearson Education

Every effort has been made to trace the copyright holders and we apologise in advance for any unintentional omissions. We would be pleased to insert the appropriate acknowledgement in any subsequent edition of this publication.

CHAPTER ONE
STRUCTURE OF THE INDUSTRY

This chapter will cover:

- The development of print media
- Business structures of print media companies
- An overview of regulatory and legal frameworks governing print media companies
- Current problems facing print media
- Journalism training and education

Case study 1.1

ON 2 February 2011 News Corporation and Apple Computer launched a collaborative venture. Rupert Murdoch, the foremost media mogul of the late 20th century, and Steve Jobs, boss of the coolest tech company on the planet, mounted the stage at New York's Guggenheim museum to announce *The Daily*, an iPad-only news app.

Reaction varied from 'It could easily become a best friend to commuters, airline travelers, even people out for a stroll' (Tim Molloy in The Wrap[1]), through 'While the initial results are impressive enough to justify the hype, they fall short of what Steve Jobs has called "redefining the news experience"' (Paul Burkey for McPheters & Co[2]), to '*The Daily* represents a complete failure of imagination' (Shane Richmond in the *Daily Telegraph*[3]).

Clearly, whatever *The Daily* was, it was neither the saviour of the newspaper industry nor the future of what had been print journalism (not that anyone was making those exact claims). This was unfortunate as by February 2011 print journalism generally and the newspaper industry in particular desperately needed both a saviour and a secure future.

The reasons for such desperation were easy to find. Anyone looking at the first page of a research paper published in 2008 by the Organisation for Economic Co-operation and Development (OECD) – a body whose mission it is to promote policies that will improve the economic and social well-being of people around the world – would have found the following:

- After very profitable years, newspaper publishers in most OECD countries face declining advertising revenues, titles and circulation. The economic crisis has amplified this downward development.
- About 20 out of 30 OECD countries face declining newspaper readership, with significant decreases in some OECD countries. Newspaper readership is usually lower among younger people who tend to attribute less importance to print media.

- The regional and local press are particularly affected and 2009 is the worst year for OECD newspapers, with the largest declines in the United States, the United Kingdom, Greece, Italy, Canada and Spain.
- Employment losses in the newspaper industry have intensified since 2008 particularly in countries such as the United States, the United Kingdom, the Netherlands and Spain.[4]

Depressing as this may have been (for newspapers in Western economies at least; elsewhere in the world they were still thriving), it was not exactly unexpected since in 2007 a National Readership Survey (NRS) report commissioned by the House of Lords communications committee[5] found that newspaper readership had declined by 5 million over 15 years.

What *was* shocking about this catalogue of decline was the speed with which it had happened. After all, newspapers had been in existence for over 500 years, had been commercially successful for 300 years and had been a significantly profitable industrial sector for 150 years. Almost overnight, it seemed, print newspapers were toast.

Toast still capable of generating billions of dollars in turnover, it is true, but much less thickly buttered with profit. One indication of how good the good times had been can be found in traditional profit margins. For much of the 20th century the newspaper industry was expected to return over 20 per cent, and routinely did so, year after year. By comparison, a highly efficient volume car manufacturer such as Nissan or Toyota might achieve between 8 per cent and 10 per cent in a good year; in 2010 Sony – the giant Japanese electronics and entertainment conglomerate – achieved *minus* 1.38 per cent.[6]

A double shock then, comprised of a rapid slump and the confounding of expectations. How had print media reached this point?

INTRODUCTION

Karl Marx suggested (in *The Eighteenth Brumaire of Louis Bonaparte*, 1852) that history repeats itself first as tragedy, then as farce. To understand where the print media industries are going and which of those two options the destination will be, it is necessary to understand where they have come from. This is best done with a brief look at the aspects of their history and evolution that will allow informed discussion of their likely future development – and perhaps even survival.

We should also remember that print itself was once a highly controversial and massively disruptive new technology, with significant parallels to the ways digital media are seen today. Because print is so absolutely taken for granted now it is difficult to imagine it as something that threatened to turn the world upside down, but the analysis found in Elizabeth Eisenstein's classic *The Printing Press as an Agent of Change* is well worth reading for anyone who wants to be reminded of just how powerfully print has changed the world we live in:

- Political power – kings, emperors, despots, popes, archbishops, generals, all have feared the power of the press to influence the people they rule over (a power that was symbolically transferred first to television and now to the internet). One result of this has been the imposition of systems of regulation, to govern who is allowed to own what media and what they can and cannot show or tell. In many countries around the world there are still very strict restrictions

– covert, overt or both – on the ownership and operation of print media but a glance at the history of newspapers and magazines in the UK shows that our monarchs, clergy and politicians have not been shy about interfering with and exercising influence over the press.

- Financial power – with great power comes great responsibility, of course, and also the opportunity to make great fortunes. The history of print media is littered with examples of people who have profited greatly from their ownership – Lord Beaverbrook, Lord Northcliffe, Lord Rothermere, Robert Maxwell, Rupert Murdoch, Felix Dennis – but how did newspapers and magazines come to be such cash cows? And has this record of success actually damaged their ability to survive in the future?
- Social and cultural power – the shortlist of press magnates above contains three peers of the realm as well as a man who is courted by politicians of all persuasions who hope to gain his – and his newspapers' – approbation. Clearly this indicates a link between social power and the print media, but owners and their organisations also exercise significant cultural power, with the ability to affect, at least marginally, the attitudes of their readers. How is this governed? How *should* it be governed?

This chapter will show how historical development, financial structures and regulatory powers have defined and shaped the print media, what this might mean for their future and how best to prepare for a career in print media today.

KEY DEVELOPMENTS IN THE PRINT MEDIA

The print journalism industry in the UK has a history that stretches back to at least 1620, when the first English language 'coranto' was published (in Amsterdam). The 'coranto' was an early form of newspaper that contained summaries of stories about battles and other events of greater or lesser immediacy; the example mentioned was published in Holland because the laws of England were very restrictive about what could be printed in the country. Indeed, in 1632 the Star Chamber (which was essentially the king's private law court) outlawed the production of any kind of news publication.

The first milestone on the route to press freedom came a few years later when the government allowed news to be published under licence (1638) and then in 1641 King Charles I abolished the Star Chamber and ended the licensing of publications.

In 1665 the government of the day adopted the power of the press for its own ends by publishing the *Oxford Gazette*, widely recognised as the first proper newspaper in England. It soon changed its name to the *London Gazette* and is still published as an official record of government events.

Early in the 18th century the first daily newspaper arrived, the *Daily Courant*. Other 'firsts' include

- the first provincial daily (*Norwich Post*, 1701);
- the first evening paper (*Evening Post*, 1706);
- the first Sunday paper (*E. Johnson's British Gazette, and Sunday Monitor*, circa 1780).

Some familiar newspaper titles also have long histories. The *Times* first appeared in 1785 as the *Universal Daily Register* but changed its name after three years. The *Observer* appeared in 1791, the *Manchester Guardian* in 1821, the *Sunday Times* in 1822, the *News of the World* in 1843, the *Daily Telegraph* in 1855, the *Evening Standard* (London) in 1860, the *People* in 1881, the *Daily Mail* in 1896, the *Daily Express* in 1900 and the *Daily Mirror* in 1903.

Print magazines also go back a long way. Some scholars claim that *Gynaseum*, a collection of pictures of contemporary fashions published by Josse Amman in 1586, was the first fashion magazine – and thus the first specialist publication – while many others nominate the *Journal des Sçavans*, published by Dennis de Sallo in 1665, as the first science magazine. In the UK, the *Athenian Mercury* of 1690 provided a clear prototype for the type of magazine that answers readers' questions, while the *Ladies Mercury* of 1693 holds a good claim to be the first British women's magazine. The *Tatler* (1709) and *Spectator* (1711) added to the variety of magazines but the first product to actually use that word in its title was the *Gentleman's Magazine*, published from 1731 to 1914.

After that the number of magazines expanded as social and cultural changes brought more leisure, more hobbies, more clearly defined trades and professions and a richer, better educated population. Today there are over 8,000 magazines published in the UK, most of which are business-to-business (B2B) rather than consumer titles – this is the main division of types of magazine.

In the newspaper world there has historically been a clear division between local or regional papers and nationals. The Newspaper Society, which represents the interests of local/regional publishers, was founded in 1836, 70 years before the Newspaper Publishers Association was formed (1906) to represent the owners of national papers.

Although several newspaper businesses own both national and regional titles (for example, DMGT and Trinity Mirror) there is still a strong and distinct regional press sector (including companies such as Archant and Johnston Press) and there are still a number of very small publishers that produce a single paper for a single town.

Magazines and newspapers have co-existed within the same companies but the trend in the latter part of the 20th century was for companies to specialise in one print platform or the other. Recent developments in bringing the two forms back together again have had mixed results. News International, publisher of the *Sun*, set up a magazine division in 2007 and closed it again in 2008, while the Guardian Media Group (jointly with venture capitalist Apax Partners) acquired Emap's B2B magazines in 2008.

All forms of print journalism, whether magazines or newspapers, have been affected in various ways and to various degrees by the rise of the internet, and not just because of a generalised drift of display advertising to online platforms. The decline is easiest to diagnose in the local and regional press, where classified advertising, once the never-ending stream of gold that ran through the inner pages, has begun to dry up alarmingly.

Why? In the USA it is widely attributed to the rise of craigslist.org, which is easier to search and free, but craigslist.co.uk is a shadow of its American counterpart. It could be because eBay.co.uk is more fun and has an automated charging system or because FreeCycle is greener, free and is based on an ostensibly beneficial social idea. Perhaps there are many more car boot sales now. Perhaps newspaper classifieds are seen as too downmarket in an affluent age.

A CLOSER LOOK

A couple of personal anecdotes might help to explain this phenomenon. When I had a range-style oven to sell I put an advertisement in the local paper, naming the very reasonable price of £100 or offers. It attracted precisely one response, a young couple who came and looked, went away and never returned. I took some photographs and listed the oven on eBay. There were bids immediately – £100, £200, £300. It seemed to stall at £350 but a last-minute bidding war raised the final price to over £500. You have to ask – why would anyone choose to advertise in a local newspaper and risk a complete lack of interest when for about the same price it is possible to reach a national audience that is eager to buy?

> ▶ A CLOSER LOOK
>
> By contrast, when I had an old but still serviceable Belfast sink to dispose of I did not want to make any money from it so I turned to FreeCycle, the online community medium that acts like a giant exchange. It turned out that a lot of people wanted old Belfast sinks for all sorts of interesting purposes and I was able to select the person whose story I liked best.
>
> In both cases, the vendor – me – had far more control over the process than would have been possible by taking out a newspaper advertisement. And in the first instance, the river of gold flowed my way, rather than into the pockets of Northcliffe Media.

This of course raises some rather fundamental questions about what readers value in their print publications – how many people bought their local newspaper because of the classified advertising rather than because of the news? If so, what was wrong with the news that the readers did not value it? Was it not local enough? Too parochial? Just not interesting enough? Too far removed from the readers' real interests?

There is another aspect to this generalised decline too – most newspaper groups have become manufacturers. They own large industrial printing plants and large distribution organisations. They do not just provide content, they are vertically integrated commercial structures with capital tied up in manufacturing and distribution; if they have to manufacture less and distribute less that has a considerable effect on their financial structure – and on their profit margins.

Print-based B2B magazines have also been affected quite radically, but the demand from their readers for constantly updated news and analysis, along with archives of data that can be 'drilled', has meant that agile publishers have been able to develop digital alternatives and augment their brands with exhibitions or other face-to-face events. As Gary Hughes, former CEO of business publisher CMPi, told *Press Gazette*: 'We like markets rather than media formats. We like to be in markets and then work out how to make money in that market rather than say here are magazines and websites, [now] make money even though you have no face-to-face assets.'[7]

In fact 'events' – exhibitions, trade or consumer shows, special reader opportunities – are a key part of every successful magazine's business plan. Not only can they be extremely profitable in themselves, they allow direct interaction with both readers and advertisers, including the opportunity to gather data on both.

Print publishers have also started to harness the potential of digital communications, with innovations to be found in newspapers and magazines. The regional press has been among the most adventurous, with the *Liverpool Post*'s experiment in 'broadcasting' one complete working day a notable milestone. The paper's staff recorded what they did minute by minute on a live blog, they streamed video of news conferences from mobile phones, they invited readers to submit questions for reporters to ask their interviewees. In Greater Manchester, the *Manchester Evening News* uses social media tools to cover the local authority; Martin Belam reported from the news:rewired conference in May 2011 that the paper 'live blogs a lot of council meetings, bringing together tweets from councillors in the chamber, activists in the viewing gallery, their journalism and comments from the community'.[8] As ways of making the processes of publishing and of local democracy very much more transparent these are significant successes. Whether they provide any generally workable models for future development will only become apparent in years to come.

Among national newspapers, the *Telegraph* and the *Guardian* led the way in developing digital versions, though they took different routes. The *Guardian* became very reader-focused, encouraging interaction within the Comment Is Free section, while the *Telegraph* developed new working methods and moved into an expensively designed new working space to facilitate the convergence of print, online and broadband television. But despite these trailblazers, the *Daily Mail*, whose editor Paul Dacre once condemned the internet as 'bullshit.com', quickly became the most popular newspaper site when it released a revised and much enhanced version of *Mail Online* in April 2008.

Given that much of what has been dubbed Web2.0 centres around social and community-forming activities (sharing photographs or music, keeping up with friends, creating, uploading and watching video), magazines should have been in prime position to take advantage of the new digital opportunities. But, like the future in William Gibson's cyberspace (The future is already here – it's just not very evenly distributed)[9], online developments have been unevenly distributed. Some titles have augmented the print version with what amounts to a rolling news operation (featuring news limited to the magazine's specialism); some are broadcasting via a broadband tv channel; many are offering blogs and forums, or developing YouTube channels.

A few print publishers have decided to launch digital-only newspapers and magazines that have the 'look and feel' of a print title (i.e. there are 'pages' that 'turn') but which offer inter-activity on every page and run advertisements that automatically play video. Dennis Publishing was the first major magazine publisher to make a mark in this field, with the ladmag *Monkey*; since then it has launched a gadget mag (*iGizmo*) and a motoring mag.

And in February 2011, News Corporation launched *The Daily*, which brings us back to the need for a saviour.

remember

- Print has a long history and will not disappear overnight; text (writing) has an even longer history and will survive for as long as we need to read.
- Regulation will affect future development – but history shows that regulations will change as circumstances change.
- Good publishers will use the different strengths of print and digital media to complement each other.
- Journalists must be prepared to meet the challenges of new working environments and changing expectations from readers.

PUTTING IT INTO PRACTICE

The print press has a long and honourable history. Newspapers and magazines have helped to shape and even change society for the better. Journalists and the publications they work for have, over the years, campaigned for any number of good causes, reported on any number of bad practices and resisted legal and governmental pressure to conceal rather than reveal.

However, just like coal mining and steel making, the commercial and industrial processes of print publication are changing and this will have an effect on the way journalists do their jobs – and also on the jobs they are expected to do.

Knowing about the historical development of print media will help young journalists not only to appreciate the value of freedom of expression but also to understand the best aspects of the tradition they are working in – aspects it is too easy to overlook when journalism is brought into disrepute by shady practices such as unauthorised phone tapping and bribery of public officials.

Nevertheless, despite these fine traditions it is equally important to be open to change and flexible about learning news ways of doing things.

> ▶ PUTTING IT INTO PRACTICE

Activity: Read up about a successful press campaign – for example, W T Stead and the white slave trade[10] or the *Sunday Times* and thalidomide[11] – and sketch out how you could use digital media to support or strengthen the work.

THE COMMERCIAL DEVELOPMENT OF PRINT MEDIA

In June 2009 the Welsh Assembly government published a report on the Welsh newspaper industry.[12] In many ways it was typical of this kind of report, rehearsing well-known arguments about fewer readers, less advertising, the threat/challenge of the internet and the precarious financial position of publishers.

Also typical were the contributions from the National Union of Journalists (NUJ) and media academics. The union was concerned about redundancies and the effect that declining numbers in a newsroom would have on their ability to do a good job. The media academics repeated well-worn tropes about the pernicious effects of capitalist ownership on fourth estate journalism: 'newspapers have been treated as a milk cow by the major news corporations and the regional and local news companies,'[13] Dr Andy Williams of Cardiff University told the Assembly members.

In this instance it appeared that the representatives of the industry had a firmer grasp of both reality and the history of the newspaper industry:

> '**we are businesses and there is no public element in that sense. Everything has to fit the model of profitability. To date, it suited that model of profitability to get the most credible and quality based journalism that we could, because the more quality-based journalism that we get, the greater our audience and therefore the more advertising we get.'[14]**

The basic business model of the print press, whether newspaper or magazine, is very simple. On one side you have advertisers with goods and services to sell, on the other side you have readers in need (or want) of those goods and services, and in the middle you have the newspaper or magazine introducing one to the other and pocketing the introduction fees – advertising charges and cover price respectively.

This arrangement did not spring into being of its own accord as a fully perfected business model; advertising as a system required other developments, such as the industrial revolution – which both increased the production of consumer goods and the ability of consumers to purchase them – before it evolved and expanded. But the print media had never been *noli me tangere* instruments of public service and 'news' had been a commodity for as long as there were traders who could profit or lose by it. Shakespeare knew this in the 16th century – there is a news-mongering 'gossip report' in *The Merchant of Venice* (act 3, scene 1). Harris and Lee point out that by the 1700s most papers were owned by printers and 'Throughout the eighteenth century the English newspaper remained locked into the dominant economic system' (Harris and Lee, 1986: 19).

Something else endemic in the 18th century was political bribery. In his history of the British press Harold Herd notes that newspapers were often subsidised by the government:

> '**Sir Robert Walpole systematically employed bribery to secure a favourable Press: during the last ten years of his administration [1732–1742] over £50,000 of public money was paid to newspapers and pamphleteers. This practice of bribing newspapers continued until the early part of the nineteenth century . . .'. (Herd, 1952: 64)**

It may be an irony of history that a series of parliamentary acts intended to quell political unrest and quieten the press appear to have positively encouraged the growth of the news media once they had been repealed. The Six Acts of 1819 included the Newspaper and Stamp Duties Act, which imposed a tax on the publication of newspapers and periodicals, the so-called 'tax on knowledge'. It never fully achieved the political effect its sponsors hoped for, as news still circulated in a variety of forms and formats, but it did (along with a tax on advertisements and a tax on paper) put a brake on the *commercial* development of the newspaper industry.

After the final abolition of Stamp Duty in 1855 there was a 'dramatic increase in the number of titles published . . . In 1854 only five dailies were published outside London. Ten years later the figure had risen to 51 and by 1889 it was 155. The five years following repeal also saw 120 papers established in 102 towns where none had existed previously' (Nevett, 1986: 152).

Was this dramatic increase purely the result of a demand for news that could suddenly be satisfied? In part it almost certainly was, and a newspaper's general social or political complexion would help to give it a particular appeal that might help differentiate it in an increasingly competitive marketplace. However, as noted above, there are two forces that drive the print media – readers and advertisers – and those who have written about the history of the British press are in no doubt about the importance of the latter group:

> 'Newspapers were bought for their news, but often what determined the choice of paper was the sort of advertisement the reader could expect to find there. This applied particularly to those in search of employment'. (Lee, 1976: 38)

Thus the *Morning Post* was the paper for gentlemen and gentlemen's gentlemen, ladies and ladies' maids; the *Daily News* for journalists; the *Daily Telegraph* for lower middle class employment and the *Daily Chronicle* and the *Echo* for the working class. Communities of readers began to cluster around particular titles because they published certain types of advertising:

> 'the predominantly commercial position of the press was emphasized by a continuous and increasing involvement in advertising . . . The English newspapers needed advertising, not only to supplement income but also to balance their appeal and relate to the communities they served'. (Harris and Lee, 1986: 19)

The beneficially circular nature of this arrangement was understood well in the 19th century but rather than the usual and somewhat over-simplified explanation that readers attract advertisers it was entirely possible to see it the other way around. Terry Nevett quotes from a contributor to the *Gentleman's Magazine* to make this point:

> 'To a large extent it was advertising which made possible an expansion on this scale. Firstly, advertisements attracted readers. According to Daniel Stuart, "Numerous and various advertisements attract numerous and various readers, looking out for employment, servants, sales, and purchases, &c &c. Advertisements act and react. They attract readers, promote circulation, and circulation attracts advertisements"'. ([D. Stuart, Anecdotes of Coleridge and of London Newspapers, *Gentleman's Magazine*, 10 (1838), p. 25] in Nevett, 1986: 152)

And there was another, unintended, benefit derived from this new stream of revenue – it was advertising that freed mass-circulation newspapers from the kind of political patronage practised by Walpole. Once this stream of revenue had been tapped, newspaper owners and editors were free to reject bribes and slush funding, as first Harold Herd and then Francis Williams pointed out:

> 'The Press was not able to gain its independence until the growth of commercial prosperity consequent on the Industrial Revolution brought a large and increasing revenue from advertisements, and allowed the newspaper to stand on its own two feet financially'. (Herd, 1952: 64)

'[o]nly through the growth of advertising did the press achieve independence . . .'.
(Williams, 1957: 51)

Where there is one unintended consequence there are likely to be others. Once it has been established that money can be made from a particular kind of enterprise the way opens up for opportunists to enter the market in search of profit and a human form of Gresham's Law[15] comes into play. It may well have been that when newspapers were only marginally profitable, or were in fact cross-subsidised by other activities such as printing, they were owned by people who cared about holding power to account; as their commercial potential grew, however, a new type of profit-oriented proprietor appeared. Coupled with this, when advertisers realised their contributions were vitally important, they could begin to demand changes, perhaps not to content but certainly to appearance, as Terry Nevett observes: 'Gradually publishers were forced to allow advertisements which were several columns in width, breaking through the column rules which had traditionally contained them, and to permit the use of bold display types and eventually of illustrations' (Nevett, ibid.: 153).

Increased competition in the newspaper market had two other major effects: behind the scenes there was increasing centralisation of ownership as commercial organisations sought to build national networks, while the actual surface of newspapers changed as a result of the pressure on publications to make themselves positively attractive to potential readers. As seems to be the case down the years, some of those most strongly opposed to these changes were the journalists, as Herd notes:

'When innovators came along in the 'eighties and 'nineties who strongly urged that the primary task of a newspaper was to get itself read, and that there was a whole range of human interests that found no reflection in the columns of existing journals, the reaction of the majority of journalists was violently unfavourable'.
(Herd, 1952: 223)

In some respects the journalists may well have had a point. Not only was the very nature of the press changing, those innovators were drawn from a diminishingly small group. Mark Hampton summarises the situation thus: for most of the 19th century the British press could be understood as a force for education, 'part of a broader commitment to a program of elevation for the working class' (Hampton, 2004: 10) but by the end of the century it had changed to what he calls a 'representative' model in which the press did not influence readers or public opinion but reflected their concerns and interests.

Thus in the mid-Victorian period press ownership was relatively widespread: 'newspaper ownership was diffused widely enough and the spectrum of political views was diverse enough that the educational ideal could seem plausible' (ibid.) but after the 1880s newspaper ownership began to consolidate in larger press groups, as a result of 'the emergence of a mass readership, the reliance on ever more expensive machines, and the increasing dominance of advertising revenue'. Mass readership is also credited with changing the look of newspapers, including, 'the introduction of headlines, shorter stories . . . a simplification of prose, and eventually photography' (ibid.).

It seems safe to say, then, that commercial forces had begun to dominate community needs well before the 20th century and that the Welsh Assembly government's committee of enquiry was revisiting old ground: subjection to commercial pressures only becomes a problem when the commercial foundations shift, as Barrie Jones indicated above. The media academics and union officials who gave evidence to the committee did, however, have one valid point – the newspaper industry has grown used to profit levels and returns on investment that make most other industries look puny by comparison. Once those returns dropped towards more normal levels, levels that would seem normal to a profitable supermarket, for example, proprietors and shareholders appear to have taken fright.

According to journalist and NUJ organiser Martin Shipton, 'This is particularly true in Wales. Take Media Wales as an example. Over the 5 years between the start of 2003 and the end of 2007, Media Wales' profit margins averaged 34.13 per cent, peaking at 38.21 per cent for the 12 months to the end of 2005.'[16]

In 2011, Trinity Mirror's gross margin of profit was 48.37 per cent; by comparison, Sainsbury's was 5.45 per cent.[17]

remember

- News is a commodity that historically had a market value because it was scarce – this is no longer the case.
- News is also a key component in democracy because citizens need reliable information on which to base rational decisions.
- Newspapers only achieved independence when advertising revenue reached significant levels.
- The ownership of newspapers has consolidated into large, increasingly centralised, corporations that, arguably, are more concerned with profit than keeping people informed.

PUTTING IT INTO PRACTICE

Even struggling newspaper groups seem to be able to generate large profits. In his MediaGuardian column of 16 May 2011 Dan Sabbagh noted that Independent News and Media, whose *Independent* has the lowest circulation of the UK's daily broadsheets, was trading 'at a 13 per cent margin that widget manufacturers would never even hope to aspire to'.

At first sight it might seem somehow wrong that news, which is generally considered a vital element in the effective functioning of democracy, should be treated as a commercial commodity. However, the question that really needs to be asked is: if newspaper publishers were not allowed to operate in a free market, why would they bother with news at all? And if they didn't publish it, who would?

Furthermore, if we consider that at certain points in their history newspapers have been directly controlled by the government or known to take government bribes, the current situation would seem to be infinitely preferable. Surely it is far better to have rich but independent publications than have them subject to government control? On the other hand, if newspapers become too dependent on advertising revenue, the advertisers might start to exert undue pressure for favourable reviews or even on the news agenda.

Activity: Think of new or different ways that newspapers could be supported financially; write out a list of pros and cons for each method you devise.

REGULATION OF THE PRINT MEDIA

Ownership patterns of the newspaper industry in the UK have not become more diverse since consolidation became the norm at the end of the 19th century. The market today is dominated by 10 national papers originating from London with a combined daily circulation of over

11 million and almost 12 million on Sunday. National newspaper ownership is concentrated in eight companies – News International, Daily Mail & General Trust, Trinity Mirror, Northern & Shell, Telegraph Media Group, Guardian Media Group, Independent News & Media, and Pearson. Of these, the first four control over 85 per cent of the national market (35.5 per cent, 19.3 per cent, 20.3 per cent and 11.9 per cent respectively.[18]

Regional and local press ownership patterns are a mix of corporate concentration and small-scale operators – the Newspaper Society represents 87 publishers who produce 1,195 titles.[19] Thirty-nine of these publishers produce just one title but overall the market is dominated by four giants who between them control around 70 per cent of the market – Trinity Mirror, Johnston Press, Newsquest Media Group and Northcliffe Media/Associated Newspapers (the last two are separate companies but both owned by the Daily Mail & General Trust).

It is important to realise that almost all of the companies that publish national newspapers have many other business interests. A daily newspaper is clearly a major commercial operation but it is usually one among several. Strict ownership rules in the UK, intended to ensure a variety of social and political views in the media, prevent straightforward cross-ownership of both a national newspaper and a national television station but newspaper groups do have stakes in television and radio in the UK and overseas. An obvious example of this is News International, which is connected to the BSkyB satellite channel via its corporate owner News Corporation.

The Communications Act of 2003 set out the limits of cross-ownership, summarised in a report by the Canadian Radio-television and Telecommunications Commission thus:

> 'In every local area, there must be three separate media companies supplying radio, TV, and newspaper services. Nobody controlling more than 20% of national newspaper circulation may own more than 20% of an Independent TV license. Nobody owning a regional ITV license may control more than 20% of the newspaper market in that region. Nobody owning a regional ITV license may own a local radio station with more than 45% coverage of the same area. Nobody owning a local newspaper may own a local radio station where the newspaper accounts for more than 50% of the circulation within the station's coverage area.'[20]

Perhaps unsurprisingly, especially given the downturn in the fortunes of local newspapers, regional publishers have campaigned to have these rules changed. Their efforts have met with some success: in November 2006 Ofcom suggested that some changes in cross-ownership rules might be justified.[21] Then a committee of the department of Culture, Media and Sport issued a report on the *Future for Local and Regional Media* (June 2010) that noted:

> 'The evidence we have heard from local media groups about the need to modify the merger regime and cross-media ownership rules is persuasive. We welcome the recommendations made by Ofcom in their report to the Secretary of State on media cross-ownership rules, and urge the Government to implement them. However we believe more far-reaching reform is needed. In order for local newspapers to survive in a changing economic and technological world, they need to be regarded as competitors in a multi-media landscape. Despite the evidence given by the Office of Fair Trading, we believe that the current media merger regime does not fully reflect this. We recommend that the Government re-examine the arrangement by carrying out a consultation on a possible multi-media merger regime.'[22]

The Welsh Assembly Government committee looking into the future of regional newspapers made very similar recommendations:

> 'Recommendation 1: The Welsh Assembly Government should make representations to the UK Government seeking assurances that cross media rules are relaxed to allow exploration of new partnerships.

Recommendation 2: The Welsh Assembly Government should make representations to the UK Government seeking assurances that any move to relax regulations relating to cross-media ownership should be accompanied by measures to protect plurality of local media.'[23]

Beyond these measures to control ownership, however, there is no single body of law that controls the press in the UK. There are, for example, laws that govern various aspects of the ways in which newspapers can report court and parliamentary proceedings, laws to protect a person's reputation (defamation, libel) and laws to protect privacy. All laws are subject to interpretation, and understanding of the extents and limitations develops over time; this has been particularly the case with privacy cases in recent years, and European legislation has an effect in all of these areas. There is, however, no general press law of the kind found in many countries. (Freedom House publishes an interesting annual survey of international press freedom.)[24] As Perry Keller explains:

'Governments in Britain have generally been reluctant to impose regulatory controls over the press. Direct government controls over newspaper content would give an appearance of state censorship that is unwelcome in a liberal democracy and would antagonise the press industry.'[25]

One result of this was that newspapers were allowed to regulate themselves through first the Press Council (1953–1991) and then the Press Complaints Commission (PCC, 1991–2012). As evidence put to the Leveson Inquiry of 2012 demonstrated, there were major problems with this system. Firstly, although there was a majority of members with no connection to the press, the council was perceived to be dominated by editors; secondly, it was funded by Pressbof, an industry body; thirdly, membership was voluntary – so when Northern & Shell withdrew the *Daily Express* and other newspapers and magazines there was nothing the PCC could do to prevent them. In March 2012 the PCC was closed, pending formation of a new regulatory body after Lord Leveson had reported.

By contrast, television and radio stations are far more rigidly governed by the Independent Television Commission, the Radio Authority and the Broadcasting Standards Commission, as well as Ofcom to look after the overall regulatory and competitive framework.

One of the most striking differences between newspapers and broadcast media as far as regulation goes is that the former are free to be as politically partisan as they like while the latter are under an obligation to be fair and balanced in their coverage and this may be seen as both an advantage and a drawback for newspapers. The advantage is that it more or less guarantees a lively and diverse selection of newspapers, and this is certainly true of the UK where all mainstream political opinions are covered from the *Morning Star* on the hard left to the *Daily Mail* or *Express* on the right. The only limitations have been those covered by laws governing personal defamation and social issues, so an extreme right-wing newspaper that published material likely to incite racial or religious hatred could be prosecuted under the Race Relations Act or the Criminal Justice and Public Order Act.

The drawback may be that newspapers taking a particularly partisan political stance may face diminished levels of trust in their reporting. Those that focus on soft news items such as celebrity gossip and/or that have been shown to fabricate interviews, for example, or participate in underhand and illegal practices such as phone hacking, are likely to forfeit almost all trust – and trust is a major issue for newspaper journalism in the UK. In September 2010 *Prospect* magazine published the results of a YouGov survey into how much the public trust various groups to tell the truth – and journalists did not fare well. In 2003, ITV journalists had a trust rating of 81 per cent but seven years later that figure had fallen by 33 points to less than 50 per cent. BBC news journalists did marginally better even though trust in them dropped 21 points from 81 per cent to 60 per cent.

Newspapers followed an interesting hierarchical pattern: broadsheets (*Times, Telegraph, Guardian, Independent*) suffered a 24 point reduction to 41 per cent, mid-markets (*Mail, Express*) were down from 36 per cent to 21 per cent and the red-tops (*Sun, Mirror, Star*) were down from an already very low 14 per cent to 10 per cent. Looking at the full results (and methodology)[26] reveals the even more worrying corollary: lack of trust. Broadsheet journalists were *not* trusted by 51 per cent, mid-market journalists by 71 per cent and tabloid journalists by 83 per cent – even worse than estate agents (79 per cent). To summarise, no category of newspaper journalist was trusted by a majority of those surveyed.

It is difficult to imagine a bigger problem than that for the future of print journalism in the UK.

remember

- There is no general press law in the UK but there are a multitude of other laws that have a direct bearing on journalism (see also Chapter 9).
- It is likely that ownership rules will be changed to allow more cross-ownership of print and broadcast outlets – and whatever new medium comes next.
- Newspapers are subject to less direct regulation than television and radio.
- Journalists have lost the trust of large sections of their potential readership.

PUTTING IT INTO PRACTICE

Current regulations mean that no-one can own both a local newspaper and a local television or radio station. The reasoning behind this is to try to ensure a plurality of opinion in the local media – that is, no one person's or organisation's political or social views can dominate.

However, newspaper groups now appear to believe that it would be commercially beneficial to relax these rules and allow a multimedia mix of print, broadcast and online platforms. On this point, the Welsh Assembly government's committee on the future of local newspapers appeared to want to have its cake and eat it, recommending that cross-media regulations be relaxed but at the same time wanting to ensure a plurality of views in the media. Given that local media of all types seem to be struggling, it is possible to argue that economies of scale might reduce costs but by the same token they would also reduce plurality.

On the national and international level News Corporation – which controls many newspaper publishers and has significant holdings in several satellite broadcasters (it owns Sky Italia outright) – wants UK ownership regulations to be relaxed so it can buy a controlling holding in BSkyB, and thus Sky News.

At the same time, public trust in journalists has sunk to a very low point, not helped by widespread evidence of illegal phone tapping by journalists on the News International-owned (and now closed) *News Of The World*. Would combining all news journalism into one corporate body tend to increase trust or not?

Activity: Think of useful combinations of media that would support local communities *and* increase trust in journalists.

JOURNALISM EDUCATION AND TRAINING

The YouGov figures cited above may look both disturbing and depressing but lack of trust in journalists and journalism is nothing new. Apart from any political regulation of the type already discussed, the distrust has also been reflected in popular culture – both Ben Jonson, in his play *The Staple of News* (1631), and William Congreve, in *The Way of the World* (1700), portrayed newsmongers and shorthand takers in a very poor light. On the other hand, no matter what the historical era, critics always see journalism as being in decline from some mythical golden age: Adrian Bingham gives a good corrective to the perceived loss of serious newspaper coverage in his paper *Monitoring The Popular Press: A Historical Perspective* (**http://www.historyandpolicy.org/papers/policy-paper-27.html**).

After the Stamp Duty and its associated 'tax on knowledge' had been repealed, governments never again tried to regulate the press in the same way or to the same degree but there were still very real concerns about political bias in the newspapers and the power of the press barons. This came to a head after the Second World War, when a Labour government was returned with a landslide victory despite almost unanimous newspaper support for the Conservatives and their leader Winston Churchill, the *Daily Mirror* being a notable exception. In 1947 a Royal Commission on the Press investigated the way newspapers were financed and run. After taking evidence the Commission recommended that an external body should be established to regulate the press and in 1951 the Press Council was established (it would later morph into the Press Complaints Commission).

The Royal Commission also looked at the recruitment and training policies of newspapers and made a further recommendation that this area be tackled in a more comprehensive and rational manner, 'because on the quality of the individual journalist depends not only the status of the whole profession of journalism but the possibility of bridging the gap between what society needs from the Press and what the Press is at present giving it'. The outcome of this was the creation of the National Council for the Training of Journalists (NCTJ) in 1951. Although the Commission saw a need to train journalists on every type of newspaper, resistance by the Newspaper Publishers Association (NPA), the trade body for national papers, meant that in effect the training only applied to recruits in the local and regional press. However, a restrictive agreement between the NPA and the National Union of Journalists (NUJ) ensured that only university graduates could get a job on a national newspaper without having first served an apprenticeship (called indentures) in the regions – and given that at the time less than 10 per cent of the population went to university this measure excluded a significant number of people.

Founding the NCTJ was a positive response to the Royal Commission's criticisms by a large sector of the newspaper industry and because it imposed certain standards it could also be seen both as a means of shoring up trust in journalists and as a step towards making journalism a profession. But for all that it aspires to the condition of a profession, like medicine and the law, journalism can more accurately be categorised as a craft, not least because there are no formal qualification requirements: anyone can become a journalist regardless of whether they have a PhD from Oxbridge or left school with no GCSEs. There is no equivalent of the Law Society or the General Medical Council to impose standard conditions of training – in fact there are four different bodies that accredit journalism courses, each recognised by different sectors of the media industries. This can cause some confusion and certainly gives rise to competition, not always helpful or useful, between the bodies:

- NCTJ – established to oversee newspaper journalism training, the National Council for the Training of Journalists sets its own prescriptive curriculum and exams. There are modules covering all aspects of newspaper practice and the NCTJ has added modules in an attempt to extend its coverage to magazine and broadcast journalism.

- PTC – the Periodicals Training Council is the training arm of the industry body for magazines, the Professional Publishers Association. The PTC does not set a prescriptive curriculum or run its own exams; it audits courses thoroughly and accredits only those that meet its standards.

- BJTC – the Broadcast Journalism Training Council represents the main employers in the television and radio industries, from the BBC to BSkyB. The BJTC operates like the PTC in the way it audits courses and accredits those that meet its standards.

- Skillset – a slightly different kind of organisation from the three above, Skillset is the Sector Skills Council for the creative media industries. This covers a much wider range of business types – TV, film, radio, interactive media, animation, computer games, facilities, photo imaging, publishing, advertising, fashion and textiles. It is more concerned with influencing policy, including training policy across the whole range of educational qualifications, than with specific curriculum development.

As noted above it has been possible to become a journalist without having any formal qualifications at all[27] but the reality is that having some training under your belt gives you a much better chance of getting a foothold in a highly competitive work-market. Employers will naturally tend to prefer someone who knows the laws of libel and defamation, someone who can find their way around the law courts, a local council or national government, someone who has acquired the basic skills of interviewing and reporting, to another candidate who may have a flair for writing but none of the craft-capital – the skills and knowledge specific to journalism.

Newspapers used to offer extensive in-house training opportunities, but now would-be journalists are largely expected to bear the costs of training themselves by taking journalism undergraduate or postgraduate degrees. A few companies still offer traineeships or graduate schemes, though numbers are limited and competition is fierce.

On the other hand, an increasing number of media companies offer internships, paid or otherwise, to those looking for a foothold in the industry. There is a good deal of controversy around this subject as some observers believe that companies are simply taking advantage of interns rather than offering them any useful training or a realistic prospect of getting a job. However, it is still a good idea to undertake work experience placements as a way of preparing yourself for the workplace or for a journalism course. Just being in an office watching journalists at work should provide a realistic understanding of what the job actually entails, as opposed to any romantic notions you might have, and a good placement will almost certainly result in your getting work published, even if it's something short and simple. Nothing beats the feeling of seeing your words on a page and it will all add to the portfolio you should be compiling to support job or course applications.

So many courses claim to offer some sort of journalism training it can be confusing, but there are a number of ways to filter out the also-rans from the possibles. Any course worth doing must offer a thorough grounding in practical journalism techniques, rather than a critique or theoretical overview. This should include plenty of practice at writing in different genres (news, features, online), effective interviewing techniques, production skills from sub-editing through page design to uploading via a content management system, use of audio and video (even for print journalists): in fact, anything and everything that a modern journalist has to be able to do.

Beyond practical skills, the course must be bang on top of media law concerning privacy, libel, defamation and reporting privileged information from courts and parliament.

A CLOSER LOOK

The need to understand parliamentary privilege and how to report it was brought into sharp focus at the end of May 2011. Once again a footballer was rumoured to have been having an affair with a model but a superinjunction prevented both the media and his paramour from naming him. This gave rise to the very strange situation wherein Imogen Thomas, one half of the equation, could be interviewed but was not allowed, under threat of legal sanction, to mention her lover's name, while simultaneously that name was being spread virally via Twitter. Nevertheless, both print and broadcast media stuck by the letter of the law until on 23 May John Hemming MP took advantage of parliamentary privilege to name Ryan Giggs and then the name was everywhere, reported under the qualified privilege that parliamentary proceedings allow, even though the court orders were still in place.[28]

Another important area that journalism courses should cover is what the Americans call civics; in the UK it tends to go under the name public administration. The subject covers knowing what you are entitled to know, as a citizen and as a journalist, about government, governance and governors, whether that is a local council, the Privy Council or the Council of Europe. This has an obvious application for those who have to cover those bodies, but it is relevant to every journalist, whatever their specialism, for who knows when a council will reject, or approve, a planning application for a music venue, a football ground, a restaurant, business premises and so on.

Finally, a good course will go beyond the bare remit of teaching journalism practice and consider the ethical implications of journalism and its effect on individuals and society. There may be some reactionary journalists, old in heart if not in age, who scoff at this venture into philosophy, but it is impossible to be a journalist for any length of time without coming across some situation that requires you to make an ethical judgement, even if it is about whether to accept a free meal at the restaurant you are reviewing.

A checklist applicable to courses might look like this:

- Accreditation – is the course accredited by the BJTC, PTC, NCTJ or Skillset? This does not guarantee absolute quality (there will always be a range of provision) but it does mean essential standards have been met. The NCTJ accredits far more courses than the other industry bodies, but if you really want a career in broadcast or magazine journalism look for the industry-specific stamp of approval; their websites will provide up-to-date lists of accredited courses.
- Industry reputation – if you include work experience placements in your preparation (as you should), talk to other journalists, editors and publishers about the courses they rate highly. If they did a course themselves get the inside story – after all, curiosity is one of the defining attributes of a journalist.
- Employment record – good course providers should be able to tell you how many of their graduates have got journalism jobs, what kinds of job and where.
- Cost – some courses, such as the postgraduate qualifications offered by Cardiff and City universities, are expensive, and this means a substantial number of people find them unaffordable. Don't bankrupt yourself in the attempt to get qualified but do look at value for money. Ask what facilities are available to students, how much contact time with tutors there is, whether there is a full-time course leader.
- Bursaries and scholarships – does the course provider, college or university offer student bursaries or scholarships? How many, how much, how are they awarded?

- Play the field – don't put all your eggs in the basket of one course. Apply to several, even if you really only want to get into one of them. Not only will this broaden your chances overall, it will also mean that you might be able to use an offer from your less-favoured choice as leverage on your first choice.

Finally, never make the mistake of thinking that your course can teach you everything and once you have graduated that's it. Even when you have acquired an accredited qualification, you will not have finished learning about being a journalist. No course, no matter how highly regarded, will be able to expose you to every situation you will meet; the law is in a constant state of revision and evolution, and new technologies and modes of communication will guarantee that your career continuously reshapes itself. If you think you can stop learning, and thinking, about what you do, then you might as well give up before you start.

This section began with a reminder that journalism has a somewhat chequered history when it comes to trust between writer and reader, but now the situation is more complex than ever before – journalism today is a two-way process, so it is vital to listen to and engage with the readers. The most exciting, and the most frightening, thing about this is that no-one knows how best to do it. Journalism needs a new way to boost its trustworthiness and it could be you – not Rupert Murdoch or Steve Jobs – who discovers a route to salvation.

remember

- Newspapers, magazines and broadcasters all used to offer traineeships or graduate schemes. Now the industries largely expect would-be journalists to pay for their own training.
- Get as much work experience as you can and start to build a portfolio.
- The accrediting bodies all have slightly different emphases. Research what they represent and decide which offers the best standards for the job you want.
- Getting a qualification will not automatically get you a job; you still need to persuade an employer that you have the right mix of personal and craft skills.
- A qualification is just the start of a lifelong learning process.

PUTTING IT INTO PRACTICE

Not so very long ago, newspaper journalists stuck to newspapers, magazine journalists to magazines and broadcast journalists to broadcasting. There were clear lines of demarcation and not a little looking down on each other. Now the situation is very much more fluid. Not only is it far easier and more common to move from one platform to another, both print and broadcast media have in common the need to work online.

Many journalism skills are clearly transferable – knowing how to find information, interview sources, identify the heart of a story and, crucially, how to *tell* the story.

That said, there are still craft-specific skills attached to each medium, whether that is the ability to create a clear news story from a jumble of background information, to write a long feature that holds the reader's attention, to use a variety of camera shots that stitch a visual narrative together or to employ search engine optimisation that will make it easy for potential readers to find your story among the mass of material online.

Activity: If you could design a training course for journalists from scratch what would it include and why?

CHAPTER SUMMARY

- Print journalism in developed economies has been in decline for at least 15 years, though it thrives in many parts of the world.
- Nevertheless, the print media still generate substantial turnover and profit.
- Newspapers and magazines have broadened their output to incorporate websites, apps for smartphone and tablets like the iPad, and social media such as Twitter and Facebook.
- Strong democracies need a reliable flow of information to allow citizens to make decisions, but newspapers and magazines are commercial entities with no statutory duty to fulfil a fourth estate role.
- Advertising revenue allowed newspapers to free themselves from political patronage and bribery but may leave them open to other pressures.
- Newspaper journalists – in fact journalists in general – have lost a significant amount of trust from many people.
- Although anyone can be a journalist, journalists need certain skills and knowledge to work effectively and restore lost trust.

THINKING IT THROUGH

Print vs digital

To think of this as a contest is to approach the issue from completely the wrong angle – it is not a matter of either/or because journalism exists in both physical and digital formats and readers expect to access it in the medium of their choice. To reach any constructive position, that 'vs' must be replaced by a '+' and declarations of intent must be replaced by a series of questions that cover general and specific grounds:

- What properties does print have that digital does not, and how can these properties be used to take journalism forward? (And *vice versa* – the answers may or may not mirror each other.)
- How can the power to measure what readers want to read be harnessed in journalism's favour?
- What does tablet-based publishing offer that traditional print newspapers and magazines do not?
- Given the global spread of mobile phones, their increasing smartness, and people's apparent willingness to pay for their services, how can journalism make an impact on this miniature screen-based platform?

In fact that last point can be taken even further, into an examination of what journalism means in this context. Are the mobile services that give Indian farmers or fishermen information about current market prices journalism? If you think they are not, ask yourself how they differ in principle from what the *Financial Times* or the *Wall Street Journal* do. Does it make a difference that one concerns perishable material goods belonging to poor people in a developing economy and the other (more usually) the abstract concept of share value to rich people in a highly-developed economy? Or that one concerns simple data presented in a straightforward way and the other involves simple data wrapped up in jargon and complicated syntax? If one of the things that characterises journalism is the provision of reliable or verified information then there are grounds for including such mobile services in journalism's big tent without regard to simplicity or complexity.

▶ THINKING IT THROUGH

But perhaps simplicity works better in some contexts than others and, when considering it in relation to the decline of print newspapers, we might be looking in the wrong direction. Rather than the form of the medium (i.e. print), perhaps it is the form of the content that should be under question. In his book *Everything Bad is Good for You*, Stephen Johnson suggests complexity is the new goal – computer games, for example, 'have become more challenging at an astounding rate . . . games are growing more challenging because there's an economic incentive to make them more challenging – and that economic incentive exists because our brains *like* to be challenged' (2005: 182).

If we accept this premise it could be taken to mean local news reporting is too simple but perhaps that is, itself, too simple an inference. Instead, it might be more helpful to think of ways in which complexity of the sort found in video games could be added, or better still built in, to journalism. Potential solutions would need to be contextual – that is to say, no single answer will fit every situation; they must be thought through on their own merits and needs – and wide-ranging. It would be ridiculous for journalism to ape video games by adding virtual rewards to news stories, discovery and collection of which would take readers up to new levels – or would it? Readers of print newspapers have certainly responded to physical rewards in the past (discounts, reader offers, sets of encyclopedias) so there is no reason why the principle should not work if the right digital rewards are offered and applied in the right way.

Ask yourself: what information do readers want and how do they want it? Use as broad a definition of 'reader', 'information' and 'want' as you can.

Profit vs public good

Or to put it another way, how can the apparently contradictory demands of capitalist commerce and fourth-estate journalism be reconciled? After all, newspapers and magazines need to make money if they are to be able to pay for the raw materials and industrial processes that go into them, not to mention the journalists they employ to create content. The question is whether they should be considered purely commercial entities or if there is some special quality that demands greater protection.

This is a far from simple question and there are no pat answers. Barrie Jones, quoted earlier in this chapter, made a very interesting point when he said: 'To date, it suited that model of profitability to get the most credible and quality based journalism that we could'.[29] Read one way this statement can be seen as an admission that 'credible and quality based journalism' is no longer such an important consideration, that perhaps celebrity gossip has filled the gap, but read another way it can be seen as an acknowledgement that there is considerable doubt and confusion about what will now support a 'model of profitability'.

This leads in turn to numerous other questions, among them:

- Why do people *buy* newspapers?
- Should newspapers be owned by the people who read them or by some kind of trust rather than by profit-seeking companies?
- Should the state provide subsidies to newspapers (for production) or to their readers (for consumption), the reverse of a tax on knowledge?
- To what extent do people *want* to contribute to their newspapers?
- How important are advertisements to readers?
- What should the relationship between profit and investment be?

▶

> ▶ THINKING IT THROUGH

Ask yourself: Would it be more dangerous to have state-subsidised newspapers than to allow the free market to determine content and which would promote greater trust in the product?

Regulation vs trust

The YouGov/*Prospect* survey of trust cited earlier in the chapter revealed a distinct difference between television and newspaper journalists; the broadcasters had a significantly higher level of public trust. One of the questions this raises must be: does television journalism have more trust because it is more heavily regulated? Does the fact that output is overseen by the Independent Television Commission, the Radio Authority, the Broadcasting Standards Commission, the BBC Trust, as well as Ofcom itself, give people more confidence in its reliability?

This may have been something print media should have considered more seriously *before* the Press Complaints Commission brought an end to its own existence in March 2012 during the Leveson Inquiry. The PCC had positioned itself as a mediator rather than a regulator, it only responded to complaints rather than initiating its own investigations, and it had no statutory powers of enforcement. Membership was not even compulsory, so when Richard Desmond's company Northern & Shell refused to pay the levy in January 2011, the *Daily Express, Sunday Express, Daily Star, Daily Star Sunday* newspapers, along with *OK!, New!* and *Star* magazines were no longer subject to PCC rulings and the PCC dropped all outstanding complaints against them. There have been a number of proposals for a new regulatory body (the Royal Society of Arts recorded a debate on the topic that can be viewed or listened to here: **http://bit.lv/leGqZd**) but nothing will be decided until Lord Leveson has published the findings of his inquiry.

Of course, loss of trust in newspaper journalists may also have arisen from the fact that some of those working for publications that did subscribe to the PCC performed illegal acts such as phone tapping, some undertook morally dubious forms of entrapment by dressing up in exotic costumes and some just treated their sources in an extremely shabby way or simply fabricated quotes and events (for example Juliet Shaw's experience at the hands of the *Daily Mail*).[30] When things like this occur the new news media – blogs, Twitter, Facebook – allow victims to spread the word about what happened to them instantly and globally. As Jeff Jarvis notes of a politician embroiled in scandal, how can anyone 'still be stupid enough to think that the coverup won't be what kills them'.[31] Given this dichotomy between media forms, how would the demands for cross-media ownership rules to be relaxed work in practice? If effected, relaxation would allow the same person or company to own local newspapers, television stations and radio channels so, hypothetically speaking, not only could all local media share a social or political viewpoint, a vindictive proprietor could conduct a campaign against an individual in regulated form on television and radio and in unregulated form in print.

Ask yourself: If cross-media ownership were allowed, would newspapers gain trust from their association with more regulated media, would television and radio lose trust because of their association with unregulated media – or would the majority of viewers/readers not notice or care?

What makes a journalist a journalist?

When George Brock, the Head of Journalism at City University (London), considered that question in his inaugural lecture[32] he identified four essential characteristics that

▶ THINKING IT THROUGH

could separate *journalism* from the mass of information that has become available to everyone all the time:

- verification – the elimination of doubt about what has happened;
- sense-making – provides context or values; may go under the labels of reporting, analysis, comment or opinion;
- witness – many situations are still best captured, with whatever technology is available, by an experienced eyewitness;
- investigation – hidden stories require skill, experience, patience and resources to tell.

(He also has an interesting take [pages 9–10] on what might be considered 'complexity' in Stephen Johnson's sense, discussed above.)

These are not the only things that journalists need to be able to do, but they are the things Brock regards as the 'pillars of trust'; things he considers to be most important in the attempt to distinguish *journalists* from those who simply provide information or raw data.

Notice what is missing from that list – there's no mention of shorthand, for example, no mention of the need for a qualification in Public Administration; in fact there is practically nothing that could be found directly on a journalism course syllabus. But that doesn't mean those skills or qualifications aren't there – a moment's analysis will show that shorthand fits very neatly into 'witness' (it's a way of recording information quickly and accurately, not an end in itself) and knowledge of how civic affairs are conducted could fit into both 'sense-making' and 'investigation'. Rather than clogging up his analysis with detail Brock focused on the larger building blocks, which allowed him to strip away the superstructure and leave only the essence.

Brock makes good and defensible points about all of these characteristics, but in the end none of them actually defines either what *journalism* is or what a *journalist* should be able to do:

- Verification only requires questions to be asked of the right sources – lawyers, accountants, doctors, shop assistants, garage mechanics do it all the time.
- Sense-making is something that anyone telling a story of any kind does; a good teacher can turn a jumble of facts into sense for her pupils.
- Witness – we are all witnesses and journalists increasingly rely on non-journalists for their first-hand accounts, as well as their photographs and videos.
- Investigation – it is possible to make a strong argument that many journalists are in the worst possible position to undertake a deep investigation. Many lack the forensic skills to interpret financial data, for example, while specialist reporters may be too compromised by their relationships with important sources to risk delving under the surface. Investigation might well be handled better by an accountant or a scientist.

We have already established that journalism is not a profession; there is no standard corpus of knowledge that all journalists must know, there is no single body to which journalists are answerable, there is no way of preventing anyone from calling themselves a journalist. Furthermore, there are ever-increasing numbers of people doing what journalists have traditionally done and there is no way of stopping them.

Ask yourself: the question – what makes a journalist a journalist?

NOTES

1 http://www.thewrap.com/media/column-post/daily-review-stunningly-beautiful-probably-addictive-and-just-little-fluffy-24403?page=0,0

2 http://mcpheters.com/2011/02/02/the-daily-impressive-but-hardly-innovative

3 http://blogs.telegraph.co.uk/technology/shanerichmond/100006286/the-daily-ipad-app-review-a-complete-failure-of-imagination)

4 http://www.oecd.org/document/48/0,3343,en_2649_33703_45449136_1_1_1_1,00.html See also http://www.guardian.co.uk/media/2010/jun/17/newspaper-circulation-oecd-report

5 Available at: http://www.publications.parliament.uk/pa/ld200708/ldselect/ldcomuni/122/12202.htm; or at (pdf): http://www.publications.parliament.uk/pa/ld200708/ldselect/ldcomuni/122/122i.pdf

6 http://www.stock-analysis-on.net/NYSE/Company/Sony-Corp/Ratios/Profitability

7 http://www.pressgazette.co.uk/story.asp?sectioncode=6&storycode=41326

8 http://www.currybet.net/cbet_blog/2011/05/newsrewired-liveblogging-panel.php?utm_source=feedburner&utm_medium=feed&utm_campaign=Feed%3A+currybet+(currybetdotnet+-+Martin+Belam's+blog)

9 http://en.wikiquote.org/wiki/William_Gibson

10 http://www.spartacus.schoolnet.co.uk/REwhite.htm

11 http://books.google.co.uk/books?id=OPANAAAAQAAJ&lpg=PA184&ots=wNe0XJXJ_s&dq=sunday%20times%20thalidomide%20campaign&pg=PA184#v=onepage&q=sunday%20times%20thalidomide%20campaign&f=false

12 http://www.assemblywales.org/cr-ld7563-e.pdf

13 Ibid. p. 9.

14 Barrie Jones, Editor-in-Chief of NWN Media, publisher of newspapers in the north of Wales, ibid. p. 7.

15 http://en.wikipedia.org/wiki/Gresham's_law

16 WAG report, National Union of Journalists – Martin Shipton, Oral evidence 22.01.09, http://www.assemblywales.org/cr-ld7563-e.pdf

17 http://markets.ft.com/tearsheets/financialsSummary.asp?s=TNI:LSE; http://markets.ft.com/tearsheets/financialsSummary.asp?s=uk:SBRY

18 http://www.publications.parliament.uk/pa/ld200708/ldselect/ldcomuni/122/12207.htm

19 http://www.newspapersoc.org.uk/regional-press-structure

20 http://www.crtc.gc.ca/eng/publications/reports/mcewen07.htm

21 http://stakeholders.ofcom.org.uk/binaries/research/media-ownership/rules.pdf

22 http://www.culture.gov.uk/images/publications/govtresponse_futurelocalregionnews_CM7882_rep.pdf

23 http://www.assemblywales.org/cr-ld7563-e.pdf

24 http://www.freedomhouse.org/template.cfm?page=251&year=2010

25 http://www.britishcouncil.org/china-society-publications-media.pdf

26 http://today.yougov.co.uk/sites/today.yougov.co.uk/files/YG-Archives-Pol-PublicTrust-190810.pdf

27 The Leveson Inquiry inspired a number of ideas about the accreditation of journalists. See: http://bit.ly/IpPRBJ and http://bit.ly/IgqJTn

28 There is an interesting summary of the situation at: http://www.bbc.co.uk/blogs/seealso/2011/05/daily_view_2.html

29 See note 14.

30 http://nosleeptilbrooklands.blogspot.com/2011/01/true-story-of-daily-mail-lies-guest.html

31 http://www.buzzmachine.com/2011/06/07/i-was-wrong/

32 http://www.scribd.com/doc/28560140/George-Brock-Is-News-Over

WEBLINKS

http://georgebrock.net/   George Brock is the Head of Journalism at City University, London. His blog frequently carries interesting think pieces about how journalism is evolving and how journalists can prepare themselves.

http://www.buzzmachine.com/   Jeff Jarvis, a former journalist, teaches journalism at the City University of New York, has devised some very innovative courses, is a vigorous commentator on the media scene and, among other things, wrote *What Would Google Do?*

http://tabloid-watch.blogspot.com/   As its sub-heading declares, this is a blog about bad journalism. Read it and begin to understand why trust has seeped away.

http://www.theatlantic.com/magazine/archive/2011/04/learning-to-love-the-shallow-divisive-unreliable-new-media/8415/3/   A thoughtful look at the past and future of journalism by James Fallows. It focuses on American media but has a universal relevance.

http://www.niemanlab.org/   The Nieman Journalism Lab, based at Harvard University, posts a wealth of news and analysis to its website. Worth looking at for the onward links alone.

http://www.poynter.org/   The Poynter Institute is a school dedicated to teaching and inspiring journalists and media leaders. Content on the site reflects its American location but there is a wealth of relevant material.

http://pressthink.org/   Jay Rosen is a journalism professor at New York University. You might not always agree with what he writes but you cannot ignore it.

http://blogs.lse.ac.uk/polis/   Charlie Beckett is the director of POLIS, a journalism and society thinktank.

http://www.nctj.com/   NCTJ website for newspaper qualifications.

http://www.ppa.co.uk/training/   PTC website for magazine qualifications.

http://www.bjtc.info/   BJTC website for broadcast qualifications.

RECOMMENDED READING

Conboy, Martin (2011) *Journalism In Britain: A historical introduction*. London: Sage.
A wide-ranging and comprehensive overview of the many factors that have shaped and changed journalism in the UK.

Eisenstein, Elizabeth (1980) *The Printing Press as an Agent of Change*. Cambridge: Cambridge University Press.
A key text for anyone interested in how print has affected the world.

Franklin, Bob (ed.) (2008) *Pulling Newspapers Apart: Analysing print journalism*. London: Routledge.
Takes a scalpel to newspapers and examines the various component parts.

Griffiths, Dennis (ed.) (1992) *The Encyclopedia of the British Press 1422–1992*. London: Macmillan.
An extensive history of print journalism.

Holmes, Tim and Nice, Liz (2012) *Magazine Journalism*. London: Sage.
An essential introduction to all aspects of print magazines and magazine journalism.

Keeble, Richard (ed.) (2005) *Print Journalism: A critical introduction*. Abingdon: Sage.
Gives a thorough insight into the skills needed to work in print journalism, with chapters by selected experts.

REFERENCES

Lee, Alan (1976) *The Origins of the Popular Press in England*. London: Croom Helm, p. 38.

Hampton, Mark (2004) *Visions of the Press in Britain, 1850–1950*. Urbana and Chicago: University of Chicago Press.

Harris, Michael and Lee, Alan (eds) (1986) *The Press in English Society from the Seventeenth to Nineteenth Centuries*. London and Toronto: Associated University Presses.

Herd, Harold (1952) *The March Of Journalism: The Story of the British Press from 1622 to the Present Day*. London: George Allen & Unwin Ltd.

Nevett, Terry (1986) Advertising and Editorial Integrity in the Nineteenth Century, in Harris, Michael and Lee, Alan (eds) *The Press in English Society from the Seventeenth to Nineteenth Centuries*. London and Toronto: Associated University Presses.

Johnson, Steven (2005) *Everything Bad is Good for You*. London: Penguin.

HMSO (1962), *Royal Commission on The Press 1961–1962*. London: HMSO.

Williams, Francis (1957) *Dangerous Estate: The Anatomy of Newspapers*. London: Longmans, Green & Co.

CHAPTERTWO
RESEARCHING

This chapter will cover:

- Research skills
- Interview techniques
- Digital research essentials
- An introduction to social media and data journalism

Case study 2.1

MEDIA Wales reporter Ciaran Jones had been on weekend calls – and had been told by police that nothing had happened across the weekend. So he carried on with the other stories he was working on, only to be confronted by an angry news editor on the Monday morning asking why Ciaran didn't know about a number of incidents which the paper had been told about by contacts.

Ciaran had a conversation with other members of the team and found that there had been other weekends when emergency services were saying nothing had happened. So he decided to spend some time researching this and finding out if it were true.

Across the weekend of 18 and 19 September 2010 the Media Wales weekend team logged every call made to South Wales police and recorded the details of who they spoke to, the times and any incidents – which turned out to be zero, essentially that no crimes of any importance had happened. Knowing that this couldn't possibly be true in the area – bearing in mind that the city of Cardiff alone has an estimated population of more than 305,000 and the South Wales police covers the area from the borders of Newport (Gwent Police) over to Swansea – Ciaran made a request under the Freedom of Information Act.

The resulting information from police showed that there were, in fact, 491 crimes on that particular weekend:

- 118 violent crimes,
- 3 sexual offences,
- 24 domestic burglaries,
- 23 other burglaries,
- 3 robberies.

This led to a series of interviews with members of the Welsh Assembly and a criminologist to set the scene on police transparency for a story for the paper and the website.[1] Since that point relations have improved, with the police being more transparent with a newly established team of crime reporters who are working for the newspaper group.

Ciaran said: 'In the whole time we were told there were no incidents whatsoever but we found there were burglaries, sex offences which would have been relevant for them to tell us about. The point was to expose things that were going on but things they weren't telling us about.'

INTRODUCTION

The key thing about research is that it offers the opportunity to build a network of tools, people and ideas that will allow you to find answers to questions effectively, the right person for a quote or even if something is of interest to your readership. Research for both news and features starts from the same point, even though the styles of writing and approaches will differ later. Although each journalist will have their own favourite techniques for researching a topic, which will be dictated by experience, their topic area and their organisation, it can be argued that research starts from answering one basic question: what do you need to know to get this story done and in front of your audience?

Most people will then think about how they're going to do their research, which contacts they like the look of to add depth and suggest other avenues. They'd be totally correct – but they are jumping the gun.

GETTING STARTED

Story research needs to be tackled in a staged approach and seasoned journalists are automatically building this into their daily lives – but it is worth stepping back every once in a while to think about the basics.

These are the things you need to know before you begin your research:

- who your target audience are;
- who the commissioner is – your own organisation/the commissioning body;
- where to get a story;
- how to build on a story idea.

YOUR TARGET AUDIENCE

You need to know your audience inside and out. Any media outlet that charges for content or advertising will have an intimate knowledge of its customer, and anyone engaging in freelance work or running a hyperlocal website – a community news site – will also understand who they are providing content to.

There are several techniques you could employ to do this:

- knowing your media outlet;
- getting beneath the surface – media packs and advertising;
- using search optimisation as a market indicator.

Know your media outlet

Magazines call this 'getting into bed with your reader' and will know their readers down to the nth degree. Magazines are niche products and need this understanding to be able to target appropriately, so they are getting the right readers, readers are getting the correct content and the adverts are appropriate to both: for example there's no point approaching an eco-magazine about how great Formula One is (unless they've just invented solar-powered race cars).

Websites that focus on specific communities of interest work in the same way. They will have a devoted following keen for news around their interest rather than something the writer thinks is interesting. Newspapers also know their customers extremely well, but their base is more varied than magazines as they are serving either a community of interest (for example, the *Daily Mail* has a very certain type of reader) or a geographical community (for example, the *Manchester Evening News*, the *Standard*, *Bristol Evening Post*, etc.).

Getting beneath the surface

If you are trying to find out about a target audience then start with the people in the know – the journalists working for the organisation. Another way is to look at a media pack, essentially a breakdown of the product and its audience for people wanting to advertise. The same information will help you if you are looking to gain work experience or you are applying for a job, as the media pack will give you a clear insight into what the organisation is all about – and will show the interviewer you've done your homework. Media packs are usually on the website, or you can track down the company's phone number and ring for one.

A CLOSER LOOK

GETTING INTO BED WITH THE READERS OF *VOGUE*

Interestingly for a women's magazine, 16 per cent of the readership for the first part of 2010 was male.[2] However the average age of the majority of the female readership (927,000) was 36 and they come from a professional background (33 per cent of the readers are from the AB demographic and 70 per cent fall within the ABC1 demographic – have a look at the National Readership survey for details about these groupings).[3] And just to give you an idea of what that means, according to the media pack, *Vogue* readers spent £1,977 million on fashion during the 12 months to publication of the pack.[4]

The News from Portsmouth

In the second half of 2010, the number of copies of *The News*, Portsmouth, were averaging 42,833 per day with an average of more than 287,000 monthly unique visitors to the website.[5] The pack also gives details of all

> ▶ A CLOSER LOOK
>
> the other products within the portfolio – the local weekly newspapers, and information about each of the sections of the paper. Newspapers will often talk about a readership figure – essentially a figure based on how many people read each copy of the paper that has been bought, which is separate from the sales figures. So in *The News*'s media pack it's stated that they sell approximately 42,833 copies of the paper a day – but the readership is quoted as 108,442. This is a crucial detail for anyone looking to get into the industry to know, not only for an understanding of the audience, but also for impressing an employer.

Another way to understand the audience is to look at the adverts being displayed on the page: they are a good clue as to what kind of readership an outlet has. *Men's Health* magazine is not likely to run adverts for pies, while magazines like *Harpers Bazaar* are very aspirational. Stories are part of what is on offer from a newspaper or magazine, but adverts are very closely targeted so you can read them as part of your attempt to understand who you are working for.

Search optimisation as a market indicator

Search engine optimisation techniques – a way of trying to ensure your website is at the top of the search results – are also very helpful for unpicking who a site is being targeted at. By having a look at the code underlying the page (or viewing the source code as some browsers call it) you can see what key words are being attached to all of the pages. (In Firefox this is done by going to the View menu and then going to page source. In Google Chrome you go to the View menu, then the Developer sub-menu and select view source.)

Near the top, in what is called the <head> of the page, will be some code that looks a little like this

```
<meta name="description" content="The phrase that appears at the top of your web browser" /> or <meta name="keywords" content="Key words to describe the content for search purposes">
```

So for the *Guardian* site the key words are:

```
<meta name="description" content="Latest news, sport, business, comment, analysis and reviews from the Guardian, the world's leading liberal voice" />
```

FHM magazine, on the other hand, offers the following:

```
<html xmlns="http://www.w3.org/1999/xhtml">
<head id="ct100_Head1'><title>
    FHM Men's Magazine | Sexy Girls, News & Men's Fashion | FHM.com
</title><meta http-equiv="X–UA–Compatible" content="application/xhtml+xml;
charset=utf–8; IE=EmulateIE7"/>
    <script type="text/javascript" src="http://video.bauermedia.co.uk/files/js"></script>
<meta name="description" content="Check out sexy girl galleries and funny videos from around the web brought to you by FHM.com, the men's entertainment magazine online." >
<meta name="distribution" content="UK">
```

```
<meta name="copyright" content="Bauer Consumer Media LTD">
<meta name="dateoflastmodification" content="23/10/2011 09:57:33">
<meta name="keywords" content="fhm,fhm mag,fhm magazine,fhm magazine
UK,fhm online,fhm uk,fhm.com,mens magazine">
<link rel="shortcut icon" href="/App_Resources/Images/Site/favicon.ico"/>
    <script type="text/javascript" src="http://ajax.googleapis.com/ajax/libs/
    jquery/1.3.2/jquery.min.js"></script>
    <l--<script type="text/javascript" src="/app_resources/scripts/site/
    jquery.min.js"></script>-->
    <script type="text/javascript" src="/app_resources/scripts/site/
    iepnqfix_tilebq.js"></script>
```

The information above – a truncated form of the actual web page which removes some of the code to show the elements we are interested in – actually tells us quite a lot about the audience and the content on offer. So the <title> offers information that the content is going to include 'Sexy Girls, News & Men's Fashion'. The description of the content shows the site offers the opportunity to: 'Check out sexy girl galleries and funny videos from around the web brought to you by FHM.com, the men's entertainment magazine online.' We know that the content is copyright of Bauer Consumer Media Ltd – the parent company for the site – and that the keywords relate around a variation of the name, the location and the word magazine.

Both the *Guardian* and FHM are using these bits of web code to allow search engines to find and index the pages, and then make them easy for people to find on the search page. It will also help you work out what they are looking for.

THE COMMISSIONER

Experienced journalists will not even start a job before they know what is expected of them. They need to know deadlines and word count for each story – they are often tightly set as the production of a media product is part of a pretty sophisticated industrial process. The longest print piece many newspaper journalists will ever write is a feature (see Chapter 4), which can run to about 2,000 words. Page leads – the key story on a news page – can vary between 250 and 500 words, depending on the product you are working for. You will not be popular if you go over the word count, and it's not often that a news desk will let something run on beyond an allocated amount of words for the page it will be going onto.

Magazines may appear to have longer deadlines for stories and longer word counts than newspapers, but it is still vital for you to know what is going on to be able to slot into the production cycle.

Deadlines and word counts may well change if your organisation follows a web-first policy – breaking the story online before putting it into a printed edition – or if you are expected to produce one story for a number of products, for example if you are working in a converged newsroom that covers a variety of newspapers and a website. You need to know how many updates are required across the day. Is this a one hit story, or a rolling/breaking story where the page will be updated across the day? Deadlines are key, not only to ensure your work is done to time – but as part of the larger process. Remember, the writing side is just one cog in the wheel: if you are late then the whole system is late, and that costs money.

Gavin Stacy, regional Managing Director of Newsquest (Wales & Gloucestershire), estimates that he would lose 1,500 sales for every 15 minutes' delay in his paper hitting the streets.[6]

PUTTING IT INTO PRACTICE   THE COMMISSIONER

- Learn how to prioritise – the news desk will have priorities, but there will be times when you need to make judgement calls and put one story or angle before another.
- If your are out in the field you need to know how to get copy back into the system – do you have a laptop, a keyboard for your smart phone or do you just write it in your notebook and then phone it through? You need to know the procedure.
- Know what kind of budget is available for covering a story. It may be that you can get the cost of transport to the High Court in London or it may be cheaper (but more disappointing for you) if your editor gets an agency to cover it.
- Do you have an output quota? How many stories do you need to write per day, and at what length? So is it three leads, and as many shorter stories, or is your diary clear to produce that killer feature? (Trust us, that never happens, but you need to know.)

remember

- You need to remember the target audience you are writing for.
- Find out about any angles or takes on a story that will be required.
- Find out about the organisation you are working for through questions and primary research.
- Ensure you know what is expected of you – how many words, when by and whether you have to sort out your own images.

GETTING THE NEWS

There are those who think news just pops out of thin air; others see it as a mystical process where some journalists can just walk into the street and find a story – and to an extent they are correct. But to understand where news comes from you have to understand what it is.

One great definition of news has been attributed to former *Sunday Times* editor Harold Evans, author of *Essential English for Journalists, Editors and Writers*. He said (1963: 64):

> 'News is people. It's people talking and doing. Committees, cabinets and courts are people; so are fires, accidents and planning decisions. They are only news because they affect and involve people.'

Why is it a good definition? It is simple, effective and helps answer where news comes from – people. People are interested in other people: people doing things – from the mundane to the extraordinary, people expressing their thoughts on events, people being people. Yes news can be about things, but often it uses the people behind the event to help tell the story. After all we might not know what a quantum-flux generator is, but we understand that a former schoolboy from Sutton Coldfield has just created something quite amazing.

So how do we tap into those people, how do we find them? Obviously there are two ways of approaching this: offline and online. This will depend on the story you are working on, but a systematic approach should combine both. And for each of those routes it depends whether you are covering a geographical beat (news about an area) or a subject beat (news about a topic). This section will look at the offline ways of finding stories; online will be covered in more detail in the section on computers and research.

Sources of news

Knowing your audience will help you to know what news is, as news means different things to different people. So let's start with the geographical beat – or district reporting as it is sometimes called.

Traditionally, local and regional newspapers had a head office and a number of district offices to provide local news. Not everyone works this way anymore; a lot of papers have centralised and closed down their district offices. Some have district reporters working miles from their patch in the head office, others have roving reporters who use free wi fi in coffee shops to send their stories back to the head office. However it is organised, district reporting is about one thing – getting to know the people and the places. The easiest place to begin get to an understanding of district reporting is to use your own town as a starting point.

Although the nature of an area will vary, given its history, population and geography, there are some fundamentals that can be got to grips with quite easily. Journalists need to know about where they are, where they work and what is important to the local readership.

PUTTING IT INTO PRACTICE

One of the most important, and sometimes overlooked, ways to get to know an area is to go for a walk and see what is around you in the community. Some journalism training courses will take people out into the local area for a seemingly innocuous walk around, before asking them to recount the kind of issues that they spotted which people in the area would be interested in.

Key places to look include noticeboards, shop windows, the local history museum and the tourist information office. Some kind of street atlas is a must have, as is access to the phone book, be it the local directory or Yellow Pages and these can be a physical copy or on your smart phone or tablet if you have one.

Life can be a bit different being a district reporter, as one of your key story sources is the people you will have to work with every day – something that Chris Broom (chief reporter in *The News*'s Fareham office) knows very well.

A CLOSER LOOK

VIEW FROM THE FRONT LINE: CHRIS BROOM, *THE NEWS*, PORTSMOUTH[7]

'You have a degree more independence as a district reporter – I found you were a bit spoon-fed and more reactionary than proactive when at head office. This is no reflection on the reporters, but when most calls come into a central hub and are dished out from there, or you have to respond to breaking news, it makes it difficult to build your own independent contacts/stories. In a district you stand or fall more on your own abilities.

'You get the chance to foster your own contacts and networks. You get a greater sense of "ownership" over your patch. The district is "yours", and we can get very territorial. I think this sense of ownership encourages you to find the great stories that are out there somewhere. If that means some serious face time, or popping along to a village fair or whatever, so be it. I'm not suggesting it's my whole life, but I have turned up to the occasional event, just to finally meet someone face-to-face I've been talking to on the phone for ages. I know through putting in the effort I have squeezed the opposition out of some stories, so they will now always come to us first, and not go anywhere else.

'Dealing with the emergency services – now this is a tough nut to crack in our neck of the woods. A bit of a personal bugbear this one. It is easier to build relationships with some of the beat officers, sergeants and inspectors – but many of them still seem to see us as a dirty crutch they need to call on every once in a while, when it suits them. We have a local chief inspector who is the bane of my life – he remembers every negative police story, and has even written to me more than once on "perceived injustices" against his force.

'And when I point out to him the positive ones about police achievements and initiatives they seem to fall on deaf ears. That and the man doesn't seem to realise how a paper works, and refuses to believe that a reporter has no say on what the headline is.

'Suffice to say, fostering good relations with your local police/fire service can pay major dividends when it comes to turning copy out sharpish!

'Ditto for councillors – there are always some who you suspect are in it more for personal glory, and seeing their name in the paper, but regardless of personal political affiliation, they can be gold mines. Their residents often come to them first with problems and issues; they in turn will come to you (if you have them well trained!). They can be a whole extra set of eyes and ears in the community, where they probably also live.

The beat reporter

Beat reporting is different from district reporting. It involves developing specialist knowledge in an area rather than being a good generalist like the district reporter or the general news or feature writer. Again, it doesn't matter whether you are a beat reporter (or feature writer) who works for print or online – this is all about getting to grips with a complex subject area and can be even more important for those covering trade magazines and B2B journals.

Examples of beat are:

- health,
- crime (police/court),
- education,
- business,
- technology,
- arts.

These areas are often covered by specialists who can write about them with authority, having built up a strong network of sources and understanding of their topic. The key issue is to build up the specialist contacts you require – not just the PR people, but the people actually involved in working your beat. Here are some initial tips to start building a beat:

- Find who the expert players are, and how to contact them. If this is your permanent topic area then you should also introduce yourself.
- Build expertise – read journals, B2B publications, websites and blogs that specialise in your area.

- Know the calendar for your area – crucial times of year, conferences, etc.
- If you report on public bodies, for example, find out where the public accounts of the police, council, etc. are available for inspection.
- Join social networking sites, forums and groups to help research your beat. (If you do join then you must learn the etiquette.)
- Use laws such as access to public documents, Freedom of Information or the Environmental Information Regulations to help you find out more.

A CLOSER LOOK

Back in August 2009 Richard Orange of Orchard News Bureau (ONB) used the audit regulations to inspect Lincolnshire County Council's financial documents. He found that the authority had paid a claim by a councillor for over £1,000 for late-night calls to a mobile which was essentially a phone line provided for constituency business. No response was given by the councillor involved and the research led to a story in *Private Eye's* Rotten Boroughs section.

A follow-up inspection 11 months later showed the councillor involved had paid back £452.

The ONB site (**http://www.orchardnews.com/accounts.htm**) has some great guides on using the legislation surrounding public accounts for both councils and the police forces.

PUTTING IT INTO PRACTICE

- How does your organisation define a particular beat, or area?
- What does it actually cover: is it a single niche or a number of related issues?
- Who can you go to for information within your own organisation? From within sibling organisations?
- What are the key texts/research sources for this area? Are there trade journals, B2B magazines, books or websites?
- What other resources are available: can you find listservs, groups, social networking sites or blogs that offer key information in your area?
- Who are the key players, and the key sources within them? Are there trade bodies or unions that can be helpful here?
- How often should you phone or meet them?
- Can you map your beat – either in terms of its key locations or a mind/concept map?
- What training or support do you need – either informally or through your organisation's training scheme?
- Learn to speak the lingo – every industry has its shortcuts/jargon that allow concepts to be quickly shared. This will help you fit in, so find out how to talk the talk and any other idiosyncratic rules that may go along with these areas. The military, for example, are very hot on hierarchy, so again know how this works and how to talk to the people you will be working with. For example a captain is in commond of a ship, but a Commander can be a captain, but then so can a Captain – the rank is different from the name of who is in charge of the vessel. It would also be quite embarrassing to be a technology reporter and keep having to get someone to explain what SCSI (scuzzy), USB, Firewire or Thunderbolt drives are. It makes you more credible to be able to converse in the language and concepts being used by your contacts.

One key point with this kind of reporting, or any other, is not to let yourself get limited. So if you are covering the council, don't just spend your time at the town hall talking to the officials and councillors. Instead go out into the wards and speak to the people who live there, the very people who are affected by these central ideas.

Keeping up with the Joneses (and all of your contacts)

Storing contacts is vital and backing up information is crucial. It doesn't matter whether you use a paper phone book or a computer database, you need a strategy. It doesn't matter what tool you use, as long as contacts are stored in a format that makes them easy to find and restore if problems happen.

PUTTING IT INTO PRACTICE

How should you store this information? You need to think about whether to store contacts by name – obviously – or also by what their role is and what interests they have. So for example if you have a councillor you would put them by name, ward and then any other role they fulfil (for example, school governor, guide leader, microlight club member) to ensure they are easy to find.

remember

- All story types will vary but you need to identify your best sources.
- Build contacts and ensure you know how to find the key information sources.
- Store your contacts in a way that is easy for you to find.

HOW TO BUILD ON A STORY IDEA

Take a look at the diagram opposite. It all looks pretty straightforward. Get a lead and then follow the paths outlined to get enough information to arrange and then conduct an interview. But life is never that easy and it will take a number of steps from within this process to get to the bottom of a story.

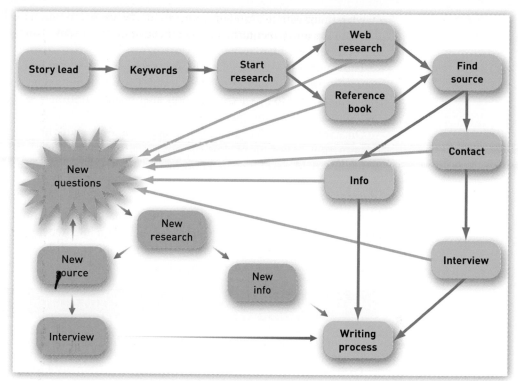

A workflow diagram detailing some of the processes involved in generating stories

We'll start with the interview.

INTERVIEWING

Like anything else in journalism, interviews are all about people. It is a chance to get first-hand accounts, colourful background and interesting quotes – all the things that mark the difference between a second-rate story and something that people will want to read. Like developing a writing style, interviewing is intensely personal. No two journalists will carry out an interview in the same way. Some use a little humour (in appropriate circumstances, remember no cracking jokes in stressful circumstances), others will prefer a very simple and straightforward approach. One thing that all interviews have in common are the people skills required when dealing with interviewees who may, unlike senior police officer or politicians, not be used to dealing with the media. There are also slightly different strategies for different types of interview – is it an ad hoc interview on the doorstep, is it a planned interview for an in-depth feature or is it an email interview? All of these things have to be taken into account. This section will look at some of the basic techniques that will help you get the best out of the interview.

Preparation

Contrary to what most people think, the interview process doesn't start when you shake hands or get shown into someone's office; it has to start much earlier. Preparation is everything and can lead to a successful interview, or an embarrassing episode, which may not offer much in return.

First things first – do your preparation. Media organisations will have some form of database (be it in paper form, on microfiche or on the intranet) and you must look at this to get an idea of what has been done before.

The internet provides a whole host of useful sites, some of which are listed on the companion website to this book – but be careful. The web is not a value-assessed reference library and sources need to be selected carefully after quality control. (See the section on computers and journalism for some guidance.)

Once you've done that you need to prepare some questions in advance. Remember though, this is part of an organic process and not a straitjacket. Interviews are all about human interaction and rigid use of prepared information can sometime hinder rather than help.

Whatever kind of recording device you are going to use – be it a notebook and pen, video camera, audio recorder, smart phone, etc. – needs to be in working order and ready to go.

Are there any legal issues likely to crop up? What about the ethical implications of a tricky interview? Is this covered by your sector's code of conduct? Obvious, but something you need to know. And blindingly obvious, but equally important, make sure you know who you are interviewing, where you are meeting and at what time.

EXAMPLE 2.1	HOW NOT TO DO IT

'My least favourite interview was with comedian Stuart Lee, who was then part of the tv partnership Lee and Herring. And the most annoying part was that it was my fault. I'd arranged the interview for just after deadline, but we'd had a production fault, which meant I was late and hadn't got to read the background on the pair. Worst of all I'd lost track of time.

The phone rang, and a very cheery voice said, 'Hi, it's Stuart.' Without thinking, and because I have four friends called Stuart (each of whom usually uses their nickname or surname as part of their introduction), I replied 'Oh hi, which one?' I then looked at the clock and my heart sank; it was 1.30 p.m. and obviously had to be my interviewee.

This was confirmed when a voice, which carried the icy tones of the north wind, replied 'Stuart Lee'. The interview was a disaster: Stuart had taken umbrage and attempted to close down my questions and wasn't prepared to give much away. My only saving grace was that his partner Richard Herring thought the whole incident was hilarious. Instead of the two-handed interview I'd wanted, I was left with quotes and information to do a piece based around Richard – much to my embarrassment.'

People skills

Films and tv often give a very unrealistic impression of journalistic interviewing. Hollywood loves confrontational interviews where people shout at each other, because they are fun to watch. Similarly it's fun to watch *Newsnight's* Jeremy Paxman grilling some politician or listening to John Humphrys giving someone a hard time on Radio 4's *Today* programme. These are appropriate tools for them because of the medium they use to connect with their audience. It wouldn't be appropriate for a lot of interviews that require the written word for communication.

Why not? Put simply, we can't convey the nuances of voice or show an image of the situation – how someone looks under pressure has to be seen. Besides, big organisations are used to getting a grilling from the media, and are able to work things in their own way. Police, politicians and company CEOs are given media training which helps them work out how to deal with a difficult interview. For members of the public it will probably be the first and last time they will deal with a member of the media – in what is often one of the most stressful periods of their lives – and you need to bear that in mind.

So, your first step is to build a rapport – after all you are a human being, despite what some people might think about journalists. Everything your mum and careers teacher ever said to you about first impressions is true: you will probably be judged within seconds of walking into a room or speaking on the telephone. Again, simple but obvious – if you are going to a face-to-face meeting you need to dress appropriately. Introduce yourself and check you are speaking to the right person.

You need to convey that you are interested in the subject under discussion, but that shouldn't be hard as you will have hit the database to get information, and that you are interested in the person you are speaking to. You need to use eye contact and simple manners to get the best out of the situation. If you spot something that allows you to express a personal connection, then do so. If the interviewee has a photograph of a pet dog, ask about it. It will allow you to build a bit of a bond with them.

Be empathetic rather than sympathetic; sympathy can be taken the wrong way. To put it simply, empathy is showing you understand. You'll also need to steer the conversation at points, but politely. We aren't talking to them for a simple chat but we do need to allow leeway to explore situations. Finally, do ensure that you allow the interviewee to talk and don't try to put words in their mouths or anticipate the responses.

Active listening

It is one thing to listen to what is being said and record it (but active listening is something else entirely. The distinction is there because it is a different skill) and one that requires some practice. Active listening is about picking up on what is being said and allows you to develop the interview in a way that responds to what is happening rather than being straightjacketed by your pre-prepared questions. It isn't easy to do and sometimes there's the temptation to try and read something into what isn't said. If that happens, ask the question; don't just assume your interpretation is correct. And if they do tell you something; don't just accept it. Be prepared to ask questions like 'How do you know that?' And if they say it is from a document make sure you ask for a copy, or find out where you can get it from.

Rules of engagement

Some reporters like to set out the ground rules before they start, others as they go. You'll develop your own way with practice. But one important thing to remember is when to introduce your chosen form of recording device. Tell them that you would like to take notes, or record the interview and explain that this is so that you can ensure you've got things right. Many newspaper reporters will put their notebook on the table while they are making small talk, that way it is already part of the situation and needn't be threatening. Audio and video recording is a bit more difficult as it requires set-up, but if you explain what you are doing as part of your small talk it will be natural and part of the process.

Tips for multimedia interviewing

Carrying out interviews is one of the most important things you need to be able to do well as a journalist. It's also one of the most stressful things you have to do. There are countless books and manuals full of advice about how to do a good interview, but the essence of it is, as Lynn Barber said, 'Be punctual, be polite and ask questions.'[8]

How you tackle interviews will ultimately come down to your personality, the personality of the interviewee and the subject matter. Like everything else you will get better with practice. But, as a journalist, you should try to develop the necessary social skills to be able to talk naturally to both down-and-outs and millionaires. And you should learn to become a compulsive questioner, however nosy this might seem.

Preparation is crucial but try to avoid the temptation of using the interview as a chance to show off how much you know about a subject. Far better, I think, to use it as a licence to be averagely stupid. Asking questions that might superficially appear to be dull is often the best way to get good answers. Obviously, you don't want to come across as an idiot in front of your interviewee, but remember you are there as the representative of the viewers or listeners who will never have the opportunity to ask questions in the way you have. So, are you asking the questions they would want answered? Or are you asking the questions that will make you appear knowledgeable?

PUTTING IT INTO PRACTICE

- Make sure you're interviewing the right person.
- Get them to spell out their name and their correct designation on tape so you can check it afterwards.
- Try not to agree questions in advance but it's OK to let people know what areas you want to cover.
- Use a combination of fact and emotion/opinion questions. Remember, it's the answers to the latter that will generally end up as your clips.
- Open questions generally produce better answers than closed ones: 'Why?' and 'Why not?' are brilliant questions. Ask them often.
- Keep your questions to the point and focused on a single idea.
- Don't be afraid to look a bit stupid. If somebody says something you don't understand, ask them to explain what they mean. Never fake understanding simply to appear 'professional'.
- Play devil's advocate, if you have to. 'What do you say to those people who think . . . (you are a moron/cheat/liar/fraud/etc.)?'
- Watch your body language. Try to maintain eye contact.
- Stay polite. Don't get into an argument. Don't allow the interviewee to take control.
- There may be one key answer you want. Don't be afraid to ask the same question several times until you get an answer that works. It might be an idea to warn interviewees that you will be doing this.
- Sometimes silence can be a useful tool.
- Don't rehearse the entire interview, though there's nothing wrong with letting the interviewee know what the first question will be so they can mentally prepare. If the subject matter is non-controversial and they are nervous, arrange a code with your camera operator (a cough, perhaps) that tells you they are recording. You can then gradually ease into the interview, rather than saying 'Here we go then . . .' and terrifying them. Clearly this is not the right approach if the interviewee is likely to say something they would later not want broadcast. But if it's just a question of overcoming nerves, people generally perform better if they don't realise the camera is turning over.
- Never say 'Last question . . .' because you will invariably think of another one and then look silly. But once you have exhausted your questions you can always say: 'Unless there is anything you'd like to add?'
- Last but absolutely not least – and probably the hardest one of all . . . Try to listen to what they are saying.

Source: Tony O'Shaughnessy, documentary producer/director and journalism trainer

Questions

Good questions are key to a good interview so they need to be well thought out, well crafted and flexible. They also need to be clear, simple and targeted. Have you ever noticed how the responses you get differ according to how you phrase a question? This is one of the most important things to remember during the interview process. There may be a lot of subconscious psychology going on during the interview process. Whole books have been written about questioning and interviewing for different careers and outcomes. It is an area of study in its own right, but some of the basic principles are worth thinking about. One thing to consider in this process is what makes a bad question, then it should be easier to frame an effective one. Here are a couple of negative questions and the responses invited by the way they are framed:

- 'I don't suppose you could tell me?' **No, I couldn't.**
- 'Do you mind if I ask . . . ?' **Yes, I do actually.**

Why are they bad questions? Because they allow an element of choice on the part of the interviewee and they could opt not to tell you. Think of how salespeople work – they give you the product, put it in your hands and tell you how great it is for you, personally. It is an effective tool – because the scenario paints you as part of the image. This will work for you in an interview too.

So ask the question, don't ask if you can ask it. Try something like: 'Tell me about the situation.' Simple, straightforward and doesn't leave much leeway for refusal. The interviewee has been painted into the picture, so is less likely to want to back away.

Another difficult form is the closed question and again here are some examples and explanations of the difficulties relating to them:

- Do you think . . . ?
- Is it . . . ?
- Are you . . . ?

Why are these examples of bad questions? Because they can lead to closed answers – literally allowing the interviewee to say yes or no. Ask open-ended questions – these often start with our old friends who, how, why and what. If you do ask a closed question you need to follow it up in a way that allows the interviewee to open up a bit more.

Another danger is overloading a question, as in this example: 'In light of the situation, given that your company is involved, do you think this is a bad thing and what are you going to do about it?' Which part of the question do you want them to answer first, and which part will be ignored by the savvy interviewee? The best thing to do is ask one question at a time. Be like a politician during Prime Minister's Questions: ask your main question but keep your killer supplementary for after the first has been dealt with. Save your toughest questions until near the end of the interview. Instead of being booted out, this way you'll have built some rapport and got information to develop your piece before the killer question gets introduced.

Don't just ask questions in the interviewee's technical language, get them to explain things to you as a layperson – you'll get better answers and you'll ensure that you understand what is going on. But you need to understand the technical language in order to tell the story properly as highlighted in the section on 'The beat reporter' earlier (pp. 32–34). Another thing to remember is that conversation is not one way; you don't need to interrupt but do ensure that they know that you are interested in what they are saying. The occasional nod, or a 'really?' helps a lot.

Finishing the interview

Never be afraid to ask to review what you've gone over and check your understanding. If you are clear about why you want to do this – because you want to ensure that this is fair and accurate – then there will be no problems. And one of the key things to ensure you do at this stage is to check spellings, particularly names. People get absolutely furious when stories are inaccurate; it can also weaken any legal case you may find yourself in.

You also need to ask what is sometimes termed as the bucket, or catch-all, question: 'Is there anything else I/my readers should know about this?' Once you've checked these things there are a couple of other things to remember: ensure you know where they are going to be later in case of any other questions or you need to organise a photograph; and don't forget to say thanks!

PUTTING IT INTO PRACTICE

There are some important things to bear in mind that may crop up in an interview. These examples are just some of the problems you may come up against:

- No comment. Sounds weak from them and makes you sound weak to your audience. Start exploring the situation more and try to get some decent answers, even if it is only that they are currently investigating and can't talk about it for legal reasons. If they still won't talk to you ask who can, or simply go and find someone else yourself. Don't ever walk away from a story because one person in the chain is not prepared to speak to you.
- Is this off the record? This is a minefield for the unwary. If you agree to being off the record, what can you use? Be clear with your interviewee and ensure that they are being clear about what they can tell you and what they can't officially tell you. And remind them that if you get the same information from someone else you will use it and this will not be affected by their going off the record.
- Can I see it before it goes to print/live? Again a dangerous one for the young journalist. There's no problem with fact checking information but allowing them to have a say on the story before printing can lead to editorial censorship and will not make you popular with your employer.

remember

My former colleague Garry Edwards introduced me to a little mnemonic, which nicely sums up the stages of an interview:

I Introduce yourself.
N Niceties, small talk before the interview.
T Tell, get them to tell you about the incident you are interested in.
E Expand or explore the situation.
R Review what has been discussed.
V Verify, facts, figures, names, etc.
I Introduce the killer question.
E Exit from the interview itself, check where they will be, picture opportunities, leave a business card.
W Wait, many people will feel more relaxed when the interview itself is over and will chat. Just make sure you have a record of what was said.

COMPUTERS AND JOURNALISM

The world is awash with information in electronic format and one of the tasks of a savvy young journalist is to understand how to get the best out of it as part of the research and story-gathering process.

Journalists are learning how to master search techniques, engage with social networks, master database and spreadsheets, and even programming languages. Not every journalist needs to be an expert in all of these, but there are some simple but important ideas it's vital to get on top of early in your career so this section will touch on some of the most accessible. However, don't think that these techniques are a replacement for some of the offline techniques outlined earlier in this chapter; they aren't. They are there to augment them and give you access to information you might not easily get any other way. As American journalist Margaret H. DeFleur rightly said: 'The computer is a tool that can be used with great effectiveness by a reporter but it must be supplemented with a basic "shoe-leather" approach.'[9]

Mastering web searching

'The secret weapon of the Internet – the killer app, to use the jargon – is not shopping, gambling or sex, but people. There are people out there with huge amounts of experience and expertise; you just have to find them and get them to talk.'[10]

Contrary to what many people think, the World Wide Web (or simply the web) is not the same thing as the internet. The simplest way to describe it, and one that is often used, is that the internet is the rails that a number of different services run on. The internet is home to:

- the web;
- search engines (e.g. Google);
- human-maintained directories (e.g. Open Directory);
- email;
- mailing lists;
- newsgroups;
- wikis;
- file transfer protocol (FTP);
- older services such as gopher, telnet, moo, muds.

Many of these can be useful to journalists and can be searched as part of 'the hidden web' – because although Google, Bing, Yahoo and the other search giants do a great job, not everything is actually indexed. But rather than the hidden web, we're going to focus on getting the basic search engine techniques right, which is more important on a day-to-day basis.

Search engines are sometimes called machine indexes – literally because computer software does all the hard work. Search engines generally use small pieces of software called spiders which crawl around the web indexing pages, literally known as web crawling. They look at words within the individual page, where they occur and how frequently and follow links from within a site. They will also explore links coming in to the site in order to find out how popular it is with people. This will then be returned in the form of search results.

There are an awful lot of websites on the internet: in May 2011 the Domain Tools site put the number of active registered domains at 130,894,938. In fact during the daily update for 4 May 2011 134,083 domains were registered and 88,241 were deleted.

So, given there is so much information on the web, how do you find what you are looking for? The first step is to ask: what do you want to know? You'd never go into an interview without having done your prep. It's rude, inefficient and can land you with some really weak answers. Would you walk into a library and demand an answer from the first member of staff that you happen to find? No. Because they may not be the specialist in your field, they may just point you to a section and leave you to have a look through on your own, or more likely they will start to ask you a series of questions that will help sort out what you are looking for.

So why do we go onto the internet and do just that? Poor search techniques often start with poor preparation. Blind Googling is one thing, and a thing we all do in our spare time, but it isn't appropriate for a journalist. To get the best out of a search engine you need to learn how to phrase questions – think about it as interviewing a source rather than just shouting at a machine. And one of the keys to that is understanding some of the basics of search.

PUTTING IT INTO PRACTICE

Look at this search term – Tom and Jerry.

Do we mean the loveable cartoon cat and his mouse friend, are we talking about two people or a company? A search engine wouldn't know. It would use a series of sophisticated algorithms to try to return an answer. In this case search engines would assume you were talking about the cartoon duo due to the frequency of key words and how many people link to sites containing these key words. But what if you weren't? A Google search for the words returned 17,600,000 results: that's a lot of pages to sort through.

Another problem is the term itself. Some search engines will not look for the word 'and' as it crops up too frequently. So in reality it is actually looking for the frequency of the words Tom Jerry, but not necessarily as part of one phrase.

Here's another problem for a computer: the word 'Bass' – fish, guitar or beer? Search engines will not know the difference and this is where power searching comes in.

Learning how to power search

As stated earlier, web searching should be far more methodical than just randomly throwing words into a search engine. As well as understanding what you are asking for there are advanced search options that can be used. Each search engine uses its own so you will have to learn different ways of working for different search sites, but it is well worth doing. We'll look at some of the advanced tools for Google as an example.

We know Google ignores words such as 'and', 'the', 'a', 'for': the technical term for this is 'stop words' – they aren't required as part of the search process. Google will try to find the sites which most frequently return your key words but it can also help if you are searching for a specific phrase. Putting double quote marks around your search term (i.e. "search term") is a way of telling Google that you want those words in that order. Officially Google looks at the order of the words and their proximity anyway, but it is still a useful filter technique if you are finding a lot of search results coming back to you. One note of caution though: Google will look for that specific result and ignore related ones. Here are some other pointers:

- **Site.** This allows you to search within a specific site to find your search terms, a particularly useful technique as not all sites have their own search tool.
- **Search site: whatever.com.** Can be used to look at types of site, so in this example we're looking at UK government sites for the key word Flu, e.g. Flu, site:gov.uk.
- **Exclude terms.** The use of the minus sign (–) tells Google you don't want that word to appear in your results. It must be right in front of the term to be excluded and not include any spaces so bass–beer.
- **Wildcards.** The * can be used to replace words.
- **OR.** Does exactly what it says on the tin – this is part of the search term rather than looking for the word or (e.g. recycle glass OR plastic).
- **Define.** Helps turn your Google search into a definition. What is/what are also work here. For example, **Define: computer assisted reporting** will give you several definitions of computer assisted reporting on the web; e.g. 'Database journalism was born in the 1950s as a synonym for computer-assisted reporting. Since then, computers have become ubiquitous, to the . . .' **en.wikipedia.org/wiki/Computer-assisted_reporting**
- **Filetype.** This is particularly useful and allows you to get a specific file type (you'll have to know the file extensions, for example .pdf is a portable document file (PDF), .doc is a document file, and .xls is a spreadsheet file). It becomes even more powerful when used as a search to find data relating to a story. If you are looking to get data for analysis this is really important to know.
- **Link.** Find pages that link to a page so, **link:news.bbc.co.uk** will return links from pages that link to the news site.
- **Cache.** Cached versions of a page – useful if something disappears, although this will only stay for a while. There are other sites that can help here. One of the best is **http://www.archive.org** also known as the Wayback Machine.
- **Info:** Find out about a page.

PUTTING IT INTO PRACTICE

Combinations of these advanced search tools get really powerful. For example, we know that a council keeps lists of empty properties for council tax or business rates monitoring. These kinds of documents are often stored as an Excel spreadsheet (.xls) so we could combine some of the power search tools to try to get the raw information.

For example, if we want to look for empty homes data from freedom of information requests in a spreadsheet format we could style our question **empty homes foi filetype:xls**. This returns 119 results while **empty homes freedom of information filetype:xls** returns 150, but it is worth noting that the search **empty homes foi filetype:pdf** returned 2,690 results.

PUTTING IT INTO PRACTICE

- Imagine what the ideal (hypothetical) page you are looking for would look like. What language and terminology would the author of that page use to describe the thing you are looking for? Those are the terms you will need in order to find what you are looking for, not necessarily those terms which you (and we all) initially think of.
- Always use a thesaurus when doing subject-based research. Google's ~ operator is good, but fairly limited at the time of writing.
- Go for the cached option (where available) in your web search results. This is what the page looked like (including the terms it contained) when it was last indexed by the search engine. This is a good way to avoid the frustration of clicking on search results only to find the terms you were looking for have disappeared (but to be absolutely sure, and avoid results where other pages containing your search terms 'point' to that page, use + signs before every term).
- If you're searching for people (who aren't in the public eye), always use 'phrase searching'. But just as importantly, if you are searching for people don't rely on Google alone. Try one of the other free, bespoke, people finders out there – like 123 people, Pipl or Yasni. More generally, don't rely only on Google for every type of search: different engines have very different indexes, and you are always best to maximise the catch.
- Use advanced operators and get to grips with search logic: Google (and other search engines) offer a range of operators to help either expand (**OR, ~**) or refine (**–**) your search according to page content. In these days of information overload, anything that can give you more control over your searching is invaluable – use the advanced option (most engines offer them) if you are unfamiliar with search logic.
- Use advanced functions: Google (and other search engines) also offer a range of search functions to help you refine by type of result. For example, the domain function (**site:.org.uk**) which lets you refine by a particular (or type of) domain, and the filetype function (**filetype:xls**) which lets you search by type of file – useful, for example, when you are after statistics (often published in .xls format).
- If you are doing in-depth research, keeping on top of a subject for a while (rather than a one-off story), turn all your best searches (in Google Blogs, Twitter, Yahoo News, etc.) into RSS feeds. But don't worry too much about doing this in straight Google or Yahoo searches – pages will need to have a very good search ranking to break the top few pages of results for that search, and end up in your feed reader.
- Save all your favourite pages online for later (using delicious, Stumbleupon, reddit, etc.). Don't rely on bookmarking things on your PC locally – if you end up hot-desking, or use more than one computer (or are a mobile worker) you'll have to replicate all of those pages on every computer you use.
- Don't let the hidden web give you the slip. The 'hidden' or 'invisible' web includes all content that Google (and other engines) can't index for various reasons (paywalls, password-protection, forms, dynamic content, etc.). The Internet Archive and governmental databases are among the most obvious examples here. But does you local library (or university library or employer) subscribe to a newspaper cuttings database (like Lexis Nexis, Factiva, NewsUK or Newsbank)? These are essential in all walks of journalism – so see what's available to you.
- Mind your privacy: if you are doing investigative research, or looking for information in parts of the web where you'd rather not publicly declare you are a journalist, anonymise your presence, whether in search (i.e. using Anonymizer) or in your access to sites (i.e. The Cloak).

Source: Murray Dick. University lecturer and journalism trainer, has worked with the BBC and was the information officer at the Centre for Investigative Journalism

Found it! Now what?

Once you've got a result you need to check whether it is actually appropriate or if some hoaxer has put it up to trick the unwary. One way to do that is to see who is linking to the information by using Google's **linkto:** operator. It will tell you who is actually linking to the page you are interested in.

Another way is to look for who is behind the site. This could be listed on the About page of the site but it might be appropriate to run what is termed a whois search. This is a search of web registers looking for who registered a website. Although site owners can pay for this to be hidden, it is well worth getting to grips with.

PUTTING IT INTO PRACTICE

Here's an example whois search. You've been asked by your editor to do a feature on the band Pitchshifter, but going via the venue hasn't got you anywhere. A colleague suggests putting the URL into the domaintools whois search tool, **http://whois.domaintools.com/**.

As you can see from the results returned we've now got an address, phone number and a name for the technical support and administration behind the site – and for those that have already done their initial research, that contact is actually the band's lead singer J.S. Clayden.

This doesn't always give a result though, as the same search at **http://www.allwhois.com** shows no results other than

> Registered through: GoDaddy.com, Inc.
> (http://www.godaddy.com)

so the simplest way forward is to go to the godaddy site, find the whois search tool and run the search again.

remember

- Go beyond standard searching by thinking carefully about what you are looking for.
- Learn power search terms.
- Think about the kinds of format that people store information in, and how you can find it.
- Verify all sources.

SOCIAL MEDIA

A category of sites that is based on user participation and user-generated content. They include social networking sites like LinkedIn or Facebook, social bookmarking sites like Delicious, social news sites like Digg or Reddit, and other sites that are centred on user interaction.[11]

Web 2.0, the so-called interactive Web, has brought about a number of changes in the way journalists use the web for both research and publishing. One of the key changes is the use of social media – social network sites such as Facebook and Twitter, to name just two of a myriad of tools being used by people to engage in conversations about their personal lives, their interests or their work. At all times of the day and night people are engaging with networks of family, friends, colleagues, peers and even strangers to share, chat and generally hang out online.

The use of these tools is a key area for the digitally aware journalist and the underpinning technologies have allowed for the development of what has been termed networked (or collaborative) journalism. Networking is not a new idea for journalists – after all every time we go to a meeting, conference or just talk to a contact we are engaged in networking. However, there are a number of differences – some of the terminology is different and the possible reach of a journalist engaged in a social network is increased exponentially through the network effect. Like any tool, social media needs to be thought about carefully. At the moment there are mixed views on whether it is acceptable to take content from social media sites – although the laws of copyright apply every bit as much online (see Chapter 9 for more details) – and this is covered later in this chapter.

Using social media for research

Key tools to get started with are:

- Twitter,
- Flickr,
- YouTube,
- Facebook,
- MySpace,
- Blogs.

One of the key things about using social media for research is that it allows you to track people either by what they are talking about or where they are based. So, if you are interested in the buzz that is happening in Twitter you can add the term to a search engine, although this is simpler to do in Twitter's own search tool **http://search.twitter.com/**, and using RSS can make it even more powerful than just Googling and looking for ideas.

Using Twitter

Twitter is a social media/social networking tool that divides a lot of people – just look at how newspapers and even BBC's *Newsnight* were talking about the service in 2009. It was even discussed in the Houses of Parliament as part of the investigation surrounding how super injunctions can be used to bind the press.

In 2011 Twitter became one of the first sources about the US raid on the hideout of Osama Bin Laden in Pakistan – an IT consultant was putting out updates about military helicopters in his area way before the media got hold of the news. In response, the BBC's Rory Cellan-Jones said: 'A journalist who does not use Twitter is now like one who abjures the mobile phone.'[12]

There are a number of simple steps to getting the best out of Twitter and people who often decry the service are usually those who have tried it but not understood what is going on. What they didn't realise is that like any other network of contacts or information a lot of work is required to get the best out of it.

PUTTING IT INTO PRACTICE

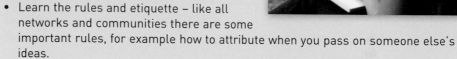

- Get an account by logging on to twitter.com.
- Get phone activated – this means you can tweet from your phone, even if it is by just sending a text message to the server, or by installing an app on your smart phone.
- Get a desktop client – this is one of the key things about Web 2.0 technologies, you no longer have to go to the website to access the service.
- Learn the rules and etiquette – like all networks and communities there are some important rules, for example how to attribute when you pass on someone else's ideas.
- Find people – there are all sorts of ways of finding people. **search.twitter.com** will allow you to find people tweeting about things or in a geographical location. Twitter's lists function allows you to look for lists of people – and there are a lot of journalists engaging in these tools listed in these areas.
- Follow people – this is crucial. If you are in an empty bar you will never meet anyone, this is partly how Twitter works. So add people to your network, listen to them and then . . .
- Get tweeting, talk about what you are researching, working on and trying to discover.
- Engage in conversations – be human in public. This is key. Be yourself and don't just expect to receive. Researchers in forums will often lurk; do that on Twitter and you will miss out on a great deal of the power of the network.
- Be aware of any company guidelines if you are running a work-based account.
- Ensure you have an avatar (picture identifier) and some biographical details attached to your account.
- It is very easy to fabricate a profile for someone and what is constantly amazing is how journalists seem to be falling over themselves to get stories published which turn out to be fake. One way to get round this is to do what the BBC's user generated content team does in order to check whether an image or video is as it should be: contact the person who owns the account. Arrange for a phone number and then ask them to shoot a section of video or image from where they are and MMS it to you – that will reduce the likelihood of getting it wrong.

Twitter as a real-time search engine

The nature of Twitter means that people are constantly updating the service with snippets, links and images they think are important and relevant to their network. And given the speed and ease with which you can use a mobile device – a smartphone or just a text or image sent from your mobile – it means that the web is alive and kicking with information which can be of value to a reporter.

There are a number of useful tools:

- Smart phone apps are a brilliant way of getting to grips with the network from your smart phone or your tablet device. Twitter has a pretty good app which runs on most of these devices.
- Monniter – a web-based Twitter search tool which allows you to monitor what people are talking about by subject or by proximity to a location (this works from a user's specified location from within their profile).
- Tweetdeck – a desktop client for Twitter which gives the option to filter and create columns in a similar way to Monniter. Although desktop based this does allow cloud syncing between machines based around your account. Tweetdeck also has a tool which allows Tweets to be translated into English, which works pretty well.
- Search.twitter.com – the advanced search option from within Twitter allows some very powerful options. It allows you to refine searches and even to look for conversations between particular users or within a certain distance of a given location.
- A key point to note is that Twitter Search can be hacked to return an RSS feed for your query – meaning that you can set up the perpetual search talked about earlier to allow you to keep up to date with your chosen topic (see **http://bitly.com/tweetrss** for a guide).

PUTTING IT INTO PRACTICE

Tools such as Google blog search and Twitter search allow you to get or create RSS feeds for your search term. And there are lots more that allow you to take an RSS feed of the search you are working on and make it your own.

These can be imported into an RSS reader such as Google Reader or Netvibes and provide constant results for searches. (see **http://www.commoncraft.com/video/rss** for a handy guide).

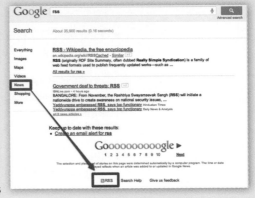

A CLOSER LOOK

ETHICS AND SOCIAL MEDIA

It's often tempting for journalists to think about people's social network profiles as nothing more than websites which are an open source of images and biographical details to be used at whim. This has been an ethical issue that has needed much closer attention since the Virginia Tech shootings in 2007, when a student killed 32 people and injured many more before killing himself. Up until 2006 Facebook had been a closed platform for students, but that changed and the service saw a massive influx of members, meaning that a large number of people were sharing personal information and images – which they often perceive as private. Academics interested in web interaction will often talk about this as private in public.

In the UK the reporting of the deaths of 20 young people in Bridgend County in Wales – which had been wrongly described as a suicide cluster – raised concerns after journalists lifted biographical details from their social networks.

▶ A CLOSER LOOK

The story was reported as a suicide cluster – with much of the media's reporting implying that the deaths were in the town of Bridgend rather than the county. Pictures of a number of the youngsters were taken from social networking sites and published. This led to an update in the Editors' Codebook – a newspaper and periodicals industry code of practice that is enforced by the Press Complaints Commission (PCC):

'Publications of photographs without family consent: Using pictures supplied by friends or from social networking sites, without the close family's consent, can cause unintentional distress.

'There can be no hard rules in such subjective areas. These and similar measures can only be discretionary. But the lessons of Bridgend are that, by bearing them in mind, editors faced with difficult judgements at critical times could avoid causing unintended offence or exposure to accusations of insensitivity.

'Social networking sites: Material from such sites published without consent can raise privacy issues. The PCC will take into account a variety of factors under the Code: how private the material is; how it was used (i.e. in cases involving grief or shock, would it be insensitive?); how accessible it was to third parties – including whether the person concerned had restricted public access to the profile; whether the individual knew it was being used; and, importantly, whether the subject matter concerned a child.'[13]

| EXAMPLE 2.2 | DUNBLANE AND AFTERWARDS |

In March 1996, Thomas Hamilton walked into a primary school in Dunblane, Scotland, and killed 16 young pupils and one of their teachers before turning one of his guns on himself. The media industry went into overdrive, reporting on an event which was unprecedented in UK history. As with any story, it was followed up in terms of the inquiry that ensued and how that eventually changed the law on possession of handguns in the UK.

For 13 years, the youngsters went about their lives, learning to deal with this traumatic event out of the limelight. In March 2009, the Scottish *Sunday Express* carried an anniversary piece looking at some of the young people who were now turning 18. Nothing unusual there, anniversary stories are a staple part of the journalism world.

The story was based on posts from some of the survivors' profiles on the Bebo social network, and splashed with the headline

ANNIVERSARY SHAME OF DUNBLANE SURVIVORS
Internet boasts of sex, drink and violence as youngsters hit 18

It took some pictures and quotes from their profiles, claiming this shamed their dead classmates, and painted them as writing 'foul-mouthed boasts about sex, brawls and drink-fuelled antics'.

Three of their parents complained to the Press Complaints Commission that this breached Clause Three of the code – invading their privacy. The paper stated that

▶ EXAMPLE 2.2

all of the information they used was publicly accessible on the social network and the young people had been named at the time. The *Sunday Express* apologised and published the apology in print and on the web, but the families were still unhappy.

The PCC ruling was that there were times when it was appropriate for the press to publish information from social media sites – even if it was only intended for a small group of people rather than a mass audience. However, in this instance the PCC ruled the boys were not public figures and had been presented in a way that set out to humiliate them.

'Publication represented a serious error of judgement on the part of the newspaper. Although the editor had taken steps to resolve the complaint, and rightly published an apology, the breach of the Code was so serious that no apology could remedy it.'[14]

These are important points for anyone involved in social network research to remember. First, what the journalist may perceive as public may be viewed in a very different way by those who are posting the information. Secondly, you need to be careful of your online reputation. Paula Murray, the journalist who wrote the piece, came under fire from bloggers who posted drunken pictures of her on the web.[15]

The story has since been taken down, but you can find it easily by searching for the title above – plenty of bloggers have put it onto their sites.

remember

- Social media is a big area, and there are millions of people online – so you need to ensure you are using advanced search for functions to find your beat or community.
- If you are going to use social networks as part of your research you need to ensure that you are regularly involved in what is going on rather than just turning up once in a while to ask questions.
- Consider everything to be fabricated, unless you can prove otherwise.

DATA JOURNALISM

This section will focus on the use of software or web tools to gather, analyse and display information in a way that makes sense – rather than just presenting a table of numbers to your audience. Skills used in this field of research range from the relatively simple, to the complex – and it is a field that is well worth starting to get to grips with.

Over the past few years the terminology used to describe this area has changed. It was previously called computer-assisted reporting and focused on using spreadsheets and databases to analyse data. Data journalism does this and a lot more besides, as there is also a focus on how to present the information gleaned from the approach or even how to mix multiple sources of information to get a bigger picture – known as mashing.

The MPs' expenses scandal[16] is essentially a data story; the discovery of extreme rendition flights by Stephen Grey was also a data story – which resulted in the book

Ghost Plane. But it can have much more everyday uses: there have been great stories in Birmingham and Cardiff of journalists requesting parking fine data and being able to map parking fine 'hotspots' in terms of location and time of day.

So what is it all about? What makes data journalism any different from any other type of reporting? The simplest answer is there is nothing different. The whole point is to interrogate a source and come up with information, figures and leads for stories – in the same way as any other journalistic reporting. One of the defining things about this type of research and output is what it sets out to do and what tools it uses to get the job done.

Data journalism can be quite simple, and using tools like Google Documents allows you quickly and easily to start setting up your own spreadsheets which you can analyse and check. A good journalist to look at is James Ball, currently a data journalist at the *Guardian*. James worked with the Bureau for Investigative Journalism before working with Wikileaks and later joined the national newspaper.

> **'Data is definitely getting more and more important. Three years ago, pitching any data-based story was difficult-bordering-on-impossible. That's clearly changed, especially in the investigative field after a year of WikiLeaks scoops.**
>
> **Even outside of investigations, though, the volume of government and business data appearing is increasing exponentially, and too few journalists really know how to make data sing.'**[17]

One of the key things to think about with any kind of data-driven story is that this will not be a slow process. Data had to be found, or made into a machine-readable format, then checked for errors – what is known as cleaning dirty data – before analysis can be run. Advice often given by experienced CAR/data practitioners such as David Donald, database editor at the US Center for Public Integrity, is simple – work on the data to see if there is a story before bringing it to the news conference.[18] This is not a quick process and will require skills-building on your part and an understanding news editor.

You'll also need to make sure your maths and statistics skills are up to date. This is often a tricky one for journalists as many come from an arts or humanities background.

Proficiency in areas of this kind is beyond the scope of this section but a good starting point can be found in *The Online Journalism Handbook* by Paul Bradshaw and Lisa Rohumaa. Media Wales journalist Claire Miller is also blogging about her progress in developing data skills.[22] She's been putting together some posts about what she's learning and they are a good place for anyone looking to start in this field.

PUTTING IT INTO PRACTICE

You may not realise it, but the section on advanced search was designed to get you going with data journalism – using advanced search functions can provide an awful lot of data that a lot of people do not realise they have put on the internet. You need to carry out Activity 4 at the end of the book and then open the spreadsheet that you find.

1 Then open up your web browser and go to Batchgeo.com.
2 Come back to the spreadsheet and check to see if you have postcodes; you can then copy the data from the spreadsheet and paste it into the box on the site.
3 Batchgeo will then geocode (find the addresses) and create a map based on your area. It will allow you to see if there are any clusters of empty properties in particular areas.
4 You can then embed this in a website.

Congratulations, you've just done your first data visualisation.

A CLOSER LOOK

Journalist Nicola Hughes is blogging about her transition to developer journalist at datamineruk.wordpress.com. Nicola is now a Knight Mozilla Fellow at the Guardian, but she previously worked with Scraperwiki.[19] While at Scraperwiki she helped gather the data that led to a Channel 4 story on debt,[20] and there's an interesting post on Scraperwiki's blog on how it was done.[21]

Nicola's advice for getting started

Although 'data journalism' can encompass infographics, interactives, web apps, FOI, databases and a whole host of other numbering, coding, displaying techniques; the road less travelled-by has certain steps, turns and speed bumps. In that sense, here's a list of things to tick off if you're interested in going down the data journalism road:

1   Know the legal boundaries – get to know the Data Protection Act 1998 and the sections on access to personal data and unstructured personal data held by authorities. Do not set foot on your journey without reading the section on exemptions relating to journalism. Use legislation as a reference by downloading the Mobile Legislate app.

2   Look at data – get to know what is out there, what format it's in and where it's coming from. Places like Data.gov.uk, London Datastore, Office for National Statistics and Get the Data are good places to start for raw data but don't forget, anything on the web is data. The best data is often hidden. Data can be text and pictures so even mining social media and catching the apps built from them can give you insight into what can be done with data.

3   Read all about it – to make data and stats accessible you need to know how to frame them within a story. In that sense, you need to know how to understand the stories they tell. That doesn't mean going on a stats course. There is a lot of accessible reading material and I would recommend *The Tiger That Isn't*.

4   Get connected – find HacksHackers near you and join Meetup groups to point you in the right directions. Data journalists' interests and abilities are unique to the individual (much like programmers) so don't take text of advice as set in stone (the web changes too quickly for that!). Find your own way and your own set of people to guide you. Go to courses and conferences. Look outside the journalism bubble. Data is more than just news.

5   Spread your bets – the easiest way to sort data is by using spreadsheets. Start with free options like Google Docs and OpenOffice. Industry standards include Microsoft Excel and Access. Learn to sort, filter and pivot. Find data you're interested in and explore the data using your eyeballs. Know what each piece of software does and can do to the data before mashing it with another piece of software.

6   Investigate your data – query it using the simple language SQL and the software MySQL. It's a bit tricky to set up but by now you'll know a hacker you can ask for help! Clean your data using Google Refine. There are tutorials and a help wiki. Know how these function, not just how to navigate the user interfaces, as these will change. These products go through iterations much more quickly than the spreadsheet software.

7   Map your data – from Google spreadsheets the easiest way to build a map is by using MapAList. There is a long list of mapping software from GeoCommons to

▶ A CLOSER LOOK

ArcGIS. Find what's easiest for you and most suitable for your data. See what landscapes can be revealed and hone in on areas of interest. Understand the limitations of mapping data; you'll find devolution makes it difficult to get data for the whole of the UK and some postcodes will throw up errors.

8 Make it pretty – visualise your data only once you fully understand it (source, format, timeframe, missing points, etc.). Do not jump straight to this as visuals can be misleading. Useful and easy software solutions include Google Fusion Tables, Many Eyes and Tableau. Think of unique ways to present data by checking out what the graphics teams at news organisations have done and also what design sites such as Information is Beautiful and FlowingData are doing.

9 Make your community – don't just find one, build one. This area in journalism is constantly changing and for you to keep up you'll need to source a custom-made community. So blog and tweet but also source ready-made online communities from places like the European Journalism Centre, National Institute for Computer Assisted Reporting (NICAR), BuzzData and DataJournalismBlog.

10 Scrape it – do not be constrained by data. Liberate it, mash it, make it usable. Just like a story, data is unique and bad data journalism comes with constraining the medium containing it. With code, there is no need to make the story 'fit' into the medium. 'The Medium is the Message' (à la Marshall McLuhan). Scrape the data using ScraperWiki and make applications beyond story-telling. Make data open. For example check out OpenCorporates, Schooloscope and Planning Alerts.

remember

- Understanding where data comes from is essential, even if it means creating it yourself from information you gather.
- Data journalism is like an interview: find the right source, learn how to ask questions and remember to check everything.
- Even a simple visualisation like a map can add to a story, but you need to make sure it is in context.

CHAPTER SUMMARY

- Good research starts with an understanding of the reader and the product.
- Research must be systematic and targeted, as you may end up showing your notes in court.
- Learn how to find people and then ask them questions, and store that information in an appropriate form.
- Keep a contacts book.
- Learn how to make the best use of your computer and the internet to assist your research – but don't forget that the best stories aren't all done from your desk.

THINKING IT THROUGH

Finding the right medium

One of the key things to remember about researching stories is to be systematic. The point of being a journalist is to develop tool sets of people, skills and software that will help you to get the best out of contacts and sources. Ensure you set up a contacts book or database; check with sources regularly; and keep up with your news feeds. Research is not a static process, and over-reliance on a set of contacts or sources can lead to weak stories and a very limited set of responses to an issue.

Ask yourself: What is the right medium for me to carry out my research? Clearly there's no right answer here but what will be clear is what kind of starting point you need. Is this a breaking story that can be crowd sourced to try to find out if anyone is on the scene and can tell us more or share pictures? Or is this more suited to a phone call? Do we need to Google search or do we have access to our own archives to get things going?

NOTES

[1] http://www.walesonline.co.uk/cardiffonline/cardiff-news/2010/10/25/call-for-more-openness-from-police-force-91466-27536319/

[2] http://www.vogue.co.uk/voguemediapack/swfa/?

[3] http://www.nrs.co.uk/lifestyle.html

[4] http://www.vogue.co.uk/voguemediapack/swfa/?

[5] http://bit.ly/pompey_mediapack

[6] Talk at Cardiff University journalism school, 2011.

[7] Interview with the author.

[8] 'The Art of the Interview' in Stephen Glover (ed) *The Penguin Book of Journalism*: Secrets of the Press (2000). London: Penguin.

[9] Margaret H. Defleur (1997) *Computer-assisted Investigative Reporting*. London: Routledge.

[10] John Morrish, freelance journalist and trainer, *Press Gazette*, 6 December 2002.

[11] http://searchenginewatch.com/define

[12] http://www.bbc.co.uk/news/technology-13257940

[13] http://www.pcc.org.uk/advice/editorials-detail.html?article=NTU4MQ==

[14] http://www.pcc.org.uk/news/index.html?article=NTc5Mw==?oxid=a8ea2047270292dc8f98ec bcb23a6d0c

[15] http://www.bloggerheads.com/archives/2009/03/paula_murray_drinks.asp

[16] http://www.telegraph.co.uk/news/newstopics/mps-expenses/

[17] http://www.journalism.co.uk/news-features/-there-was-never-an-average-day--james-ball-on-being-wikileaks-in-house-journalist/s5/a542552/

[18] Conversation with the author, 2009.

[19] http://datamineruk.wordpress.com/

[20] http://www.channel4.com/news/could-selling-off-britains-assets-cut-the-debt

[21] http://blog.scraperwiki.com/2011/03/08/600-lines-of-code-748-revisions-a-load-of-bubbles/

[22] http://clairemiller.net/blog/

WEBLINKS

Given that data journalism is a new and exciting field of research, the recommended links will focus on that area.

http://www.ire.org/   Investigative Journalists and Editors – an international organisation although with a US focus, which offers training and support for investigative journalists.

http://datajournalism.stanford.edu/   Journalism in the Age of Data – this series of videos was created as part of a research fellowship from the Knight Foundation; well worth a watch.

http://www.gijn.org/   Global Investigative Journalism – A group of non-profit organisations who produce stories, conduct training and provide resources. The organisation also runs conferences.

http://www.tcij.org   The Centre for Investigative Journalism – a UK-based charity that runs training and summer schools for journalists; well worth a look at the resources available on the site.

RECOMMENDED READING

Bradshaw, Paul and Rohumaa, Liisa (2011) *The Online Journalism Handbook: Skills to survive and thrive in the digital Age*. Harlow: Pearson.
The chapter on data journalism is a good place to get started with this area – there are also some good points about social media and how to use communities in your research.

Brooke, Heather (2007) Your right to know: a citizen's guide to the Freedom of Information Act. London: Pluto Press.
Arguably *the* book that every journalist should own when it comes to using Freedom of Information as a research tool.

Harcup, Tony (2009) Journalism: Principles and practice. Abingdon: Sage.
Don't be put off by the slightly odd formatting of this book; the section on the journalist as investigator is well worth a read.

McKane, Anna (2006) *News writing*. Abingdon: Sage.
Very much a newspaper journalist's take on research, but some useful and interesting points.

Quinn, Stephen (2008) *Online newsgathering: Research and reporting for journalism*. London: Focal Press.
A good book with plenty of information for those wanting to get the best out of their computer. Given its age it tends to talk about computer-assisted reporting rather than data journalism – but the only difference is semantics.

REFERENCE

Evans, Harold (1963) 'Getting the Facts', in J. Dodge and G. Viner (eds) *The Practice of Journalism*. Oxford: Heinemann, p. 64.

ACTIVITIES

1 Having worked through this chapter answer this question: what is news? For this exercise speak to five different people (not journalists) and make a note of what was said. Then look at pages 30–31 and see how it compares. How many of them have mentioned war, crime or national politics as key ingredients in the mix?

2 Try answering these questions about where you live or study, without using a reference source.

   a. Who is your local MP?
   b. What is the political composition of your local council?
   c. Who are the ward councillors for the area you live in?
   d. What is the name of the school that scored highest in the A Level or GCSE league tables?
   e. What is the name of the owner/manager of your local corner shop/ convenience store?

3 Note down 50 potential sources of news from your local area – yes, many of them will have a web presence, but this exercise is not about finding their press releases on their websites.

   Here are a few obvious examples to get you going:

   ☐ the local courts – magistrates, Crown and civil;
   ☐ emergency services – police, fire, ambulance, mountain rescue, coastguard;
   ☐ local government.

4 Run a power search for empty properties spreadsheet in your local authority, and then open up the spreadsheet and have a look at the results. Does this seem a lot to you? Make notes of who you could speak to develop this story further.

5 Put your favourite site's URL (web address) into the whois search at domaintools and try to find a phone number or address. Then try to verify that address by using simple steps (e.g. Google maps) to check if the address actually exists.

CHAPTERTHREE
NEWS WRITING

This chapter will cover:

- Writing intros
- Story structures
- Key content and story elements
- Use of language, punctuation and quotes

Case study 3.1

IT'S a routine morning in a weekly newspaper office when the phone rings. It could be a reader calling with news of a school play or a summer fête but this time it's different. The caller has seen a taxi driver shot in the town centre and the gunman has driven off with police in pursuit. Another phone rings and another and another.

Before the call few people have heard of Derrick Bird; within a few hours his photograph is plastered across media around the world and the small town of Whitehaven is at the centre of a major breaking news incident.

The first shooting in public is at 10.33 a.m. on Wednesday 2 June, 2010. The death toll is reported – rising from at least 2, to 10 then to 12 and finally Bird shoots himself. Then the identities begin to emerge – the well-known rugby player, the gunman's brother. Twitter feeds claim his own mother is among the victims but this is quickly corrected. The list gets longer and the search for explanation begins. Some of Bird's victims appear completely random – pensioners out walking in this scenic part of the Lake District; but others are targeted – a fellow taxi driver, his solicitor and others against whom he was believed to have held a grudge.

Witness accounts of the killings keep coming; reporters are dispatched to the scenes of reported shootings; emergency services create a gold command emergency control base inland in Penrith; police issue statements but initially with scant detail. They are covering more than 30 crime scenes. Unarmed police in a standard van lose track of the gunman who has shot about 10 people and injured more than 20. The wanted man is identified as Derrick Bird, a 52-year-old taxi driver, and his photograph is released. A Facebook group is reportedly established calling for him to be shot. The public are warned to stay indoors across a swathe of Cumbria and the nearby Sellafield nuclear power plant locks down. Bird has driven south, shooting and killing along his way. He is on the run but no-one knows exactly where. Then a pub landlord reports hearing shots in nearby woodland at Boot. By 2 p.m. Bird is dead.

Police recover a gun and a body, believed to be that of Derrick Bird. Shortly after 3 p.m., the all clear is sent for the public to come out of their homes but it takes several hours before Bird's death is confirmed.

Some time in every journalist's career – even on a small community newspaper – a major news story of shocking magnitude is likely to break. In this heightened atmosphere, a reporter's news-gathering skills and particularly the network of local contacts are put to the test but so too are news-writing abilities. On such an adrenaline-fuelled day reporters may well feel they are operating on auto-pilot but this is when previous training and experience comes to the fore. When a really big story breaks the copy turnaround times become tighter and tighter. In print-only days, a daily reporter would bash out a stop press newsflash, turn around a first take for the next available edition, and look to update for as many extra editions as the press would print. With multiple platforms at hand, a reporter needs to send RSS feeds and Tweets to break and update the unfolding story; flash the news on the website, write a few paragraphs of outline and begin rapidly to flesh out the story, with a core report and as many extra dimensions and links as possible. Reactions whether by phone or digital media need to be handled and fed into the reports, adding graphics, visuals, sound and video as they become available.

If that sounds like too much work for one person, it often is. Sometimes a lone reporter has to do their best; ideally a well-organised newsdesk marshals extra resources as the story develops. Some reporters will be at the scene; others will be digging around for background or chasing witness accounts and one reporter will be holding the ring, shaping and prioritising the information from many sources and sharing the most accurate, illuminating version possible with readers.

Just as police called in every armed officer in the county to track Bird and hospitals called in emergency cover to try to save the shooting victims, so journalists will be drafted in from sister offices, called in from days off and diverted from some other stories to meet the insatiable demand for information from a stunned local and international audience.

The pressure in those first 12 hours is intense but, especially for local media, the story runs on and on. Derrick Bird's shooting spree will be a catalyst for news in and around Whitehaven for weeks, months, indeed generations to come.

See 'The disappearing deadline' in the Thinking It Through feature at the end of this chapter.

INTRODUCTION

One of the killers of two-year-old James Bulger is back in prison after breaching the terms of his licence.

Thousands of people are feared dead after a devastating earthquake struck the Caribbean island of Haiti.

Along with the Derrick Bird killings, these were two of the biggest stories of early 2010 and they offer helpful pointers to the skills of news-writing.

Each is told in fewer than 20 words; indeed fewer than 140 characters. Any journalism student – indeed most people under 30 – will know the significance of the 140. That is the maximum number of characters that can be sent in an individual Tweet. Texting using SMS has a slightly more generous quota of 160 characters. Knowing the formats of mobile media is increasingly significant for journalists especially those reporting news. Accessing information on the go is on the rise all around the world and, for instance, more Africans have access to mobile phones than to computers.

The addition of iPads and all manner of other portable electronic screens is accelerating the delivery of text-based information away from newspaper and on to digital platforms. Newsprint may be pleasurable, convenient and require no expensive electronic reading device but the competition to provide 21st century means of delivery suggests it could be eclipsed by the alternatives. So what impact do the emerging platforms have on the journalist writing news?

Online news certainly opens up new ways of packaging stories; ways of breaking up and layering information and of providing new combinations of text, sound, stills and moving images. Readers have more obvious choices about how to navigate the content and crucially they have the opportunity to interact with the material, its creators and other audience members.

But the public does still need to be given the news and given it as clearly and concisely as possible. There are now many more choices of where readers go from there but they need the core news first. This chapter will focus predominantly on the telling of a basic story – how we break news to an audience.

In many ways the 21st century technology reinforces the basic skills of news-writing. Traditional journalists are branching out into multi-media story-telling and the reach of their text has never been greater. Where every word must count to earn its space in the printed newspaper, so every character must have something to contribute to a text message. In a world of fast-moving, mobile communications, our audience wants it all and it wants it now. So we cannot waste our time or theirs by using words wastefully.

Writing news is about communicating as effectively as possible in text to engage the audience interest and convey an accurate message. A news story has to tell the audience something new: something they don't already know. Most often that means reporting an event, a decision or a change that has just happened. But it can include information about the past as long as it has just emerged. Stories based on government documents released under the 50-year rule are a classic example. Where information has been kept secret, the true story is news even though the events were decades ago.

A news story also has to tell readers something they want to know. Traditionally, many news organisations focused on covering what they felt readers needed to know and such sentiments cannot be lost given the value to a democracy of reliably informed public opinion. However, readers always had the choice to turn the page or not buy the newspaper at all.

In the 21st century, although the range of information available is broader than ever, it is also even easier for the audience to filter out anything it thinks it doesn't want. Using Twitter, RSS feeds and search engines, readers can choose to keep themselves in the dark. The chances of slipping some of what the audience needs in with what it wants are diminishing, so news providers need to work even harder to engage potential readers and be sure of remaining in their information mix.

To connect with our audience we need to understand what will grab and sustain readers' attention. We need to think about what is in it for them. Why would someone read this story? Why does it matter? How is it relevant to my audience? The interactivity of online actually helps us there as we can track like never before what content is being read and for how long. Quite how we respond to charts which are dominated by sport, celebrity and quirky animal stories is part of a wider debate on news values but it does help to explain how readers connect with the content. Those still wanting to provide meaningful coverage at the very least appreciate how hard they must work to meet the challenge, as the American Committee of Concerned Journalists puts it, of making the significant interesting. Much of that impacts on what we write about, whose news we cover and how we package it. But is also puts an even greater premium on how that news is written. The ability to write clear, unambiguous text that can be read and understood in one pass by our audience is of immense value in the information age.

Often journalists will be writing for a clear niche audience where certain prior knowledge and familiarity with jargon can be assumed and that can include specialist news reporting. But in this chapter we focus on what would be seen as general news, aimed at the general public, at a mass audience of ordinary people who want to know what is going on in their world. To do that, we have to know how words work and be able to use them as precision instruments to tell our stories.

remember

- Make every word count.
- Write as clearly and concisely as possible.
- Write for your audience.

WRITING INTROS

Where better to begin than at the start. News journalists call the first sentence of the story the 'intro'; it may also be called the lead. Either way it is the first element of the narrative; the first text that is fully read rather than glanced at as headlines are. It has a vital role to play in conveying the news but also drawing readers into the story so they read on.

Writing news is upfront and out there. The classic approach to news is to blurt it out; to tell the whole story in a nutshell. News reporting is not generally about building suspense or working up to a punchline (see later for the exceptions). News reporters give it all away in the opening sentence. The focus is on the latest situation and the outcome rather than on chronology. Think of it as starting at the end of the story rather than the beginning.

PUTTING IT INTO PRACTICE

Take the example of an armed raid on a jewellery shop. We wouldn't write:
'It had been a quiet day in Morgan's jewellery shop and the staff were preparing to go home when a customer arrived at 5.20 p.m. and asked to see a watch from the window display. A few minutes later a second man came in and inquired

> ▶ PUTTING IT INTO PRACTICE

about jewellery repairs. One assistant went out to the rear of the shop to check with the owner leaving the other assistant alone with the two customers. When she came back into the shop one of the men was pointing a gun at the male assistant and telling him to empty the trays of stock into a bag, etc. etc.'

This blow-by-blow chronological narrative reads like a stilted police witness statement and would turn readers off long before they learned that one of the assistants had been shot challenging the gunman and that the robbers had escaped with half a million pounds of jewellery.

The classic news intro for a Welsh audience would read:

> 'Armed robbers shot a shop assistant who tried to stop them escaping with £500,000 from a Cardiff jewellers this morning.'

or

> 'A brave shop assistant was shot after challenging armed robbers who escaped with £500,000 jewellery from a Cardiff store today.'

Both of the news-style intros convey the overall story in both human and financial terms. In both cases the use of a monetary figure provides a scale and we locate the event to a city. Both provide the basic gist of what has happened and, although still broad brush, do make sense alone.

The first option benefits from powerful, vivid opening words and puts the focus on the main actors in the drama. Readers can immediately visualise the story. The journalist is effectively painting a word picture for them. In our mind's eye readers create an image of two men (nearly everyone would subconsciously make them men), the brandishing of a gun and an injured shop assistant (probably pictured as female).

The first words of an intro are particularly important and ideally convey some drama or significance that will help the reader connect with the story.

The second option in our jewellery raid example focuses on the victim and personalises the story in a way that might appeal particularly to a local readership who may know the shop and staff caught up in the crime. So this time the reader would visualise the story through the eyes of the shop assistant accosting the armed raider.

Choosing between the two would require a judgement on which angle of the story would resonate most with readers.

Activity: Select a couple of newspapers and/or news sites. Examine the intros and consider their main focus. See how they measure up to the checklist on page 64 and re-write them if you think you can do better.

When writing an intro, a reporter also needs to consider the answers to the six classic questions: the who, what, why, when, where and how. Readers will want them all to be answered in the story as a whole and some traditional newspapers pushed to weave all six into an intro. That could make for long, cumbersome intros and did not allow for the fact that some stories rely more heavily on some of the answers than the others. An intro will answer the most significant questions; not necessarily all six. At least three is a popular rule of thumb. Some say one is enough as long as the ensuing story answers the others. Rather than cramming in as many answers as possible, run through the list for each story to isolate the elements that are most important.

In breaking news we may not even have all the answers. Many early reports rely on the what, who, where and when. The how and very often the why may take longer to determine. If a leading politician dies in hospital, the 'who' and 'what' may be the emphatic focus of the breaking news. If a leading politician dies in a brothel, the 'where' demands to be in the intro too.

This process also highlights the importance of drawing out in the intro what is unique and extraordinary about any story. The best formulas and checklists are not employed to make every intro the same but to work through the information to identify what is most exceptional about each one.

Another way of describing intros is as single, double or triple headers. This refers broadly to the number of ideas or angles included in the intro. So a politician dying is a single header – a one idea intro. A politician dying after a police chase would be a double header and a politician dying after a police chase and triggering a general election would be a triple header.

Another example would be:

- Single header: 'The Pope is dead'.
- Double header: 'The Pope made a final plea for peace before dying early today'.
- Triple header: 'The Pope has died, making a last plea for peace and indicating his preference for a doctrinally conservative successor'.

On some stories an intro will almost write itself. On others a journalist will wrestle with the words and sequencing to try to capture the essence of the story in an elegant sentence. Generous colleagues will put their heads together to help each other out when it just doesn't flow. Two distinguished journalists' contributions to the dialogue on intros (and much else) are well worth acknowledging: Harold Evans, the former editor of the *Northern Echo*, *Times* and *Sunday Times*, and David Randall, a vastly experienced UK national newspaperman (see Recommended Reading at the end of this chapter).

Harold Evans, in *Essential English for Journalists*, says (2003: 93):

> **'The skill is in achieving brevity without depriving an intro of precision . . . Filling it with just the right amount of detail is where the skill is needed . . . The intro must concentrate on the effects, on one news idea. It must contain some identification but origins, sequence and chronology are all subsidiary to what resulted in the end.'**

The approach here is helpful in terms of focusing on the upshot of a story – and indirectly having to consider why it matters to readers. The line about the right amount of detail is a particularly interesting way of describing the balancing act required in writing an intro. Some specifics are required to make a connection but too much detail bogs down the reader so that the grand sweep of the event is lost.

Wording an intro is about the dynamics of expression too. A clear, concise sentence with a simple structure has pace. Convoluted sentences slow the reader down, so slow the action too. An effective intro is also likely to be written in active mode with a clear action. So: 'Armed robbers shot . . .' is a good example of a direct sentence with an active verb. The focus is very clearly on the armed robbers.

David Randall's advice in *Universal Journalist* includes:

- Never start a story with a subsidiary clause.
- Never start a story with a number in digits.
- Never start stories with official names of official bodies.

These 'nevers' all stress the importance of the opening words. A direct sentence that begins with a clear subject to drive it is much easier to grasp than one that opens indirectly. So it would be much more confusing to read: 'Having fought off and been shot by an armed robber, a Cardiff shop assistant was critically ill in hospital today.' Readers are left hanging until half way through the sentence. Without a clear subject to focus on from the start, readers take a lot longer to build up a mental picture of what has happened and may well have to read the intro twice to make sense of it.

Starting a story, or indeed a sentence, with a number in digits doesn't work either because readers absorb meaning through word shapes. A numeral is a subconscious sign to expect figures and data; not a word sequence from which we create meaning. A numeral at the start of a sentence can 'throw' the readers and the story flow is lost.

Opening a story with the official name of an official body is downright lazy. So for example: 'The Metropolitan Police Service announced today that it has . . .' is a turn-off for readers. There is not even a hint of anything unique or extraordinary here. Where is the news? The Metropolitan Police Service will have done umpteen things in London on any one day. A good intro should cut to the chase and focus directly on the news in the opening words.

Similarly, imagine we wrote an intro for our armed robbery: 'Police are investigating an armed robbery at a Cardiff jewellery shop where £500,000 was stolen and a shop assistant shot.' The focus is on the police and the first mental picture created for readers is of generic police officers pounding the streets or driving around in their cars rather than of the drama of the raid.

For most stories, the news is most likely to lie in what has been announced not in the act of announcing it. The intro may need to identify the body making the announcement by way of attribution but this can usually be woven in towards the end of the intro. So: 'Armed robbers who shot a shop worker and escaped with £500,000 from a Cardiff jewellers should not be approached, say police.'

Newspapers vary widely on the degree of attribution included. Certainly if a claim is being made or opinion expressed, an attribution is needed. So: 'Britain was wrong to go to war in Iraq, says a former Tory minister.' Some news organisations, particularly agencies, make a point of attributing as much as possible so the audience knows the precise source of information.

One final intro model worth noting is the **delayed drop**. This is a more oblique style of story opening associated with lighter news. Here there is a brief element of suspense, perhaps a slight teasing of the reader on a quirky story with an unexpected angle to it. The opening paragraphs may lead them in one direction; then the reveal springs the surprise in maybe the third or even fourth sentence.

A good reporter will have the delayed drop in the mix but use it sparingly. The *Daily Mail*, for instance, makes regular use of the device when it runs a softer story on page three, such as an off-beat animal tale. So: 'A strict diet of fruit and veg has helped Roger lose two stone and made him the talk of his weight-loss club. He's now down to his target weight and feeling fitter than ever – which is good news for the six-year-old Rottweiler.'

One aspect of intros on which there is little agreement is appropriate length. Measured in words, somewhere in the 20s is normal but many news organisations' styles expect intros to be routinely shorter or longer. In the age of microblogging, an upper limit of 140 characters would make sense allowing for automatic transfers. Or where text may be appearing on paper or on screen, a character limit may be required to fit a website template that automatically picks up the intro for the home page. Some newsrooms have very fixed limits for print as well as online. As a reporter, knowing how a story is going to appear to the audience can set some helpful parameters.

Otherwise counting words cannot tell you whether an intro is good or bad per se but it can be a useful guide to whether the balance is right. If an intro comes up under the norm, check if there is enough information in it. Would it be better as a double header rather than a single header? Does it need a little more specific information to grab attention? If an intro is more than 30 words, check the other way. Is there too much detail? Are there superfluous words or ideas? Could the structure be simplified to help the readers absorb the information in one go? In either case if the intro reads clearly and unambiguously and conveys the most important angles of the story, the readers – and your news editor – should be happy. (See also 'Buzz words' in Thinking It Through at the end of this chapter.)

remember

The intro checklist is as follows:
- Does it give the main news?
- Is it a potted version of the whole story? Could it be published alone?
- Does it attract the reader's attention?
- Does it make sense?
- Is it accurate? Does it fit the facts? Are all the words spelled correctly?
- Is it the right length – commonly between 18 and 25 words, but varies from publication to publication?

STORY STRUCTURE

A news story sets out its main points as succinctly as possible. It needs to lead the reader through the information, adding to the picture with each sentence and flowing easily from point to point.

Structuring a story has been described as the art of telling the reader what they need to know next which seems obvious but is harder to achieve than it sounds. Certainly the writer has to be able to see the story from the audience perspective. The danger for any journalist is that they become too absorbed in the investigation and familiar with the material. A journalist needs to remember that this is news to the reader who is coming to the story cold.

A CLOSER LOOK

A STYLE GUIDE

More good advice from within the industry comes from *The Economist's Style Guide* – which is published in book format. The bullet points on the dust jacket alone are well worth noting.

- 'The first requirement of *The Economist* is that it should be readily understandable.
- Clarity of writing usually follows clarity of thought. So think what you want to say then say it as simply as possible.
- Use the language of everyday speech.
- Do not be hectoring or arrogant. Those who disagree with you are not necessarily stupid or insane.

Various models exist to help structure a story. Again none provides the Holy Grail for all stories and all outlets but they can help to shape an otherwise amorphous mass of facts and figures. The most common still is the inverted triangle (plus permutations). Others teach to a WHAT formula and some news organisations have established their own expectations on structure. Sometimes as a reporter you will be obliged to follow a set pattern, particularly for web templates, otherwise it is a matter of establishing which models work best for you to help your stories fall into place.

The inverted triangle

News intro gives the big picture

Details added in descending order of importance

Finer detail

The idea of the inverted triangle is that width symbolises significance. This helps those new to news writing by emphasising the ways in which this form of story-telling differs from fictional forms or essay writing. The top of the triangle, the widest part, is the all-encompassing intro; the big picture version of the story. The meat of the tale is in the opening paragraphs. As the story develops, the reporter works down to the finer detail and to the less significant aspects of the story. Eventually the story ends – with a whimper rather than a bang. A news story just peters out with no grand finale, no conclusion, no witty pay-off line. Again this differs from most text formats so the inverted triangle helps to stress the contrasts.

To some extent the inverted triangle approach is the product of old print technology. When text was typeset in slugs of lead and not so easily manipulated by journalists, the simplest way to make stories fit a printed page was to cut from the bottom. A technician could do it rather than a journalist. As long as the reporter had followed the inverted triangle structure, the story would still make sense and only lesser detail would be lost. In its advanced form, a reporter would write a story tying up loose ends as they went so that any article could be cut at the end of any sentence without confusing readers.

The advent of digital technology has made this seem something of a crude approach that is no longer necessary now production journalists can adjust any character and cut any phrase from anywhere in the story until the required space is filled. However the inverted triangle lives on and not just in the copy of ageing hacks. Perhaps this is because it actually tends to produce stories that suit the readers.

When news emerges, offering the story in a nutshell then fleshing it out with layers of detail is an effective way of communicating information because it is easy to absorb. Some will read all the way to the end; others will skim the opening paragraphs and feel they know enough. Losing a few finer details won't prevent the reader from understanding the gist. That is actually quite a neat way of making a story work for a range of different readers in print as well as online.

Also, even with the added sophistication of digital production, the fastest way to make a story fit is to cut it from the bottom. In a news environment anything that saves time has its temptations.

remember

- Give readers the big picture news upfront.
- The more important the information to the audience, the sooner it should be introduced.
- Work through to the finer detail.
- Let the news story just end; don't add a conclusion or summary.

The WHAT formula

The WHAT formula builds on the who, what, where, when, how and why questions and can be useful because it offers a general description of the most common sequence of information found in news stories:

- The **W** is for what, stressing that news is most often about what has happened as the intro. There are likely to be elements of who, where and when too.
- The **H** is for how, often the next tier of information, which develops the intro and, over the next one or two sentences, wraps up the main elements of the story and at least begins to answer any of the remaining six key questions.
- The **A** is for amplification. This is a useful phase of the story to consider. The outline has been developed in the opening paragraphs. Now we can move into the detail. So here we might have supporting quotes, some of the sequence of events and specifics of the news.
- The **Tie-up** is for background information, for loose ends and for routine elements of what happens next.

So for a road accident the pattern might be:

- **What:** Two lorry drivers died in a five-vehicle pile-up in thick fog on the M4 this morning.
- **How:** David Jones, 45, from Cardiff, and Michael Martin, 32, from Portsmouth, were killed when their trucks collided and overturned on the westbound carriageway near Newport at 8.10 a.m. Three other people were seriously injured.
- **Amplification:** Firefighters took two hours to free one of the victims from the wreckage of a red Ford Ka which ran into the back of the two lorries. Mr Jones, a driver for Brain's brewery, and Mr Martin were pronounced dead at the scene. Police say the truck driven by Mr Martin crossed the central reservation and hit the Brain's lorry, knocking it across the carriageway and into the path of three other vehicles. (Plus quotes and information on three seriously injured.)
- **Tie-up:** Warning about driving in fog; disruption to traffic; any diversions, etc.

Again the formula helps to stress the contrast between the fiction form and a news story.

PUTTING IT INTO PRACTICE

Fiction form

When electricians wired the home of Mary Jones, of Smith Grove, Cardiff, some years ago, they neglected to install sufficient insulation at a point where the wires crossed a gas pipe and a short circuit occurred early this morning.

Contact with the gas pipe created a blaze which ignited the woodwork. The flames worked up through the cellar stairway and soon the entire lower floor of the house became an inferno.

Mrs Jones, her 10-year-old daughter Alice and James, her 5-month-old infant, were asleep in the second floor rear bedroom. They had no means of escape and perished in the flames.

News form

- **What**: A Cardiff mother and her two children died today in a house blaze.
- **How**: Mary Jones, her 10-year-old daughter Alice and baby son James, aged 5 months, were trapped in a second floor bedroom as flames swept through the Smith Grove house.
- **Amplification**: The fire began in the cellar where firefighters have established that faulty electrical wiring caused a short circuit near a gas pipe. The Jones family were asleep when flames worked up through the cellar stairway and enveloped the entire lower floor of the house . . . etc.
- **Tie-up**: Further inquiry into cause. What happens next?

Activity: Look up three front page stories and see if you can spot an inverted triangle or WHAT structure to them. *Daily Mail* hard news stories often have a classic structure to them. See if the stories appear differently online.

---

remember

- Think WHAT.
- What, How, Amplification, Tie-up.

Other structures

Some news organisations are known to have a favoured story structure. News from the main UK agency, the Press Association, was written so that the first three paragraphs presented a coherent version of the story. This was in the spirit of both the inverted triangle or WHAT formula and was adopted with the news organisation's clients in mind. A major story on farming, for instance, might be run in full in a rural newspaper but much more briefly in a big city title. Page editors knew they could take the first three paragraphs and confidently cut the rest without checking through line by line to make sure readers wouldn't miss out on crucial information.

News agency Bloomberg, for example, focuses on a four-paragraph format which can convey the story and fit neatly onto a single view of a computer screen. Bloomberg's prime clients are business users who pay for a company terminal on which the news flashes up. So the awareness of the platform on which the news is to be read is crucial. Reporters are expected to follow the sequence.

- What is new?
- How do we know? Give the source.
- Why does it matter? Provide the context and significance within the big picture.
- Back it up with a quote from someone with a strong stake in the news. The bigger the stake the better.

Whichever model you employ to help structure your story, it is worth paying conscious attention to the second paragraph. Many a great intro is let down by the aimless or repetitive sentence that follows it.

It can help if the second sentence has the same subject as the intro. So if we opt for the intro that focuses on the armed robbers, the second paragraph might read: 'The two gunmen fled on foot from Morgan's High Street jewellery shop with a haul of diamonds, pearls and designer brand watches.' An intro focused on the have-a-go shop assistant could be followed by a second paragraph: 'Eighteen-year-old Mary Jones was shot twice by gunmen who held up Morgan's High Street jewellery shop just before closing time.' Either way this helps develop the reader's mental picture of the event. But don't be tempted to repeat the exact pattern of the intro with just a couple of specific details added. Do move the action of the story on with every new sentence.

Following a double or triple header intro, a decision needs to be made about what to focus on next. The next one or two sentences need to introduce all the angles. Then, in the amplification, the various aspects have to be prioritised in the most logical sequence. Sometimes an angle backed up by a strong quote might take precedence. Be sure to provide enough context for each quote. Don't let your sources get ahead of the reader.

Non-linear story-telling

The dynamics of online have led some to challenge the value of linear story-telling. Online readers tend to scan and graze news; they may link to it from outside the site, typically from Google search; they want to click through to pursue their own individual preoccupations and priorities. Writers are advised to keep stories short and sweet, provide headings, pull quotes and break reports up into lots of separate 'chunks' to create multiple entry points and multiple routes through the story. Navigation is key. However, at the heart of most story packages there is still a core news report run in classic linear style. When relying on the immediacy of the web, linear works well to establish the essence of the news. As we move into exploiting the interactivity and depth, coverage is more likely to spin off into non-linear elements. Witness accounts can be separated out; different perspectives and responses can be told in a looser narrative style.

What online has emphasised is the need for a journalist to be capable of writing in a variety of styles and formats and be able to choose the most appropriate approach for each new story. (See also 'New dimensions of news' in Thinking It Through at the end of this chapter.)

remember

The news story checklist is as follows:
- Has the story answered the questions: who? what? where? when? how? why?
- Does the story amplify the points of the intro in order of importance?
- Does the story give both sides if concerning a potentially contentious issue – is it objective?
- Have all the loose ends been tied up?
- Does the story structure suit its platform and its audience?

KEY STORY ELEMENTS

News-gathering skills are about asking the right questions and questioning the answers you get. The best reporters keep questioning until they emerge with an effective set of notes from which to write the news. This chapter concentrates on the skills of news writing rather than news-gathering but in practice they are tightly interwoven. News reporters are already shaping the story during an interview and writing it in their head: building up a picture of the event, filling in the gaps until the account makes sense.

When reporting on complicated incidents it can help to draw a diagram – initially for your own benefit and then potentially to share with your audience as a graphic. Ask yourself: where are the missing pieces?

A reporter can be prepared both for the questioning and the writing up by recognising the different key elements of different types of story. What is likely to be most important about a fire? What do readers want to know about an inquiry report? A checklist in each case can help to ensure your report covers all the angles. The danger could be that the stories become overly formulaic as a result. But if you guard against that, applying the checklists to a particular fire or inquiry report can tease out and highlight its unique elements.

Particular events

What follows are some of the regular types of news story and the particular aspects to cover in each. It obviously cannot be exhaustive but it should exemplify an approach and offer a useful tool for those eager to develop a facility for news writing. A good story will answer these questions for readers. As you will see the 'people' elements loom large throughout.

Fires

Key elements to cover in the story are:

- People? Deaths, injuries, rescues, escapes, witnesses on the scene; any broader dangers such as noxious fumes. Who normally lives there? Where were they? Even in a pet-obsessed country, news of the impact on people is likely to be most important.
- Animals? Deaths, injuries, rescues.
- Property? Spread, state, value of damage, impact on neighbours.
- Heroics? Firefighters and/or public.
- Tackling fire? How many fire appliances, breathing apparatus, rescue vehicles, spread, numbers of crew. State of fire when they arrived, how long it took to bring under control (doesn't mean it is out).
- Cause?
- Warnings? Smoke alarms, candles, unattended chip pans, something new.
- Impact? Domestic: how the occupants cope. Business: who was on shift? Who was called? How does the business recover?
- Remember firefighters also deal with rescues, flooding, etc.

Robberies

Robbery is defined as theft by force or threat of force which immediately points a reporter in the direction of possible key angles.

Key elements are:

- What was stolen or what were the robbers trying to steal?
- What force was used or threatened?

- Who against? What injuries were sustained?
- Were the robbers challenged?
- Who did the haul belong to?
- Hunt: anyone arrested? Any appeals? E-fits?
- Longer-term impact on victim?
- Security: what was in place, what happens now?

Murders

Key elements are:

- Victim? ID, how and when found, and who by?
- Cause of death?
- Weapon? What it was and if it has been recovered.
- Suspect? Nature of murder inquiry, any arrests, any police appeals for information.
- Events in days/hours leading up to death.
- Biography of victim: family, neighbours, workmates, school.

Accidents

News reporters are very likely to cover road accidents and more rarely train and plane crashes.
Key elements are:

- People? Dead, injured, affected; drivers, passengers, sometimes crew.
- Vehicles? Sequence of collision(s); possible cause but beware attributing blame.
- Rescues? Heroics by rescue services or bystanders.
- Wider impact of road closures, service cancellations.
- Dangers: part of a pattern?

Shootings

Mass shootings were seen as an American phenomenon but Derrick Bird was not the first and he will not be the last in the UK. Look at some of the reports of the Cumbrian shootings and see if you would add to the list.
Key elements are:

- People? Dead, injured, escaped, affected.
- Perpetrator? Gunman, weapons, how many shots, gunman alive/dead.
- Investigation?
- Motive?
- Impact on location – (e.g. school, shopping mall).
- Where did the weapons come from?

Court trials

Court reporting is covered in both Chapters 7 and 9 but here we include a very basic skeleton for trial coverage.
Key elements are:

- Defendant's name, age, address and occupation.
- Formal charge and detail of the allegation.
- Plea.
- Prosecution and defence statements.
- Key witness evidence.
- Judge's summing up.
- Verdict – by jury.

- Sentence – by judge.
- Names of counsel, judge, court.

Inquests

Inquests are inquiries led by coroners into sudden, unnatural or unexplained deaths. The legal purpose of an inquest is to determine who died; where, when and how and 'the particulars to be registered' which provide some sort of cause or explanation, such as suicide or accident. Accusations are not generally made against specific individuals but there may well be consequences from an inquest which, for instance, decides that the death was as a result of negligence. Some are highly controversial, such as that into the death of Ian Tomlinson at the G20 protests in London in 2009 after he was struck by a police officer. The inquest jury in 2011 returned a verdict of unlawful killing.

Key elements are:

- Who died and how?
- What were the possible explanations? The inquest will probably work through a range of versions of events.
- What verdict is reached?
- Any comment from the coroner?
- Any comment from relatives of the deceased?
- Any criminal implications?
- Any response to concerns raised by the coroner?

Employment tribunals

Employment tribunals exist to safeguard fairness at work. They rule on disputes between employers and employees such as claims for unfair dismissal and over legal rights, for example to redundancy money or pay in lieu of notice. Employees may claim discrimination on grounds of race, sexual orientation or disability. Workers, particularly women, can bring complaints of sexual harassment or unfair treatment when pregnant.

Key elements are:

- Who are the parties? Employee and employer.
- What is the grievance? Claim and rebuttal.
- What is the tribunal's finding and the remedy?
- Union involvement? The employee may be represented by a union which may act for others in similar circumstances.
- Any anonymity orders? These can be granted in complaints regarding sexual conduct or those brought under the Disability Rights Act.

Company results

Key elements are:

- Profits, turnover.
- Changes.
- Compare – with last year, with others in sector.
- Impact on business, CEO, directors, shareholders, staff.
- Future plans and prospects.
- Small print.

Inquiry reports

Various forms of public inquiry can be set up by central or local government or to examine a particular issue, for example the Neuberger Report by the Master of the Rolls on the use of superinjunctions reported in May 2011. Inquiries can be held into major planning disputes, say over an airport. And inquiries are held into disasters such as rail crashes or the death of an abused child.

Key elements are:

- Findings: executive summary.
- What are the recommendations?
- Was anyone at fault? Who or what needs to change?
- Reactions of the parties scrutinised.
- Reactions of the 'victim'.
- What are the outcomes? Sackings, resignations, new policy.

Golden and diamond weddings

Local papers and websites commonly mark the 50th wedding anniversary of couples in their area. Some only feature marriages that hit the 'diamond' standard of 60 years. People are living longer but the divorce rate is high so it's not clear whether numbers will be going up or down. This is a classic area where the challenge is to use the checklist to tease out something different – something unique to each couple.

Key elements are:

- Details of the couple.
- How are they celebrating?
- Fifty years ago – How did they meet? Where did they marry?
- Highs and lows.
- What family do they have? Are reunions planned? Is anyone flying from afar?
- Secret of a successful relationship (if they say 'give and take' ask again).

Factory or other business closure

Key elements are:

- Number of job losses.
- Reason for closure.
- What happens to workers?
- What happens to site?
- What are the knock-on effects? – suppliers, customers, etc.
- What's the financial position of the company and the staff? Is it solvent?

PUTTING IT INTO PRACTICE

These core elements provide a starting point for both news-gathering and news writing. As information unfolds, follow-up questions will point you in the direction of different angles or a unique twist in the tale. Once you begin to write, the checklists will help ensure you don't omit a crucial angle.

Activity: Take the BBC or local newspaper website, look for archive stories in the various categories and see which elements are covered and what more the reporter has discovered in each case. Also, what might the key elements of a report of a burglary be?

- Develop checklists to ensure the key story elements are covered in your write-up.
- Use the formula to isolate the exceptional aspects of the individual news item.
- Don't resort to cliché.

USE OF LANGUAGE, PUNCTUATION AND QUOTES

- Careless words cost readers.
- Clarity, economy and vigour go hand in hand.
- Let the facts speak for themselves.

These are just three of the many adages to emerge from the welter of advice a journalist receives over the years. Some – hopefully the best – stick with you. The first is perhaps the least used but merits examination. Carelessness lets in errors which can be expensive both in legal terms and in alienating readers. Sloppy use of words also costs in time if some sub-editor has to re-write work to make sentences more concise or to remove redundant words and phrases. Worse, if the careless words are not rectified they reach the reader. Even if a story is not wrong or misleading, if it isn't carefully crafted the chances of its being read are much reduced.

Readers are renowned for 'grazing' online. They glance at an intro then move on if they aren't interested in more. Readers on paper can be picky too. Wordiness slows down the intake of the story and a reader frustrated by poor expression is likely to abandon what would otherwise be relevant news.

The solution is to make every sentence add to the story and to make every word within it count. Learn to convey as much information as possible in sentences that are simply structured but tightly packed with information. Never say in four words what you can say in one. When it comes to sweating the language, much can be learnt from careful examination of mass market tabloids such as the *Sun*. For the more upmarket titles, publishing longer stories to capture complexity and report in depth is entirely justified but no news story should be longer than it needs to be. There is no reason to waste words in any news environment.

Inverted sentences should generally be avoided. If you need to use them, perhaps to vary the rhythm of your story, use them sparingly. Make sure you don't link two separate thoughts or two separate subjects. 'Born in Cardiff, he was an expert on Dostoevsky' suggests he is a Dostoevsky expert because he was born in Cardiff. On the other hand, 'Trained at the Royal Welsh College of Music and Drama (RWCMD), Gareth went on to sing with the Welsh National Opera' is both grammatical and sensible. 'Trained at the Royal Welsh College of Music and Drama, Welsh National Opera gave Gareth his first professional role' is not grammatical because the qualifying clause relates to the wrong subject – Welsh National Opera did not train at RWCMD.

The advice that follows takes a conventional text-based approach to issues around language. Obeying grammatical rules provides consistency which tends to aid clarity, especially where the reader has only text to rely on. Editors take various stances in this realm. Some insist that grammatical rules have to be applied rigidly in text to protect against ambiguity. But sentences that capture more of a spoken style can be easier to read. Significantly for journalists, language changes and editors have to decide how the title's approach should evolve – slightly behind or slightly ahead of the curve. In some instances, particularly of spelling and hyphenation, there is not an established right or wrong. It would, for instance, be confusing to read of a '**gray** car' in a headline and a '**grey** car' in the text. A title chooses one to use throughout.

Language pointers

Reporters who keep a clear focus on how to communicate most effectively with their audience are likely to negotiate the minefield of language to best effect. The following points may help.

Absolutes

What is absolute can't be qualified. Something unique has nothing like it so can't be quite unique. Other examples of misuse include 'first ever' and 'one of the premier'.

Clichés

A cliché should be anathema to journalists. A reporter seeking to stress the unique and extraordinary elements of news needs consciously to avoid falling back on well-worn, stock phrases. If reporters have written them a million times, readers have read them a million times so any original impact is lost. The worst clichés used in text would never crop up naturally in normal conversation. Giving the green light or thumbs up, hitting out, blasting opponents, living in fear, facing heartbreak, and sparking rows are contrived descriptions. Just say what you mean and move closer to common parlance. Avoid referring to anger and fury or indeed making any assumption about the emotional responses of those involved in stories unless you have direct evidence.

Collective nouns

A collective noun should be followed by a singular verb, for example the company is, the government is. Most text reporting stuck rigidly to the rule although in conversation few people adhere to it. But because the BBC reports on radio and television using the conventions of normal speech, then transfers scripts online, the usage on websites is mixed and tends to make them plural.

Common exceptions in print:

- The plural is used in sport (e.g. City are, the club are, Wales are). This convention is very widespread and tends to include mentions of sport on news and features pages too.
- Bands and theatre companies are plural (e.g. the Prodigy are, U2 are).
- So are the police, the public and the media.
- Also the couple are, the duo are, the trio are.

Don't mix singular and plural in the same sentence. Writing 'the company makes an announcement after they receive interim figures . . .' doesn't make sense.

Compound adjectives

Words linked to form adjectives must be hyphenated. Without hyphens such compounds can at best confuse readers and in the worst cases do not make sense. Ages used as a compound adjective are hyphenated. So a story can involve a 20-year-old woman, but she is 20 years old. In many compound nouns the hyphen has disappeared with usage, and the two words are now written as one, as in bathroom. Some examples may be in your company style guide, or publications will have a favoured dictionary to arbitrate on whether the hyphen is needed or not.

Each

Means every one, separately. It takes the singular pronoun, as in 'Each had her own style' rather than 'Each had their own style'.

Euphemisms

Journalistic writing should be direct and upfront. Euphemisms mask meaning so are rarely desirable. Talk plainly and explicitly to your audience. In news stories people die; they don't pass away.

If

When 'if' introduces the conditional, take care over tenses. 'If I **were** an MP, I would challenge injunctions in the public interest' is correct. 'If I **was** an MP, I would challenge injunctions in the public interest' is not. The usual singular becomes plural.

Jargon

Journalists relying on the written word need to communicate effectively. When sources use specialist technical terms or, worse, empty, grandiose-sounding language, it is the reporter's job to translate it into plain English. Turn other people's gobbledygook into more familiar wording everyone can understand. It is a journalist's job to find out what is meant and restate it clearly and concisely. One PR officer's 'ongoing industrial relations situation' could well be a journalist's 'strike'. Find out and be specific.

None/neither

None means not one and so it is singular, as is neither. So 'none is sure of the outcome' or 'neither the Prime Minister nor the Chancellor has an answer'. But if the second noun is plural the plural verb is needed as in 'neither the Chancellor nor the Ministers are available'.

Only

Use 'only' close to the word it qualifies. So: 'he had only one excuse' rather than 'he only had one excuse'.

Or

Two or more singular subjects joined by 'or' take the singular. So: 'Bronwen or Sally **is** being promoted.'

Pronouns

Don't assume the generalised person you are referring to is male. It is better to write the sentence in the plural to avoid the need to refer to both genders. If you do opt for the singular, it is preferable to refer to him or her, his or hers. Strictly speaking you should never use 'their' as a substitute for his or her as it is a plural pronoun and should not be used as a singular. However, this united use is becoming more common to avoid endless repetition of 'he or she' etc. Check the publication's guidelines if in doubt.

Preposition at the end of a sentence

Most text output has abandoned the original grammatical rule not to end a sentence with a preposition. Where a preposition sounds right at the end of a sentence, or offers the least contorted phrasing, don't move it. If it reads awkwardly, move it to earlier in the phrase. So: 'I don't know where it came from' would be far more natural than the archaic 'I know not whence it came'.

Puns

Infamous headlines such as 'Stick it up your junta', addressed to the Argentine military government during the Falklands war, have made the *Sun* newspaper forever synonymous with the use of puns. Sports pages on many titles are another breeding ground. Puns are admired and condemned in roughly equal measure. Beware journalists more caught up with impressing colleagues with their wit than finding the best way to project a story to the reader. If a pun doesn't come easily, stop trying. A genuine pun does not change the spelling of any words so some editors would ban the likes of Easter 'egg-stras' (see also Clichés). A real play on words can also be understood literally. Generally they are better suited to light-hearted stories.

Superfluous words

For editors, corrections were traditionally made in blue pencil but trainers of print journalists are renowned for covering submitted drafts of news stories in red pen. For one regional trainer the most venom was reserved for redundant words. The judgement 'superfluous' scrawled against a word or phrase meant the reporter was guilty of writing without due care and attention.

Delete words that are used only in casual conversation and waste space. In the following, the words in brackets are redundant and should not be written into copy:

(around) about	meet (with)	(regular) monthly meeting
(eye) witness	(new) development	7 p.m. (in the evening)
(future) plans	(on a) daily (basis)	(successfully) passed
(in order) to	(ongoing) campaign, row	(totally) destroyed
in three days (time)	(past) experience	

remember

- A journalist is a wordsmith.
- A news story is a piece of precision engineering with words as the raw material.
- Every word counts.

Use of punctuation

Effective, consistent use of punctuation is particularly important in text. The reader of the written word has only the text from which to make meaning. Unlike a radio or TV reporter, the print journalist cannot rely on timing or intonation to convey the information. In text, punctuation takes the role of the voice in pacing the story to aid understanding. Punctuation is a key part of phrasing and can be treated like taking a breath. The length of pause is determined from short to long; from commas, through semi-colons, colons and dashes to full stops.

Commas

The comma provides the shortest break in the flow of the text. A pair of commas can work like brackets – indeed they are then referred to as parenthetical commas. When you write 'who' it will often need to be preceded by a comma. The commas top and tail the extra information slotted in to the sentence but the sentence would still make sense without that phrase. So: 'The minister, who comes from Scotland, moved to London with his family . . .' Omit the parenthetical commas only if you are writing about 'the minister who comes from Scotland' as distinct from other ministers.

The pair of commas is often needed for people's job titles, addresses or other biographical detail. So: 'Helen Mirren, who starred in *Prime Suspect*, said . . .' Or the information can be used instead as a label in which it could become: 'Prime Suspect star Helen Mirren said . . .' which does not require commas.

A comma cannot link two sentences to make one. Copy that reads 'The robbers ran out of the shop, they did not remove their masks' is really two sentences, each with its own subject and different verb. As its name indicates, a conjunction is the only means of linking two sentences. When this is done, a comma may be needed before the conjunction to avoid confusion.

When linking clauses, a comma may or may not be required. It is not needed in the following sentence: 'The editor decided to drop the story and tell the reporter to find out more.' It is needed in the sentence: 'The editor decided to drop the story, and the reporter was disappointed.' The subject has changed after the 'and' so the comma is used to create the necessary break.

Semicolons and colons

The semicolon is next up in the hierarchy; signalling a break slightly longer than a comma. The semicolon is typically used in a list of items or names, such as candidates in an election. So: The candidates are Brian Brown, for the Conservative Party; Fred White, for the Labour Party; and George Black, for the Liberal Democrats.

A colon goes one step further. Many publications use a colon to introduce a quote. So: Mr Smith said: 'I will.'

Dashes

A dash is most effective when used to give a punchline effect – say in a delayed drop intro, as discussed earlier in the chapter. So: 'He splashed out £100,000 on the wedding – and that's not even including the honeymoon.'

Don't over-use them. A dash is too often a cop-out by those who aren't sure whether a comma or full stop is required. Learn how to punctuate properly instead.

Full stops

A full stop brings the reader to a temporary halt so is the most emphatic of the breakers we use in print to pace the information. Sentences should be kept short and simple. Check any long sentence to see if it should be broken up, either to avoid grammatical error or to make it easier to read. A sentence has a subject and a verb, and usually an object. If yours has more than one subject, separated by commas, consider substituting full stops to create separate sentences. Usually keep to one subordinate clause.

A full stop is traditionally called a 'point' by print journalists.

Apostrophes

The other most significant further aspect of punctuation for text journalists is the apostrophe. Frustration over its misuse was notably manifested in journalist Lynn Truss's surprise best-seller, *Eats, Shoots and Leaves: The Zero Tolerance Approach to Punctuation*. This highly emotional examination of punctuation couldn't be further from the dry old grammatical tomes previously relied upon as oracles for editors (see Recommended Reading at the end of this chapter).

- The apostrophe denotes the omission of a letter or letters. So: Isn't, can't, don't.
- It is, it has and who is are treated similarly. It's is short for it is or it has. Its is the possessive pronoun. Both are used correctly in the sentence: 'It's been a long wait, but the Government will have to announce its policy soon.'
- Who's is short for who is or who has. 'Whose' is the possessive pronoun. Confusion is common over the use of possessive pronouns that do not take an apostrophe 's'. His, her and their are straightforward before nouns such as her book but tend to cause confusion when the noun is implied. So: The book is hers not her's.

- An apostrophe followed by the letter 's' makes a singular word possessive. It must also be used when a plural word does not end in 's'. So children becomes children's and women becomes women's.
- Singular words are made possessive by the addition of an apostrophe 's'. This includes words that are singular but happen to end in 's' such as Wales. So we should not write 'Wales' rainfall' but 'Wales's rainfall'. The plural of Jones is Joneses, so we should write of 'the Joneses' house'. If a word ending in the letter 's' has to be made possessive, add an apostrophe 's' if it is singular and an apostrophe alone if it is plural.

  However some publications choose to break the rule because the s's looks untidy in print. *Media Wales*, for instance, uses Wales' as the possessive. It's an editor's prerogative to decide how to balance the demands of language and layout.
- The apostrophe is often misplaced in words like 20's and 1980's. These are plurals, not possessives. The correct form is 'a woman in her 20s' or 'an event in the 1980s'. If abbreviated the decade is the '80s where the apostrophe denotes the missing 19.

Question marks

The question mark should follow only a direct question as in: 'What is the time?'

In reported speech it is redundant.

remember

- Correct punctuation can be vital to accurate understanding.
- Correct punctuation is reader friendly.
- Punctuation in text does the work of pauses and intonation in the spoken word.
- Know your weaknesses.
- Keep a grammar guide handy and know the conventions adopted by the outlets you write for.

Use of quotes

Using quotes well can make a huge contribution to a news story. Direct quotes lend authenticity, credibility and colour to a story and allow readers to connect directly with the journalist's source. A direct quote uses a source's actual words; an indirect quote, or reported speech, paraphrases the response but attributes it.

In some news stories a direct quote is like evidence – it supports the revelation in the intro. An intro might read: 'A former Cabinet minister today accused the Prime Minister of dithering over spending cuts.' The most convincing way to justify that intro is to include a direct quote high up the story from the former Cabinet minister.

In other stories a direct quote strengthens the sense of human impact and gives emotional depth to the report. A witness quote from the scene of a catastrophe, for instance, will often capture the atmosphere and experience more effectively than a journalist, particularly if the reporter cannot be at the scene.

Sometimes a direct quote is used 'for the record'. We may want to quote an official to confirm details of an event to make it clear that the facts are directly from that organisation. But generally factual information would be paraphrased into reported speech to be clear and concise.

A direct quote tends to be more effective – and thus the better option – where a source is being more expressive. Perhaps they are describing a scene or an experience; they are revealing personal opinions or emotions. Perhaps they have used particularly colourful language (and that doesn't mean cursing!). Here words directly from a source carry great weight.

In a news story with multiple angles it can help to work through notes picking out a key quote to best support each aspect. Ensure that words used within quotes are the words actually spoken though with care you may be kind to the speaker by making the words grammatical. If you abridge a quote, insert leaders (...) to show that words have been omitted. If necessary in the interests of brevity or clarity, turn quotes into reported speech. Never turn assent or denial of a question into a direct quote.

There is a growing tendency to dip in and out of direct quote within an individual sentence. This has its uses – especially for someone whose shorthand note is too poor to capture the whole sentence. This use of what we call snatch quotes works effectively for emphasis if used sparingly. For example, when Tony Blair talked of 'bog-standard' comprehensives the significance lay in his use of that precise phrase. Quoting the whole sentence verbatim would have lost impact but relying entirely on reported speech wouldn't have focused on his controversial turn of phrase. However, attempting to combine long sections of direct quote within an over-arching sentence of reported speech is a recipe for grammatical errors and reader confusion. Representing quotes effectively and punctuating them consistently is crucial if readers are to maintain a clear grasp of the material.

In news the clearest way to use a direct quote is to identify the speaker at the beginning of the sentence. So: President Obama said: 'We will talk.' It is much easier for the reader to picture the person first and then read what they have to say. A long quote run with an attribution at the end leaves the reader up in the air.

Even when a report may have already referred to the source quoted, an explicit attribution for each new section of direct quote will help to keep the reader on track. This may be relaxed where only one source is quoted but is particularly helpful where new voices are introduced. If one quote follows another without initial attribution, the reader will subconsciously attribute it to the first source rather than the new one and be taken aback when they finally reach the new name.

Here again, anything the journalist can do to avoid forcing the audience to re-read any part of the story makes the communication more effective.

PUTTING IT INTO PRACTICE

For example:

- Michael Jones said: 'I will live out my life in Paris. Life is easier than in Britain.'
  or
- 'I will live out my life in Paris,' said Michael Jones. 'Life is easier than in Britain.'

When continuing a quote from one paragraph to the next, close quotes are not needed between paragraphs; only at the end of the quote.

> He said: 'It came as an enormous shock to all of us. I just can't understand how it happened.
> 'She was a marvellous teacher. We will all really miss her.'

For a quote within a quote, use double quotation marks to distinguish it from the overall quote. (But note that some publications employ the reverse rule, i.e. they use double quotation marks and then single quotation marks within. So, again check with the publication's house style.) For example:

> He said: 'She was so cross she said, "Stop being so sloppy."'

> ▶ PUTTING IT INTO PRACTICE

However, avoid ending the sentence with a quote within a quote because it looks so awkward.

Direct quotes should be in a separate sentence from indirect speech. For example:

Neighbour Doris Pickle thought the dead woman Sylvia Carnegie was on holiday. She said: 'Everyone is stunned by the news.'

It is wrong to write:

Neighbour Doris Pickle thought Mrs Carnegie was on holiday: 'Everyone is stunned by the news.'

Once you have attributed the quote to a person there is no need to keep repeating the attribution unless you go from direct into indirect reporting. For example:

Indirect/reported speech: Michael Jones said it was not part of his department's responsibility to arrange a demonstration.
Direct: 'I suspect this is a ploy to close the department,' he added. 'My fear is that they will succeed.'

If a snatch quote appears at the end of a sentence the full stop goes outside the inverted commas, as in: Tony Blair said too many schools were 'bog standard'. This looks odd in print so should be avoided. This can be done by re-ordering the wording but generally it is better to use either indirect (reported) speech or a full sentence of direct speech (quote).

Activity: Check how a big news story is covered by a variety of sources and consider how each uses quotes within the story and how they are punctuated. If you lose the thread of a story part way through, think about whether poor or inconsistent punctuation has hindered your ability to absorb the information. Is it always clear who is being quoted? What do the quotes add to your appreciation of the news?

Reported speech

The tense of the first verb in a sentence determines the tense of those that follow. Reported speech is written in the past tense, so other verbs in the sentence take the past tense. So: 'He said the fundraising was going well.' Don't be tempted to alter the tense if the fundraising is continuing. It is wrong to write: 'He said that the fundraising is going well.' It would be correct, though, to write as fact: 'The fundraising is going well.'

remember

- Quotes add authenticity to a news story.
- Quotes can effectively capture atmosphere and human responses.
- Attribute quotes at the first available opportunity.
- Keep direct and indirect speech in separate sentences.
- Use snatch quotes sparingly.
- Punctuate quotes correctly and in accordance with house style.

CHAPTER SUMMARY

CHAPTER SUMMARY

- News has to be new.
- Write for your reader.
- Make every word count.
- Focus on people.
- Clarity of writing usually follows clarity of thought.
- Determine the strongest intro and let your story flow from it.
- Read your reports thoroughly for meaning and accuracy before making them public.

THINKING IT THROUGH

The disappearing deadline

'Deadline? No-one said anything about a deadline!'

That's a corny speech bubble in a cartoon of a shocked monk labouring for years on the fantastically elaborate lettering of an illuminated manuscript. In times of instant internet communication, a long-standing weekly newspaper reporter could be forgiven for a similar shock at the change in timescale expectation for turning around work.

In an age of 24/7 online news, there arguably is no deadline any more. A story is ready when it's ready. Editorial staff accustomed to building to one shared deadline for a print edition of a monthly magazine, say, are now breaking news on Twitter. Even for daily newspaper journalists this is a brave new world.

Staff reporters are now working very much as agencies always have. Stories break when they break. A flash is followed by a snippet, a three-par version, a 250-word version with extra angles and quotes added a couple of paragraphs at a time. It is a perpetual flow and the challenge is to be as fast as possible.

Being first is obviously of considerable commercial value especially in the business field. Reuters and Bloomberg move mountains to try to beat each other by seconds to flash stories up on traders' terminals.

But ethical considerations come into play too. Being first runs a higher risk of being wrong. Sky News is prepared to gamble for the sake of a reputation for breaking news.

John Ryley, head of the satellite broadcaster's news service, said:

"News does not usually break cleanly. Big stories emerge in dribs and drabs, bits of information from many sources often conflicting and confusing . . . when a big story breaks we report new information, clearly attributed to its source, even if things turn out differently."[2]

Or as detractors would call it: 'Never wrong for long.'

The BBC, with a higher premium on credibility and different audience and funding pressures, is more cautious.

However tight for time, a reporter must not be more definite than the current information allows. If information is just a report from a passer-by on Twitter, say so. Put in the caveats, the sources, an assessment of reliability. Don't run rumour as fact. ▶

▶ THINKING IT THROUGH

David Leigh, of the *Guardian*, wrote in 2007:

> 'You can get junk food on every high street. And you can get junk journalism almost as easily. But just as there is now a Slow Food movement, I should also like to see more Slow Journalism. Slow Journalism would show greater respect for the reporter as a patient assembler of facts. A skilled craftsman who is independent and professionally reputable. A disentangler of lies and weasel words. And who is paid the rate for the job. Aren't such people essential for probing the dodgy mechanisms of our imperfect democracy, and our very imperfect world?'[3]

Check out the debate between David Leigh and Roy Greenslade *et al.*[4] and track how it has evolved since.

Ask yourself: If journalism is a discipline of verification, how do you know when a story is ready to be put into the public domain?

New dimensions of news

This chapter has focused on writing a core text-based news report which works in print and online. Even in print this was often only the beginning of a dynamic process involving images, graphics, witness accounts, updates and off-shoot angles. For the 21st century news journalist, online expands those combinations significantly as well as telescoping the time frames. Compared with standard print editions, online coverage provides the opportunity to exploit its immediacy, depth and interactivity to the full.

The multi-layered approach may well include elements of non-linear story-telling, discussed earlier in the chapter. Quinn and others argue that the demands of an online audience actually reinforce the value of the inverted triangle to break news concisely (see Recommended Reading at the end of this chapter). A strictly structured story is easy to scan; a reader can stop at any point and either move to a different story or pursue a link to an extra dimension of the piece. Clarity is even more crucial when a reader has so many routes through the material.

Once the short core news is given, a news writer needs to begin the layering process. Most reporters are at the very least expected to provide internal and external links as copy is submitted. An image is a requirement of most online news templates rather than an optional extra at the discretion of the photographic department. A news journalist has to think of pictures and graphics too.

This can be considered a great opportunity to move beyond the tight confines of print editions where space can be short. One 'killer' quote may be used in the core news report but the online version can carry an extended witness account either in text, audio or video for those wanting to explore those vivid human elements or tap into the expertise of a source. Background research sources can be shared with readers who really want to dig deeper. The more permutations the merrier.

A reporter, guided by newsdesk, has always had to ask him or herself what a story is worth. In print that meant a word count and a decision on how much space would be devoted to it on which page. Now deciding what a story is worth means establishing if and how it appears on multiple platforms and how many different dimensions are provided for readers. Quinn deals interestingly with this and it is one of the many trends which have led to the creation of converged newsdesks to choose the right treatment for each story between different print titles and media platforms.

▶ THINKING IT THROUGH

Check out the reading, critically view several key websites and compare treatment of a major. Where online initially mirrored print, now in many respects print mimics online with newspaper designers providing more entry points and breaking stories up with links, fact boxes, case study panels and more. Think about the demands that places on the news reporter.

Ask yourself: How do we decide the best treatment for core news stories in print and online and what extras are appropriate for different stories?

Buzz words

In the classic Harry Evans tome, originally called *Newsman's English*, reporters were urged to include 'key' words in an intro to grab the reader's attention. 'Murder', 'hacked', 'bomb' all work; or, as in his example, 'beheaded' (see Recommended Reading at the end of this chapter). In the 21st century key words gained additional significance for attracting an audience – courtesy of search engine optimisation.

The web is a very crowded place and effective use of search engine optimisation can massively increase the chances of content being found. Early on this was often attempted through the use of key words such as celebrity names or 'in' expressions which bore no relation to the actual content being used in metatags to drive a site up the web rankings. But it is now the way of the world. This abuse prompted search engines in the 21st century to place more emphasis on the actual content of each web page and it was always arguably counterproductive to attempt to attract audiences under false pretences.

That means the buzz words need to be in the article itself. This conjures up absurdist notions of how to work Beckham, Britney, Al-Qaeda and meerkats into the same intro – a concept not lost on satirists. But in an age when readers can filter their news according to their established interests, journalists do need to consider how to increase the chances of their stories being in the mix rather than outside it.

The dominance of celebrity impacts on us all. Just as the beleaguered charity drums up a glamorous 'ambassador' to tour refugee camps or the serious playwright drafts in a movie star to sell theatre tickets, so journalists write about the big names and buzz topics to push their stories up the hit list. In all cases, some accommodation of the realities of our world makes sense; take it too far and everyone looks ridiculous. (For more on celebrity, see Chapter 7.)

One of the benefits of digital media is the ability to track an audience in a far more sophisticated way than previously possible in print. In place of circulation figures and reader research every other year, web analytics can provide timely information about exactly what is being read online or via mobile services and for how long. Sites also know how they are being accessed: whether directly or via search engines or links from other sites.

Finding clarity from the wealth of data requires expertise and it took some time for any sort of industry standard to emerge even for the basic measure of audience. The Audit Bureau of Circulation (ABC), which long monitored sales of newspapers and magazines, now offers ABCe figures for the digital audiences of its members.

Specialists in search engine optimisation are doing good business training, mainly e-marketing departments but also editorial staff, on how to find an edge in a rapidly changing environment. Journalists need to keep abreast of developments in this area including the criteria used by search engines to rank material. ▶

▶ THINKING IT THROUGH

Google is dominant and any change to its search algorithms can have a dramatic impact on where different sorts of sites and material appear in its rankings. Its Panda update in 2011, for instance, claimed to give extra weight to sites with original content and where users stayed for longer. It downgraded some 'content farms' and voucher sites, but was also accused of undermining its competitors along the way.

This could be read as a move towards introducing an element of quality over mere quantity into the rankings which should benefit original journalism but it also demonstrates the power of Google as the new gatekeeper of content. Bear in mind that 99 per cent of searchers don't look past the first two pages of results.

The consideration of quality also needs to apply when a journalist is including hyperlinks within copy. These can make a big difference to the story's reach without warping the article at all and reporters will often be expected to provide them. This is an ideal way to exploit the depth and flexibility of digital content, allowing different readers to pursue their chosen aspects of the story or move on to original source material. But, for these hyperlinks to add value for the reader, they must lead to reliable sites. Expert commentator Dan Gillmor, for instance, bemoaned the preponderance of 'lazy linking' in a *Guardian* article in May 2011.[5]

A savvy, networked reporter needs to know how to make the most of a story and use technology to help it reach the largest possible audience. Check out the Weblinks at the end of this chapter and the online updates and debates on the issue.

Ask yourself: How do I reasonably maximise the chances of my content being read in print and online? How much should content be driven by online story rankings?

What's in a word?

How does the language we use about people affect the meaning of the story? Journalists must use language as a precision instrument so it matters if our chosen words mislead or fuel prejudice. At very least journalists should be aware of the impact their choice of terminology can have, especially if it's simply incorrect. For instance, what are the reasonable ways to describe disabled people? Should we be guided by lobby groups for disabled people or by the common parlance of our readers? Is it just political correctness? These are just some of the issues addressed explicitly or implicitly in the tone and language used by a publication. That is partly why most have a more or less comprehensive, written style guide.

Some elements of a style guide are intended purely to achieve consistency, alert editorial staff to common errors and generally assist the achievement of clarity for readers. On the basics, check out the impassioned plea for why it all matters from Lynne Truss in *Eats, Shoots and Leaves: The Zero Tolerance Approach to Punctuation*. It's suitably straightforward for those without the benefit of a formal education in English grammar.

Language evolves. Words that were in limited use or regarded as slang work their way into the mainstream and thus into print. Familiarity can lead to the discarding of hyphens or capital letters over time. Editors have to decide whether to lead or follow in such changes – but they risk being too avant garde or too old-fashioned. A style guide is a balancing act in many respects. It also needs to reflect the challenges of text over speech. Sometimes a little more formality is wanted and needed to compensate for loss of inflection and the like.

▶ THINKING IT THROUGH

But other style decisions are guided by the ethos of the title and by its readers. How a title refers to asylum seekers, Muslims and travellers, for instance, can both offend the subjects of the story but also embody a neutral/supportive/hostile attitude to such groups. Another classic example is: do we use terrorist, insurgent or freedomfighter?

Check out the *Guardian* style on issues such as sexuality, swearing, disability and ethnic minorities.

Ask yourself: Is the *Guardian* style appropriate for its audience? If you were editor, would you make any changes? Compare it with the BBC, *The Economist* or other publication style guides.

NOTES

[1] Dust jacket of *The Economist Style Guide*; see also http://www.economist.com/blogs/johnson
[2] BBC 'mimicked' Sky News policy after 7/7 bombings, Oliver Luft, Guardian online, 10 February 2009. http://www.guardian.co.uk/media/2009/feb/10/sky-bbc-news-7-july-bombings
[3] 'Are reporters doomed?', David Leigh, *Guardian*, 12 November 2007. http://www.guardian.co.uk/media/2007/nov/12/mondaymediasection.pressandpublishing3
[4] 'Why I'm saying farewell to the NUJ', Roy Greenslade, Guardian's Greenslade blog, 25 October 2007. http://www.guardian.co.uk/media/greenslade/2007/oct/25/whyimsayingfarewelltothe
[5] See below.

WEBLINKS

http://www.bbc.co.uk/journalism   Great addition to the pool of advice available publicly on what constitutes good journalism and how to achieve it. Basics aren't neglected and there's also an interactive dimension to test spelling, grammar and more.

http://www.economist.com/research/styleguide/   *The Economist* outlines its style online as well as in a hardback pocket book. There's even a quiz and links to other reading, including an archive of Johnson columns discussing the finer points of the English language.

http://www.guardian.co.uk/styleguide   *The Guardian*, *Observer* and guardian.co.uk now share a style guide which is available online and in print. This is a world where being labelled a pedant is a compliment. Check out its clarification and corrections section and the regular commentaries from its readers' editor.

http://www.guardian.co.uk/media/2007/nov/12/mondaymediasection.pressandpublishing3 (Accessed May 2011) Are reporters doomed? David Leigh's plea for Slow Journalism appears under the heading: 'Are reporters doomed?' Follow it through and see how the debate has evolved since.

http://www.guardian.co.uk/commentisfree/cifamerica/2011/may/18/digital-media-social-media?INTCMP=SRCH   The web's weakest links – Dan Gillmor's plea for more considered linking to quality material.

http://www.niemanlab.org/   Harvard-based operation which describes itself as 'a collaborative attempt to figure out how quality journalism can survive and thrive in the Internet age'. Thought-provoking and leans to non-profit models.

http://www.k-1.com/Orwell/index.cgi/work/essays/language.html   (Accessed May 2011)
Orwell's classic essay on Politics and English Language from May 1945.

http://www.poynter.org   Busy site of the Poynter Institute – a school dedicated to teaching
and inspiring journalists and media leaders. It promotes excellence and integrity in the
practice of craft and in the practical leadership of successful businesses. It stands for a
journalism that informs citizens and enlightens public discourse.

http://www.societyofeditors.co.uk/page-view.php?page_id=191&parent_page_id=141
(Accessed May 2011) The Society of Editors campaigns for media freedom, bringing together
editors from all news media. The resources tab on its website includes a wealth of advice
on reporting relatively marginalised and vulnerable groups including Reporting Diversity,
Reporting Poverty and the MIND Mental Health Reporting guide.

RECOMMENDED READING

Cole, Peter and Harcup, Tony (2010) *Newspaper Journalism*. Abingdon: Sage.
Interesting mix of academic research and practical observations on the current challenges
facing print news media, including how they impact on the individual journalist.

Evans, Harold (2000) *Essential English for Journalists, Editors and Writers*. London: Pimlico.
The news-writing component of the classic Evans newspaper series, revised perhaps a little
too respectfully from the 1972 original *Newsman's English*. So, a little old-fashioned but
packed full of dos and donts and discussion of different story treatments. An extensive
chapter on headline writing will help reporters now often expected to come up with their
own for templated web or print pages.

Hicks, Wynford, Adams, Sally, Gilbert, Harriett and Holmes, Tim (2008) *Writing for Journalists*.
Oxford: Routledge.
Useful basic text with a concise chapter on writing news, a helpful discussion of style and a
glossary of terms.

McKane, Anna (2006) *News Writing*. Abingdon: Sage.
Appropriately plain-speaking and very practical guide to news writing with a generous quota
of worked examples. Encourages a healthy respect for precise use of language.

Quinn, Stephen and Filak, Vincent (2005) *Convergent Journalism, an introduction: Writing and
producing across media*. London: Focal Press.
An early offering of advice for the reporter in a converged world. This is both a useful and
thought-provoking read, applying fundamental approaches, such as the inverted pyramid,
to new scenarios online as well as in print.

Randall, David (2007) *The Universal Journalist*. London: Pluto Press.
Excellent all-round guide for the 'thinking' journalist drawing on Randall's varied experience,
particularly as a news editor. Chapters 13 onwards are particularly relevant for news-writing
tips and advice. Randall draws on the history of journalism and his own long career not to
succumb to rose-tinted nostalgia but to offer insights into how we can all do better.

Ward, Mike (2002) *Journalism Online*. Oxford: Focal Press.
One of the original guides on how to make best use of online opportunities and what it
means for writing styles and much more. Some elements are dated but it deals well with
the intrinsic challenges, particularly for anyone used to a print-only environment.

REFERENCE

Evans, H. (2000) Essential English for Journalists, Editors and Writers. London: Pimlico, p. 93.

CHAPTERFOUR
FEATURE WRITING

This chapter will cover:

- Finding ideas for features
- Researching and developing feature ideas
- Organising information
- Different writing styles and structures
- Alternative approaches to feature writing

Case study 4.1

ON a cerulean blue background five yellow circles overlap. At the centre of each circle is information about a pop song. Then, radiating from colour coded segments, a diminishing series of coloured blocks.

What is it? A two page feature about 'How the world listens to music' in *Wired UK* (June 09, p: 38/39) telling readers how releases from Bruce Springsteen, Kylie Minogue, Lily Allen and Bloc Party were played around the world on Last.fm (see the Wired image by scanning the code).

This elegant set of diagrams made a complex dataset simple enough for readers to understand at a glance; it also encapsulated three key magazine craft skills:

- presentation was perfect for *Wired* readers
- combining music and data was perfect for *Wired* readers
- execution was perfect on the page

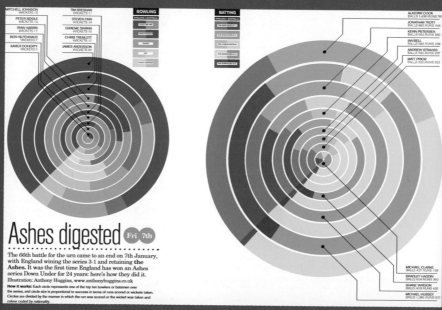

Clever graphic features are not restricted to corporate glossies like *Wired* – indy magazine *Delayed Gratification* explained the Ashes cricket series of 2011 in a similar way (www.anthonyhuggins.co.uk)

INTRODUCTION

A range of coloured circles with very little text is not what most journalism textbooks would describe as a feature but this is not most journalism textbooks. The spread I have described fulfils all of the essential requirements and contains all of the characteristics of a feature as used in modern print publications.

Before looking at what those requirements and characteristics are, there is one very important point to be made and it is essential to grasp it right away: a feature is whatever a creative mind, or set of minds, decides it is. There is no formal definition, no official criterion that sets out word counts or formats or subject matter. The easy, lazy, definition is to think of a feature as a piece of continuous prose that's longer than a news report and does not use the standard inverted pyramid structure, but a look at almost any magazine, website and an increasing number of newspapers quickly shows this rigid convention simply does not hold true – although for a non-paper, screen-based platform that would seem to lend itself to pictures, there are an awful lot of words published online.

In traditional newspaper terminology, a feature was basically anything that was not a news story, so the term included crosswords as well as longer pieces by star writers. Magazines traditionally used a form of feature in which a story was told in a continuous narrative, usually illustrated with photographs; length could vary enormously but the implication was that a single topic would be dealt with in depth. Print journalism in the 21st century, however, has to exist in the current cultural space, and that involves a different use of words and pictures, a different set of expectations from the reader – and much more competition for the reader's attention. Not only do people not want to be on the receiving end of a lecture or sermon, there are hundreds of other sources offering them an easier way to absorb information. Newspapers

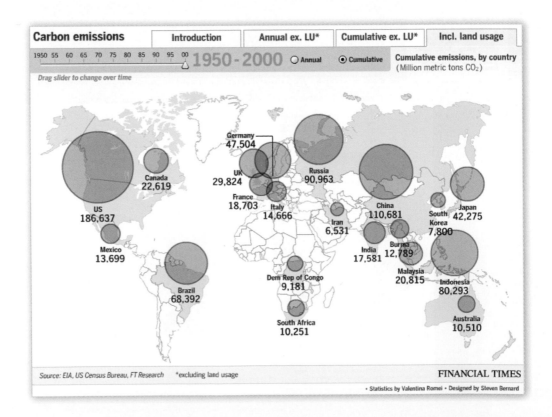

have begun to learn this, as seen by comparing the graphic from the *Financial Times* showing global carbon emissions with the one from *Wired* described on page 87.

If it has become accepted that a range of coloured circles with very little text can be a feature, there is little point in trying to insist on traditional methods and structures only. In 21st century print journalism, which of the following could not be a feature?

- a 2,000 word piece of prose backed up with deep research;
- a double-page spread occupied mainly by a set of overlapping graph lines;
- three pages of pictures accompanied by small blocks of text;
- a page of five, short, autonomous articles linked by an overarching theme;
- a photograph with a caption.

The answer is that they all could be, but the 2,000 words of prose is, for the purposes of this example, a government report. Of course it might just as easily have been a feature, especially in a serious newspaper, a periodical like *The Economist* or even *Wired*, but all the others can definitely be categorised as features, and they have all appeared in real-world print publications. Even a brief session in WH Smith flicking through a selection of magazines will bear this out.

READERS' NEEDS

So, if the feature can no longer be defined simply and unproblematically, if all these possible variants are now legitimate, how can any journalist/editor/art editor know what to choose? The answer is simple – look at what your readers want, what they expect and how far their expectations can be pushed. In short, we are back on the firm ground of traditional journalism theory, usually expressed as 'know your reader'.

Although this has become a commonplace, it has more traditionally been associated with print magazines because magazine journalists down the years have had one lesson drummed into them above all others: write for the reader, not yourself. Most newspapers, after decades of dishing out what the editor or proprietor thought most appropriate, have also learned that lesson, perhaps because readers have grown weary of being lectured (although the *Daily Mail* seems to have mastered the trick of giving its readers what they want *and* lecturing them: neat). This reader-centric lesson is important for all forms of journalism but it is especially relevant to feature writing: whereas news should be valuable data in and of itself, to be consumed quickly and used immediately, a feature demands more attention and may not offer an instantaneous payback. Features require a different compact between reader and writer.

If readers are not interested in the topic, they won't read the feature, and if enough of the magazine, newspaper or website is not of interest they won't buy it or visit it again. People choose a newspaper because they share the same outlook that it promulgates – those with a liberal outlook read the *Guardian*, those of a more reactionary bent read the *Daily Mail*. Either of those papers may run features or comment pieces that represent a different point of view but the overall message will be consonant with the established philosophy; there is a community of interest, be it local, national or political; there is cognitive assonance to keep readers reassured that their view of the world is normal.

Magazines are also based around communities of interest but whereas newspapers are like department stores that have to stock many different types of goods, magazines are more specialised – some are fashion boutiques, some are hardware stores. In one sense this makes selecting a topic for any given magazine simple; fashionistas want fashion, DIY enthusiasts want DIY. But it also makes it more difficult, because within the ecology of magazine publishing every title has its own niche. To an outsider, *Vogue*, *Glamour* and *Elle* may appear very similar, but to a dedicated reader they represent different things entirely and the feature writer must be aware of what those differences are. The same applies increasingly to newspapers because, although broad categories were once enough to give a general shape to content and outlook, the recent combination of declining circulations and a shift of advertising to online have made each reader more valued and information about each reader more valuable. The lesson to be drawn is that it is essential to identify the correct target reader because if you don't know who you are writing for you will never write effective journalism.

There are three important things to get right when considering feature writing:

- subject matter – what to write about;
- tone – how to write about it;
- presentation – how to show it.

Of these, the first two are definitely within the province of the writer; presentation is more complicated in that it will probably lie in the hands of the commissioning editor and the art editor or designer, although the decisions they make will affect the way a piece is written and the format of the writing.

Subject matter: finding and developing features

Sometimes an idea for a feature will strike like lightning. Quite often it will be as a result of putting two unlikely things together and seeing what happens. A brilliant example of this can be found in online magazine *The Quietus*, which marked the 40th anniversary of the moon landings in 1969 by playing a selection of songs about space to eminent astronomer Sir Patrick Moore before asking his opinion of the music and the science contained in the lyrics. This feature lined up all the cherries on the feature jackpot: a widely celebrated news event, a well-known protagonist, an unexpected situation and music about which readers will have their own opinions (plus a playlist on Spotify, the online radio service, in case anyone was unfamiliar with, say, *Out Of Space* by The Prodigy). The brilliant result, which could have been an enormous car crash, can be read at **http://bit.ly/space_rock**.

When inspiration is not flowing so freely, however, more routine sources for journalistic inspiration have been covered in Chapters 2 and 3 and most, if not all, of those sources can be used to find feature material too because while a feature is not a news story the two forms share common characteristics. One of journalism's most distinctive features is that it is always about something of relevance now, at this moment, timely. On the other hand, although the development of 24-hour news channels, online publishing and social networks like Twitter ensure continuous dissemination of news and rumours, being about 'now' does not mean journalism has to cover what is happening this very second; if a new set of facts has been discovered about an event that happened many years ago, that is news. Every year the National Archives at the Public Record Office releases government documents that have been sealed for 30 or 50 years, and every year these inspire news items and features immediately after their release. Then the historians go to work on their careful analysis, contextualisation and interpretation, and that work will be published in academic journals and books some time later. It has been said that journalism is the first draft of history because it records events as they happen, but it is important to be able to distinguish between the immediacy of journalism and the contemplativeness of real history.

Sometimes the timeliness of a feature will be clear and self-evident. A newspaper will run a big piece that explains or comments on news events; a weekly like the *Economist* will run in-depth analyses of political or economic trends. These have a clear connection to current affairs. But even consumer magazines that have no apparent immediate connection to world events run on an agenda of timeliness and novelty. Fashion magazines have to keep up with constantly changing trends, while any title concerned with the consumption of new products (gadgets and cars, for example) needs to monitor innovation. Magazines aimed at hobbyists (classic cars, steam engines, anglers) tend to operate more on the 'what you don't yet know is news' agenda; this can apply equally to newly discovered artefacts, newly completed restoration projects or the latest big fish landed.

In all cases the feature writer has to be able to come up with an answer to the standard question, 'Why *this* story *now*?' If we can call this element of immediacy 'timeliness', we can add it to the other major element that must be at the heart of any piece of journalism (and especially a feature) – reader interest. Thus we end up with three major planks that have to be in place before even starting to write:

- reader interest *plus*
- publication suitability *plus*
- timeliness.

These three elements should be in place whether the feature has been commissioned or is being pitched freelance. In fact freelancers should always go through a self-commissioning process to increase their chances of success. One of the best ways to succeed is to show that you know the publication very well, in terms of what it has covered and how those topics have been covered. Your feature idea needs to fit into the publication's world view and style. It should also have an appropriate tone of voice. Do not make the mistake of thinking it is your duty to make readers expand their world view; people buy print publications because they have a particular world view or a specific interest and while it is often possible for a skilful feature writer to stretch those views or interests readers do not want *your* convictions rammed down *their* throats.

Tone

It is essential to establish the correct tone of voice for a feature – right down to the way sentences are constructed and individual words chosen.

Let's take an extreme, if unlikely, example to explain why. You have been commissioned to write a feature about downloading music for *Top Of The Pops*. The magazine is aimed at a female teenage readership, it is big on visuals and it tries hard (usually successfully) to be down with the kids. By a stroke of luck you have simultaneously been commissioned to write a piece about the effect of downloads on the music industry for *The Economist*. Great – the research and story-telling synergy that every efficient freelance craves.

But how much crossover would there be in reality? *TOTP* does cover serious issues but for its readers downloading is probably just something they do without giving much thought to the economic or technological background. In fact, within the context of the magazine, what could you tell them that they didn't already know? About new or better download sites? About improved MP3 players or mobile phones? Perhaps if the Jonas Brothers had been complaining about pirated CDs or *High School Musical* had suffered from knock-off DVDs you'd have an opening to discuss wider issues, otherwise the approach and topics covered will need to be discussed in great detail with the commissioning editor. And what kind of language would you use? *TOTP* demands a good grasp of language acceptable to teenagers; if you try to fake it you will quickly be found out.

The Economist then, perhaps an easier bet after all – but can you master its language? Authoritative, dry, concise, sometimes verging on the stuffy and pompous but generally avoiding it. How about the research? Do you have a contacts book that will get you the top level sources you need? *Economist* readers want to hear from the people at the top of the information chain and they don't expect to read a rehashed aggregation of existing material with recycled quotes. If you can't get Edgar Bronfman and Thom Yorke to return your calls you're probably playing in the wrong league.

Even if by some miracle you could draw on the same research for both features, can you imagine the mental gymnastics needed to structure and write two such different pieces? That is because *The Economist* and *Top Of The Pops* employ highly contrasting modalities. To simplify a term used in semiotics, modality describes the specific way in which information is encoded for presentation to a particular audience. It becomes a useful word here because it can encompass and incorporate all of the variables that different publications and their readerships expect and require. *The Economist* as a publication comes with a specific set of expectations, *TOTP* with a completely different set; content in either magazine is subject to certain formal requirements of composition and a particular approach to the use of language; subject matter falls within certain parameters; and so on. (See also Publication modality later in this chapter.)

The Economist's New York bureau chief Mathew Bishop passed on a few useful tips for PR companies wanting to work with the publication, but they apply equally to freelancers trying to pitch story ideas:

> 'A bad way to work with *The Economist* is to just send a press release or make a standard pitch by phone. A really bad way is to show you've never really looked at *The Economist*, and it is astonishing how many people pitch us material that could never appear in *The Economist*.
>
> What we are looking for is two things. First, a PR professional who has understood the kind of stories we've been following. On any given subject there's probably going to be a whole period of stories going back many years and there will be a fairly consistent narrative. The challenge is to go to us with a story that challenges or fits in to our narrative.
>
> If you can show knowledge on our narrative and how your pitch fits into that and takes it forward, you will get immediate attention. PR should also understand, if I'm typical of *The Economist*, I am getting 500 emails a day, many of which are completely redundant.
>
> The ideal thing is where the subject of an e-mail is personalised in some way. The first couple of sentences will have to show very quickly understanding of *The Economist*.'[1]

In addition to catering for specific reader needs and interests, there is another compelling reason to make sure your feature is interesting: advertisers. Once again, conventional journalism textbooks tend to avoid this aspect of print publishing but it is a fact that newspapers and magazines rely on advertisers taking space with them so that there is money to pay for paper, ink, printing time and content – that is to say, your fee or salary. One reason why newspapers and magazines are in such well-publicised financial difficulties is because advertising revenues have dropped off alarmingly. Some of this is due to the normal cycles of economic activity, some is due to the extraordinary economic downturn of recent years and some is because advertisers believe they can use their money more effectively online (or even that advertising generally is not all it's cracked up to be). Advertising income has been the most important income stream for print publications for the past century and the best way to attract advertising is to attract readers.

Professor David Abrahamson of the Medill School of Journalism at Northwestern University came up with a neat definition of the relationship between magazines and advertisers that applies just as well to newspapers. He said a magazine contains 'specific information in a specific form that can be expected to appeal to a definable segment of readers'; once their attention has been captured, the publication becomes capable of 'delivering those readers to a group of manufacturers or distributors with the means and willingness to advertise their products and services to them'.[2]

If we unpick that a little for the benefit of feature writers, the important aspects are the first: 'specific information in a specific form that can be expected to appeal to a definable segment of readers'. In Abrahamson's formulation, the readers come first and the advertisers follow them, and that is the best sequence to bear in mind. Advertising departments will always lean on editorial departments to curry a few favourable mentions; that's the way it always has been and always will be. The important thing is to have a strategy for dealing with it. Agreeing to publish a double-page spread about every advertiser is going too far in one direction and never agreeing to publish anything at all about any advertiser is too far the other way. It is entirely possible that your readers will genuinely be interested to learn more about a particular product or service, and it is not beyond the bounds of possibility that writing about an advertiser's business operation could give rise to an interesting feature. But readers are skilled at detecting bullshit and toadying and if you put advertiser interests before reader interests too often they will leave you, followed swiftly by those advertisers you were trying to please.

Angle

Lest there is any doubt here, the readers must always be at the centre of what you do as a journalist. The tone and subject matter, as discussed above, are key but just finding a topic to write about will probably leave too broad a field to cover. Let's follow this through by taking music as a topic. In his book *The Rest Is Noise: Listening To The 20th Century*, Alex Ross was able to consider a massive range of music and composers, from Shostakovich to Sonic Youth, but he had over 600 pages in which to do so and even then there was a preponderance of music from the classical tradition. *BBC Music* might, possibly, offer a similar range of interests but even *Mojo*, famed for its lengthy pieces like the 17-page Bob Dylan special in the December 2010 issue, cannot possibly include everything about everything.

Journalists therefore have to focus more narrowly, have to select a part of the broad topic to write about and this narrowed selection forms the *angle* – the particular lens through which the subject matter will be viewed. Even Bob Dylan, to continue the *Mojo* theme, cannot be completely contained within 17 pages; it is entirely possible to write a 283-page book about just one of his songs, as Greil Marcus did in *Like A Rolling Stone: Bob Dylan At The Crossroads*. Finding the angle that will allow you to tell the story in the right way – bearing in mind the reader's interests and the publication's style and outlook – is therefore essential.

Two questions will help you to locate the angle; one follows from the other and between them you can actually define several angles from the same topic – a boon for freelancers. The questions are:

* Who cares about this?
* What am I going to tell them?

The first does not mean 'who cares' in a 'whatever' sort of way, it means who are the individuals or groups that have some kind of a stake in knowing more about this subject? The second refines any given individual's or group's need for the specific information that will affect their lives or the way they act.

Let us imagine that you, as a journalist, have found some information about literacy levels among school leavers that shows many young people have a problem with reading and writing (not a hard act of imagination, sadly). Ask yourself that first question and you should quickly be able to come up with several answers:

* parents of children at school or who have recently left;
* teachers who want to improve the situation in their school;
* employers who have to recruit from the pool of school leavers;
* local councillors or school governors who have responsibility for running schools.

That gives you four different angles. Why different and why angles? Because it is unlikely those four groups want or need the same information. Parents will want to know how to judge or improve their children's reading and writing; teachers will want to know about specific schemes to improve delivery; employers will want to know the extent of the problem and how they might be able to tackle it in the workplace; councillors and governors will want to know what powers they have to ensure improvement. There will probably be a bit of overlap but there will also be considerable divergence.

Once you have got the answers to those two questions you can use a spidergram or MindMap (see page 96) to draw out all the possible fields of research and investigation. This, in turn, will lead you towards the specialised sources you need – individuals, experts, groups and organisations that will help you find the facts and knowledge you need to tell the story.

For a short word, *angle* produces a disproportionate amount of confusion among learner-journalists but it's actually a simple concept – it's the version of the story that will attract the specific readership you are targeting. Vern Pitt, a staff journalist at *Community Care* magazine, defines the angle as, 'The most interesting side of a story for your readers' and you could also take that a step further to say 'The most interesting *interpretation* of a story for your readers.' A great example of what this means can be found in a story Andrew Orlowski wrote about CD sales for online technology magazine *The Register*. The normal angle for a story like this – the music retail industry angle, if you like – would focus on the decline in sales and how badly record companies and record stores are doing as a result. But Orlowski takes a completely different angle by pointing out:

> **'People continue to buy pre-packaged plastic music discs – most containing as little as one album – despite the rise in digital album sales, the cheaper option of listening on demand, and the risk-free option of downloading entire discographies in one go.'[3]**

In other words, the decline is not surprising but the resilience of the physical product is – that's the angle.[4]

Angle in this sense does not imply partiality or bias. However, as it is also a professional term which can be accepted unthinkingly, in the wrong hands it can end up meaning just that. Fox News in the USA trademarked the phrase 'fair and balanced' as the motto for its clearly right-wing output but when the organisation tried to injunct Al Franken for using the words in the title of his book *Lies and the Lying Liars Who Tell Them: A Fair and Balanced Look at the Right* the judge threw the case out, perhaps demonstrating that a journalist should never confuse *biased partiality* with an *angle*.

PUTTING IT INTO PRACTICE

In her book *How To Write Successful Magazine Articles*, Camille Davied Rose recounts the experience of Margaret Cousins, a journalist on *Good Housekeeping* whose editor made her submit 25 ideas for articles every week. As a result, wrote Cousins, 'I cannot walk down any street or go anywhere to this day that my mind does not consciously store up impressions, observations, dialogues, attitudes and a dozen things which could be turned into articles for magazines' (Rose, 1967).

Put this into practice for yourself by keeping a notebook for a week and aim to jot down 25 ideas for features. Keep your eyes and ears open, sharpen your curiosity and powers of observation so that everything you see, or overhear, becomes a source of interest and a potential feature.

At the end of the week, review your notes and find at least one strong feature idea that you could develop. Think carefully about the angle, or angles, you could take.

Activity: Select one feature idea from your 25 and develop it further. Try to create two distinct angles that will serve two distinct readerships.

- You are always writing for the readers, not yourself.
- The style and tone of your writing should be right for the target publication.
- Finding a fresh angle will allow you to develop new features from old subject matter.
- All media thrive on fresh ideas and stagnate on recycled ones.
- Whatever you think is the right way to do things – including anything you learn from this book – is not right if it's not what the readers want.

Once you have worked out the readers' needs, subject matter, tone and angle, the sequence of operations to follow runs like this:

- idea – (subject matter, etc., see above);
- information gathering – research;
- organising – selecting the best research;
- writing.

INFORMATION GATHERING

Whatever the subject of your feature you will need to be informed about it. Interviewing a celebrity will require you to have a good idea of what they have been up to and when, how their last film/record/book went, the state of their marriage and so on. Much of this information – perhaps all of it – will be available in the public domain, probably in newspapers and magazines or on gossip websites such as **perezhilton.com** or **3am.co.uk** (though it may not all be accurate). On the other hand, if you are covering a heavyweight topic, or writing a long feature or even a series of features, the burden of background reading will be commensurately heavier. You may even need to do a small literature review to see what books and articles have been published, what information they have uncovered, what angle they have taken and who has contributed to the sum of knowledge.

The formula for success when thinking about sources is:

- Always look for the people who can help you to tell your story.
- Use their stories to illustrate the points you need to make.
- Combine your research with their stories to create a compelling narrative.
- Human interest + background + analysis + structure + narrative = success.

How do you find out what you need to find out?

Preparatory work to determine the angle of the feature should have given you an understanding of the type of information you need and then the type of person or organisation likely to have that information. As an example, take the general topic of climate change. Unless you are writing a book, you will not be able to cover every aspect of this phenomenon; however, as a journalist you will be writing for a specific readership and that will give you your initial guidance. Climate change will affect almost everything in some way, so the range of potential communities of interest is enormous: gardening, boating, diving, angling, farming and birdwatching are just a few of the hobbies or jobs that could be vulnerable to change. Readers interested or involved in them will need, and expect, different sets of information: the

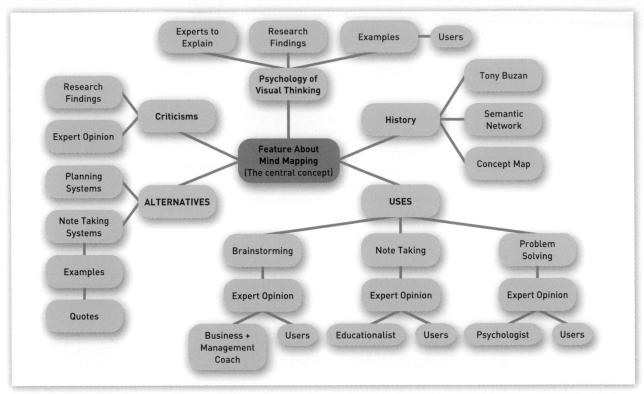

underlying causal phenomenon is the same but the specific interpretation will be different and if you find an expert who can explain the effect on rose plants you are unlikely to be able to use that information in an article about fishing. The readership's requirements guide you to the general field and then the publication's specific niche will guide you to the particular experts; for instance, boating may cover ocean sailing, pleasure cruising or kayaking, and you will need to find different experts for each category.

Some people find that drawing a MindMap or spidergram helps. These are essentially the same thing, except that Tony Buzan has registered MindMap as a trademark to protect his commercial interests in the idea. To create such a diagram, put the core idea in a circle at the centre of a piece of paper and then surround it with related ideas, phrases, possible sources, etc.

In the early stages it does not matter how the information is arranged or whether it is all relevant or useful: a MindMap/spidergram is simply a tool to help generate ideas and for this it is very useful. However, brainstormed material must then be sorted and arranged more rationally, otherwise there is a danger that users will transfer the chaotic randomness into the feature.

Your reading, thinking and graphics should lead you to identify potential human sources, people you can talk to who know something (hopefully, a lot) about the subject. You may need to consider the best order in which to see these people: if there appears to be a particular spider at the centre of a web of intrigue, perhaps you should speak to a few of the flies associated with 'the spider' to gather intelligence for a set-piece confrontation. You will certainly need to think about the questions you are going to ask. It seems an obvious rule that you should not ask questions that have been answered elsewhere, but it is still worth stating. Previously published profiles or interviews (though they may contain inaccuracies), reference works such as *Who's Who*, social networking sites like Facebook or LinkedIn and specialist aggregators like Pipl.com, 123people.com and YoName.com can all provide facts and clues about your interviewee. (For advice on how to use these services, see **http://bit.ly/people_finders.**)

If you are interviewing someone for their expertise rather than their personal life, it is a good idea to know at least something about their special subject and your background reading should provide the groundwork. However, it is equally important not to imagine that your reading will have made you an expert capable of arguing back, although lack of expertise should never stop you from asking commonsense questions, or questions that help to fill in the gaps in your knowledge.

How do you get hold of people to interview? In the normal ways – telephone, email or even letter. Although there are many resources online (see journolist.com for sound advice on sleuthing the web) don't forget obvious sources such as the telephone book, professional directories or electoral rolls (now conveniently searchable thanks to 192.com). An author, actor or performer may have an agent or PR you will have to contact.

After all your reading, interviewing and note taking you should have far more material than you could ever hope to use, and if you don't, you probably haven't done enough. What follows is one of the most difficult stages of feature writing.

ORGANISING

Journalists are always told to avoid clichés but phrases become clichés because they contain an element of truth. Thus, the saying 'Those who fail to plan, plan to fail' is worth repeating in this context because planning is a key to success in writing features. We have looked at the need to plan the information-gathering process and now we need to consider how to process the information that has been gathered. When Sir Arthur Quiller Couch wrote:

> **'Whenever you feel an impulse to perpetrate a piece of exceptionally fine writing, obey it – whole-heartedly – and delete it before sending your manuscript to press. Murder your darlings.'**[5] (1916)

he was advising on style, but the same must apply to much of the background research and many of the quotes you have so painstakingly gathered. However, I would modify the saying to 'Murder your second-class darlings' because the very best material must be kept.

Organising a feature starts with outlining a structure. This may have been specified in the commission or you may have the liberty to decide it yourself. Even so, whatever the actual form the piece will take, you should develop a clear idea of what order the information will follow and write this out or draw a diagram that should not look at all like a spidergram. There are many possible structures for a feature and many ways of representing them. The following is a fail-safe archetype for a piece written in continuous prose, from which you will be able to derive many variations including types that do not have a linear narrative, such as box-out features.

Intro section

This is where you must grab the reader's attention. There are a million other things for people to do, so it's your job to make sure reading your feature comes top of their list. When you are gathering information keep alert for potential intro material. In a non-linear feature this section should include the headline, standfirst and textual introduction (if there is one).

Bridging section

This is the link between the intro and the main body of the feature. Lead the reader from the excitement of the opening to the thoughtful mid-section.

Argument

The main body of a through-written feature. This is where you will draw on background research and quote your sources to help tell the story. The story you tell should have a sequential, but not necessarily chronological, narrative and the arguments you make must be logical and grouped, so that you do not jump around from A to B to C to D and than back to A because you forgot something (but if your jump back to A is a clever trick of rhetoric, that's fine).

Contra section

It can include counter-arguments that put the opposite point of view, or there can be a contra section. You could repeat the argument/contra sub-structure as often as necessary or you can put the two together and have a series of pro/con paragraphs.

Summary section

Optional place to go over the main points of the argument once more.

Outro

Just as you came in with a bang, so you should go out with a bang. Don't allow the feature to peter out, bring it to a definite conclusion with a specially saved quote or a brilliant observation – as with the intro, keep alert for outro material. Working in a reference back to the intro can be highly effective, giving a fully rounded feel.

A CLOSER LOOK

The best-selling novelist Julia Gregson, a successful journalist before becoming an even more successful author, has a simpler guide to structure. It goes:

- HEY!
- SAY
- NAY
- SAY
- HEY!

Filled out, that means grabby intro followed by main point(s) followed by counter argument(s) followed by restatement of main point(s) followed by memorable outro. She also advises that if you are having trouble actually writing a piece to imagine it as a letter to a good friend: Dear Fred, you'll never guess what I've just found out . . .

THE FIRST 'HEY!' – A GUIDE TO INTROS

There are many ways of starting a feature and although there is no rigidly scientific way of categorising them it is useful to have some kind of framework to describe them. The following types of intro are all found in newspaper, magazine and online features.

Focus on a person (aka the specific human intro)

Start by focusing on a person whose experience underlines what the story is about. Readers will be able to empathise more easily with human experience than with an abstract theory or a parade of facts. Human interest can also liven up what might otherwise be a dry story, so this can be a useful technique to use in business stories, or stories about social change. A good example of this type of intro was used by James Meek for his *Guardian* feature about Icelandic company Decode Genetics and its mission to create a DNA databank of the entire Icelandic population. The data would then be used to discover 'disease genes' and thus lead to enormous profitability.

How do you begin to write about an entire nation? Start by focusing on an individual whose life has been affected, and if that individual has another incident in his background so much the better. Meek's first sentence runs:

'Before the cyclist hit him in 1996, Hinrik Jonsson was a strong, skilled, energetic craftsman, a 35-year-old with a young family, whose hand-made furniture could be seen in houses all over Reykjavik.'[6]

These 35 words give us not just a huge amount of background but a human drama too – a life-changing accident.

In the second paragraph Meek tells us about Jonsson's compensation and how he invested it:

'In the spring of 2000, he walked into a state-owned bank, the National Bank of Iceland, where a broker swapped his money for shares in the hottest Icelandic company on the country's thriving but unregulated grey market, Decode Genetics, at $56 a share.'[7]

The third paragraph brings the intro to a conclusion:

'Earlier this year, Jonsson returned to the bank to sell his shares. They were worth not much more than a 10th of what he had paid for them . . .'[8]

Having grabbed our attention by telling us about one person, Meek can now move on to the more corporate part of the feature. (To read the complete feature go to: http://bit.ly/specific_human)

Use an anecdote

An anecdote is a short, self-contained story with its own beginning, middle and end. It must be relevant to the subject and the end should tie into the bridge of the story. Anecdotes usually also focus on people. The example here is a piece that Michael Hastings wrote for *Rolling Stone*, a feature that led to General Stanley McChrystal being stripped of his position as the commander of US and Nato forces in Afghanistan, a clear indication of the power of print journalism to make a difference. But it starts – with a quote (see below) – by recounting a small event during McChrystal's visit to Paris:

' "How'd I get screwed into going to this dinner?" demands Gen. Stanley McChrystal. It's a Thursday night in mid-April, and the commander of all U.S. and NATO forces in Afghanistan is sitting in a four-star suite at the Hôtel Westminster in Paris.'[9]

Hastings then gives a fuller context for the general's visit to Europe, recounts the full exchange with his Chief of Staff and gives us a stack of telling detail:

'The tables are crowded with silver Panasonic Toughbooks, and blue cables crisscross the hotel's thick carpet, hooked up to satellite dishes to provide encrypted phone and e-mail communications. Dressed in off-the-rack civilian casual – blue tie, button-down shirt, dress slacks – McChrystal is way out of his comfort zone . . . The general hates fancy restaurants, rejecting any place with candles on the tables as too "Gucci." He prefers Bud Light Lime (his favorite beer) to Bordeaux, *Talladega Nights* (his favorite movie) to Jean-Luc Godard.'[10]

More detail, more dialogue and then the payoff to this anecdote, which brings Hastings himself into the scene:

' "Who's he going to dinner with?" I ask one of his aides. "Some French minister," the aide tells me. "It's fucking gay." ' [11]

(To read the complete feature go to: http://bit.ly/anecdotal_intro)

The common denominator

This is a way of taking a common experience and using it to introduce a more complex topic (and thus may be similar to a specific human intro). It can be a useful way to start stories about finance, the law or science. In the example here from *Reader's Digest* (December 2009), Jerome Burne's actual topic is cognitive neuroscience, looking at how the brain works. The feature quotes heavyweight scientists from the likes of the Karolinska Institute and cites academic journals, but it starts with a scenario that many readers will be familiar with:

'Like millions of other teenagers my 14-year-old daughter Kitty is often to be found on the sofa, laptop on her knees, checking facts for the essay she's writing. The TV is on and occasionally she scrolls through Facebook. She texts, makes calls on her mobile and takes her iPod headset on and off.'[12]

We have an unthreatening scene, a named person performing routine actions, and then a little personal reflection by the author about how things used to be. This then leads into the intro's punchline: 'The question a lot of experts are now asking is: *how is this way of working affecting their brains?*'[13]

Narrative

Open the story with a chain of events unfolded in a dramatic, chronological way. This can be very effective in an action story but it does require good writing skills if it is to work properly. The first example is by Kitt Doucette from *Men's Journal* (May 2009) and displays a very Hemingway-esque direct narrative style; the second, by Sarah Woods from *Wanderlust* (December/Jan 2009), is equally direct but not so visceral.

'Deep in the Sawtooth Mountains of central Idaho, skis strapped to my back, an ice ax in one hand and the faint taste of bile in my mouth, I stare down the Horstmann Couloir and try not to throw up. The couloir, a 55-degree strip of snow wedged between two vertical rock walls, looks more like an elevator shaft than anything remotely related to a ski run . . . Now add the fact that you're eight aerial miles from the nearest road, 60 from the nearest hospital, 9,900 feet above sea level, and surrounded by 216,383 acres of unforgiving wilderness. Swallowing takes a lot of effort. I'm in way over my head.'[14]

'Suddenly, without warning, Hernan raised his hand, silently grinding to a halt – a pile of puma droppings at his feet. They were fresh – alarmingly so – and bore signs of a large peccary kill. Hernan scrutinised the leafy depths, ears pricked and eyes narrowed, while I held my breath. Puma are more likely to attack a human than, say, a jaguar is, so when we discovered new tracks on the forest floor we marched on in eerie silence, flinching at every snapped twig or birdcall.'[15]

Setting the scene

An intro that establishes where the story is taking place, who the main actors are and what they have been doing can be very effective. It is often used to recap information in a feature that follows on from a previous story, to recall a historical figure. In the first example from *Reader's Digest* (March 2009), Adam Nicholson recalls Vita Sackville-West, his grandmother:

> 'The other day I was looking through the old filing cabinets at Sissinghurst, meticulously arranged by my father before he died . . . when in the drawer labelled "V. Sackville-West" I found a file marked "Gardening Correspondence Course 1956". Vita was by then famous as a gardener. She had been writing *The Observer* gardening column for seven years and had made at Sissinghurst a garden that was already known and loved.'[16]

Tim Bouquet uses a similar technique to to establish a sequence of past events in this feature from *Reader's Digest* (September 2009). The feature is well worth reading for the way Bouquet structures the chronology:

> 'It is one o'clock on Saturday, October 2, 2004, and the City of London is deathly quiet. Two men – one bearing a laptop, the other sporting a ponytail – arrive at the locked doors of the European headquarters of Japan's Sumitomo Matsui Banking Corporation. The inside man lets them in, having already adjusted the motion sensors on the CCTV cameras so they won't be witnessed.'[17]

Description

This can work well in a travel story, for example, but it requires the description to be of something out of the ordinary, or a familiar scene written about from a new perspective. Whichever, it must be striking and well-written. The two examples are from *Wanderlust* and demonstrate that this type of intro can be used to both vigorous and contemplative effect. Alex Robinson (Dec/Jan 2010) throws us instantly into the heart of a vibrant Brazilian street party:

> 'There was a river of dancing people between the pastel-painted houses and the ornate church facades of the narrow street in Olinda, on Brazil's far north-eastern coast. Bearded old men in white cotton suits and young black girls with aquamarine eyes and swishing baroque dresses two-stepped along the cobbles. Gym-pumped men as hard as pit bulls under their Marge Simpson wigs pressed up against me in the tight crowd. "Bem-vindo cara!" they roared, embracing me in a vice-like hug and handing me a can of Bohemia beer – "Welcome, friend!" '[18]

Paul Bloomfield (May 2010) takes us to a much more serene location – but note the final sentence that adds a touch of grit and intrigue:

> 'In a peaceful glade lined with swaying bauhinia trees, the barest whisper of a breeze set singed red banknotes fluttering under a rock atop a grave.
>
> Graceful arms sweeping around the broad, chair-shaped monument stretched eastwards towards the sea; elegant gold characters embossed on the headstone's rich red sun disk honoured its resident. Smaller memorials – tiger and dragon, flanking the central grave – marked the resting places of lesser family members, while clusters of incense sticks sprouted alongside the scorched remains of that spirit money. And the charred remnants of a mobile phone.'[19]

Up the garden path

An intro which appears to be going in one direction but then doubles back on itself to confound expectations – these examples are taken from features written by undergraduate journalism students:

1 Feature about homelessness

> 'I'm sitting in a quiet cafe in the centre of Cardiff. Mary, a bright, attractive 17-year-old, is nursing a warm mug of coffee opposite me. Mary has nine GCSEs and two A-levels. She plays the violin. Mary is also homeless.'

This was very effective but there was a major problem with it – the student had made the whole thing up.

2 Feature about child poverty in Wales

> 'Dropped through the letterbox amongst the daily post comes a Save The Children envelope. The letter inside reads: "Living in poverty is a daily reality for millions of children around the world . . . Together we can give thousands of children a head start to escape poverty." '

'So where would you expect your requested donations to go? Children in Sudan? Rural Tibet? Vietnam? Wales?'

Intros to avoid

The quote

Quotes are very often not self-explanatory to the reader. You will know the whole context of the conversation and thus understand why these few words are so important, but the reader does not have that benefit. Unless a quote is very strong, very funny or particularly relevant, don't use it to open a feature. Think 'Why should I use this quote?' A good answer would be if you have an anecdote like the one Michael Hastings uses to start his *Rolling Stone* feature (see above).

The rhetorical question

Unless you are careful, a rhetorical question can either seem patronising, or invite a negative answer.

'How much do you know about money laundering?' would not be a good way to start a feature about that subject. Those who did know something might think they knew a lot and didn't need to read your article; those who didn't know probably wouldn't be interested enough to carry on and would miss out on all the valuable information you had found for them.

The 'Imagine' gambit

Don't ask your reader to 'imagine' something – it's your job to provide the words that will conjure up the image. A good example of this was provided by one of my former students. Here is her first attempt to describe the library in a workingmen's institute:

> 'Imagine a room where the musty smell of old books instantly hits you. They are rich green, red and black, and bear the battered marks of age and over use. They line the walls meticulously in no particular order.'

You might see nothing wrong with that but I believe asking the reader to 'imagine' actually imposes a barrier between reader, writer and imagined subject – you are demanding an action before having established a relationship.

Here is the revised version, which comes across so much more directly it's hard to think that only a few words have been changed:

> 'The musty smell of old books hits you instantly. They are rich green, red and black, and bear the battered marks of age and over use. They line the walls neatly, but in no particular order.'

An opinion

Unless you are a recognised authority on the subject, don't lead with your own opinion.

A CLOSER LOOK

HOW FAR CAN AN INTRO TAKE YOU?

In January 2011 *Time* magazine published an article by Annie Murphy Paul about so-called Tiger Moms, Chinese mothers who drive their children relentlessly and even ruthlessly. The intro focused on Amy Chua, a professor of law at Yale university who had published a book about her authoritarian parenting and as a result appeared all over the media. The intro gave examples of her behaviour, cited other interviews and features, used colour details to describe her, and generally seemed to be heading towards (yet) another profile of Chua.

Then, nine paragraphs in, Paul uses a bridging section to switch direction. She writes:

> 'With a stroke of her razor-sharp pen, Chua has set a whole nation of parents wondering: Are we the losers she's talking about?
>
> Americans have ample reason to wonder these days, starting with our distinctly loserish economy.'

Suddenly this feature has turned into a discussion of the economy, educational standards and American self-confidence in general. A specific human intro has allowed the writer to move quite naturally into a much broader set of sub-topics.[20]

THE ARGUMENT: MAKING IT PERSUASIVE

When trying to persuade readers of something – making an argument – there are some well-tested guidelines that can be closely aligned to the Hey-Say structure shown above. In the 1930s, Alan H. Monroe, a professor at Purdue University, systematised the stages of persuasion that a good speech should follow but there is no reason why Monroe's Motivated Sequence, as it is called, cannot be used in a written piece. The sequence runs:

- Attention: grab the reader's attention by using a strong case study, dramatic statistic, or, less commonly, a quote.
- Need: demonstrate the extent of the problem, its significance and that it requires an active solution. Use facts and examples from your research to persuade the reader of the need for action.
- Satisfy: suggest solutions that could solve the problem, be it at national, local or personal level.
- Visualisation: show the reader the results of following and/or not following your suggested course of action. Use specific, concrete details.
- Action: tell readers what they can do to help solve the problem (aka Call To Action).[21]

All of these elements can be used in a feature but be careful about calls to action. It may be appropriate to encourage readers to make a next step or it may not. Use your understanding of the editorial context, the magazine's aims and the reader's need to judge.

OTHER FEATURE GENRES

Sometimes, of course, your feature will not be making an argument of any kind. It may be a:

- **How-to** – showing people how to do something step-by-step from beginning to end, from simple to complex. Peter Walsh's feature *Conquer Clutter Room By Room* for the online version of *O, The Oprah Magazine* (January 2006) explains the most effective ways to declutter, for instance, using a structure that takes readers from master bedroom to garage.[22]
- **Straight story** – following a chronological time line from start to finish, though you may want to use a dramatic moment out of sequence for the intro. This kind of story is ubiquitous but *The Economist* ran a nice example on 14 July 2011 looking at the prospects for News Corporation – and Murdoch père et fils – in the wake of the *News Of The World* phone hacking scandal. Check out the simple but effective graphics and timeline too.[23]
- **Recommendation** – comparing or classifying; for example, testing products or services against stated criteria. There are examples of this everywhere but a classic use of the form is in multi-car tests like the example from *Car*.[24]
- **List** – list features are used for many purposes, ranging from a collection of answers to a particular problem (The Five Best Ways To Diet) to a purely comparative list (The Best 100 CDs Of All Time). The example from NME falls into the latter camp.[25]

When you have your structure and an outline of the points you need to make, you can start to align your research material with those points. Most of the time, and certainly for shorter articles, you can jot these alignments in your notebook, especially if you have identified the points with numbers or letters. For more complex features, or if you are writing a series, solutions range from colour coding with highlighters to creating a card-index system such as that laid out by Vicky Hay in her classic book *The Essential Feature* (1990).

You must be ruthlessly selective with the research material and save only the best and most relevant. It always seems a terrible waste to discard hard-won quotes or references from a densely argued academic paper but it is even worse to over-pack a feature with citations at the expense of the narrative: remember that in the end you are telling a story. Compare this task with a photo editor's – there may be dozens or scores of images from a photoshoot but only a few can be used: think of the difference between a feature illustrated with loads of thumbnails and one that uses a few large and dramatic images.

A possible solution to the problem would be to use the overmatter online, something that has already happened with photoshoots. Consider making full transcripts, or recordings, of interviews available – not only might this offer extra value to readers, it also creates extra transparency for the journalistic process by allowing readers (and the interviewee) to understand how you have selected and used material. Make sure, however, that online space is not just used as a dumping ground; there must be a real value for the reader in publishing this extra material.

WRITING A SERIES OF FEATURES

If you are writing a series of articles around a common theme you will have the opportunity to use more research material but the structure becomes even more important. In addition to planning the form of each individual feature you have to plan a meta-structure that guides the whole series.

Working on the assumption that a series is likely to be about an important topic, one that will have many aspects that can be investigated and written about, you should draw up a spidergram with the overall subject at the centre and spin off all of the possible sub-topics that you can think of. Take chocolate as an example.

Chocolate might appear to be a trite subject. You want a treat, you go down to the newsagents, you hand over some money and you consume the product. It's just there. But of course, it's not just there, it had to get there. If you begin to work backwards from that shop, ideas snowball. Here are a few:

- How did it get there?
- Who decided on the price?
- How is the retail price split up?
- And among how many?
- Where are the confectionery factories?
- Who owns them?
- How do they get the raw materials?
- Who trades them?
- Is it profitable?
- Where does cocoa grow?
- Who grows it?
- What conditions do they work under?
- How much do they get paid?

There are many more, but this simple list has taken us from a newsagents at the end of your street to the plantations of the Coté d'Ivoire and possible issues of child labour. At every stage someone is making money from this product, creating a pyramid of profit built on the labour of those who get paid least of all.

Once you have all the questions down you can separate them into sub-topics or related themes. In this instance we might decide to follow production from the cocoa plant to the shop counter. This could give us a series of four features that looked at the growers, the traders, the manufacturers and the retailers/consumers. Each feature would have a separate focus, each would require its own set of sources, contacts and background readings, each would stand alone as a self-contained piece of work that did not overlap greatly with, or repeat, what had gone before, but that together would provide a comprehensive picture of this apparently simple subject.

Whatever the initial topic or subject that you want to research and write about, find a way to define the meta-narrative, then define and separate the narratives of each feature. Think of the process as following a chain of interlinked events. Say the topic is the effect of fashion photography on eating disorders among young women in China – what is the chain of events here? Context is very important – the setting is China, so it will first be necessary to understand the specific cultural and social conditions of young women there, how fashion is produced, displayed and consumed, and so on.

When it comes to planning the series you could start at the fashion house that supplies samples of the clothes in its latest collection for magazine photo shoots; then move to the photo session, which would allow you to write about models and photographers; the images then move along to the magazine's editorial team, where the art editor and/or photo editor will select and (in all probability) alter or manipulate them; then the final feature could show the magazine being consumed by its readers and the immediate effect on them. At each stage you could draw on experts of various types and background research, as well as the people immediately involved in the action.

In *All The President's Men*, the feature film based on the investigation of Watergate, the political scandal that eventually brought down President Richard Nixon, a source known as Deep Throat tells *Washington Post* reporter Bob Woodward to 'follow the money'; detectives in fiction are often given the advice, 'cherchez la femme' (an expression first used by Alexandre Dumas senior in his 1850s novel *The Mohicans of Paris*). Whether it is money or a love interest, you must find something to follow through your discrete but connected features.

PUTTING IT INTO PRACTICE   ANOTHER NOTEBOOK

Once you have chosen the story idea to follow up (see Putting it into practice on page 94) start a new notebook that will be dedicated solely to that story. In this notebook you will record everything you find out – facts, names, phone numbers, leads to further information, background reading of books or articles, details about the people you interview you can use to add colour to the feature, sketched ideas for a layout – everything.

Not only will this dedicated notebook save you from having to keep masses of scraps of paper together, it may also save your legal bacon. Journalists should keep their source material for at least a year after publication in case it is needed to defend a legal action – or even as evidence in a prosecution. Novelist and journalist Julia Gregson was able to head off trouble after a disgruntled interviewee claimed the two had never met; the copious details Julia had noted down about the woman's house, where the interview had taken place, was accepted as evidence they had met and the complaint collapsed.

One more advantage of this method – it will allow you to show how much work you have put into a piece should there be a dispute about payment.

remember

- Your feature will only be as good as the research that underpins it.
- Finding the right contacts and sources is a key journalism skill.
- Be prepared to discard a lot of research material and keep only the best.
- Develop a range of writing techniques and feature structures.
- If you are writing a series find the narrative arc that will carry the story through.

WRITING THAT KEEPS READERS INTERESTED

We have already looked at the expectations of a publication and its readership as regards use of language, tone or style of writing and choice of vocabulary. These considerations will guide, and also set specific boundaries on, the way you write.

There are, however, some rules that can be applied across all kinds of journalism and the two most important are to be concise and precise. The notion of concision contains within it the principle of using as few words as possible but also conveying as much information as possible with those words. The English language, thanks to its constant reinvention and refreshment by other tongues (among them Anglo-Saxon, Old Norse, Latin and Norman French, along with a good few useful items from the former British Empire), is blessed with a large and varied vocabulary, so it should always be possible to find exactly the right word for the job. It is also a general rule, given a choice, to use a short word rather than a long one, and if possible a short, old word, which is why I have used the word 'word' instead of 'lexeme'. The saying 'short words are best and the old words when short are best of all' is attributed to Winston Churchill by many authorities, including *The Economist Style Guide*. Jakob Nielsen, the guru of web usability, expanded the apothegm to 'precise words are often better than short words'.

Churchill could usefully have added something about concrete words, too. That is to say, the kind of word that prompts a definite sensory reaction in the reader, a word that taps directly into a reader's imagination and allows an immediate mental experience of or empathy with what is being described. Peter Jacobi, in *The Magazine Article*, contrasts the power of 'nouns and verbs' to show a reader what has occurred with the tendency of 'adjectives and adverbs' to merely tell, thus failing to engage the imagination: 'Nouns and verbs carefully used show. They intensify the material of the article because they immerse the reader.' (1991: 79).

Concision is important, but never forget the power that cumulative detail can have. There is a great example of this in Tom Wolfe's *Mau-Mauing the Flak Catchers*. Introducing an out-take from the story in his collection *The New Journalism* Wolfe calls this technique 'the downstage narrator' (1990: 412) and acknowledges his heavy dependence on 'details of status life to try to draw the reader inside the emotional life of the characters' (ibid.). Judge for yourselves from this description of an official working in the 'poverty office':

> **'All you have to do is look at him and you get the picture. The man's a lifer. He's stone civil service. He has it all down from the wheatcolour Hush Puppies to the wash'n'dry semi-tab-collar shortsleeves white shirt. Those wheatcolour Hush Puppies must be like some kind of fraternal garb among the civil-service employees, because they all wear them. They cost about $4.99, and the second time you move your toes, the seams split and the tops come away from the soles. But they all wear them. The man's shirt looks like he bought it at the August end-of-summer sale at the White Front. It is one of those shirts with pockets on both sides. Sticking out of the pockets and running across his chest he has a lineup of ball-point pens, felt nibs, lead pencils, wax markers, such as you wouldn't believe, Papermates, Pentels, Scriptos, Eberhard Faber Mongol 482's, Dri-Marks, Bic PM-29s, everything. They are lined up across his chest like campaign ribbons' (ibid.: 424).**

The effect depends not just on an accumulation of detail, but the precision of that detail – the brand names and particular types of pens and pencils – and the fresh metaphor of the final sentence that combines nerdy detail and creativity.

Individual words and strong metaphors are important elements of readable journalism but they have to be put together well. Just as a good feature must have an overall structure and rhythm there must also be structure and rhythm within the paragraphs: macro-structure and micro-structure.

Reader must feel that they are being taken on a journey, so there is that beginning and middle and end, but there also need to be clear landmarks and milestones along the way that allow readers to feel in safe hands. This will often take the form of good pick-up – trailing a word or phrase or idea late in one paragraph and picking it up in the next so there is a clear connection and feeling of continuity. These are what make the difference between a feature being like a stack of plain building blocks, ready to tumble over at any second, and a stack of Lego, stabilised by the pips and indents in each brick.

A CLOSER LOOK

A LONG, CONNECTED FEATURE

For a good example of a long feature that employs milestones and landmarks effectively, take a look at 'Learning to Love the (Shallow, Divisive, Unreliable) New Media' written by James Fallows and published in *The Atlantic*, April 2011. It starts with a recap-anecdote that establishes the context for the piece and runs over the arguments about decline in the media, bringing in Barack Obama to add weight and a recognition factor. The feature moves into more personal opinions until Fallows suddenly takes the reader by the hand, leads us to a new scene and cements us into the new environment:

'To show why, let's visit Gawker . . .

Nick Denton, the founder, owner and CEO of the dozen or so Web sites that make up Gawker Media . . .'[26]

This technique is repeated throughout the sections of the feature, Fallows trailing phrases or quotes at the end of one paragraph and picking them up in the next. Look out for these phrases, examine the paragraphs around them and note how they both recall what has gone before and predict what is to come:

'Scary or not, is this in fact worse than journalism as we have previously known it? . . .

The news business has never been stable . . .

In this turbulent media environment, let's remember something we saw early this year.'[27]

A TYPOLOGY OF FEATURES

Styles of writing, as well as the number of words required, will vary depending on the type of feature being written. Determining the *type* is different from determining the *genre* (as discussed earlier); a feature's type is determined by its general characteristics, appearance and treatment whereas the genre is determined by what the content is intended to do – explain, improve, compare, etc.

Features come in many sizes, shapes, styles and types. There is no official method of categorising them but most will fit into one of the following:

Analytical feature: 1 – precision journalism

If the book has been the dominant symbol of Western culture for the past 500 years, the analytical feature is its journalistic equivalent. Analytical journalism, in its strictest sense, is an attempt to underpin journalism with the methodological approaches of the social sciences. The key text in this movement, if such it can be called, is Philip Meyer's *Precision Journalism* (written in 1969, first published in 1972 and revised and republished in 2001), subtitled *A Reporter's Introduction to Social Science Methods*. In it, Meyer emphasises the relevance of understanding how to use and interpret statistics so that journalistic research can be put on an objective, scientific, footing. When he wrote the first edition, this approach contrasted strongly with the 'new journalism' of Tom Wolfe and Hunter S. Thompson (to name just two of its practitioners), which took its cues more from the techniques of fiction: Truman Capote's *In Cold Blood*, a work based on fact but imaginatively interpreted, would perhaps stand at the opposite end of the journalistic spectrum from Meyer's analytical approach.

However, an analytical feature is very often a much simpler artefact than the introduction of mathematical or statistical principles would imply. In fact, an analytical feature is usually just a piece of fairly standard journalism that examines a given situation or topic and presents its findings on that topic in a standard journalistic format. If there is any kind of qualitative difference implied by the title, it will generally be realised by application of the concept of 'depth' but this word is somewhat problematic as it has many aspects and possible meanings. In the context of an analytical feature it could be taken to mean:

- Length – although quantity may or may not relate to quality, analytical features are generally quite long, sometimes up to several thousand words.
- Breadth – a wide range of related or quasi-related sub-topics are mentioned; if they are relevant it may well lead to a deeper understanding of the overall topic.
- Quantity of research – broad background reading or other briefing, intended to give the writer a more complete contextual understanding of the topic that can then be transmitted to the reader.
- Quality of research sources – the writer has gained access to people or organisations that are considered to have the 'real' information needed to make sense of the topic or get the 'inside story' and thus give the reader valuable and exclusive knowledge.
- Expert – the writer is an acknowledged expert in the field and has excellent access to high-level sources of information because of that. However, this can be a mistaken assumption as anyone who read Sir John Keegan's profile of Donald Rumsfeld – a profile that told us practically nothing new or interesting, despite Keegan's professed long acquaintance with the American politician – in the February 2003 issue of *Vanity Fair* will realise. (Go to **http://bit.ly/vf_rumsfeld** and find PART ANISTON, PART BEZOS, ALL RUMSFELD for further explanation.)

A much better example is John Lanchester's feature for the *Guardian* (13 July 2011) about the turmoil in the Eurozone caused by the Greek economy. Lanchester established his credentials in this field with a book about the global financial crisis, *Whoops!: Why Everyone Owes Everyone and No One Can Pay (2010)*, that extended his reputation as a novelist into non-fiction and showed his ability to explain complicated issues to the lay reader (see **http://bit.ly/analytical_1**).

Note: One thing to beware of with the analytical feature is that it can become somewhat essay-like and turn into *hybrid-academic-journalism*, a form that is to be avoided as it has neither the rigour of academic writing nor the vigour of journalism.

Analytical feature: 2 – data journalism

Over the past few years 'analytical journalism' has taken on a new meaning, thanks to organisations such as the Institute for Analytic Journalism (IAJ). The IAJ website's welcome message describes analytic journalism as:

'Critical thinking and analysis using a variety of intellectual tools and methods to understand multiple phenomena and to communicate the results of those insights to multiple audiences in a variety of ways' . . . analytic journalists consciously and constantly survey all other professional disciplines searching for methods that can be used by journalists to do more insightful, meaningful stories. The disciplines range from accounting (forensic accounting and performance measurement) to medicine and public health (epidemiology) to zoology (measuring relationships between species and resources).

There are some similarities between computer-assisted reporting (CAR) and analytic journalism. Both typically retrieve and analyze quantitative data, or translate qualitative data into quantitative data for more precise analysis, especially over time. Analytic journalists, though, seek methods beyond crunching numbers on a spreadsheet or running filtering algorithms on a database.'[28]

In some instances, this takes us right back to where we started, with features illustrating datasets. For an interesting explanation of how this can be applied to journalism, download the PowerPoint lecture notes from **http://bit.ly/analyticslides**. Examples of this type of feature are increasingly common on newspaper websites – for example, the *Guardian* (**http://bit.ly/analytical_2**) and the *Financial Times* (**http://on.ft.com/analytical_4**) – but Stanford University's visualisation of how journalism travelled west with the pioneers is a lovely specimen (**http://bit.ly/analytic_3**).

A CLOSER LOOK

CREATIVE USES OF DATA

Brilliant examples of this kind of work can also be found at:

- **http://www.gapminder.org/** – Gapminder was founded in Stockholm by Ola Rosling, Anna Rosling Rönnlund and Hans Rosling. Its mission is to become a 'fact tank' that promotes a fact-based world view by creating videos, Flash presentations and PDF charts showing major global development trends with animated statistics in colourful graphics.
- **http://www.worldmapper.org/** – Worldmapper is a collection of world maps, where territories are re-sized on each map according to the subject of interest. The maps are equal area cartograms, also known as density-equalising maps, and the cartogram re-sizes each territory according to the variable being mapped (Population, Education, Health, etc.).
- **http://www.informationisbeautiful.net/** – run by David McCandless, who describes himself as an author, data journalist and information designer. His passion is visualising information – facts, data, ideas, subjects, issues, statistics, questions – all with the minimum of words. 'I'm interested in how designed information can help us understand the world, cut through BS and reveal the hidden connections, patterns and stories underneath. Or, failing that, it can just look cool!'
- **http://visual.ly/** – launched in July 2011 as a hub for data visualisations and a place for data visualisers to share their work and connect with those who want to commercialise them. The site launched with over 2000 visualisations in a wide range of categories, from sports and technology to the economy. Its partners in the publishing world include CNN, *National Geographic*, the *Wall Street Journal* and The Next Web.

Blogs and sites that aggregate this kind of material include: **http://chartporn.org/**, **http://news.designlanguage.com/** and **http://flowingdata.com/**.

Standard narrative feature

Although it will share many of the characteristics of the analytical feature (type 1), the standard narrative feature does not of necessity have the serious import of its heavyweight cousin. The majority of features written as continuous prose can be classified in this category: for example, this piece about crop circles from *The Economist* – yes, you did read that right (7 July 2011: **http://ind.pn/standard_narrative**).

Words and pictures feature

May be a long feature but the defining characteristic is that words and pictures will be given equal weighting, and this may affect the writing format if the words are closely linked to specific illustrations. *The Economist*'s lifestyle cousin *Intelligent Life* made sure that Giovanna Dunmall's words coincided with the appropriate images in *Waste Not Want Not*, a feature based on an art exhibition about dirt at the Wellcome Collection (**http://bit.ly/words_and_pix**).

Pictures and words feature

In this type of feature the words are definitely subordinate to the pictures, and may be little more than informative captions. However, this does not mean what you write is not important: a picture may be worth 1,000 words, but your 100 words will guide the reader to an interpretation of the picture.

Ruth Morgan's feature *Born Free*, about freerunners, occupies 12 pages of the May 2011 of *Red Bulletin*, Red Bull's extraordinarily good promotional magazine. Over nine of those pages, 75 per cent, are taken up with photographs but without the text there would be no feature. (**http://bit.ly/pix_and_words_1** – starts on page 30).

By contrast Ryan Tatar's piece *CWC: The Final Chapter* runs over eight pages of *Huck* magazine's March 2011 issue and the proportion of photography to text is probably closer to 85:15. In fact it would also be accurate to describe the piece as a photo-essay, but again the words are essential to a full understanding of what you are looking at (**http://bit.ly/pix_and_words_2** – starts on page 50).

Composite feature

The composite feature is best described as a series of short, discrete, features (perhaps no more than 200 words each) that are linked together by their common theme. For example, in its February 2009 issue *Reader's Digest* ran a six-page spread of stories about heroic animals – each of the stories is self-contained but together they create a unified whole (**http://bit.ly/composite_1** – starts on page 38).

Similarly, the *Guardian Guide* of 9 July 2011 ran a piece by Justin Quirk about a series of exhibitions held throughout the West Midlands, all dedicated to heavy metal music; the events are all separate but connected by theme and intention (**http://bit.ly/composite_2**). The writer selected and described a single object from each exhibition to draw the feature together, a structural device that draws on the popular Radio 4 series *A History Of The World In 100 Objects* (**http://www.bbc.co.uk/ahistoryoftheworld/**).

Longitudinal

This describes not so much a categorisation as a description of how Web 2.0 media can extend the reach of a feature and transmute it into other fields. If we take the *Guardian*'s graphic of global road transport emissions as an example, we find the graphic itself and its associated analytical feature (a good instance of types 1 and 2 converging). We can also find links to blog posts and comments, and if we look further afield we can find links to other places, such as favouriting sites (Digg, Reddit, StumbleUpon) and tweets on Twitter that take the original feature well outside the *Guardian*'s purlieus.

Jeff Jarvis has called the tendency of some features to take on a new life 'process journalism' (**http://bit.ly/process_journalism**) and has also argued the case for the fundamental building block of journalism to be not the article but the topic:

'I want a page, a site, a thing that is created, curated, edited, and discussed. It's a blog that treats a topic as an ongoing and cumulative process of learning, digging, correcting, asking, answering. It's also a wiki that keeps a snapshot of the latest knowledge and background. It's an aggregator that provides annotated links to experts, coverage, opinion, perspective, source material. It's a discussion that doesn't just blather but that tries to accomplish something . . . It's collaborative and distributed and open but organized.'[29]

On 10 August 2011 Jarvis's prayers were answered (possibly; the man is quite picky) in an article by Lewis DVorkin, introducing *Forbes* magazine's 'new article page for the era of social media'. This would, DVorkin explained, be:

'the next step in the iterative rebuild of Forbes.com. It's a key component of our unfolding strategy to put our authoritative journalism at the center of a social experience by providing reporters and writers with the publishing tools and audience data they need to connect with consumers. If you total up our FORBES staffers and contributors, we have 850 topic-specific experts using our platform to do just that . . . Today's article page release tightens the author-audience relationship and furthers our effort to build a scalable content-creation engine of individually branded journalists, authors, academics and other qualified contributors.'[30]

PUTTING IT INTO PRACTICE

As should be becoming clear now, features come in many forms and styles, and have many aims and intentions. It is a great idea to have a scrapbook in which you can keep examples of features that you think are particularly good, effective, imaginative or plain weird.

You can also use a bookmarking service such as delicious (**www.delicious.com**) to make a cloud-based scrapbook of features you find online or in digital/digitised publications.

Activity: Look for features in as many different types of print publication as you can and try to fit them into a category. Use the categories given here, add to them or make up your own system.

remember

- Journalism is not a static system, it is always evolving.
- There is no single way of presenting information to a readership.
- Read as much as possible.
- If a piece of writing strikes you as particularly good or bad, effective or ineffective, take the time to analyse it.
- Learn to appreciate different formats even if you do not intend to use them.

A TYPOLOGY OF FEATURES, FROM READERLY TO WRITERLY

As the world has become more visual and the print media have developed more interesting ways of using words and pictures, the form of the feature has become increasingly fluid. This has led to the type of non-traditional interpretation of the feature idea seen earlier in this chapter. For the sake of practical guidance, and to establish a sound footing in what is likely to be an evolving area of journalism, it is worth attempting a taxonomy of feature types before looking in more detail at how to create, research, structure, write and present them. Any kind of categorisation requires an analytical structure and to provide a framework for this analysis I draw on the work of Roland Barthes, the French literary theorist. Barthes developed many ideas in his productive lifetime but the one he is probably most widely known for is an essay on the 'death of the author', wherein he argued that language controls the writer rather than vice versa. In his book *S/Z* (1970) he proposed the idea of 'readerly' and 'writerly' texts. To oversimplify, a readerly text is one that attempts to impose a fixed meaning determined solely by the author, whereas a writerly text allows the reader to contribute to the creation of meaning.

In the context of this chapter, a readerly text could be characterised as a long investigative feature that presents a series of facts in a sequential timeline of continuous prose, and a writerly text as something like the *Wired* graphical feature described at the start of this chapter. The former claims to reveal a certain fixed reality; the latter makes no single fixed claim and allows an infinite number of interpretations.

My initial attempt at categorisation starts with the most readerly type of feature and proceeds to the most writerly. It is important to note that this is not a completely scientific method and that the order of presentation does not imply an intrinsic order of value or worth.

READERLY		
	Analytical	Ties reader to the set of facts presented as definitive by author
	Standard narrative	Tells a story in which the author attempts to make a definite truth claim
	Words and pictures	The hegemony of the word is disrupted by visuals that allow interpretation
	Pictures and words	Visuals become dominant, though captions still offer definitive explanation
	Composite	A collection of separate but related pieces that operate under a defined heading
	Data visualisation	Visual presentation permits wide range of interpretation
	Longitudinal	Discussion of original piece expands into blog links, Twitter, Facebook
WRITERLY		

Although categorising feature types in this way might seem to be adding an unnecessary layer of complexity to a relatively simple concept, it is, as I have emphasised already, essential for journalists working in print – but who will almost certainly not be working *only* in print – to stop thinking in traditional terms. Although a feature can still accurately be described as a longer piece of journalism analysing a topic in depth, that is only one form of feature, and not always the best choice. Journalists working in print need to find new ways of thinking about how to make arguments with information and data, and using Barthes's theory is a way to do that; you don't have to believe it, but you could try it out as part of the commissioning or creative process – or find your own new way to look at things.

The point I have been trying to make in this chapter is that journalists (and those who train and educate them) need to move on from thinking about features as being a given number of words in a certain format. This does not mean we need to jettison all traditional concepts of feature writing because many of the basic principles apply whatever the final form. If we list the essential elements of the feature, that list will look very familiar and include a combination of the following.

Length

'Length' is a tricky word. It carries the implication of extended appearance but can also describe brevity. A feature may well be long, but it can also be short. Ekow Eshun, whose CV includes being editor of style magazine *Arena* and artistic director of the Institute of Contemporary Arts, got his start in journalism by writing a 200-word feature on the cultural significance of Kickers footwear. On the other hand, the 'new journalists' of the 1960s – Tom Wolfe, Hunter S. Thompson, *et al.* – were noted for their hyper-extended pieces for *Rolling Stone* and their books. A small graphic can be rich in data, just as a photograph can still be worth 1,000 words.

Depth

This is somewhat less tricky. A feature should tell the reader as much as possible about a topic; sometimes 200 words is enough, sometimes 5,000 only just does the job and sometimes words are not the main focus at all. The difficulty is for the commissioning editor to judge how much information in what format is appropriate and for the writer/creator to pack as much into the available space as possible.

Completeness

As with depth, the feature should tell readers everything they need to know. The topic could be how to bake a perfect apple pie or the Chinese government's economic policy; in either case the reader needs to understand both by the end of the piece.

Illustration

Features need to be illustrative, which can mean being accompanied by photographs, artwork or graphics, or that the writing uses a lot of examples and case studies, or that the artwork and graphics predominate. Often it will mean some combination of all three, but the important principle is to think of how the piece generates or uses images.

Involvement

No-one needs to read a story, especially not your story (or mine), so you need to give it something extra that will get and keep the reader's attention; you need to make it involving. Sometimes this comes from great story-telling, sometimes from the overall package of words and pictures, sometimes from superb graphics.

Distraction

Although no-one *needs* to read your story, there is a strong and widespread desire to be entertained, or distracted, through the medium of words and pictures. Human beings love stories and story-telling but one of the important things to realise is the variable timespan this can involve. Millions of people are prepared to devote hours to the Harry Potter books but when Dutch academic Joke Hermes researched how women use print magazines, she found one of the most important attributes is that they are easy to put down. Break off from an involving novel and you risk losing both the narrative thread and your place; break off from a magazine and you can easily find where you were.

Utility

Another thing Hermes found was that print magazines are valued for the way they can add to a person's 'repertoire'; put more simply, you can learn stuff from them. It doesn't have to be big stuff – if you want to learn how to bake that perfect apple pie and your magazine tells you, that feature has done its job. If you want to be more informed about the Chinese economy and that long analysis leaves you confused, it has failed.

These categories and essential elements may prove to be useful but there are other considerations that a feature writer has to take into account before deciding what specific form the work should take. Luckily, a Scottish media baron summarised these choices in a pithy saying – 'educate, inform, entertain'. That was the vision Lord Reith, the first Director General of the BBC, had for the public service broadcasting organisation he was in charge of and it is still part of the BBC's mission statement: 'To enrich people's lives with programmes and services that inform, educate and entertain.'

Features can be positioned along a scale of functionality that relates to Reith's dictum, running from didactic purpose to informative purpose to entertaining purpose. The correct form of functionality should be decided on at the very start of the feature writing process and it will depend on a number of factors, the most important of which are the readers' needs and the publication's modality.[31]

Publication modality

The vocabulary may be different but this is also traditional turf: know your publication. If you don't, you won't be able to create a piece specific enough for any given title.

Modality, as applied to print publications, has four main factors:

- reputation or aura – the brand image, sometimes built up deliberately, sometimes the result of organic evolution;
- expectations – what a reader expects to find in the publication;
- use of language – the tone, vocabulary, jargon, etc. of the writing;
- subject matter – may be wide ranging or narrowly focused.

Put into a table, the factors of modality look like this:

Modality – type → – degree ↓	Reputation/ aura	Expectations	Use of language	Subject matter
	Trustworthy	Well sourced	Formal	Restrictive/ deep
Didactic	Reliable	Informative	Dry	Intensive
			Direct	
Informative	Interesting		Allusive	Wide ranging
			Slangy/ jargonesque	Extensive
Entertaining	Experimental	Fun	Informal	
	Flakey		Chatty	Random

THE FUTURE OF FEATURES AND FEATURES OF THE FUTURE

When the Readership Institute, a research centre of Northwestern University, undertook a survey of newspaper readers in June 2001, it found that one of the strongest responses to a question about what would give greater satisfaction was – features (specifically, news stories told using a more typically feature structure). Magazines are quite naturally built around features, and websites – where everything we read is in *type* – include a great deal of feature material. The future of the feature appears to be safe and healthy and it is not taking much of a risk to hypothesise that, as long as people want to read, they will want to read features.

I noted earlier in this chapter that 'a feature is whatever a creative mind, or set of minds, decides it is' but there is something that needs to be added to that statement – a clear understanding that the set of minds includes the readers. We have seen above how the development of a 'longitudinal' feature moves away from the author and publisher into the public sphere and that is a trend that is likely to grow. Indeed, a clever author or publisher will find a way to harness that process for both creative and commercial reward.

Finally, some advice from one of the most able magazine publishers in the industry. Nick Brett, editorial director of BBC Magazines, has a career that spans local and national newspapers, the editorship of BBC flagship *Radio Times* and the development of the BBC magazine brand into a global force. He is well aware of the time-tested maxim about writing for the reader and he has moved beyond it, persuading his editors always to put the reader at the heart of what they do and then to 'let the reader in'. What does this mean? It means listening to their suggestions for content; it means asking them for feedback about what they like and don't like; it means inviting them to participate in the making of the magazine in clever ways, for example a reader of *Good Food* challenging Gordon Ramsey to better the dish that he or she makes best, with the results blind tested by a panel of *Good Food* readers; it means readers of *Lonely Planet* sending in 'postcards' of the high-quality photographs they took on holiday for reproduction on a large scale in the magazine.

You can admit the reader in print as well as online and editors who discover how best to do it for their readership find it benefits their pubication greatly. The feature writer of the future must look for ways to let the reader in: in a nutshell, make your features writerly.

PUTTING IT INTO PRACTICE

Write a commission for an article you would like to write or to read. Include all of the following elements:

- topic – the basic subject matter;
- angle – the precise approach to that subject matter; the specific aspect(s) you will write about;
- sources to include – the people it is vital you contact for information;
- sources to avoid – perhaps those who have proved unreliable in the past;
- format – how the piece is to appear on the page will shape the way you write it;
- illustration – as noted above, the visuals are very important;
- ways to make it writerly;
- deadline;
- payment.

Cultural or literary theory rarely works well when inserted directly or undiluted into journalism. Critical analysis can, however, provide new insights into journalism – *your* journalism. Whatever anyone tells you, especially journalists, there is great value in *thinking* about what you are doing as opposed to simply following old rules of thumb or established working practices. But . . . not all rules of thumb or established working practices are necessarily bad or in need of revision.

CHAPTER SUMMARY

In this chapter we have looked at some of the many forms and varieties feature writing in print can take. Even without breaking into multimedia/digital interpretations, we have seen that features can range from very simple words on a page to quite complex and conceptual formats.

Despite this variety there are some considerations that must be remembered above all others. The story you are telling must be:

- as interesting to the readership as possible;
- as well researched as possible;
- told according to the readership's needs and expectations;
- appropriate for the publication's remit and modality.

At a basic level, feature writing is as straightforward as it always has been – accurate facts marshalled into a strong, often entertaining, narrative. Paradoxically feature writing is also as complex as it always has been – the best story-tellers may not seem to be trying too hard but the seductive surface of the narrative conceals the effortful mechanics of structure and form. The complexity factor has only been increased by the extra choices of presentation and platform.

This chapter looked at how to:

- find ideas for features;
- research and develop those ideas;
- organise research information;
- write in different styles;
- use different structures.

It also looked at alternative ways to analyse feature writing because just as the events of July 2011 – when the News International phone tapping scandal began to bring down journalists, editors and police officers, and left some politicians indelibly tainted – demonstrated the value of a strong ethical code, so developments in feature writing and presentation make it worth having a conceptual framework for critical thinking to help guide writers through the confusing maze of possibilities.

THINKING IT THROUGH

One of the questions buried deep in that maze of possibilities must be, 'What is a feature?' As we have seen in the preceding sections it is almost unanswerable, such is the potential variety of forms, formats and content. However, we could take some advice from earlier in the chapter and look for an angle that could take us further. As often happens, once you start looking for an angle you discover several.

Long news reports vs features

One useful line of enquiry might be to trace the boundaries between feature writing and extended news writing. Two books recommended in the list at the end of this chapter, the *Faber Book of Reportage* and the *Granta Book of Reportage*, provide numerous examples that can be used as case studies. The introductions to each book, by John Carey (an academic) and Ian Jack (a journalist), are essential to a full and contextual understanding of the definitions used, the processes of selection – and each editor's understanding of the value of eye witness observation. Sometimes, but not always, this is called journalism; sometimes, but not always, it is done better by someone who is not a career journalist.

To undertake this exercise, start by selecting a piece of reportage – the Granta book may offer a more accessible range in terms of recent events, although they are all quite long – and read it through at least twice. The first time will tell you what happens, the second time will allow you to observe the writing.

Ask yourself: At what point does reportage morph into feature writing – or does it not matter?

Subjective vs objective

In his Introduction to the Granta book, Ian Jack touches on the 'journalism of attachment', a genre, or approach to reporting, popularised by Martin Bell that argues journalists should record the human and emotional costs of war rather than acting as mouthpieces for government or military sources. As a result journalists hope to affect policy, motivate public action to do something about the situation and participate in the public debate about the conflict.

Practitioners of the journalism of attachment see this as an indispensable aspect of good journalism. The genre can be a powerful force for good but its adherents can also slip into clichéd tropes and forms of delivery. Although Bell reported for the BBC, an institution noted for its even-handed approach, he justified the rejection of journalistic neutrality as a consequence of a moral imperative to stand up to evil-doing.

Beyond that, when journalism slips into the personal, is there a danger of first person reportage/writing becoming contaminated with subjective opinion and defective or selective memory? There are plenty of examples in both books of the reporter/writer taking centre stage (writing as 'I') – select a couple to compare and contrast.

Ask yourself: Would the writing be better or worse, more or less convincing, without the writer at the heart of the action?

Journalist vs writer

One of the common myths of journalism is that journalists are (or somehow should be) 'unclubbable'; they are mavericks who go against the flow, kick against the

> ▶ THINKING IT THROUGH

pricks, don't take no for an answer, won't stay under anyone's thumb, and so on. At the same time, a competing myth makes journalism the greatest freemasonry in the world and places journalists among the most serious thinkers of the day: it's a massive club of like-minded, high-minded, seekers of truth and justice. Plus they all know shorthand, the laws of libel and have an unwavering belief in objective reporting.

However, both books of reportage demonstrate convincingly that some of the best journalistic writing has been done by people who are not, or would not describe themselves as, journalists. It has long been recognised that non-fiction writing can benefit from some the techniques of fiction writing but is it possible to take that idea further? Are there times when being 'a journalist' can actually get in the way of telling a powerful story? Thinking about this also begins to touch on the topic of the citizen journalist and user generated content

Ask yourself: Can journalism training get in the way of good story-telling?

What does 'reading' mean?

If we turn from the writer to the written, from the creator to the content itself, several more questions arise in the context of feature writing. They are all worth considering further, in the light of this chapter and your own research. You will need to own or have access to an iPad but it is well worth having a look at *The Atavist* (**http://atavist.net/**), which publishes original non-fiction stories that are longer than normal magazine features but shorter than the average book for Apple's tablet. Stories are published through an app and although they start off looking like a print-based feature, they actually make full use of the multimedia capability of the device: video, audio, additional layers of information, and many other features.

Ask yourself:
• How can serious topics be tackled in non-traditional formats?
• In what ways have print layout and online displays affected or influenced each other?
• Does multimedia story-telling add to or detract from the 'reading' experience?

NOTES

[1] http://bit-ly/bishop-pitch
[2] Abrahamson, David (1996) *Magazine-Made America: The Cultural Transformation of the Postwar Periodical*. Cresskill NJ: Hampton Press, Inc., p. 28.
[3] http://bit.ly/register_cd
[4] My thanks to Robert Andrews of PaidContent UK for directing me to this story.
[5] Sir Arthur Quiller Couch (1916) *On the Art of Writing*. Cambridge: Cambridge University Press. Available at http://bartelby.org/190/
[6] James Meek (2002) 'Decode was meant to save lives . . . now it's destroying them', The *Guardian*, 31 October.
[7] Ibid.
[8] Ibid.
[9] Michael Hastings (2010) 'The Runaway General', *Rolling Stone*, 22 June.
[10] Ibid.
[11] Ibid.

[12] http://bit.ly/RD_commondenominator – navigate to p. 52.

[13] Ibid.

[14] http://bit.ly/narrative_intro_1

[15] http://bit.ly/narrative_intro_2

[16] http://bit.ly/scenesetter_1 – navigate to p. 76, copy starts on p. 78.

[17] http://bit.ly/scenesetter_2 – navigate to p. 76.

[18] http://bit.ly/descripition_1

[19] http://bit.ly/description_2

[20] http://ti.me/tiger_mom

[21] Additional information about effective use of rhetoric can be found at http://www.artofrhetoric.com/rhet_elements.html

[22] http://bit.ly/Oprah_How_To

[23] http://econ.st/Straight_Story

[24] http://bit.ly/supercar_test (the link shows the opening spread only)

[25] http://bit.ly/NME_100_greatest

[26] http://bit.ly/long-connected

[27] Ibid.

[28] http://bit.ly/aboutiaj

[29] http://bit.ly/building_block

[30] http://onforb.es/forbes_update

[31] In semiotics, a modality is a particular way in which the information is to be encoded for presentation to humans, i.e. to the type of sign and to the status of reality ascribed to or claimed by a sign, text or genre (see http://bit.ly/feature_modality).

WEBLINKS

http://www.johnmorrish.com/journolist/   John Morrish is a journalist and writer; he maintains this very useful site as a service to all other journalists and writers who need to use online resources effectively.

http://www.faganfinder.com/   Fagan Finder is a collection of internet tools, that describes itself as 'the best of the web . . . each page or section is built using or linking to the very best resources in that category'.

http://pipl.com/, http://www.123people.com/, http://www.yoname.com/   These 'people finder' sites use publicly available information such as Facebook pages, Twitter accounts, Amazon wishlists and so on to aggregate personal details.

http://www.192.com/   192.com started by aggregating information gathered from UK Electoral Rolls (a long-established source of information for journalists) and making it searchable. It has since added many other services.

http://www.yell.com/   The *Yellow Pages* in online form – often overlooked.

http://www.thephonebook.bt.com/   Directory Enquiries without the charge.

RECOMMENDED READING

Bernstein, Carl and Woodward, Bob (1974) *All The President's Men*. New York: Simon & Schuster.
A classic account of journalism at its investigative best.

Carey, John (ed.) (1987) *The Faber Book of Reportage*. London: Faber and Faber.
Magnificent historical overview of factual writing, ranging from Thucydides in 430BC to James Fenton in 1986.

Hay, Vicky (1990) *The Essential Feature*. New York: Columbia University Press.
One of the most detailed guides to feature writing ever written, although some of the advice is specifically relevant to the USA.

Hermes, Joke (1995) *Reading Women's Magazines: An Analysis of Everyday Media Use*. London: Polity Press.
A readable academic account of how magazines become important through their very disposability.

Hicks, Wynford, Adams, Sally, Gilbert, Harriett and Holmes, Tim (2008) *Writing for Journalists*. London: Routledge.
Lays the foundations for sound writing in the different genres of journalism.

Jack, Ian (ed.) (1998) *The Granta Book of Reportage*. London: Granta.
Superb collection of 20th century long-form journalism, often not by career journalists.

Jacobi, Peter P. (1997, 2e) *The Magazine Article: How To Think It, Plan It, Write It*. New York: John Wiley & Sons.
Jacobi's slightly offbeat advice makes this an excellent companion to Hay's more straightforward account.

Wolfe, Tom and Johnson, E. W. (1975) *The New Journalism*. London: Picador.
A superb compendium of writing from the '60s and '70s when journalists were not afraid to experiment and editors not afraid to let them. Worth reading for the Introduction alone.

REFERENCES

Jacobi, Peter (1991) *The Magazine Article*. Indiana, p. 79.

Rose, Camille Davied (1967) *How do Write Successful Magazine Articles*. New York: The Writer.

Wolfe, Tom (1990) *The New Journalism*. London: Picador, pp. 412, 424.

CHAPTERFIVE
PRODUCTION

Case study 5.1

IT'S a beautiful photograph of a praying mantis. The creature, mainly light green but with a white thorax and some brown highlights on the forelegs, has been captured in a very unusual pose – the two rear pairs of legs on a thin twig and the front pair raised in threat or supplication. In fact it looks like an upright stick man with a large bustle; or, considered in a different way, it looks as though it's dancing.

Certainly that seems to have been what the production team on the *Metro* newspaper thought when they published the picture on page 31 of the Thursday 22 September 2011 issue. In the print edition they came up with a caption that referenced John Travolta in the 1983 film *Staying Alive*:

'Praying Alive: You can tell by the way he uses his walk, this praying mantis is a disco fan. Snapped in Cyprus by HasanBaglar, the insect appears to mimic John Travolta's Staying Alive dance.'[1]

The online edition used the same photograph but went with a different popular culture referent in the headline and standfirst before getting more serious in the main copy:

'Mantis shows it's fun to pray at the YMCA with bold dance move' [headline][2]

'With its arms in the air and what looks like a grin on its face, this praying mantis could well be performing the YMCA dance.' [standfirst][3]

'But although the bug appears to be having fun as it mimics the moves invented by the Village People to accompany their 1978 hit, it is probably trying to scare off predators.'[4]

Harmless stuff, surely, the kind of thing a production team comes up with all the time. Page 31 is not a place for the most serious news and in any case newspapers are as concerned to entertain their readers as they are to inform them. The picture stands as a great image in its own right and the caption might add a smile to the experience of reading the paper. The production team, obviously in a jokey mood and with music on their minds, probably didn't exactly hide behind the anonymity of the role but they almost certainly didn't expect what happened next.

On page 50 of the following Monday's edition, under the heading *Was it a pun too far* and illustrated by a smaller version of the photograph was this letter:

'Regarding the picture of the praying mantis (Metro, Thur), was it necessary to include such an inane caption on what was an otherwise fantastic piece of photography?

It is ridiculous in the extreme to suggest the insect was dancing to a Bee Gees song and to start the caption off with some of the Stayin' Alive lyrics. It was a joke, perhaps, that might have even been funny with the disastrous sentence at the end, stupidly adding or suggesting "it appears to be dancing". I have, regrettably, forgotten the exact words of the sentence but your silly titles and attempts at witty captions may on this occasion have gone too far.'
W. Hardcastle, via email

Either W. Hardcastle really did feel the words spoiled the image, or had a catastrophic sense of humour failure, or the letter is tongue in cheek, or – and this is unlikely but far from impossible – the letter was made up by a mischievous person on the *Metro* team and smuggled onto the letters page. Whichever is the case, and whatever the intention, the production team was taken to task in a manner that was both very public and quite unusual.

Production is a job that has traditionally been undertaken by journalists who did not expect to be picked out by the spotlight of fame and yet it is the work of these skilled people that brings the finished product, the newspaper or magazine, into the hands of the readers. Changes in the political economy of print publications have meant that the production role is now more widespread and less specialised than before – in short, as dedicated production teams dwindle, so more non-specialists are expected to get involved.

The episode of the facetious praying mantis caption contains several useful lessons for production journalists that will be covered more fully in this chapter: lessons about reader expectations, about working with images, about not trying to push a pun too far and about not being able to predict reactions or use the anonymity of the production desk to hide from their consequences.

INTRODUCTION

Talk to any newspaper journalist of a certain age about their favourite memories and one is almost guaranteed to feature in every top 10. It will include variations on the words 'rumble', 'shake' and 'printing press' and recalls the moment when the printing press, usually installed in the basement, started up. Presses are large pieces of machinery, with components sufficiently weighty for their operation to cause a discernible tremor through the fabric of a building. It was a routine that encapsulated – and symbolised – an important point in the journalistic process: a forewarning that the reporting, telephoning, researching and writing was about to become public; the sweat and tears that underpinned the stories were about to undergo transubstantiation into paper and ink.

Nowadays presses have become so large and so expensive that they are housed in their own mega-sheds, usually on an outlying industrial park that allows easy access for the lorries that bring in reels of paper and take out pallets of newspapers and magazines. But in the alphabet of print journalism, A represents the first sniff of a story, Z represents the printed product and B to Y are all the things that lie in between – including the complete production process.

'Production' is one of those words that covers a huge territory. At one time – and well within the memory of working journalists – it would have involved a typewriter, a sheet of paper, a photo-composing machine, a scalpel, a steel ruler, a pot of Cow Gum, a large static camera, red, blue and possibly black pens, several pairs of hands and a couple of trade union-authorised rubber stamps.

All of these things, in various permutations, were needed to prepare a publication for print long before the presses were brought into action. The journalist would feed a sheet of paper into the typewriter (probably two sheets, with a sheet of carbon paper as the filling in a sandwich), bash out a story, remove the paper and hand it on to the next person in the chain. That person would decide whether, when, where and how to use the story and pass it on to the next pair of hands, or use their own, to make a series of squiggles on the paper that would indicate to the next person in the chain (the typesetter) how to set the piece up in type.

Once this had been done, a proof on photosensitive paper would be printed out and returned to the editorial department for checking. There a sub-editor would check and correct the words (sometimes using a system of red, blue or black pens to indicate who the mistake could be charged to, editorial or production).

In the meantime, a layout sub-editor or designer would take a photocopy of the proof and and the prints or transparencies of the photographs that had been selected to accompany the piece and by clever manipulation of scalpel, steel rule, Cow Gum and tracing paper (to size and shape the photographs) would create a page layout on a specially printed cardboard grid that showed the columns and margins of the final page.

This would be sent to the compositors, who were in charge of sticking the copy in the right place, making the halftone images that would reproduce the monochromatic photos (colour was another thing altogether, and usually had to be sent out to a special repro house) and final placing of the page components, before photographing it all on the static camera to turn it into a large piece of film that could be sent to the print works to be converted into a printing plate.

Remembering all this, it sounds ridiculously complicated – without going back further to the even more mechanical age of hot metal typesetting – but because of the historical and commercial imperatives that shaped the printing and publishing industries, it was what happened. The trade unions that were originally formed out of necessity, to protect the interests of employees against employers, seemed after the Second World War to become drunk on the power to hold proprietors to ransom. At certain points in history, they were prone to take strike action that could be financially ruinous, particularly to those who owned newspapers. Compositors and printers belonged to separate trade unions and work had to be rubber stamped at various stages to prove that it had passed through the hands of those authorised to undertake that aspect of the process.

It not only *sounds* ridiculously complicated, it *was* ridiculously complicated – and now it is history. Everyone is authorised to do everything and the person doing most of it is a journalist. To an extent that would have been unimaginable 50 years ago – even 25 years ago – it is now the journalist who is responsible for most of the pre-print production processes.

An important factor in this change can be attributed to shifts in social and political trends (the Thatcher government's desire to tame the unions, increasing numbers of 'ordinary' people who owned their own houses) but these would be nothing without the technological advances that have put the power to publish into the hands of literally anyone with access to a computer. Journalism has never been a closed shop in the way that printing and graphic art once were; it has always been open to anyone with a news for nose and a 'little literary ability' (to use Nicholas Tomalin's famous dictum) but there are still significant differences between an amateurish job and a professional job, and this distinction can be learned – as the rest of this chapter will show.

WHY SPELLING MATTERS

There is a single word that sums up the changes in print production outlined above: Wapping. It was Wapping that ensured most journalists – and certainly all entry-level journalists – are now expected to have the skills that enable them to contribute to the production process. It is not an opt-out any more, not that it it ever was in truth, and Wapping also provides a classic example of that.

Wapping was the dockland district in east London, well supplied with former warehouses and other large adaptable spaces, where Rupert Murdoch, head of News International, set up a fully equipped newspaper plant under the guise of launching a new evening paper (the *London Post*) and then moved his daily and Sunday newspapers literally overnight. One day the *Times* and the *Sun* were put together in Fleet Street (or rather New Printing House Square in Gray's Inn Road and Bouverie Street respectively), the next they were produced in Wapping. The revolution was not only televised (with pictures of picketing strikers), it can also be dated exactly to Friday 24 January 1986.

Put simply, it was a revolution over keystrokes – literally, the act of typing. Before Wapping journalists were not allowed to use computers to create finished copy; they could bash it out on a typewriter, or even key it in on a computer but then had to print it out and hand it over to a member of the National Graphical Association (NGA) to be re-keyed. It is hard to imagine a less efficient system, and it typified much of the print production process: lots of at best duplicated and at worst wasted effort. The buildings at Wapping had been equipped with the latest computerised production systems and the journalists who moved there (not all of them chose to do so) immediately began to input their own copy, with no more re-keying.

Even so, many of the old mechanical processes still needed to be done because neither computer hardware nor software was then capable of doing it. Without the print craftsmen (and some craftswomen) to complete these tasks the journalists and their bosses (almost all newspaper people) had to do them. Roy Greenslade, now a professor of journalism at City University but then assistant editor of the *Sun*, has more than once recounted a tale from the very early days of Wapping, when he bawled out someone he thought was working too slowly only to discover it was actually Rupert Murdoch bent over the composing table. On Wapping's 20th anniversary the *Independent* ran a piece asking participants for their memories. Ivan Fallon, who was deputy editor of the *Sunday Times*, recalled:

'I woke on a camp bed in the old rum store that had become our new HQ – one of half a dozen executives charged with producing a paper on which normally several hundred journalists laboured. The recumbent figure beside me was Rupert himself, grabbing a few minutes' sleep. He was everywhere that weekend – cutting copy and bellowing instructions.'[5]

So it is possible to see that production skills were not only already well engrained in many newspaper journalists, from then on they became essential. The same is true for journalists working on magazines – indeed, it is possible to make a good argument that magazine journalists have *always* been closer to the production process than newspaper journalists simply because of the more highly designed nature of the product and the fact that magazines have much smaller staff numbers; if you're working across from designers, you are much more likely to take an interest in what they do to make your words look so great.

One media academic has gone as far as to say that newspapers have learned many of the skills that allow them to appeal to particular readerships from magazines:

> 'The main source of the innovations in the publishing industry that created the modern popular press was magazine and periodical publishing . . . in fact, a key and continuing aspect of the history of twentieth century newspaper in Britain and the United States is a process of magazinization of the press in which publishers increasingly cater to a range of different audiences and different interests.' (Tulloch, 2000: 139)

It is also possible to observe how newspapers have learned from magazines in matters of presentation and use of photographs and illustrations. Sometimes this is direct imitation, as with the pioneering *Sunday Times Magazine* (launched on 4 February 1962 as the *Colour Section*) but it can be seen more generally in the way that photographs and graphics are used on the page, and with the adoption of breakout boxes and sidebars to liven up the copy.

As for print on screen, it is impossible not to be involved with the production process. You cannot put copy or pictures into a web page, blog or content management system without becoming an integrally involved part of the procedure. Many journalists, and not always just the younger ones, now have the skills to shape the look and design of their digital output.

ACCURACY ABOVE ALL

Whatever Wapping did to change the skill set required of print journalists, there are other, more basic, factors that persist throughout technological turmoil. If journalism is to be trusted, never mind believed, it must be accurate; journalists rank low enough in public surveys of trustworthiness for every aspect of what constitutes accuracy to be vitally important and the very basis of accuracy, the foundations on which everything else must be built, is accuracy in the use of language.

If you haven't worked it out already, this is our old friends – spelling and grammar. Language can be used for many purposes – to move people to tears or to action, to teach new skills, to entertain – and if it is to achieve maximum effectiveness, it must communicate with the widest possible number of people. The rules (or conventions) of spelling and grammar have developed to enable a widespread commonality of understanding: when good journalists use a particular word and place it in a particular place within a sentence, they do so because they want, and expect, it to be interpreted and understood in a particular way. Getting these things right is not a moral issue, although sometimes it seems to be taken that way, nor should it be an excuse to beat young people – those who have not benefited from a complete education, or those who have a persistent or specific difficulty – around the ears.

In fact if there is one thing that has been consistent down the years it is criticism of current standards of spelling and grammar, usually by an older generation of a younger generation. When I first started working in journalism education (1995) one of the documents left in my office was a report by an examiner making just such a criticism. According to him these young students could neither spell nor construct a good news story – I forget the exact date it was written but it was not recent even then. In the research for this chapter I also came across a paper delivered to the Canadian branch of the Association for Education in Journalism, entitled *Spelling and Grammar – Their Importance to Journalism: What Journalism Schools Are Doing*, dated August 1975. The author, Thomas A. Bowers, began:

> 'Fifteen years ago parents and elementary school teachers worried because Little Johnny and Little Jane couldn't read well. Now Little Johnny and Little Jane have gone off to college, and something akin to full-scale alarm is developing over their deficiency in using the English language.'[6]

Fifteen years before 1975 takes us to 1960 – and that's my generation of Little Johnny and Little Jane. I would be willing to bet that in 1960 an equivalent of Thomas A. Bowers was writing something very similar and I know for a fact that 15 years after (1990) other people, and possibly even myself, were voicing similar concerns. It is no different now (2011 at time of writing), and it seems that no matter when we actually live, we are always in decline from a golden age of better standards.

There is always something happening in popular culture that will make matters worse:

- Elvis Presley's rock'n'roll,
- the Beatles,
- television,
- computer games,
- rap music,
- text-speak,
- Twitter.

All have been blamed in their time for a perceived decline in standards. Some future-gazing moaners, perhaps modelling themselves on the Red Queen in *Alice in Wonderland*, have even blamed them in advance of any evidence. Like any persistent noise, it risks becoming part of a general racket in the background, unlistened to and almost unnoticed.

But there are two very important things to note despite this constant level of criticism: first, correct spelling and grammar *are* important and, secondly, it seems that people spell better as they get older and it is definitely possible to take steps to improve your work in this respect.

The importance of clear communication

On the first point, if there are no widely recognised standard ways of spelling and putting words together to form sentences and paragraphs, eventually all writing will consist of 'mutually unintelligible idiolects' (a phrase coined by Tina Blue of grammartips.homestead.com, who explains that an idiolect is 'a "dialect" spoken or written by only one person'.[7] This is the exact opposite of what journalism should aim to do. Daniel Defoe (1660–1731), the author of *Robinson Crusoe* and *Moll Flanders*, is widely recognised as one of the first journalists in Britain (Harold Herd called him 'the first professional journalist of major standing . . .' (1952: 46)). When asked about the best way to communicate, Defoe answered:

> 'If any man was to ask me what I would suppose to be a perfect style or language,
> I would answer, that in which a man speaking to five hundred people, of all common and various capacities, idiots or lunatics excepted, should be understood by them all.'
> (Herd 1952: 51)

That should be the aim of all journalists, whether reporting the news, writing a feature or sub-editing other people's work – and it starts with spelling and grammar. Not only is it important to be able to communicate clearly with as many people as possible, it is perhaps even more important to ensure the basic facts are correct: basic facts such as spelling a person's name correctly, using the correct words to describe an action or situation, and putting those words into the correct order for maximum effectiveness. Without that basis, the rest of the production process becomes irrelevant.

Why is this so important?

- Poor spelling creates a bad impression.
- It's the first thing a reader notices.
- It's the first thing an editor notices.
- Readers and prospective employers place greater importance on spelling than many teachers or lecturers.
- Anxiety about spelling can inhibit your writing, especially your choice of words.
- Incorrect spelling of common words, names, places, etc. raises doubts about factual accuracy.

The Wapping revolution broke the power of the print unions, removed several layers of craft work from the production process and put power *and* responsibility in the hands of journalists. It harnessed social change to technological advances and provided the grounds for those advances to speed up. It also started a chain of consequences that are now beginning to erode the demarcation between journalism jobs; in the not very distant future there may be no 'reporter' and 'sub-editor', no distinction between providing words and crafting them into a readable state in print or digitally. At one end of the scale this means all journalists will need advanced computer skills and at the other it means all journalists will need to be able to spell better than anyone else.

PUTTING IT INTO PRACTICE

Spelling and grammar are important to all journalists, especially now everyone is expected to contribute to the production process. What can you do to get up to speed with them?

The first and most obvious thing to do is to use the spellcheck on your computer. This will clean up simple mistakes but beware – **all spellcheckers are essentially stupid**. If you have used the wrong word but spelled it correctly, your spellcheck will not pick it up. It cannot tell the difference between 'hare' when you meant 'hair', or 'there' when you meant 'their'.

There are a number of methods to improve your spelling that have been tried and tested over the years by teachers, tutors and autodidacts.

Read as much as possible

Books, newspapers, magazines, comics – anything as long as you pay attention to the words you are reading and how they are arranged in sentences. If something is difficult to read, work out why. If it is easy, or pleasing, work out why.

Write as much as possible

Golf champion Gary Player is credited with saying, 'The more I practise, the luckier I get' and the same applies to writing. If you read something you like (see above) try to copy the style. But it is important that you check your written work and ideally get someone whose judgement you trust to check it too.

> ▶ PUTTING IT INTO PRACTICE
>
> **If you are not sure how to spell a word, look it up**
>
> Use a good dictionary; I recommend any of the Oxford dictionaries although Chambers is my favourite. If you are checking in an online dictionary make sure it uses UK English spelling not US English.
>
> **Good ways to improve your spelling**
>
> - Learn commonly mis-spelled words.
> - Learn the common rules of spelling.
> - Learn good spelling strategies.
> - Identify mis-spelt words in your own writing – keep a list or spelling log and learn those words.
> - Draw pictures to imprint a spelling on your mind.
> - Use mnemonics (a rhyme or a pun) to remind you of difficult spellings.
> - Use a blank card as a bookmark and write the words you have problems spelling on it.
> - Buy an indexed notebook and use it to write words you want to remember.
> - Try using a spelling workbook or spelling dictionary.
>
> **Play word-based games**
>
> Such as:
>
> - anagrams and word searches,
> - crosswords,
> - Scrabble.
>
> **Test yourself**
>
> Create your own spelling and grammar tests and do them against the clock. Score yourself and keep a record of your scores.

remember

- Accurate spelling and grammar are basic skills that every journalist must have.
- A feel for the use of words is especially important to production journalists.
- There are ways to improve improve spelling and grammar.

LIVING IN COMPUTER-LAND

If you need an outstanding example of the all-round, multi-skilled journalist there's no need to search; just look back to the good-old, bad-old days of Fleet Street, when print publishing was dominated by restrictive union practices. The person you seek is Harold Evans, who started his career at 16 years old on a local weekly, went on to edit the *Northern Echo*, achieved his greatest glory as editor of the *Sunday Times* from 1967 to 1981 and was knighted for services to journalism in 2004. He was noted for his energy and meticulousness; Maurice Wiggin, who worked with Evans, recalls him:

'whizzing through the office like a flame; literally at the double, in his shirt sleeves . . . He is the complete working newspaperman, and when I see him bringing his galvanic perfectionism to bear on every detail of the paper, I am irresistibly reminded of those far-off days when I, too, really loved the craft of newspaper production . . . it does me good to see the old enthusiasm permeating every cranny of the paper, the restless perfectionism, the personal touch, the insatiable inquisitiveness and above all the zest and the contagion of his zeal.' (Wiggin, 1968: 203)

That passage is a great guide to how to succeed in almost any career, but especially print journalism. For most people, overseeing every detail of one of the world's great newspapers – which at that time was turning out some life-changing investigative journalism – would be enough. But Evans was made of different stuff; he wanted to pass on the lessons he had learned and the techniques he had developed and between 1973 and 1978 he wrote *Editing and Design: A Five Volume Manual of English, Typography and Layout* comprising:

- Book One: *Newsman's English* (revised and republished in 2000 as *Essential English for Journalists and Writers*);
- Book Two: *Handling Newspaper Text*;
- Book Three: *News Headlines: An Illustrated Guide*;
- Book Four: *Picture Editing* (republished in 1997 as *Pictures on a Page: Photojournalism, Graphics and Picture Editing*);
- Book Five: *Newspaper Design.*

These five books are a perfect summary of the state of print newspaper production. They are by no means a bible for modern methods but a testament to the power and importance of attention to detail; with a little tweaking their topics can be used as a guide to what all journalists need to know now.

There is, however, a significant omission from the content of Sir Harold's great manual. Although small personal computers, the mouse, the internet and email had all been developed by 1971 (and the first Apple was made in 1976) most people's idea of a computer was still a massive machine that used software stamped into big reels of punched tape, had to be housed in special rooms and took all night to process information. They were the province of nerds, geeks, boffins or hobbyists, certainly not common in offices and if the *Sunday Times* had any they were probably in the accounting department.

This situation, of course, was to change with astonishing rapidity. In 1983 *Time* magazine gave its Person of the Year nomination to the personal computer as the 'machine of the year'. There are Fleet Street tales of journalists who could not even use a typewriter and phoned all their stories through to a copytaker but a journalist unable to use a computer would not even get a job today. The personal computer, in either Microsoft or Apple flavour, dominates the desktop and is capable, within its small footprint, of replicating most if not all of the many tasks previously undertaken by the army of craft workers.

What this means for anyone aiming to be a contemporary Harold Evans is that they will need complete mastery not only of the traditional basic skills but also of ever-changing computer hardware and software. To some it will seem a natural progression, others may feel sad that a measure of technical ability must now be added to the 'little literary ability' but to a third group it will be positively frightening. To understand why, we can usefully introduce the concept of the 'digital native'.

It's actually very simple. In 2001 Mark Prensky published an article in *On The Horizon* suggesting that people who have grown up with digital technology interact with the world, including processes of learning, in a significantly different way from pre-digital generations: 'today's students think and process information fundamentally differently from their predecessors'. Using the metaphor of nationality, he called these people 'digital natives' ('all "native speakers" of the digital language of computers, video games and the Internet') and those who had come before 'digital immigrants' ('Those of us who were not born into the digital world but have, at some later point in our lives, become fascinated by and adopted many or most aspects of the new technology').

Prensky elaborates this theme into a proposal for changing pedagogic techniques to suit the new generation (he even goes as far as to suggest that digital technology actually has the power to change the way the brain functions) but there are a number of points that relate directly to journalism's new requirements. First, the concept of legacy skills and future skills:

> '"Legacy" content includes reading, writing, arithmetic, logical thinking, understanding the writings and ideas of the past, etc. – all of our "traditional" curriculum. It is of course still important, but it is from a different era. Some of it (such as logical thinking) will continue to be important, but some (perhaps like Euclidean geometry) will become less so, as did Latin and Greek.
>
> "Future" content is to a large extent, not surprisingly, digital and technological. But while it includes software, hardware, robotics, nanotechnology, genomics, etc. *it also includes the ethics, politics, sociology, languages and other things that go with them*'. (Prensky, 2001: 4; italics in original)

However, it is important to realise that not all digital natives speak the language with the same facility; some will be more gifted than others, some will be more interested than others. If we extend the metaphor of nationality, there are different accents, different occupations, different attitudes. Harold Evans's skills fall firmly into the legacy category and it is likely that those attracted to 'writing' – which is one of the most common reasons given for wanting to go into journalism – will probably be more inclined to value legacy skills over future skills. It is not universally true that all members of the digital native generation are comfortable around computers and every journalism educator can tell you about students who describe themselves as 'technophobes', who don't see the point of computer games or social media and who put up either a spirited or a morbid resistance to the very idea of engaging with this stuff.

But, at the risk of repeating myself, if you want to get a job as a journalist, you have to. Fortunately, as with spelling, there are ways to change attitudes and improve abilities. Prensky's idea has been taken up by a number of researchers, including Ofer and Azzia Zur of the Zur Institute, who came up with three category distinctions:

> 'It is important to realize that not all digital immigrants and not all digital natives are created equal. While most digital natives are tech savvy by default of their being born around technology, others do not have a knack for technology and computers, nor an inclination. Similarly, Digital Immigrants fall into three major groups: Avoiders, Reluctant Adopters and Enthusiastic Adopters . . .'. (http://bit.ly/internet_addiction)

Thus just as not all digital immigrants are technologically inept, so not all digital natives are comfortable with technology, and the categories can be applied to both natives and immigrants. The important thing is to recognise and acknowledge which category you fit into:

- *Avoiders* tend to have the bare minimum of technology in their lives (the standard example is only landline phone and a television).
- *Reluctant adopters* understand technology is needed in their lives and work but avoid it as much as possible (mobile phone, word processing, email).
- *Eager adopters* have enthusiasm or a talent for technology that sees them experimenting with devices and software (digital video, smartphone, tablet computer, blogging, Twitter, Foursquare, Gowalla, etc.).

The examples attached to each category are only suggestions and can be tweaked endlessly to keep pace with technological change. They can also be adapted to journalism jobs: an avoider might have to use word processing and a content management system; a reluctant adopter might get into taking and processing digital photographs and using desktop publishing software; an eager adopter would probably be shooting and editing video and audio, as well as running the blog/website/social media community.

And the thing is, you can change category. Just as every journalism educator can tell you about the technophobes, they can also tell you that those same people began to adopt and adapt, started using and experimenting with new kit and suddenly found they were not technophobes after all. It might be a struggle, it might take some time, but it can be done. As the German philosopher Friedrich Nietzsche noted, 'What does not destroy me, makes me stronger' (1895: 8) and finding out how digital technology can help you communicate certainly won't destroy you even though it might change your opinion of yourself.

If the component parts of *Editing and Design* were brought up to date, what might they look like? A comprehensive manual would still have to include information and advice about using words, using pictures, combining the two on a page and adding attractor elements (such as headlines and box outs). An index might look something like:

ESSENTIAL LEGACY SKILLS

- Using words
- Using pictures
- Creating shapes on a page

CURRENT SOFTWARE SKILLS

- Word processing
- Desktop publishing
- Photo editing
- Content management system
- Basic HTML

VALUABLE FUTURE SKILLS

- Video shooting and editing
- Audio recording and editing
- Scripting and narration

Of these elements, probably only the basic legacy skills will remain unchanged. The ability to manipulate words and pictures and combine them into packages that will please readers is fundamental to all journalism and has particular application to production.

Software skills will be constantly evolving and as a result the valuable future skills will also always be changing, usually because, as the future becomes today, the skills become current or even essential. That's the thing about new media – it's *always* new and as journalists we are *always* having to keep up with it.

A CLOSER LOOK

DIGITAL IMMIGRATION

My own experience as a digital immigrant has been of having to learn – and abandon – numerous bits of software: Amstrad's *PCW* word-processing system, *Ventura Publisher* dtp and *QuarkXPress* all sit somewhere in my subconscious. *Photoshop* has been a constant (although its iterations have been many), *InDesign* tops the dtp pile for the moment and a smattering of *HTML* allows me to perform basic tweaks to web-bound material. I can cut and shape video with *iMovie*, although I have played

▶ A CLOSER LOOK

with *Premiere* sufficiently to see it offers a richer experience, and tinkered with *Audacity*, the free audio editing software. I can use a couple of different content management systems, as well as setting up and customising a *Wordpress* or *Blogger* blog. I know how to use my phone to take pictures, movies and audio and how to transfer them to a computer for further work.

But all equipment becomes old and inadequate even though it may still be working perfectly; all software dates and is updated regularly. There are many proprietary production systems available and publishing companies may decide to switch from one to another. Although it is good to become as expert as possible in whatever you are using, it is also good not to make a massive personal investment in any given system. Regard all such knowledge as a transferable skill.

Like all digital immigrant journalists, I had no idea that all this unknown territory lay over the horizon and, frankly, it's not a big deal. Everything listed is a tool and while great craftspeople undoubtedly love and cherish their tools, it's only really necessary to know how to use them and to realise that next year, next week or tomorrow, it may be necessary to learn how to use a different tool. You don't have to commit to them for life and you can't break them in the same way you can break a physical tool. They may stop working for mysterious reasons, or do something unexpected, but that's a different matter. Learning how to do basic reboots and fixes is another valuable tool – but the most basic lesson of all is still remembering to save your work regularly.

PUTTING IT INTO PRACTICE

When it comes to learning how to use equipment and software there's a useful legacy saying to remember: practice makes perfect – or at least competent. At the top end of the scale of practice would be taking a general course, such as one that leads to the European Computer Driving Licence (ECDL), the Europe-wide qualification demonstrating competence in computer skills, and at the other would be taking a course that trains you in a specific piece of software.

However, there are many other things you can do to make yourself more comfortable and more skilful. Here are six suggestions.

1 Play

Or, to put it another way, familiarise yourself with hardware and software by engaging with it. The more you use it, the less frightening it will seem.

2 Don't forget the Help menu

Most software now has a mass of useful how-to information, either within the program itself or via links to a website.

3 Look online

Not only do many software providers have dedicated websites to help users (often with forums where one can ask specific questions or browse for relevant answers), there are guaranteed to be independent sites and forums for any widely used program. ▶

▶ PUTTING IT INTO PRACTICE

4 Ask somebody who knows more than you

If you are sitting near someone who clearly knows how to do something you're stuck on, ask. Most people love to show off their ability – but don't overdo it. You could also consider paying the person to give you some tuition.

5 Set yourself a series of challenges

Start by trying to do something simple (say, just make a page with a headline and picture in a dtp package) and continue by adding to the complexity (resize the picture; make box outs; automate the page numbering; take one story and adapt it for print, web and mobile platforms). You don't have to go crazy; set your own pace.

6 Read

Teach Yourself . . . , . . . For Dummies, the entire output of Peachpit Press – there are hundreds of books dedicated to teaching people how to do things (just typing 'Adobe Photoshop' into Amazon brings thousands of hits – use crowdsourcing to filter down to the best titles). One of the most useful traits for any journalist to have is autodidactism. This is what old-fashioned libraries are for; use them.

remember

- Production journalists need a mixture of legacy, current and future skills.
- You have to be computer literate, that's just the way it is.
- You don't have to *love* computers, but you do have to be willing and able to use the software they run.
- Being able to use them does not make you a geek, nerd or boffin.
- The best way to get better is to practise.

WORDS, IMAGES AND MORE

Maurice Wiggin, whose description of Harold Evans in full editor flow was cited earlier, really got into the swing of being a journalist when he was appointed features editor of the Birmingham *Evening Despatch*. It was a small paper with a small staff, so he had to be 'copy-taster, ideas man, sub-editor, rewrite man, headline writer, caption writer, typographer, layout man, picture editor, and often writer as well' (1968: 147). This is an interesting list for two reasons – first it comprises all the jobs that had to be done then and have to be done now (which we can categorise as legacy skills) and, secondly, it describes the state to which newspapers (and magazines to some extent) are returning as the number of journalists they employ shrinks. What it misses out are the extras, the future skills, that lay some 50 years on from when Wiggin was writing.

The legacy skills of production still involve working with copy, creating headlines and other page furniture, visualising and often executing layout and checking at every stage that all is as it should be. Perhaps the only unfamiliar job description from that list is 'copy-taster', but it is actually quite descriptive – someone whose job it is to select or approve copy suitable for publication; many people would think of this as a section editor's job.

There is one other major difference between the way Wiggin did his job and the way a current production journalist would do it. Current journalists would do it all on computers at their desks and not have to work in a 'composing room . . . the nearest thing in journalism to a factory' (1968: 148). The composing room was where the craft workers did their stuff – typography, paste-up, camera work – and while it may seem an advantage to have got rid of the duplicated key strokes and labour intensive production processes, there was something of great value to be found in the composing room: the education of experience. As Wiggin acknowledges, the printers 'taught me first the basic grammar of print, the rudiments, and thereafter quietly egged me on to ever more reckless ventures . . . our pages took on character, vitality and energy, and ultimately a quite high gloss finish . . .' (1968: 148–9).

It is still possible to benefit from the education of experience but not in the same way. The newspaper industry has cut right back on training schemes and the magazine industry's record of provision is patchy (although the Professional Publishers Association and its training arm the Periodicals Training Council have established a variety of successful paid-for courses); the composing room has been absorbed into a desktop computer, the printworks is likely to be far distant from the editorial office and the days of journalists having the time or opportunity to hobnob with print workers are long gone.

What has happened is that instead of the employer paying for, or providing the means of, the enhancement of skills, the burden of cost has been transferred to the employee or would-be employee. In their survey of journalism training provision, Simon Frith and Peter Meech found that 'few editors now have the resources to provide any sort of on-the-job instruction themselves' (2007: 141) and as a result (or possibly as a cause) 'the costs of access to journalism careers in both the press and broadcasting are now borne, almost entirely, by the trainees themselves' (2007: 157). Hence an explosion in the numbers of courses claiming to offer journalism training – education of experience at your own expense.

What the employers are seeking, of course, is someone who knows what the business involves, who can be trusted to get on with the job without causing any great ructions or disturbance and, preferably, someone who can, and is willing to, learn on their own.

If we use Wiggin's list as a starting point, the production journalism skills you need to know about and then put into practice fall into two main categories – working with words and working with visuals. On top of that, and outside Wiggin's ken, is another layer of future skills.

Working with words

The absolute bedrock of this has already been discussed above – rock solid spelling and grammar, along with the means to improve if necessary – but there is plenty of superstructure to be raised on those foundations. The production journalist has many important duties but they start with the ability to take a piece of writing and make it better. Now 'better' is a value-laden word and it needs to be interpreted carefully and within a specific context; the wide reading recommended above will enhance critical faculties and widen appreciation of different writing styles but in this case the context must always be 'better for the readers of this particular publication' and will include:

- an appropriate vocabulary;
- an appropriate writing style;
- an appropriate level of information;
- an appropriate format.

Many of these factors should have been agreed when the piece was commissioned by the editor or section editor (see Chapter 4) and the production journalist should check that the brief has been met. Some work will need very little revision but in other cases production journalists will have their work cut out to bring it up to scratch. (See Chapter 6 on sub-editing for more on putting this into practice and Chapter 4 on feature writing for more about writing, commissioning and formatting.)

The next stage involves thinking about the way the piece will look on the page, how best to attract a reader's attention, and providing multiple points of entry into the story. The major elements to consider are:

- taking information out of the main body to provide box outs or sidebars (if necessary);
- creating a headline that sells the story;
- creating a standfirst (also known as a sell) that adds to the headline and draws the reader into the story;
- finding strong phrases or sentences to use as pull quotes (also known as blown quotes or out-takes) that will give readers another point of entry into the story;
- writing captions for the photographs or illustrations that are informative and in an appropriate style (serious, flippant, descriptive – there should be a definite and distinct house style for captions);
- there will also be some elements of page livery – regular logos or flashes, page head or tail, page numbers.

Once we reach this stage, the page elements are beginning to overlap with visuals.

Working with visuals

The specific skills and abilities required of a production journalist in this field (covering type, layout and visuals) will vary considerably from one publication to another. A small magazine or newspaper may expect the production journalist to undertake every single stage of the process whereas larger organisations may have dedicated designers who take on the more complex technical or artistic functions. Even in this case, the production journalist may have to complete routine tasks such as fitting content into a pre-determined page layout grid.

In practice it is important for every journalist to be able to visualise how their story will look on the page, especially on magazines. Matt Swaine, the ex-editor of *Trail* magazine, was in charge of editorial training at Bauer Consumer Media in Peterborough and at the PTC's 2010 Academics & Industry Forum he gave a presentation on the skills that magazine employers look for in young journalists. At the top of his list came 'great understanding of design' because:

> 'Good writers need to be able to visualise exactly what a feature is going to look like at the feature meeting phase. They need to be able to brief photographers when out on a job. They need to get their ideas across to designers. They need to write with a clear visual end result that they are working to . . . as an editor, I want writers who understand print media and its full potential. I want people who instinctively reach for a pencil and pad at the commissioning or feature idea stage and sketch out exactly what they want their feature to look like. The ability to visualise features generates stronger features, that have visual impact and it seriously speeds up the creative process. It communicates things quickly to those around them and that means other writers can start enhancing and improving features immediately rather than waiting for a final on the page proof to be presented . . . The person who pulls out a pencil and paper and starts sketching a feature idea in a job interview is definitely going to pique my interest as a potential employer.'[8]

Since this book is about print journalism, and since *everything* that we read, whether it is on paper or on screen, has to be presented in text, an obvious place to start with visual skills is type and typography. Most people who have used word-processing software will be aware that they can change the shape and size of the letters on the screen by changing the font, and the selection of fonts available on even a basic program gives a hint of the extent of this subject. In fact, typography is a field of study in its own right that could easily occupy a person's whole life but even without going to those lengths it is axiomatic that all journalists should be interested in the way their words will be presented, and production journalists should take that interest to a deeper level. There are excellent, easy-to-read, books that cover the history and will impart a fundamental appreciation of type.

Turning more specifically to Matt Swaine's advice, an appreciation of type should be allied to an appreciation of how it is used on the page, along with all the other elements included in that page. There are a couple of very useful exercises to help develop this appreciation.

PUTTING IT INTO PRACTICE   TWO USEFUL EXERCISES

1 Deconstruct a published layout by identifying and listing all of the different things present, even if you do not know their technical names, and observing where they are placed on the page and how they fit together (their spatial relationship).
2 Collect layouts that appeal to you, not just from the magazines or newspapers you normally read but from others that you might buy as a sampling exercise. When Matt Swaine was teaching journalism at Cardiff University his name for this kind of collection was 'Project Magpie' and he incorporated it into the formal curriculum.

Given the number of page layout systems in use, it is difficult to cite specific skills with any accuracy. It is safe to say that Adobe InDesign and QuarkXPress are the two most commonly used desktop publishing systems, and that one or the other is often (but not always) the layout engine incorporated into more complex systems like Tera, Atex and GoPublish. However, the basic functionality is the same whatever the system: you set up a page and within that page you manipulate boxes that hold either text or pictures. The basic skills that you learn on one system will be transferable to another, even if the actual software menus and key combinations are different – and the Help menu is there to, well, help.

Matt Swaine summed up thus:

> 'Make it a requirement of all early drafts of features to come with a suggested opening spread. Headlines shouldn't work in isolation but should be written to link the opening picture, the angle of the feature, the intro. In conjunction with the opening picture the headline needs to be strong enough to make people stop and read.'[9]

One very important page element that we have not yet considered is the actual visual element – photographs, illustrations and other graphics. Normally the production journalist will be working with given material, but bear in mind the advice above that all journalists must be able to communicate with photographers and graphic artists. It is relatively common for journalists working on specialist magazines to take their own photographs, especially for something like a travel or adventure feature, so this is another area of knowledge and skill that can usefully, and even profitably, be expanded.

At the very least, a production journalist must know how to use photo editing software (such as Adobe Photoshop) to resize, crop and perhaps boost the colour or contrast of an image, as well as knowing how to save an image in the appropriate file format for its publication platform.

The skills discussed above would be familiar to Maurice Wiggin, even if the means of executing them is different, which leaves us with the future skills.

FUTURE SKILLS FOR PRODUCTION

In truth, it is impossible to predict what future skills will be necessary but what we can do is look at some skills that have become established and others that are becoming mainstream.

- Website management – there are very few print publications without some kind of online presence. Generally the skill will be knowing how to keep a predetermined content management system-based site updated and how to upload text, graphics and movies, but at the outer edges it could involve building or tweaking a site.
- Video skills – knowing how to operate a camera, the basic repertoire of shots with which to construct a narrative, and the ability to use editing software.
- Audio skills – ability to use recorders, basic script-shaping for podcasts, knowing how to edit sound files using common software.
- Social media skills – how to use Twitter, Facebook and whatever may be around the corner to communicate with existing readers, build communities with readers, reach out to new readers, allow readers to communicate among themselves and so on. As with everything else, this must be appropriate for the specific readership and take into account their preferences. For example, at present it seems that older audiences prefer to get involved in conversations using forums, rather than sending 140-character messages via Twitter but this is another thing that will be constantly evolving.

Future skills are where being a digital native can really pay off. There is no established tradition within digital media, no single way of doing things for a newspaper or a magazine, and the way is open to try new things. Matt Swaine foresees a future of opportunities for digital natives ('they') making their way into print media currently dominated by digital immigrants ('we'):

> 'Web does things differently to print and students should be encouraged to think about the potential of the web and they need to allow print to play to its strengths and make sure that digital is being used to fulfil clear reader needs.
>
> What can different platforms do for readers? How different platforms can best meet my readers' needs has been a pressing question for me over the last three years as editor of *Trail*. In professional terms this is a vital question and one that needs some serious thinking time. Students should be made to think about this and should be really challenged on it.
>
> Encourage experimentation. We are NOT the experts here anymore. They understand the technology and we should be the ones who get them to think about how it can best be used. They may be able to see the potential in new platforms. How do you do this? By being asked to be creative and not taking a prescriptive approach.'[10]

PUTTING IT INTO PRACTICE

There are three categories of skill to practise in connection with this section: words, visuals, future. All will benefit from a strong professional interest in print publication – you should consume different publications voraciously looking for ideas to copy and adapt.

Words

1 Read as widely as possible but read everything – body copy, headlines, captions – with a critical eye. If you think something works, analyse why; likewise if it

> ▶ PUTTING IT INTO PRACTICE

doesn't work. A very useful exercise is to deconstruct a published layout by identifying and listing all of the different elements present.

2 Cut the body copy from a printed article and come up with your own headline and other page furniture, then compare your work with the original. Put yourself under pressure by doing a number of stories against the clock.

Visuals

1 Start your own Project Magpie folder by cutting out good examples of layout – everything from single stories on a newspaper page of stories to complete spreads from a magazine. This should build into a reference library of how words, page furniture and photographs/illustrations fit together within the boundaries of a page. Make sure you include examples of different page sizes (broadsheet to pocket-sized) and see how they work differently.

2 Copy pages you like using page make-up software. Make sure you set the right page size to begin with otherwise the proportions will not work – but you can also set the wrong size page and then try to make it work. Even if your facsimile is not perfect, the practice will improve your skills.

Future

1 Play with all the kit and software you can get your hands on, including exploring every function on your phone, and think about how you could use it to enhance a specific publication – keeping the readers in mind at all times. Make little movies, edit them, upload them to YouTube and review them.

2 Start a blog and customise the look and features. Specific services will change continuously but at the time of writing Wordpress offers a lot of customisable functions and Tumblr is favoured for its simplicity. Link to, or incorporate, your Twitter and Facebook accounts. Make the exercise more realistic, and more useful as a CV point, by blogging about a specialised topic.

BRINGING IT ALL TOGETHER

Newspapers and magazines have been going through an extended period of upheaval and change over the past few years but the disruption has not been uniform and neither has the response to it: as cy-fi novelist William Gibson told the *Economist*, 'The future is already here, it's just not evenly distributed.'[11] Although a lot of the public discussion has focused on decreased advertising and falling readerships contributing to lower revenues, production systems – never a glamorous topic of speculation but essential to all publications – have been as greatly affected as anything else. The general trend has been to attempt increased efficiency by reducing numbers, combining roles and introducing new ways of working. Specific instances, however, range from sacking a few subs to completely reorganising the production process but the main variants can be encapsulated in three categories: traditional, revised traditional, radical.

Traditional

A traditional production system would see raw material (copy, pictures) coming in via a commissioning editor, copy-taster or reporter, being passed to a sub-editor for processing, then on to a designer or layout sub who would produce a proof that went back to a sub for checking and correcting where necessary and finally onwards to a more senior person for final checking and signing off, after which it could be delivered to the printer.

This system can work very well and is good for catching mistakes in that a piece of work is (or should be) checked over several times. From the employer's point of view, however, it seems quite wasteful, especially when technology and training can combine the sub and designer roles, and secondary checking can be reduced to a single pair of eyes or even left to the sub/designer.

There is also no natural place to fit 'future' content – audio, video or online.

Revised traditional

This can take a couple of forms, production centre and hub-and-spoke.

Production centre

The production centre is pretty much what it sounds like. Rather than having a specially appointed designer in-office, a magazine or newspaper will send collated content to a studio area where work will be assigned among a group of production journalists. This has the advantage (from an employer's point of view) of being more efficient, inasmuch as workflows can be maximised rather than having one team member hanging about waiting for work to come through from colleagues. It also allows for degrees of specialisation so, for example, photo manipulation or web design can be sent to workers with the right expertise.

However, looked at from the other side, there are a number of potential disadvantages. Purist editors may feel that dividing work among a team of more or less engaged sub-editors may result in work that is mediocre rather than driven by loyalty to a specific title; furthermore in the deadline driven atmosphere of a newspaper it may cause delays and prevent last-minute changes. Members of the production team will have to get used to working with a number of different house styles for copy and design styles for layout. This can be overcome with good documentation and training but it may also contribute to the feeling of distance between where the material originates and where it is processed.

Hub-and-spoke

This is a system that was brought to popular notice in the UK by the *Daily Telegraph* when it moved to new offices in 2006. The intention was to integrate print and digital publishing interests, locating reporters and production staff from all departments on a single editorial floor; the daily and Sunday editions of the newspaper, the website, and other digital products, including audio and video interviews, originate from this unified space.

Although the *Daily Telegraph* did not invent this system, which owes a debt to the IFRA Newsplex experimental newsroom developed at the University of South Carolina, it has implemented it in an interesting way. Heads of departments (or sections) sit in the middle of the open newsroom and each news section (home, business, sports, international and so on) is aligned with its own 'spoke'. Describing the arrangement to editorsweblog.org, Rhidian Wynn-Davies pointed out that the spokes are actually curved lines of people in charge of either content, design or production. 'Those curves are quite important to us, they kind of work as internal triangles,'[12] he told the website. Content-producing teams that are less dependent on breaking news – supplements, magazines, feature content – are situated at the sides of the open floor, along with production studios for video and audio.

The advantage of this system is that it is a logical way of dealing with the exigencies of modern newspaper production; the disadvantage is that is takes a massive space to do it properly.

Radical

The *Daily Telegraph* has been radical in the way it has taken the traditional idea of 'benches' – a literal metaphor of the way newspaper production spaces used to be organised – and completely rearranged them. In 2009 the *Financial Times* came up with a more symbolic new system for the creation of 'web ready workflow', based on the principles of create, craft and complete – a system that does not necessarily imply a total reorganisation of the workspace.

A CLOSER LOOK

CREATE, CRAFT, COMPLETE IN ACTION

I was so taken with the C-C-C idea that I developed it into a system used for the production of a student magazine that incorporates print, online and multimedia (including a YouTube video channel). The system was piloted and found to work, with a few tweaks, very effectively and efficiently – each team has clearly defined responsibilities, there is little or no duplication of effort but it is still possible to build in checks at different stages, so that more than one pair of eyes sees the work. As far as pedagogy is concerned, it also allows the groups of students to rotate teams so that everyone gets a go at doing everything.

My version of the triple-C system is as follows; the specific elements relate to our course magazine so feel free to adapt it.

Create

The Create Team provides raw material for magazine content: news, stories, features, interviews; photographs, videos, sound clips.

- Reporters/writers research and prepare their commissioned content (copy, still photographs, video clips, audio clips, graphics) and take responsibility for adding hyperlinks and other Web 2.0 extras – as well as running spell/style checks and writing draft headlines, standfirsts and captions.
- Features for print = 800 words; for online = 400.
- News stories, reviews, etc. = 125 words print and online.
- Front cover concept, cover lines, selection of images.
- Conceptualise back cover.

Craft

The Craft Team converts raw material into publishable content.

- Make print story packages with copy, pics, graphics in InDesign (to final proof stage).
- Make online story packages for CMS/website with copy, pics, graphics, slideshows, video, audio, etc. (to pre-publish stage).
- Make digital narratives for IP-TV Channel (to pre-upload stage).
- Edit content, check hyperlinks, etc.
- Refine headlines, standfirsts and captions.
- Manage designated web pages.
- Link online stories to print pages.
- Sub and revise as appropriate.
- Complete front cover, choose image.
- Complete back cover.

Complete

The Complete Team is responsible for final proofing, final legal checks (libel, copyright), printing out the InDesign pages, publishing the online material and uploading IP-TV material.

- Proof and/or revise content for print and online.
- Proof and/or complete story packages.
- Print final output of print edition.
- Upload and publish final output of CMS/Web edition.
- Upload digital narratives to IP-TV Channel.
- Manage any changes or amendments, including ensuring enriched web 'master copies' are fully updated.

There also needs to be a fully worked out and documented administrative system underlying the workflow. The one used at Cardiff, which could undoubtedly be improved on, looked like the following.

THE PRODUCTION SYSTEM IN ACTION

The production system has at its core three main folders: Create, Craft, Complete. Within those folders there may be sub-folders for Copy, Pictures, Movies, Sound Files, etc.

- The Create Team files straight to the Create folder.
- The Craft Team makes a duplicate copy of material and moves the duplicate into the Craft folder (there must always be an original file in its original folder).
- The Complete Team makes a duplicate copy of material and moves it into the Complete folder.

File naming system

The file naming system identifies the magazine (L360), the issue (1, 2, 3), the story name (e.g. walestravel), the initials of the person who worked on it (e.g. AB) and the Group identity (Create, Craft, Complete). For example:

CREATE
L360_1_storyname_creatorinitials_create.doc

CRAFT
L360_1_storyname_crafterinitials_craft.doc

COMPLETE
L360_1_storyname_completerinitials_complete.doc

Example

In the first issue there is a feature called Wales Travel, created by Alfred Black, crafted by Cecilia Dow and completed by Effie Forest. Its progress through the folder and file system would look like this:

> ▶ A CLOSER LOOK
>
> - Alfred creates the document and then saves it in the Create folder as:
>   L360_1_walestravel_AB_create.doc
> - Cecilia is assigned the file to work on. She makes a duplicate copy and saves it in the Craft folder as:
>   L360_1_walestravel_CD_craft.doc
> - Effie will complete the process. She makes a duplicate copy and saves it in the Complete folder as:
>   L360 _1_walestravel_EF_complete.doc
>
> **Pictures, video, extras**
>
> Picture files, video files and other material must be saved using a similar system:
>
> magazinename_storyname_picturename_initials_team.ext
> e.g. L360_1_walestravel_dragon3_AB_create.jpg
>
> All still picture files must be saved at 300dpi and in jpeg format.

STYLE GUIDE

There is one other thing vital to the smooth running of the production side of a publication and that is a style guide. This is a document everyone should be able to refer to when there is any doubt about how things should be written out. For example, when referring to a person's job, should capital letters be used or not? Should the titles of books and films be set in italics or left plain? Should writers use 'dispatch' or 'despatch', 'jail' or 'gaol'? These sound like trivial details until you have to ensure uniformity throughout a newspaper, magazine or website.

The style guide need not be long but it will inevitably have to cover more than you might imagine. Excellent models are freely available from the *Guardian* (**http://www.guardian.co. uk/styleguide**) and *The Economist* (**http://www.economist.com/research/StyleGuide/**) and if you don't have the time or resources to create your own guide, adopt or adapt one of these. Make sure that staff and freelance writers, as well as everyone connected with production, know about the style guide – and use it.

PUTTING IT INTO PRACTICE

Although there are some good new production models to learn from, there is no universal tried-and-tested system. Think about how you would want your publication to work and then come up with your own fully integrated production system, making sure that you:

- Break down the tasks.
- Make it practical.
- Document the underlying administration.
- Try it out.

CHAPTER SUMMARY

The production process is often overlooked in favour of apparently more glamorous and creative forms of journalism such as news reporting and feature writing. However, not only does production offer a well-established route into journalism for entry-level workers, it can also be highly creative on many levels and, most importantly, without it there would be no news or features.

If there is a single word at the heart of production it is 'accuracy' – from the basics of spelling and grammar through to the manipulation of computers and software to achieve the best possible results – and if there is one phrase, it must be 'for the reader'.

Production is a continuously evolving field as new hardware, new software, new systems and new fields, such as social media, are incorporated into legacy media such as print titles, used to create new standalone digital publications, or help to form new communities of interest.

Digital natives are well positioned to find new ways of using technology to benefit and extend print brands. While you should not allow 'play' to interfere with your assigned tasks, you should not be afraid of playing with kit and ideas – after all, the future is waiting to be produced.

THINKING IT THROUGH

Consider the following questions:

- Would it matter if everyone spelled and wrote differently?
- What difference have computers made to journalism?
- How many tasks can one person do? How many can one person do well?
- What is the best system for production – i.e. the one that works most efficiently and catches the most mistakes?

NOTES

[1] http://bit.ly/metromantis

[2] Ibid.

[3] Ibid.

[4] Ibid.

[5] The *Independent*, Sunday, 22 January 2006, available at http://ind.pn/wapping_memories

[6] Available at http://1.usa.gov/spelling_grammar

[7] If you want to learn more about idiolects, a good starting point would be the Open University webpage: http://oro.open.ac.uk/5930/

[8] Matt Swaine presentation at the PTC's 2010 Academics & Industry Forum.

[9] Ibid.

[10] Ibid.

[11] 'Books of the Year' (2003) *The Economist*, 4 December.

[12] http://bit.ly/newsroom_design

WEBLINKS

http://www.spelling.hemscott.net/, http://www.open.ac.uk/skillsforstudy/spelling-strategies.php   These two sites offer practical ways to improve your spelling.

http://www.dailygrammar.com/, http://www.bbc.co.uk/skillswise/words/grammar/ These two do the same thing for grammar.

RECOMMENDED READING

Betteridge, Anne (2008), *Adult Learners' Guide To Spelling*. Edinburgh: Chambers. Offers practical exercises and stratagems for improving.

Evans, Harold and Gillan, Crawford (2000) *Essential English For Journalists, Editors & Writers*. London: Pimlico.
A classic of the journalist's genre.

Hicks, Wynford (2006), *English For Journalists*. London: Routledge.
This slim volume offers easily understood rules of grammar and composition.

Hicks, Wynford (2009) *The Basics Of English Usage*. London: Routledge.
As above but not just for journalists.

Hicks, Wynford and Holmes, Tim (2002) *Subediting For Journalists*. London: Routledge.
The best available book on the subject; a second edition is due in 2012.

Keeble, Richard (ed.) (2005) *Print Journalism: A Critical Introduction*. London: Routledge.
Chapter 13 is the crucial one.

Steinberg, S. H. and Trevitt, John (1996) *Five Hundred Years of Printing*. London: British Library.
Very informative, very readable and another classic.

REFERENCES

Bowers, Thomas, A. (1975) 'Spelling and Grammar – Their Importance to Journalism: What Journalism Schools are Doing', Paper presented at the Annual Meeting of the Association for Education in Journalism, August 16–19, Ottawa, Ontario.

Frith, Simon and Meech, Peter (2007) 'Becoming a journalist: Journalism education and journalism culture', *Journalism* 8(2): 137–64.

Herd, Harold (1952) *The March of Journalism: The Story of the British Press from 1622 to the Present Day*. London: George Allen & Unwin Ltd.

Nietzsche (1990 [1895]) *Twilight of the Idols*. London: Penguin.

Prensky, Mark (2001) 'Digital Natives, Digital Immigrants' in *On the Horizon*, MCB University Press, Vol. 9, No. 5, October 2001, at **www.marcprensky.com**

Tulloch, John (2000) *Tabloid Tales: Global Debates over Media Standards*. Oxford: Rowman & Littlefield Publishers Inc.

Wiggin, Maurice (1968) *The Memoirs Of A Maverick*. London: Quality Book Club.

Zur, Ofer and Zur, Azzia (2010) On Digital Immigrants & Digital Natives: How the digital divide creates conflict between parents and children, teachers and students, and the older and younger generations. Online Publication. Available at **http://www.zurinstitute.com/ internetaddiction.html**

CHAPTERSIX
SUB-EDITING

Case study 6.1

ON 9 August 2011, Rob Williams went in at 6.30 p.m. for the night shift as sub-editor for the *Independent* online. Normally this shift requires a number of admin tasks to keep the site updated and ensure the content from the paper is optimised for online and ready to go live at midnight.

Headlines need to be optimised for the search engines, developing stories need monitoring via social media and other news outlets – allowing the online sub to ensure that stories from the day are updated to keep readers informed throughout the evening and into the early morning. The job is also about responding to readers' comments and engaging with people around them.

> 'The thing that strikes me about the modern job of subbing online is just how much you need to understand the basics of how the internet works. You need to know something about HTML, tags and SEO but vastly more important than that is the understanding that the internet is built of people.
>
> If the old sub of the past was someone hunched over the desk – an anti-social pedant, it won't get you very far online. You have to like people and be responsive to things. It's easy to misjudge it and become the star of a Twitter storm.'

The overnight content also gives the site the chance to respond to international readers, and the Indie's online sub has to keep an eye on the time zones to make sure that content on the site is also appropriate to those awake – with the American market being an important part of that.

However, given that this was the third night of the London riots – it was going to be a busy night. A 600-word story regarding Home Secretary Theresa May's condemnation of the London rioters was put on the site, and sent live. Throughout the evening Rob could hear sirens from outside his window, so knew that events were ongoing and kept track of the wires and social networks to keep on top of what was going on.

'If you are looking at developing stories like the London riots you need to be reacting quickly to atmospheres and online attitudes. You need to be pre-empting the direction in which the news is going.'

The *Independent* doesn't liveblog – update the site in a minute-by-minute fashion – but stories are monitored for timeliness, comment threads checked to see if they are getting readers engaged and that stories aren't just up-to-date but going in the right direction for the audience.

By 8.30 p.m. there were six or seven lead stories available, and it was impracticable for them all to go on the site – not only would this create an information overload for readers, it becomes too much for the night sub to keep updated. So information was combined and refined to ensure the site was up-to-date. At that point it was announced that Prime Minister David Cameron was coming back from holiday for a meeting at the Cabinet Office Briefing Room (also known as COBRA to the media, essentially a crisis management meeting) – something that Rob picked up from social media networks. His task was then to update the story and move the story about the Home Secretary off the front page to allow the copy on the Prime Minister's return to go on the front page instead. The story developed from an initial update to a fully-fledged story from the Press Association, which needed to be looked at regarding the *Independent*'s style, before writing a standfirst, search engine optimising the content and adding an online headline. Stories from the evening had to be regularly updated to keep them fresh – one of the worst nightmares for an online sub being that people commenting on the site are more up-to-date than the news stories. It was also a case of sourcing good images – there were a lot available – and checking for other multimedia content, including uploading video of a burning store to one of the reporter's blogs.

The shift finished at 3.30 a.m., allowing Rob to leave the site ready for the day shift, which would start shortly after.

INTRODUCTION

Sub-editing is seen as a vital part of the production process of any medium that puts text in front of an audience – be that in a newspaper, magazine or online. At its simplest, the sub stands between the journalist and the reader as part of a quality-control process.

There are those who would argue that the sub's job is one of the most important in a media organisation as they clarify for the confused, add legal safety to the defamatory and add polish to what could be a mundane piece of work. Others see them as a legacy from an age of hot-metal printing presses that are not required in the current media environment.

One thing that is clear is that an understanding of the skill set is vital for any journalist, whether you edit a page, design one or write the content for any platform – and particularly if you put text in front of an audience while publishing solo on a site or blog.

There are a couple of major misconceptions that need to be cleared up at an early stage. The first is that the title 'sub-editor' implies that they assist the editor, or are in a management hierarchy below them; however, this is a role rather than a position of power within the newsroom. Subs are actually responsible to the chief sub-editor.

The second is that subs just correct English – although this is part of the role it is not the only issue that they have to deal with.

Traditionally, sub-editors were seasoned journalists who had learned the key lessons that have been outlined in this book:

- what a story is;
- where it comes from;
- good writing – including fundamentals like spelling, grammar and basic accuracy;
- the legal and ethical frameworks that journalists operate within;
- the readership;
- good subject knowledge – be that a topic or a local area.

There are also different aspects of the role – some sub-editors are responsible only for the text (they are sometimes referred to as copy editors or downpage subs), some design while others have combined the role to handle both text and layout. Some journalists also fulfil part of the sub-editor's role, by inputting their stories straight into the text boxes on page templates.

WHY LEARN ABOUT SUBBING?

Not all journalists set out wanting to be sub-editors, but many of those who become subs find they have developed strong skills in the areas outlined above. Although not all journalists will become subs, the skill set is a vital one for any young journalist to have.

Many subs have fallen victim to the job cuts of recent years, regional subbing centres have been created by newspaper groups like Johnston[1] and Newsquest,[2] and journalists often find themselves writing straight into pages rather than writing in a word-processing package. In the magazine industry it can be quite common for young journalists to be involved in the production process if there is only a small team putting the product together.

And online, journalists will be often be blogging or filing copy without the safety net of a more seasoned set of eyes looking at the copy – meaning that an understanding of the journalist's skillset from a sub-editor's point of view is extremely important. This is something that has been recognised by the industry training councils – both the Periodicals Training Council and the National Council for the Training of Journalists have sub-editing/production elements within their syllabus.

QUALITIES OF THE SUB-EDITOR

A variety of skill sets are attributed to a sub-editor, so it is worth looking at these in the light of this chapter.

A common set of skills listed for a sub are:

- Sharp news sense – tailored to the newspaper on which you are working.
- Orderly mind – can assemble a clear and logical sequence of facts from a muddled account written by an inexperienced reporter or put together an orderly story from copy coming in from a number of sources.

- Obsession for accuracy – even the smallest mistake can damage a newspaper's credibility. A careless sub is a liability.
- Respect for the writer – every alteration must be for a purpose. Only change a reporter's copy to correct or improve it. Don't change a story just because it is not in your personal style. Unnecessary rewriting wastes time, damages the writer's morale and increases the risk of error.
- Feeling for the story – be well informed about readers and key issues within your circulation area or niche so you can weigh the significance of story angles.
- Good general knowledge – keep up with national and international news, again that relates to your coverage area rather than always being about global news.
- Ability to work at speed – a perfect story is no use if it misses the edition. You must learn to work accurately to deadline and know how to prioritise.
- Ability to write captivating headlines – learn how to tell a story in very few words. Extend your vocabulary to write headlines, which fit the story and the space available.
- A sound legal knowledge – you need to spot and remove legal risks in copy. Remember headlines can be legally dangerous too.
- Ability to achieve visual balance – weight headlines to suit the significance of the story and the visual impact on the page.
- Sound knowledge of production methods.
- Ability to write crisp, clear English – each story must be understood by all readers. It must be comprehensible at a single read. Look at every story from the reader's viewpoint.
- Resilience – be calm in a crisis. Don't flap when the pressure is on.
- Enthusiasm – be excited about news. Be interested and willing to learn.
- Sense of humour – you will need it to stay sane.

THE ROLE OF THE SUB-EDITOR, THEN AND NOW

Sub-editors are often seen to be part of the industrialisation of the news process in newspapers – essentially a relatively modern phenomenon. A number of writers have tried to capture what the sub is and does over the years. A large part of the role still remains rooted in the historical core skills, as the following highlights show.

1950s

Back in 1950, Alexander Nicol wrote a chapter on the sub-editor in *The Kemsley Manual of Journalism*, which outlined the job of the sub-editor and some of the key skills. One huge difference between then and now was the printing process and the ability to use the tools for the job. Nicol said that subs should be 'Able to use the tools of the trade to complete the job – pencil or ball-point fountain pen, scissors and gum pots.'[3]

But a lot of the core skills outlined by Nicol are clearly recognisable today:

- condense the news into the space available;
- taste copy (in other words read it to get a flavour of what is going on);
- ensure accuracy;
- headline writing;
- adherence to deadlines;
- good English.

1960s

One of the books still seen as a key manual and guide to sub-editing was *The Simple Subs Book* by Leslie Sellers. Again, although Sellers first wrote in the late 1960s the key concepts he outlines could easily be applied to the sub-editor of today:

- make sure stories are easy to understand;
- check everything, then check and check again;
- ensure the text is legally safe;
- make sure that copy is in house style and fits the size of space;
- create headlines, captions and design the pages.

1980s

By the mid-1980s these skills were being reported[4] as the ability to:

- correct all errors of fact and expression in the copy being handled – checking;
- clarify the meaning of the story;
- condense (or amplify) the story to fit the space available;
- make it conform to the typographical and literary style of the newspaper;
- improve the story;
- mark the copy for the printer;
- write headlines and crossheads.

1990s

By the mid-1990s the discussion of sub-editor had moved on to the idea of the page editor – the single production journalist who was able to fulfil a number of roles that had previously been handled by specialists. As outlined in Chapter 1, the digital printing process and desktop publishing revolution changed journalism massively during the 1980s and 1990s, and gave journalists the power, at the push of a button, to do jobs that had once taken teams of people.

David Montgomery – a former *Daily Mirror* editor – gave a speech in 1997 in which he spoke about the multi-skilled journalist who could:

- select stories;
- put them in order of prominence;
- design the page;
- write the headlines;
- put in and manipulate the pictures;
- edit the text;
- review the work in total;
- send the page to the printer.

> 'This effectively eliminates four or five departments . . . [and] inevitably means the death of the subeditor and the birth of the page editor.'[5]

I first started work as a sub-editor around this time – and although technically my role was that of a page editor I was still referred to as a sub. But my responsibilities were very much those outlined by Montgomery. Whether on a daily or weekly paper I was responsible for the pages I worked on and would be the last person to alter them before they reached the readers.

2000s

The role of the sub, like much else in journalism in the 21st century, is currently in flux. Several newspaper groups have centralised their subbing desks and are getting reporters to write straight into pages as outlined earlier.

The debate about the sub's role in the future of journalism even comes back to the title itself. In some places the title of multimedia desk editor has been adopted to describe how subs can now add multimedia elements to copy for websites, augmenting the original journalist's offer. They still perform the duties outlined above but have added new elements to the role, although if the aftermath of Montgomery's speech is anything to go by, most in the trade will still refer to them as subs.

The role of the sub-editor in the 21st century

This chapter will discuss the role of the sub in terms of:

- checking,
- clarifying,
- condensing,
- creating,
- augmenting.

CHECKING

A key part of any sub's job is checking the material that comes in front of them. It doesn't matter whether that is a big interview feature for a glossy magazine, the front page splash on the newspaper or a 120-word community story on a hyperlocal website – getting it right is what is important.

Although the mantra 'Trust No One' is usually associated with the TV series *The X Files*, it serves as a reminder for any sub. This isn't a mantra for the cynical to distrust everyone around them – it is, rather, a call to arms to the sceptic. It requires the sub to be the one who value judges what others are saying, and not to assume that they themselves know all of the answers.

Simple checks can stop some very embarrassing mistakes slipping through. In August 2010 the *Independent* ran a small piece on the Big Chill music festival, which had apparently originally started life as the Wanky Balls music festival.[6]

It seems obvious in hindsight that this is patently stupid and shouldn't make it through the reporter's own checks. But it did make it through, and past the subs into the Saturday edition.

Some judicious research by bloggers showed that the 'facts' of the story had been checked using Wikipedia – and that particular page just happened to have been vandalised.

This could have been spotted by some very basic checks – and the legendary sub's question 'Are you sure?'. As with any journalist, subs should be strong in local or beat knowledge, contacts and online research to ensure the quality of the product they are working on.

Accuracy

One of the key jobs of the sub-editor, highlighted by Nicol in the Kelsey manual back in 1950, is to ensure that the reader is getting a quality product, and as a result they are sometimes described as the readers' champion. But in reality they are often the last pair of eyes to see a story before it goes through the printing or web publishing process.

PUTTING IT INTO PRACTICE

The first step in basic accuracy is to check on the skills outlined in Chapter 4:

Does this story answer the who, where, why, what when and how aspects?

This can easily be converted into a very simple checklist.

Question		Checked
Who?	Are there names for everyone mentioned?	☐
Where?	Is the location evident? Does your publication promote or hide the location from the intro? Are the addresses of those involved included? Should they be?	☐
What?	Can you understand the events of this story?	☐
Why?	Do you understand why it happened?	☐
When?	Are the dates clear and does the timeline of the events make sense?	☐
How?	Do you understand how this happened?	☐

This sounds quite a simple list to work from – but, under pressure, common sense and basic understanding can sometimes go out of the window. For example, look at this intro, which could easily be improved using a checklist of this nature:

> A 45-year-old welder admitted raping a Swedish au pair at Cardiff Crown Court today.

The good sub will want to know if the welder had actually raped the au pair in court today. This wouldn't be very likely, as the where is too literal. It should be:

> A 45-year-old welder pleaded guilty to raping a Swedish au pair when he appeared at Cardiff Crown Court today.

This approach could also have saved some embarrassment at the *Guardian*. In a story about American businessman Warren Buffett, the writer said the 79-year-old billionaire:

> . . . lives in the same five-bed house in Omaha that he bought in 1938.

One slight issue there, given his date of birth Buffett would have been just seven years old at the time. A correction had to be run to clarify that he actually bought the house in 1958 at the more logical age of 27.[7]

Check, check and check again

One of the key issues with a story is that the sub, in a drive to improve a story for purely subjective reasons rather than for the key points outlined above, can sometimes add in errors. This can be fatal and lead to all sorts of problems. Subbing should be done as accurately as possible to ensure basic errors don't creep past.

Basic checks outside the story issues include making sure that any terminology used is correct. I was once working with a colleague who was designing a page that contained a piece about a rock band. During the course of the piece it said the band's former manager had robbed the band. Straight away alarm bells rang. If you check McNae's *Essential Law for Journalists* you will see robbery defined as: 'Theft by force, or by threat of force'.[8] This was factually inaccurate and could have caused problems, as a robbery is a much more serious offence than what had actually happened, which was being jailed for defrauding the band by false accounting. And the entry under theft contains the following sage advice: 'The act of theft is stealing. Do not refer to the offence as robbery'.[9]

Colloquially in the North of England burglary is often referred to as robbery – as in 'someone robbed my house last night'. Although robbery is technically a crime against property, McNae makes it clear that burglary involves 'entering a building as a trespasser and stealing or attempting to steal; or inflicting or attempting to inflict bodily harm. It is also burglary to enter a building as a trespasser with intent to steal, inflict grievous bodily harm, commit rape, or do unlawful damage'.[10]

Numbers

Numbers are often a problem for journalists, and can cause a lot of problems in the text. As outlined in Chapter 2 it is important for a journalist to be able to understand numbers. The Royal Statistical Society and Sense About Science have put together a great guide to getting the best out of statistics, something that should be on every sub's reading list. [11]

Recalculating percentages is also something all subs should do – they should work out the figures and not just accept what is put before them by reporters. Percentage literally means the rate per hundred, and it is the rate of change between figures that often causes the most problems. Look at this example:

> Car parking tickets that resulted in unpaid fines in Tameside rose from 65 per cent in 2008 to 79 per cent in 2009.

Fine, we can work that out as a percentage change. The key issue here is that this is not a 14 per cent increase – which at the first glance you might think $(79 - 65 = 14)$. It is actually a 21.5 per cent increase, worked out as follows:

$$\text{Difference between the new figure and the old figure} \div \text{The old figure}$$
$$= \text{percentage rise. So } (14/65) \times 100 = 21.5$$

Not only is it accurate but also a better story as the number of tickets has gone up by over a fifth.

Averages are also an issue – is this a mean, mode or median figure? Sounds terribly mathematical but it is important to know, as it will make a difference in what you are talking about. Each means something slightly different, and as soon as a reporter starts mentioning averages, you need to check. And watch their approximations too: 80 people isn't nearly 100.

Grouping numbers together can also be an issue. During the exam season the *Birmingham Post* ran a story outlining how

Four Handsworth pupils land 63 GCSEs between them

> Four Birmingham school pupils proved to be a class act today after achieving a remarkable 63 GCSEs between them.[12]

It turns out that three of the group got 17 passes each and one got 12. The point of the story was to show the top achieving pupils but the grouping of the numbers doesn't work properly and it sounds a bit odd put in this way. This is often used as a way of grouping criminals who have been sentenced to jail terms or for people who have been rewarded for long service in a particular job.

Another great place to get to grips with numbers is the book *The Tiger That Isn't*, by Blastland and Dilnot – again an excellent addition to any sub's bookshelf.

remember

- Accuracy is paramount.
- Check facts.
- Check figures.
- Be precise.

Correcting

Chapter 3 offers sound advice to the reporter on how to make their text smart, snappy and accurate, and is well worth reviewing at this point. And the section on use of language, punctuation and quotes is arguably more important for a sub than a reporter – as the sub is the one who will have to amend any of the errors left by the writer in the first instance.

So, a good level of understanding of sentence construction, punctuation and grammar is vital to the sub. Most people take text in its written form as a very basic skill that we learned at school, and don't have to put much effort into. But they would be doing themselves a disservice – and more importantly when you are paid to help produce a high-quality written product your customers are going to expect something quite special from you.

In it's simplest form, when we put out text in a magazine, newspaper or website, we are producing broadcast media – not in the sense that it will be on TV or radio, but in the sense that we are distributing a message to people rather than communicating as part of the process. This means that the reader will often have read the piece first, before using any of the communication tools to get back to you to raise an issue, flag up a problem or even just say how well you've done (although the last is unlikely).

Have a look at the diagram below. Although this model originally comes from communication theory, there is an important point to remember. Anything which could interfere with the communication process will affect what your reader picks up. How often have you been annoyed by signs that are wrong or the improper use of an apostrophe? Do you get upset when people say effect instead of affect (or vice versa)?

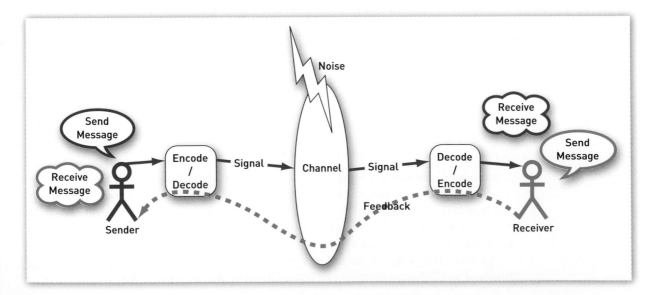

Then, congratulations, you are already on your way to being what is sometimes called a copy sub. A word of caution though – sub-editors can often feel the wrath of the writer for altering or amending copy. Sometimes for the right reasons, and sometimes for what is perceived as the vanity of the sub-editor. James Milne, in *A Window in Fleet Street*, wrote:

'Pity the poor reporter who toils all day for his story, writes it with his mind's blood and when he sees it in print he hardly knows it.'[13]

This might have been borne in mind by sub-editors on *The Times* when they altered a review sent in by the critic Giles Coren. Coren became upset that what he saw as a carefully built up joke reference to oral sex was removed by changing 'going for a nosh' (slang for oral sex) to 'going for nosh' (slang for eating). To read Coren's letter in full go to the *Guardian*'s website via **http://bit.ly/corenletter**.

PUTTING IT INTO PRACTICE

Punctuation can be a tricky beast, and is not always straightforward. It is historically seen as a way to aid people reading aloud, and affects how people consume what you are trying to put across.

Look at this text, which is devoid of any punctuation:

Dear John I want a man who knows what love is all about you are generous kind thoughtful people who are not like you admit to being useless and inferior you have ruined me for other men I yearn for you I have no feelings whatsoever when we're apart I can forever be happy will you let me be yours Harriet

It is hard to read because there is no space to pause, no opportunity to engage with what has been written. One possible version of this could be:

Dear John
I want a man who knows what love is all about. You are generous, kind, thoughtful. People who are not like you admit to being useless and inferior. You have ruined me for other men. I yearn for you. I have no feelings whatsoever when we're apart. I can forever be happy – will you let me be yours?
Harriet

What a lovely thing to say to someone, and as a message it flows, offers space to pause and gather breath and take in the message as a whole.

But what if we added in the punctuation in a slightly different way?

Dear John
I want a man who knows what love is. All about you are generous, kind, thoughtful people who are not like you. Admit to being useless and inferior. You have ruined me, for other men I yearn. For you, I have no feelings whatsoever. When we're apart I can forever be happy. Will you let me be?
Yours,
Harriet

This is clearly a very different meaning from the previous punctuated version of the text and this needs to be recognised by any sub-editor.

Apostrophes

Although covered in Chapter 3, apostrophe usage is such a common problem in newsrooms that it is worth reiterating here. Just about every newsroom I've ever worked in had the basics of how to use an apostrophe as a poster on the wall. These posters were usually a variation around this problem:

it's   its
who's   whose
your   you're

In all of these cases the apostrophe represents a missing letter and not a possessive – this is something that has to be learned by rote. Other common issues with apostrophes are caused by plural nouns. Key problem areas are words like men – this is the plural of man so the possessive becomes men's. Remember there is no plural word mens, so the use of mens' *must* be wrong. The same goes for women's and children's (the plural form of child).

One interesting issue relates to words like sheep – which is both plural and singular form, so the possessive would be sheep's, e.g. the sheep's fleece (again a good sub would now be checking to see if the copy clarifies exactly how many sheep are actually involved here).

Sub-clause

This is essentially a secondary element of a sentence and is of less importance than the main clause. The simplest way of thinking about it is, essentially, using commas to bracket off the least important part so the main sentence will make sense without it.

For example:

John drives his car, a red VW Golf, along the A470 every day.

We can actually skip the fact that the red VW Golf is here; it is secondary to the main sentence.

Another issue with sub-clauses is what is called the inverted sentence. This is essentially a literary device but one that is disliked in the newsroom as the point is to get the subject, object and verb towards the start of the sentence to ensure it is as active as possible. For example:

On entering the room, John shot the man.

Although this is a perfect example of a sub-clause there is a key issue with it – it gets the subject (John) and the verb (shoot) towards the end of the sentence. Although authors may love the device, the key advice for a journalist is to get the detail in quickly:

John shot the man when he walked into the room.

The only issue here is that it is now not quite clear who walked into the room and a good sub would need to ensure that this is clarified.

Further issues

There are a number of issues with English, grammar and punctuation that merit very good books in their own right (see the Recommended Reading for further guidance).

remember

- A sub is part of the communication process.
- Check punctuation to see if it alters the sense of the piece.
- Make sure that text is active, to the point and has the subject, object and verb at the start of the sentence.

Clarifying

The key role of the sub, when it comes to text, is often seen as improving and clarifying stories. However, this is where the issue of subjectivity creeps in – remember to be a critical friend, not the scourge of the reporter. Clear communication is important in a business that centres on informing your customers about what is going on – that's what journalism is, crudely defined.

Every year the Plain English Campaign holds an awards ceremony to praise those who communicate in simple and effective language and to highlight those who can turn the English language into something almost undecipherable.[14] The *Daily Mail* and *York Press* were two of the newspapers that topped their categories for media in the 2010 awards.

Chrissie Maher, founder of the Plain English Campaign, said:

> 'When I started the UK's first community newspaper in Liverpool, there was clearly a need for local people to be part of their local news in a way that they could understand. *York Press* has kept that spirit alive in their press where others have been swallowed up by the big boys or simply disappeared.'[15]

There are also some fantastic examples of officialese, which use the English language in such a torturous way that they become confusing for the reader. A noteworthy example of this comes from a Wandsworth Council report that states:

> 'It is proposed that 100% of an individual's personal budget be subject to an assessed contribution i.e. a means tested charge towards the cost of an individual's care. This is consistent with the charging policies developed by the London Boroughs of Richmond and Ealing. Other local boroughs are still in the process of policy development.
> The application of 100% to the calculation of a service user's maximum assessed contribution will act to promote choice; a key principle of the personalisation regime.'[16]

Needless to say this won a 'Golden Bull' Award from the campaign group and the award was made because:

> There are a little over six pages of explanation of the proposals but a lot of the wording will leave many people baffled.[17]

This kind of language is all too common in official documents, and part of the job of a sub is to ensure that any copy based around these stories is accessible and easy to read.

Jargon

Each profession has its own technical language to ensure that people can understand each other, usually based on specialist terms or acronyms. This is designed to make it easier for people to communicate quickly and easily with one another. For example, a surgeon can be clear about exactly which type of knife is required for the job, or people can understand about the state of the UK's finances by saying PSNCR rather than having to say public sector net cash requirement in full.

However, this does raise some serious issues as to how readers deal with what they are reading. We may be writing for a specialist niche audience who understand the terms – quite likely in highly specialised trade magazines, but less so in a local newspaper.

Although dating back to 1968, Leslie Sellers gives a great example of how to deal with jargon:

> 'The Indian government is giving active consideration to the containerisation and palletisation of bones exported to Britain for the making of gelatine in a bid to minimise the danger of anthrax.'[18]

This 31-word sentence is pretty hard to read and could be a lot simpler. First check that you know what palletisation or containerisation mean, and they are either considering this or not – so active consideration can go out of the window too.

So, Sellers suggested:

'India is considering improving packing for bones sent to British gelatine firms to cut the danger of anthrax.'[19]

Not only does this mean that you have saved 13 words, it is clearer and more efficient. As Sellers said: 'Not a beautiful sentence, but at any rate one that is shorter, clearer and free of all contamination by jargoneers.'[20]

Sometimes specialist language does have to be used to ensure the context is appropriate – science stories can be dumbed down too far and mean that problems occur in a story, but this is part of the job of the sub – to ensure there is enough detail in the story and not too much to make it difficult to work with.

A matter of style

Stylebooks are a key tool when it comes to ensuring consistency across a product. They sometimes cover the whole product – including the layout – rather than just how to use certain agreed forms of words or standardising translations from other languages. What is important is that this is a living, breathing document aimed at bringing consistency to a product – so all of the writers are, for example, using chief executive not Chief Executive.

An example of this is shown in *The Times*'s stylebook. Although the Indian city of Bombay was renamed Mumbai in 1995 it was still regularly referred to as Bombay in the British media. In 2008 *The Times* updated its stylebook to acknowledge these changes:

'On occasion, it will be appropriate still to use a phrase such as "formerly known as Bombay". In the meantime we will adopt a formula that talks of "Bombay, also known as Mumbai".'[21]

PUTTING IT INTO PRACTICE

Carry out a Google search for newspaper stylebooks, and see how many you can find online and then compare them. Two that are easily found online are the BBC Stylebook[22] and The Guardian stylebook.[23] You will see that both offer a wide range of information and advice, not just on the usage of words or standardising phrasing. The BBC book, although aimed at broadcast journalists, is a good source of ideas – particularly if the newsroom you are working in doesn't have one. Even a small team needs to have a stylebook to ensure that everyone is working from the same starting point.

remember

- Keep it simple.
- Be careful of jargon.
- Remember the reading age of your audience.
- Keep it in style.

CONDENSING

Simple, active sentences are part of the key strengths of the journalist. They allow the reader to get to the heart and soul of the issue quickly. One of the devices used to help in this is the word count, which will be attached to a story. Newsdesk, or the news conference that involved the production chiefs and the news team, will decide on the placing of a story – the page and what length it needs to be written to. But what happens when something changes and a breaking story occurs? Or how do you deal with word limits on the internet, when your only limitation is the storage space of a server and the bandwidth available to it – or how do you change the story to be a teaser for Twitter?

PUTTING IT INTO PRACTICE   READ ALL ABOUT IT

Practising condensing a story is a skill that every sub needs to ensure that they are using the copy to its best advantage. Reporters will sometimes try their best to get in every point they think is vital, even if that means going over the word limit. Contributors are worse; they are often experts in their field but not journalists – meaning they are not as succinct as they need to be but also may be using jargon. But it isn't just about condensing for a print product – newspaper subs still produce what are known as 'bills', the poster displayed outside the newsagent, which are designed to sum up a story in a short amount of space. This is often done on a sheet of A2 paper in a font and size that can easily be seen by the passerby. For example, the *Southern Daily Echo* in Southampton tends to use Helvetica Neue at 107pt to catch the attention of passersby.

When condensing a story to be promoted on Twitter there are a whole new set of considerations to be made. Part of the point is not just to put the message out in 140 characters (which includes spaces) but to include a link and to allow space for a reader to retransmit (known as a 'retweet') including the username of the original poster. It is also worth considering space to allow people to add their own comment – making this style of writing more akin to headlines, which will be covered in the next section.

CREATING

The creation part of a sub's job contains a number of aspects, depending on the product they are working on. They will take the copy and turn it into a page (unless of course the production system forces the journalists to write straight into the page); they may well be involved in altering the copy for the web, or adding multimedia elements (covered in **Augmenting** copy later).

There are whole books about this creative aspect of the sub's, or designer's, role. This section will give an overview of:

- layout and design,
- typography,
- headlines,
- images.

Layout and design

Software used in newspaper and magazines has changed the design process massively since the days of cutting and pasting strips of text onto a layout and then taking an image of them. Whether it is inDesign, Quark Xpress, free DTP software like Scribus or Microsoft's Publisher, they all have one simple thing in common. From a software point of view design is all about a jigsaw of page elements that can be put together however the designer wants. It allows images and text to be instantly placed together to allow an idea of what the page could look like.

What it doesn't do is add creativity, an understanding of the product and its target audience, the psychology of colours and how people read – that's the work of the designer or layout sub. In a book about computer design, this chapter would focus on terms like user interface, interaction design and other technical terms that mean one very simple thing: design is all about the way words, images and page furniture are collaged together to give the most impact and in a simple way that will assist the reader in getting to grips with the content, rather than being over-stylised to such a degree that they can't read what is going on.

This section will touch on some of the basics of newspaper and magazine design to allow you to get an idea of some of the issue involved.

Getting started

Arguably the most important rule of design – apart from the now legendary 'Keep it Simple, Stupid' (KISS) – is the idea of an entry point into your page. This can depend on a couple of important considerations. The first is how people open a print publication. The general rule of thumb is that they will open it and look at the right-hand page first. This allows subs to prioritise content between a pair of pages (known as a double page spread). So traditionally within a newspaper layout page three is more important than two and five more than four.

Once they have selected the page, most people tend to read from the top left-hand corner. So often the newspaper will have its lead story at the top of the page – it will be clearly available when the reader's eyes naturally go to the spot on the page. Often for magazines or newspaper feature pages this entry point will be an image, usually used at a large size for dramatic impact. Other times it will be the story itself that offers the most impact. This will often be decided by the executives at conference, but subs can be asked to make some of these choices themselves. One of the key considerations is the wow factor that any part of your page may have and you need to work to that in a way that will be in keeping with your design stylebook (this may be formal or may actually just be in the heads of the most senior members of the team).

Design stylebook

Some publications will have a design stylebook to ensure that the publication is kept to a consistent theme. It will say what size headlines should be – and when, and if, they should use other page elements like sub- or crossheads. One of the key things is that it will set out the typefaces, sizes of headlines for appropriate stories, teaser panels and more. As with the text stylebook this is a way of ensuring consistency among the team that will be putting the product together, something relatively easy if the sub is the only one working on a small product – but a big problem if that sub is only working on one or two pages of a big newspaper.

Modular layout

A key thing about modern print design is its modular nature – it tends to work in discrete blocks of content rather than letting them flow around other page elements. It works almost literally as building blocks on a page and is based on the rectangular nature of the page itself. The danger here is that a page can become lateral – working in one axis only – whereas good page design works around both the vertical and horizontal axes to create a balance.

Page design

One of the key things about page design is how the elements work together.

All of these pages display examples of how the page elements work together. Typography is carefully defined to ensure that the text works with the other visual elements. Images are cropped and chosen to ensure they support the story. But all of them start from the same place – whichever software you are using. (If you are interested in getting started you can download Scribus for free.)[24]

Typography

A lot of the terms from typography come from the days of the old hot metal printing presses, and although the specific processes have long gone they are still used in the digital design and printing process. Although not as immediately eye-catching as pictures, typography plays a massive role in how a magazine, paper or website feels to the reader.

Some fonts can shout, others carry feelings of weight and importance – others are zingy and fresh. So a basic understanding of typography is important for any sub as good fonts make a real impression. A lot of media companies use bespoke typefaces that differ from standard fonts to change how the paper feels, or improve the legibility.

Typography basics

Type is usually referred to as having ascenders and descenders – elements of the type which go above or below the standard-sized letters such as a or e (known as the x height).

Different typefaces have different looks, feels and – more importantly for printed and web publications – legibility. Some of this goes back to the days where the old-fashioned printing presses would fill some of the letters with ink and make them hard to read. Type comes in fonts – or families – which contain a number of variations of it. For example, the standard Helvetica comes in:

Helvetica regular

Bold

Bold Oblique

Oblique

These typefaces have a different feel to them, even though they are from the same type family. Another important point about fonts is that they are either serif, or sans serif (sans is from the French without – so literally without serif). Serifs come from the days of stone carving as the stonemasons needed a start and end point for their chisels.

A DIFFERENT TONE: A comparison of serif (Times New Roman) and Sans Serif (Helvetica) fonts. Although the same point size. Helvetica has a bigger x-height and is a wider face

Again the two different types of face will give a different feel as to what is on offer. This also changes how many lines of text can be put into the same vertical space (see Leading below).

What's your type?

A newspaper would rarely use a typeface like **Bauhaus**, as it would convey an image of being very modern and arty. It could do well as a headline font for a magazine as the 'heaviness' of the text has the power to draw the eye. But it would be hard to read a whole article in it. Similarly it would be unlikely for a lads' magazine to use 𝓛𝓾𝓬𝓲𝓭𝓪 𝓑𝓵𝓪𝓬𝓴𝓵𝓮𝓽𝓽𝓮𝓻 in an article on extreme sports; it looks more like something that would be used on a treasure map or a film about Tudor Britain.

8pt is often used as a body text size as it allows plenty of room to get text on a line, particularly in print columns

10pt is often used for intro paragraphs on lead stories as the size increase offers weight

12pt is more likely to be standfirst for a story rather then a body text size

14pt is more could be used as a small story headline, or box

18pt is often used for NIB columns headlines

24pt is a headline for small stories

30pt is a downpage headline

36pt is more important

48pt carries weight

60pt imposes

72pt=splash!

What's the point?

If you asked a sub this you'd get a different answer – depending on whether you spoke to a copy sub or a design sub. A design sub would take it that you were asking about the size of a typeface (see the font sizes using Futura box). The point size determines how much text can be fitted onto a line.

Alignment of text

Justification of text, or any text alignment, is essentially about horizontal alignment of copy within a column of text. Ragged right (where text is aligned to the left but appears to have a ragged right-hand edge) and justified (where text aligns both right and left) are the two most common forms.

Leading

Leading (pronounced ledding) was originally a strip of lead of varying width that was put in between lines of text during the days of hot metal printing, and is measured in points. The term is still used to describe the spacing between lines in digital printing. It is the same principle as the line spacing within word-processing software such as MS Word where you can specify single, line and a half, or double-line spacing. In typography there are range of sizes – again measured in points – that can be used to space text.

Remember that different fonts will look different at the same point size and leading.

Headlines

Headlines work in a number of different ways, but are aimed at doing one simple thing – attracting the attention. After the use of a well-cropped and placed image they are the most eye-catching element – and are used to make the page more typographically alluring: in other words, to stop the page looking like a huge slab of grey body text.

How this is done varies depending on the type of publication, for example the front page of the newspaper shouts, using very large and heavy typefaces. The point of all headlines is quite simple: they tell readers what the story is about and encourage them to read on and find out what is going on.

A lot of the rules below apply to headlining online copy, with one major difference – as with online body copy – the use of search engine optimisation. (This will be covered later in this chapter.)

The language of headlines

Given that headlines only have a set amount of physical space, which can quickly be filled by a large font (see the Typography section), headlines have generated their own syntax and key words. They aim to be brief and relay what is going on in a powerful, but succinct way. The key thing to remember is that they are basically a short sentence, which should contain a noun and a verb.

They also need to be active, in the same way that most news stories are. So an example of a strong headline is our old friend:

MAN BITES DOG

There is a subject to the sentence (the man), an active verb and it makes sense when read aloud.

One thing to note here is the use of bites rather than bit. Although the incident happened in the past, headlines tend to be written in the present tense as this tense carries the idea of immediacy and activity. This is headlining at its simplest and, arguably, most effective. But it isn't always so straightforward.

Have a look at this list of words and how they tend to be used in headline writing:

Axe   Close or cut, in relation to services or jobs
Wed   Marry
Blast   Can either be used in terms of an explosion or an argument

They are short words, which can be used to describe longer ideas – but there is an issue with how they are used on a daily basis. In December 2009 the BBC ran an online story with the headline:

Children's boss axed after death

Clicking through to the story it quickly became clear that the woman in question did not employ children, hadn't died or been attacked with an axe after her death. The journalese use of axe (to close or cut the job – literally sack) gives the wrong impression of the story here. The story was later re-headlined to be more appropriate to the events. What had happened was that the director of a council department, which looked after children, was sacked after the death of a two-year-old girl. Admittedly this is quite a long idea to get into a headline, but it is an important one to consider before using too much jargon. The resulting headline was:

Salford children's director fired after toddler death[25]

The only issue would be that the localisation wouldn't help much in print – if you were not from Salford, or at a push Greater Manchester, you may not be interested. Online it works well as it includes the **WHERE** as a search engine keyword.

A CLOSER LOOK

There are more serious issues that can occur due to inappropriate use of words within the headline, which can have serious and very expensive ramifications. In May 2010, the *Independent on Sunday* ran a story about Zoe Margolis – aka Girl With a One-Track Mind – who pseudonymously wrote about her sex life on her very popular blog and also penned a book about her experiences.

The *Sunday Independent*'s headline, which ran in both print and online, was:

I was a hooker who became an agony aunt

This is clearly not the case, and isn't included anywhere in the original story – only in the headline. Margolis was forced to issue legal proceedings and eventually accepted 'substantial damages' for the effect of the libellous headline to her reputation.

The *Sunday Independent*'s web headline was eventually changed to

Zoe Margolis: I'm a good-time girl who became an agony aunt[26]

There are two key issues in this case worth noting:

- how easy it would have been to get this correct;
- how the spread of both the URL – which contained the libel – and the article meant that the comments were at the top of the search engine result pages.

Margolis, speaking to the website **Journalism.co.uk** after the resolution of the case, said:

'Editors and sub editors need to check, double-check and triple check the URLs and headers of articles before they get automated to the newspaper's RSS feeds. I hope lessons can be learned by my case – but I doubt I'll be the last person to be libelled in this way.'[27]

PUTTING IT INTO PRACTICE

The art of the print headline is not an easy one, but some simple points can get you going on the right path to ensure your headlines stand out on the page.

Language checklist:		Language checklist:	
Present tense	☐	Precise language	☐
Active	☐	Strong verbs	☐
Personal	☐	Focus on one point	☐
Simple	☐	Use key words	☐

Using the checklist above we can now start to look at some of the basics of news headlines.

Present tense

Although stories tend to be written in the past tense, headlines are usually in the present tense. So a story about four people dying in a car crash the previous day should be:

4 die as cars crash *not* **4 died as cars crashed**

The classic example of an active headline is our old friend

Dog bites man *not* **Man bitten by dog**

Passive headlines are rarely used in news stories, which are designed to stir emotion.

Make every word count

As discussed earlier in the chapter, a sub's use of language should always be very specific and precise. This is even more important given the amount of words that can be fitted into a space in print (refer back to the section on Typography to help you here). So a story about the announcement of the increase in the price of a packet of cigarettes in the Chancellor's Budget speech could be headlined as:

Cigarettes are set to rise massively in Budget

but that isn't very precise.

Cigarettes to rise by £4 in Budget

would be much better.

Another point with the first headline is that the use of adjectives is relative and fairly subjective – we already know that facts and figures are correct here so it would be better to work with them.

Some more examples of precise language are:

- *witnessed* becomes *saw*;
- *depart* becomes *go*;
- *consultations* becomes *talks*;
- *commence* becomes *starts*.

This is important to remember as shorter words allow you to use headline space more effectively.

Images

Whether for the web or in print, images have a huge impact on the design of the story and its appeal to the readership. It might be a simple tight head and shoulders picture of a person being interviewed or the impressive double-page image which makes the *Guardian*'s Eyewitness section so impressive. On large newspapers or magazines, the picture desk will often size these. There are a variety of software tools used for dealing with images, such as Adobe's Photoshop, although there are free packages that will also give you the opportunity to work with images.

You'll need to know the answers to the following questions:

- What is the story?
- Is it a landscape or portrait picture?
- What size should it be? Physical size is important, but so is the DPI (dots per inch) size of the image. Screen images are shown at 72dpi while print can be around 200dpi and you'll need to know how to adapt this for each medium you are outputting to.
- Where will the image be placed in relation to the story? That will affect the size. Some web content systems will automatically place the picture in the same spot on the page.
- Is it part of a slideshow for the web? If so, all of the pictures need to be the same specification to allow the website to work effectively.

remember

- Page elements need to work together to ensure that clutter doesn't interfere with the reader's movement through the product.
- All elements should be clearly signposted.
- Typography helps set the tone of the product, and should be consistent.
- Use active, punchy and accurate headlines to support your copy.
- Images need to be appropriately sized and support your page.

AUGMENTING

One of the major implications for sub-editors involved in the web is the sheer scale of the potential audience they are faced with. A UK title may have a considerable reach, but its online edition is available to literally anyone with an internet connection. This has major implications on the design and functionality of any media organisation's website. There are crucial factors such as accessibility, what device people will use to access the content, searchability, interactivity and engagement, which anyone working on the web – but particularly sub-editors – need to get to grips with.

How much of this augmentation from print to online the sub has to do will depend on your organisation's view of interactivity and who is responsible for adding it - but think opportunities when you sub a story. There is a wide range of tools that can be used to support a story online – from Google maps, which were used extensively during the riots on 9 August 2011,[29] to things like word clouds, image slideshows, timelines and more.

A CLOSER LOOK

Neil McDonald, head of web and data development for Trinity Mirror North West, is part of a team looking after two major local newspapers and seven weekly newspapers. As a former reporter and print sub-editor, Neil understands the importance of the skills outlined in this book.

Key aspects of his role are:

- website management;
- checking stories that come through to make sure they are search engine optimised;
- ensuring that stories make sense;
- that they have pictures and videos where appropriate;
- augmenting the story with multimedia when appropriate – for example, during the 2011 election a word cloud of David Cameron's speeches were added, and maps were also added as required.

The group's reporters write into page templates which have a section for a web headline, so Neil and the team have to ensure that that is correct and properly search optimised. The team must also understand that breaking news will go live – there's a move in focus away from the next day's print deadline and towards getting the information out to the reader.

'I was amazed at how similar looking after content for the web seemed to subbing. I originally saw it as this impenetrable internet thing, but in actual fact the skills are very similar, you have to be accurate and legally safe. And SEO didn't seem that different to me, it was just another strand to the same skillset - summing up a story with the best words possible. You've got to write headlines that attract search but you are writing them for people to read.'[28]

PUTTING IT INTO PRACTICE

Andy Dickinson, a senior lecturer at the University of Central Lancashire, came up with a way of helping his students think about augmenting their copy for the web by producing the following checklist.[30]

This checklist is simple, but effective, and requires either reporters, subs or both to think about the multimedia and interactive options available to them to support the story.

Although this isn't an exhaustive list, these are some of the crucial things to consider and are regularly used by magazine, news and independent websites.

- Images – particuarly slideshows, can add a lot of impact. Most web content management systems or blogging tools will allow you to create slideshows.
- Links to background stories are an essential part of web journalism: the web is dynamic and not limited by a single edition so you are able to offer links within your own site and to the original documents or organisations you are talking about.
- Maps can be easily created using the Google maps tool, or geocoding sites (look back at the example in Chapter 5). This could easily be embedded in a web story.
- Timelines also offer an interesting perspective on events, allowing a reader to see quickly and easily how events have occurred. Tools such as Dipity[31] and Timetoast[32] allow the easy creation of interactive timelines.

▶ PUTTING IT INTO PRACTICE

Process in to content checklist
Consider the sections below when you are developing or reporting on a story.

Story	
Journalist	
Date	

Who – who are the key players in the story and do I have (or need to get) a picture or a link to bio information. More than 4 pictures? Ask your digital editor about a slideshow.

Name	Website	Image	Filename
		☐	
		☐	
		☐	
		☐	

What – What's the issue? Do I have a link to a backgrounder or other articles that fill out the context of the story?

Subject	Website

Where – note locations, with postcodes if you can, mentioned in the story. More than 4 and you may want to consider a map.

Postcode	Description

When – make a note of times and dates of key events in your story. More than 5 or 6 of these may mean that your story would suit a timeline online.

Date	Time	Event

Multimedia – do you have audio and video (or need some) that supports this story?

Type	Filename	Description

SEARCH ENGINE OPTIMISATION

Both magazines and newspapers have to worry about newsstand appeal – having catchy and snappy headlines, images or sells that will grab the readers' attention and speak to them. That's all very well when you are looking at the racks in your newsagent or supermarket – the shelves are absolutely stacked, but the amount of space is finite. Even within stores like WH Smith, which carry hundreds of titles on the shelves, there are a fixed number of products within an interest area.

But that's more difficult on the web – Google and the other search tools index trillions of web pages, so how do we ensure that we can get to our readers? Many online media sites are now finding that people are coming to them through search or social media rather than the home page. A report for the Newspaper Marketing Agency in May 2010[33] found that top referring sites were Google at 49,142,742 unique visitors as opposed to 34,503,928 for direct visits. In the UK that came in as 23,099,079 unique visits through Google search and 14,785,370 directly – and that is bearing in mind that Google is only one of a number of search channels.

One of the key things to bear in mind here is the importance of the search engine – whichever one that may be. They do work in slightly different ways and, as discussed in Chapter 5, it is well worth understanding how key tools work. Once you understand how search engines work you can help the reader find what they are looking for in the myriad of results returned by their search. This is where search engine optimisation (SEO) comes in.

A CLOSER LOOK

The following example shows that a Google search for SEO returned 938,000 pages!

SEO is often seen as a dark art of the web, where unscrupulous people spend time ensuring that sites you don't want to see are at the top of your search list. But at its simplest it is actually a way of helping readers find what you want. At the time of writing Domaintools.com put the number of active web sites at 938,000,000 but that was only looking at .COM, .NET, .ORG, .INFO, .BIZ and .US sites. Current estimates put the number of pages into the tens of trillions and Google actually stopped displaying the figure it claimed to be indexing several years ago.

But one thing all those figures suggest – there is an awful lot of content on the World Wide Web and you need to find a way to help it stand out from the crowd. This is sometimes why SEO can be seen as something of a dark art, as some site owners use dubious methods to get content to the top of the search results – hence the inspiration for this online joke:

> A man walks into a bar, pub, watering hole, dive, brewery, brewpub, public house, gin joint . . .

The joke is pointing out that an SEO spammer will use synonyms for their key words to ensure that they get the most coverage. However, with a little bit of augmentation, journalistic writing can not only be found by search engines, it can be read by the human doing the searching – one of the key issues that the spammers seem to ignore.

Very simply, we can use the traditional skills of the reporter and the sub-editor to make sure that content can be found easily by searchers. In some ways this is not a massive leap from the traditional skills of the writer or sub, but instead of using page layout and billboards we are using elements within the page to be found and read.

Key elements of SEO

One of the key points in understanding SEO is the use of key words – the words or terms that a searcher would use to be able to find the story you are augmenting. News stories are usually loaded with key words – who, what, where, when and how – names, brand names and places are all very searchable and often stories that are about topics such as sport and crime are very easy to find. But not every story you will work on is as simple to SEO as that. Experience is invaluable here, as key words are not just about using synonyms to get the best out of the available terms.

Synonyms and alternative terms are useful – for example, it's a good idea for a piece on search engine optimisation to feature the term SEO early on to increase the opportunity for its being found. However, there is another issue to think about: which market are you optimising the piece for? The spelling of optimisation means it would be unlikely to be found by a US searcher (as they spell it optimization rather than optimisation), but any search for SEO would still return a result.

Keyword	Competition	Global Monthly Searches ⑦	Local Monthly Searches ⑦
mountain bike review ▾	Medium	74,000	22,200
mountain bike reviews ▾	Medium	74,000	18,100
mountain bikes reviews ▾	Medium	18,100	5,400

Rising searches	
1. best mountain bike	+180%
2. best mountain bikes	+170%
3. trek mountain bike	+70%
4. giant bike	+60%
5. trek mountain bikes	+60%
6. mountain bikes	+50%
7. trek bike reviews	+50%
8. giant mountain bike	+40%
9. mountain bikes reviews	+40%

Google provides several useful tools for understanding how this works. The first to try is Google's AdWords keywords – although designed to see how much competition there is for a set of advertising keywords it will help you see how many people are looking for a term. This not only shows how popular it is, which could mean that you have an opportunity to be returned in the search terms, it will also show you how crowded the market is for those particular terms. Once you've tried this, you can then look at the search-based keyword tool to explore this further.

Another useful tool here is Google Search insights, which gives some interesting insights to related terms. Using the mountain bike review example as shown here, Search insights shows how other search terms in the same area are faring. And as 'best mountain bike' is faring well the use of the term in the page will work well as it was increasing in terms of popularity when the example search was conducted.

```
<html>
<head>
<title>Title at top of browser tab</title>

<meta name="description" content="The text that is displayed under the
title in the search engine – sometimes referred to as a snippet">
</head>

<body>

<h1>Usually the name of the site</h1>

<h2>A headline for content</h2>

<p>The content of the story</p>

</body>

</html>
```

Page elements

Some understanding of basic HTML is crucial in SEO, and these page elements can help improve search results. The basic structure of a page's raw html is shown alongside. Although most of this will be managed by the media company's content management system (CMS), it is worth understanding how these page elements relate to SEO.

\<title\>

This should be a unique and accurate description of what the story is about and shouldn't be too long, as search engines tend to truncate at more than about 60 characters. This may well be set up as a standfirst or excerpt box within your CMS. It is a crucial part of SEO as it appears below the headline in Google search. Again, this should be a short piece of text and research shows it counts for 43 per cent of viewers' decisions to click through to the page itself.

The title may also be the same text used by a site to display on its front page or category pages, although this can sometimes be different as it can provide off-page links from within the parent site.

Writing style

It sounds simple, but a key piece of advice from Google on SEO is that the text needs to be accurate, spelled correctly and not written sloppily.[34] This tight writing ties in with the traditional rewrite job of the sub – renosing stories is a key part of the offline sub's role, and offers an opportunity to develop the 'findability' of the piece, bearing in mind that the search engine is only one part of the searcher finding your work.

Advice varies about how much of a story will be trawled by a search engine. Some SEO sites suggest that search engines look at the first 500 words of a story while others reduce this figure to 200 words. This is sometimes used by magazine and newspaper sites to spread a longer story across a number of pages, each with a unique standfirst and headline, which means it will be more visible within a search.

Headlines

As with anything else within SEO for journalists, this needs to be written for the searcher and not the algorithm. And although keywords are important in a headline, they should not be used at the expense of the story. *Guardian* columnist Charlie Brooker wrote an excellent post on how this SEO game playing could cause problems for the media with the headline:

> Online POKER marketing could spell the NAKED end of VIAGRA journalism as we LOHAN know it[35]

It actually occupied the top spots for searches on SEO for quite a while.

PUTTING IT INTO PRACTICE

Subs offline often pride themselves on a witty headline, but that can cause problems online. A classic example of this is the now legendary:

Super Cally Go Ballistic, Celtic Are Atrocious

This is trotted out whenever Caledonian Thistle are able to beat Celtic in the Scottish Premier League, cup matches etc. As well as being a cliché, it isn't easy to search. And here's why:

- Super – doesn't offer any insight into what is actually happening here.
- Cally – the top two searches returned at the time of writing were for a female character from the reimagined *Battlestar Galactica* series and a character from the classic BBC sci-fi series *Blake's 7*. Nothing to do with football at all.
- Go – a good action word, but doesn't say if they won. Win would be better here.
- Ballistic – usually used in the context of firearms or missiles. Again doesn't really tell us anything itself, although used in the sense of being launched at the enemy in the original headline.
- Celtic – although Celtic (pronounced with a soft C, as in Seltic) are one of Scotland's top teams, a search algorithm will not know the difference between that and Celtic (pronounced Keltic – deriving from the tribes of Britain, and something you should never pronounce incorrectly to a Scottish football fan). However, the sheer number of links will put the sport's team to the top of the search engine.
- Are – again, a word without value on its own.
- Atrocious – 'lose' would be better as atrocious doesn't say why they are atrocious.

It may be boring but 'Caledonian Thistle beat Celtic' is far more searchable.

In an article for the *British Journalism Review*, the *Telegraph*'s Shane Richmond looked at how to SEO the classic Sun headline for the sinking of the Belgrano, an Argentinian battleship, during the Falklands Conflict. Shane's view was that this could not be found by a search engine given the kind of search terms that the reader would be using.[35]

Shane highlights a number of issues that are part of traditional print style, but wouldn't work online – the delayed or drop intro being one of them:

> 'The further down your story a search engine has to travel to reach a keyword, the less value it will attach to the article.'[36]

Even if you write about badgers, thermal dynamics or parachuting you will want your article to be seen by people who care about those topics. SEO techniques will give your article a better chance of being found. In fact the *Guardian* employs specialist SEO sub-editors to ensure its web content is up to speed.

Remember

- Understand your content system and check what kinds of multimedia or interactive elements are required for the story.
- Text should be as accurate and concise as for print.
- Ask whether text is to be spread over a number of pages.
- Optimise the story and the headline for search engines.

CHAPTER SUMMARY

Sub-editing is a major part of the communication process within the media. Even if you are putting your own copy live on a site or into a page you need to know the essentials of subbing:

- clear, jargon-free copy;
- strong headlines;
- good images;
- effective and simple page design;
- what multimedia or interactive elements you can use to augment a page.

THINKING IT THROUGH

1 How good is your grammar? What to change, what to leave?

In a setting where you can easily change someone else's work – be that in print or on a website – maybe the first question any sub should ask themselves is: should I? One of the key issues to look at is the word count – that may well affect the amount of subbing required on the piece in the first place. Another simple one is to look for the use of the word 'that' in a piece. It is often redundant and can be removed to quickly save space.

But after the obvious changes a sub needs to think about whether they are making changes to improve the piece they are working on – to make it shorter, more effective and in house style – or whether it is purely their desire to impose their own mark on the work. After all, there are no bylines for subs. But you need to be confident of your skills before you go wading into other people's work and, more importantly, you need to be aware of *your* shortcomings and know how to solve them.

Another issue that a sub needs to think about is the use of the colloquial. Although this wouldn't be used in a broadsheet, tabloids and local papers will use some elements of the colloquial to be part of the everyday life of their readership. This is particularly true of speech as all of us are influenced by where we grew up, and that is reflected in the way we talk and write – word usage and phrasing are a key part of that. So, does that mean that we should extend the changes in grammar to quotes themselves?

One problem with changing quotes is that it will leave you open to claims of fabrication. Some subs, depending on house style, will clean up grammar in a quote but leave the sense intact – or if it needs major attention may paraphrase. Other publications will use [sic] in brackets, almost literally to say 'it was said thus'. Is this a good way of ensuring that someone's words are not taken out of context or does it feel like a smart Alec saying, 'This person is thick and doesn't know grammatical English. Although I've not been allowed to alter it, I want you to know that I'm not responsible!'

Ask yourself: If you were to change the story, are you confident that you are being objective and dealing with issues like house style – or are these subjective changes? Are you confident that you are up to speed on your written English, and do you know where to get advice or support if you need it?

NOTES

[1] http://www.holdthefrontpage.co.uk/2011/news/jobs-at-risk-in-new-subbing-hub-plan-2/ and http://www.pressgazette.co.uk/story.asp?storycode=46625
[2] http://www.journalism.co.uk/news/nuj-considers-strikes-after-newsquest-announces-job-cuts-at-central-subbing-hub/s2/a543167/
[3] Nicol, Alexander (1950) *The Kemsley Manual of Journalism*. London: Cassell.
[4] 'The news machine: a guide to advanced techniques in journalism', *Part 2, Getting to press (sub-editing and production)*. The Thomson Foundation (1985).
[5] Hicks, W. and Holmes, T. (2002) *Subediting for Journalists*. London: Routledge, p. 6.
[6] https://katarney.wordpress.com/2010/08/09/wanky-balls-festival-or-lazy-journalists-are-lazy/
[7] http://www.guardian.co.uk/business/2010/jun/09/pass-notes-warren-buffett

[8] Banks, D. and Hanna, M. (2009) *McNae's Essential Law for Journalists*. Oxford: Oxford University Press.

[9] Ibid.

[10] Ibid.

[11] http://www.senseaboutscience.org/resources.php/1/making-sense-of-statistics

[12] http://www.birminghampost.net/news/west-midlands-education-news/2010/08/24/four-handsworth-pupils-land-63-gcses-between-them-65233-27125966/

[13] Milne, J. (1931) *A Window in Fleet Street*. London: Murray.

[14] http://www.plainenglish.co.uk/awards.html

[15] http://www.plainenglish.co.uk/awards/media-awards.html

[16] http://www.wandsworth.gov.uk/download/3752/fairer_charging_consultation

[17] http://www.plainenglish.co.uk/awards/golden-bull-awards/golden-bull-winners-2010.html

[18] Sellers, Leslie (1968) *The Simple Subs Book*. London: Pergamon Press.

[19] Ibid.

[20] Ibid.

[21] http://www.timesonline.co.uk/tol/news/world/asia/article5248351.ece

[22] http://www.bbctraining.com/pdfs/newsstyleguide.pdf

[23] http://www.guardian.co.uk/styleguide

[24] http://www.scribus.net/canvas/Scribus

[25] http://news.bbc.co.uk/1/hi/8403806.stm

[26] http://www.independent.co.uk/opinion/commentators/zoe-margolis-im-a-goodtime-girl-who-became-an-agony-aunt-1917708.html

[27] http://blogs.journalism.co.uk/editors/2010/05/20/independent-on-sunday-offers-blogger-over-hooker-headline/

[28] Interview with the author.

[29] http://www.guardian.co.uk/news/datablog/interactive/2011/aug/09/uk-riots-incident-map

[30] http://www.andydickinson.net/2009/02/12/a-process-and-content-checklist/

[31] http://www.dipity.com/

[32] http://www.timetoast.com/

[33] http://www.nmauk.co.uk/nma/clo/live/onlinenews?onlineNewsModel=18169

[34] http://static.googleusercontent.com/external_content/untrusted_dlcp/www.google.com/en//webmasters/docs/search-engine-optimization-starter-guide.pdf

[35] http://bit.ly/brookerseo

[36] http://www.bjr.org.uk/data/2008/no4_richmond

RECOMMENDED READING

Banks, David and Hanna, Mark (2009) *McNae's Essential Law for Journalists*. Oxford: Oxford University Press.
Any sub, or anyone putting text into a product of any kind, needs to be clear and up-to-date on their legal knowledge.

Blastland, Michael and Dilnot, Andrew (2008) *The Tiger That Isn't: Seeing Through a World of Numbers*. London: Profile Books Ltd.
An excellent book covering the use of numbers and statistics, which would be of great value to any journalist working with text.

Bradshaw, Paul and Rohumaa, Liisa (2011) *The Online Journalism Handbook: Skills to survive and thrive in the digital age*. Harlow: Pearson.
This book focuses on online skills and has good sections covering multimedia elements to stories and the technologies behind them.

Evans, Harold (2000) *Essential English for Journalists, Editors and Writers*. London: Pimlico.
Arguably the book for dealing with text, the legendary editor offers sage advice for both the writer and sub and the sections of using language efficiently offer a great amount to young journalists.

Frost, Chris, (2003) *Designing for newspapers and magazines*. London, New York: Routledge.
Although a book dating back to 2003, Chris Frost gives a good introduction to the art of print design in an accessible format.

Truss, Lynne (2009) *Eats, Shoots and Leaves*. London: Fourth Estate.
An accessible and useful book on punctuation and a guide on how to be really pernickety when it comes to looking at the work of other people – and your own.

WEBLINKS

http://www.senseaboutscience.org/data/files/resources/1/MSofStatistics.pdf   A good guide to the use of numbers, in what to many journalists feels like something way beyond their grasp on a day-to-day basis – well worth having on your virtual, or physical, bookshelf.

http://www.scribus.net/canvas/Scribus   A free page editing package that will allow you to start experimenting with designing for print products and put some of the ideas outlined in this chapter into practice.

http://www.bbc.co.uk/journalism/skills/writing-styles/writing-for-the-web/   The BBC College of Journalism puts a lot of training and support materials online, and this section on web writing is well worth a look; the page also has good links to sections on video and working for mobile devices.

ACTIVITIES

1 Using *The Guardian Stylebook*, look at the paper and the online version of three stories to see if the reporters and subs have applied house style correctly.

2 Take a page lead (the main story from a news page in a magazine or newspaper) and condense it into a story of around 150 words. Use the section on News writing to help you get the best out of your language and to refresh your memory on the story pyramids. Then take this story and condense it to the size of a NIB (news in brief) at about 80 words. Does it still contain that killer element that will hook the reader?

3 Take a piece of copy you have written, and then use the formatting functions of your word-processing package to change the typeface. Start with Times New Roman (a serif face) and then try a style like Helvetica or Arial. How do they look different? What do they make you feel in terms of the typography?

4 Look at the typography of a print edition of a newspaper or magazine, then compare it with the website – what does the difference in style say to you?

5 Headlines activity. Look at these front-page headlines from national newspapers and rewrite them for search optimisation. First search for the headline to see if you can find what the story actually is, then try to write a better headline for the web:

   a. Zip Me Up Before You Go Go
   b. Up Yours, Delors
   c. Your Country Needs Roo.

CHAPTERSEVEN SPECIALIST JOURNALISTS

Case study 7.1

THE global financial crisis put the spotlight on specialist business reporters like never before. Some struggled in the unaccustomed glare of attention; others such as the BBC's business editor Robert Peston became household names and a seemingly ubiquitous presence on television, radio and, notably, online for weeks. It was actually his blog that caused most controversy because his ability to report and comment so quickly caught the bankers flat-footed and temporarily made the journalist the story when he was accused of fuelling the panic over the collapse of Northern Rock.

Shooting the messenger is nothing new but the speed with which fear can spread did have an impact upon this financial crisis compared with previous ones. Peston argues that Northern Rock fared worse than other similarly beleaguered institutions because it handled its communications with depositors badly. Ordinary savers didn't understand statements issued more for the benefit of the financial sector so turned up at branches wanting an explanation. Unprepared staff were not geared up for the mass reaction so queues formed. 'It was the queues that caused the worry,' Peston told the 2008 Society of Editors conference in Bristol.[1] And arguably images of the queues – suggesting a run on the bank – were far more influential than his blog.

Peston is the epitome of today's specialist journalist, delivering content seamlessly across all media platforms and bringing experience to bear from a career that has spanned niche and mainstream print titles.

He is an enthusiastic blogger. Although the tone of a blog may be more casual and chatty than a Radio Four interview, he rejects the accusation that its content is any less rigorous. He told the conference: 'I do apply exactly the same standard of verification to blogging as to anything else I do.'

What he did appreciate – which the financial sector didn't – was that having a blog in the mix gave him a freedom to work outside and beyond the fixed radio and television bulletins. He could, and did, break stories late at night and at unpredictable times. He could also use his blog to comment and elaborate on his relatively brief main BBC interviews, and link to other sources and data.

He told the conference: 'What is fantastic about new technology is that I can do two things. I can get stuff out very quickly and it allows me to put a degree of detail out there that you can't do in a three-minute two-way.'

He also appreciates the wealth of responses his blog generates because they bring him extra information and perspectives. He said: 'Comments that people leave are incredibly valuable because they get you thinking about stories in a different way.'

The response – which includes an element of 'subveillance' – can provide specific follow-up angles and new sources but also generally serves as a reality check for journalists. High-profile cases have been highlighted where the public have exposed blatant journalistic fakery, but they benefit perfectly genuine reporters too by opening up the dialogue. For specialists, they are a useful antidote to the dangers of settling into a rut of established (and establishment) contacts and viewpoints, to which Peston alludes.

Specialists have to be versatile in other ways too. They may have a relatively narrow area of expertise but they have to operate very flexibly within it. Every journalist's first loyalty is to the public but a specialist must also forge very special relationships with contacts. In that respect they need to speak several languages – those of their sources and those of their audiences. A specialist needs to be a bridge; one who can take the insights of expert sources who talk in the jargon of their world and translate it for a reader. The reporting needs to be meaningful and relevant for the audience while remaining true to the original information.

The financial world, where some terminology surrounding 'derivatives' and the like was arguably intentionally obscure to mask the level of risk involved, is a classic example of a specialist having to operate in both spheres. Occasionally a niche audience may appreciate the jargon, but even there a journalist may need to work hard to provide clarity and get to the bottom of what is really going on.

Peston also demonstrates handsomely the value to a specialist of contacts. When the crunch came, they gave him that crucial dimension – access. He got the interviews everyone wanted because he had known these key players for years, on his and their way up. He knew where they would be; he had their numbers (literally and figuratively); and had built sufficient rapport with them to get them to talk to him. These were the fruits of a brief stint in the City followed by more than 20 years as a print journalist, starting out with the specialist *Investors Chronicle* for three years before moving across to various titles including the *Independent*, the *Financial Times* and the *Sunday Telegraph*.

Peston told the conference: 'I was a political editor and a banking editor which gave me access to people which journalists who hadn't done those things wouldn't have.'

Like other specialists, Peston was accused of becoming too close to those valued sources; so caught up in the City bubble that he didn't see the credit crunch coming. He and some other notable business journalists had pointed out that the level of indebtedness was unsustainable but few were sufficiently suspicious or pessimistic. Peston regrets that he 'didn't shout louder' but the public must take some responsibility here. We are all very adept at blocking out messages we don't want to hear.

However, every specialist needs to recognise the danger of losing independence from those they cover. Sources can become friends but they must always know that the story comes first.

Peston exhibits one final key ingredient of a specialist: passion for his subject. That comes through in person as it does on screen or in print. As a specialist, more than most, he loves his job.

INTRODUCTION

Specialist reporters like Peston are very much to the fore in 21st century reporting. Where once specialists were the favoured few on magazines and the old broadsheet newspapers, now they abound – on local as well as national titles. In text-based media, starting out as a generalist is still the norm, but across the board journalists are now likely to become specialists sooner rather than later (see Chapter 10).

Various factors contribute to this trend.

- **Issue-based reporting** – newspapers traditionally served geographical communities, but in a more transient age more content relies on communities of interest such as health or environment.
- **Niche publishing** – specialist coverage was always strong in the magazine industry but the appeal of niche has been accelerated to warp speed among an online audience. Printing on paper was constrained by the timing and cost of physical distribution making niche an expensive option. The opportunity to publish online opens up niche content to a potential global audience without the concomitant burden of distribution costs. Churn is considerable in this sector with titles launching and closing as enthusiasm and hobbies wax and wane. But, in the UK, magazines spanning print and online are tending to fare better than newspapers.
- **Analysis** – in an age driven by 24/7 news aggregators that offer free content to readers, some news organisations believe reader value no longer lies in breaking news but in analysis. The UK's upmarket print titles are most prone to this trend but most newspapers are following suit to some extent. This is good news for the specialist who can put those seemingly random events in context. They are much better placed to make sense of 'happenings' for the audience.
- **Complexity and secrecy** – the globalised world is a complicated place. Organisations, lifestyles and allegiances are more complex than ever before. Also, despite the age of spin, a Freedom of Information Act and online reality checkers, many agencies that impact on our lives are less transparent than before. Finding out what is really going on may be technically easier than it was before but the powers-that-be can be very astute at evading scrutiny not just in politics but in our schools and football clubs too. A generation of privatisation, contracting-out, the introduction of Cabinet-style local government and the development of quangos has reduced the range of decision-making routinely – and statutorily – exposed to the public gaze. The current government is pulling some quango powers back within Whitehall but at the same time envisaging more contracting out, for

example, in the NHS and the police, which is likely to reduce direct accountability or at very least make it harder to track decision-making. Specialists are needed particularly to keep tabs on what happens behind the scenes rather than out in the open.

THE SPECIALIST REPORTER AND SOURCES

A key element of being a specialist is being able to make the connections – literally with the widest possible range of contacts – but also by being able to piece together snippets of information, spot an emerging pattern and fill the gaps in what the public knows.

A generalist covering an ad hoc, one-off news story may well miss the significance of a particular event. Specialists can slot it into a bigger picture and understand why it will matter to their audience. They can understand the relevance of a throwaway remark or read between the lines of a bureaucratic report.

Once the significance is recognised, the specialist is also well placed to rise to the challenge, as expressed succinctly by the US Committee of Concerned Journalists, 'to make the significant interesting and relevant'.[2]

Contacts in the field can help to spell out the impact of any particular event, generate real-life case studies and allow the specialist to engage the audience, whether general or niche. Specialists will cover the routine 'diary' events within their field but are expected to use their contacts to bring in 'off-diary' exclusives. Specialists can help to combat the accusation of superficiality so often used as a stick with which to beat the text-based media. Providing context facilitates real understanding and moves beyond empty voyeurism.

A specialist is always on the look-out for follow-ups and needs to employ a creative streak to keep coming up with fresh treatments of often long-standing issues in their field. A specialist can also help counter the accusation against reporters of sensationalism; almost of revelling in misfortune. The suggestion that an injured elderly woman, say, is being exploited for the sake of a strong-selling headline can be countered by a follow-up that makes the title part of an attempt to seek a solution or at least an explanation. Sticking with a story also offers a sense of commitment; that the title is providing a long-term, sustained effort to provide necessary information for the public, not just succumbing to 'hit-and-run' journalism.

A specialist will often be expected to work across a growing range of formats and may span traditional departmental boundaries, say on a newspaper, between news and features. Most specialists enjoy the freedom of such a role but it does demand a mix of writing as well as news-gathering skills. Not every news reporter is a natural feature writer but a specialist may need to be.

A 21st century specialist is likely to be stretched even further – maintaining a related blog and/or being used as a pundit in pieces to camera for the title's website. Specialists are also faced with a huge volume of audience feedback. The potential for crowd sourcing is immense for specialists but filtering the wheat from the chaff is a time-consuming business.

Handling sources

Sources are particularly significant to the specialist. A wide network of contacts underpins productive output and increases the chance of securing a rapid response when news breaks and of generating scoops. In general:

- Consider all perspectives of the subject. Contacts are needed with all the key stakeholders – not just the overtly powerful but those on the receiving end of decision-making. So seek out sources at all levels within a hierarchy. Look for representative groups where one source can speak for many but be clear about who they do speak for.

- Understand the structures and powers at work. Once you know officially how a system operates find out how it works in practice. Who really calls the shots within an organisation?
- Look particularly hard for sources in under-represented areas whether it is hospital patients, unemployed youngsters or individual shareholders.
- Other independent operators are worth identifying too who might share at least elements of your quest to be non-partisan and to track the big picture in your field. Are there monitoring bodies in the sector such as inspectorates or statistics gatherers? Are there think tanks and academics researching in that area?

The list goes on and any good specialist will never stop making contacts so as to bring fresh voices to the mix. Mind-mapping is a useful technique for a specialist to employ to try to capture as many aspects of the specialism as possible within an overall structured approach. An example is given later in the chapter on page 189.

Because of the complexity and culture of secrecy discussed in the introduction, specialists need to develop trust with contacts. When taking on a specialism, do as much homework as possible before approaching key contacts. It is easier to develop rapport if you've at least done them the courtesy of conducting routine inquiries for yourself before attempting to tap into their expertise. Sources take something of a gamble every time they talk to the media so it helps if you can inspire some initial confidence. Some background understanding also allows a specialist to question what is being said. However grand your source, always subject their answers to logic, consistency and reality checks.

When building rapport with contacts, don't be tempted to ingratiate yourself by suggesting you are 'on their side'. The ideal relationship with a valued source is one of mutual respect. Your interests may coincide from time to time but you have different responsibilities and priorities. Don't base a relationship on pretence.

Attempts to suppress stories

When a reporter genuinely sympathises with or simply gets on well with a source, a conscious effort must be made to remain objective. A specialist can get too caught up in the source's agenda and forget their primary duty to their audience. Worse, a specialist can start to protect a source by editing out certain unfavourable angles or even dropping a critical story. Spin doctors and agents can also try to block coverage. The classic offer is to keep one story quiet in return for a bigger one. These are murky ethical areas. Most reporters would never say 'never' but it's a potentially slippery slope.

A journalist's presumption is to put information into the public domain. We need very good reasons to withhold it. There are some occasions where information is suppressed, sometimes for legal reasons, other times by voluntary arrangement, for example withholding information in kidnaps or where there are security implications. If in doubt, ask yourself how the audience would judge the decision to withhold information.

A source should be able to rely on reporting that is fair, honest and balanced. Aim to maintain dialogue even if the relationship is strained by reports that cast your source in a negative light.

Confidential sources

If specialists are genuinely getting under the skin of their subject, sources will start to confide in them. Sometimes sources will want to pass on information but not be prepared to go on the record. This has its uses but is a fraught area of news-gathering.

Never enter into a confidentiality agreement lightly because the ramifications can be enormous for reporter and source. This is not an area in which a journalist should ever be found wanting. Trust is an essential element for any successful journalist, particularly a specialist. The best are trusted without hesitation by audience, colleagues, editor and sources. But that trust is much easier lost than won.

Bear in mind the following points:[3]

1 Exercise extreme caution

Do this before giving any undertaking to protect the identity of a source. Once an assurance is given it has to be honoured and this may become more uncomfortable and costly than it first appears. The information has to be worth risking a career, and even going to jail, for. Enter into it with eyes wide open. Remember the Press Complaints Commission Editors' Code of Practice principle: 'Journalists have a moral obligation to protect confidential sources of information.'[4] (This is discussed further in Chapter 9.)

2 Be explicit

As soon as a source even hints at a degree of confidentiality, you must be clear about what exactly each of you is committing to and establish the ground rules at the beginning of an interview even where nothing momentous seems to be at stake. Be sure that the phrases 'off the record', 'in confidence' or 'don't quote me' mean the same to you as to your source. Even journalists don't agree on what these terms mean so it is very easy to get at cross-purposes with sources. The definitions have to be spelt out with each source.

3 Assess the source

- Are they who they say they are? Have a telephone number at least and establish that it works. A bricks and mortar address is better.
- What are their motives? It will be very difficult to defend your actions or theirs if the motive is money. Do not pay for their information if you want to rely on it in court. They could also be motivated by revenge against, say, a company that has sacked them which would also call their credibility into question. Payments may also be illegal.
- Are they in a position to know what they claim to know?
- Has what they say happened, happened? Those infamous kiss-and-tell tales involve questioning that pulls no punches about whether two people have had sex or not.
- Why do they need to be anonymous? Is their caution necessary?
- Would it be obvious that the information had come from them?

4 Critique the information

- What is the public interest in revealing the source's information? Does it have public interest value in legal and audience terms as well as being a story that will make you look good?
- What other ways might there be of accessing it? Sometimes information that appears to be confidential is actually available openly to a journalist who knows where to look, which the source might not. Also, a confidential source can often be shielded from the risk of exposure by using their information as a 'tip-off'; a steer on what questions to ask later of attributable sources so that the eventual story need make no reference to the existence of any confidential information. It may well be possible to frame the questions so as to give the subject no inkling that they are inspired by inside information.
- Is there physical as well as oral evidence? Is any documentation authentic? How would you go about establishing that it is? Is the information in it reliable?
- Is the information in a form that would lead easily to identification of the source? This may not be obvious but the informant may know. Think what will be required to protect their identity.

5 Question yourself

If the story seems too good to be true, it probably is. Take enormous care not to read what you want to read into information or images.

- What are your motives? Do you want to believe your source because you like what they are telling you? Don't allow your enthusiasm for a good story to blur your judgement. Play devil's advocate with yourself.
- What other explanations could there be?
- Are you being set up?
- What if the source, even if genuine, is just mistaken?
- What makes the story credible?
- Could the story ever be run or are there simply too many legal obstacles?

6 Finally

- Can you really protect the source's identity? Can your organisation? If the answer to either of those questions is no, you must not agree to try. Be clear that any confidentiality deal means you must not say who *isn't* your source. Ruling people out may allow the source to be identified by a process of elimination. If an organisation points the finger at the wrong person, you may be in an awkward position.
- Does the source realise what might happen next? Warn them of the possible outcomes of which they may not be aware. It is tempting not to in case it deters them from co-operating but it is the only fair way. A whistleblower may be taking a considerable risk themselves and might face dismissal or civil or criminal legal sanctions if you let them down.

The handling of confidential sources can be challenging for even the best-intentioned and well-briefed reporter. When the relationship breaks down it can have terrible consequences, as it did in 2002 in the case of Dr David Kelly, the weapons expert who was found dead, having apparently taken his own life after being revealed as the confidential source of a BBC story challenging the basis of the government's justification for attacking Iraq.

See 'Is there such a thing as investigative journalism?' in Thinking It Through at the end of this chapter.

remember

- Access to sources is crucial – develop the widest possible network of contacts and keep renewing it.
- Share your passion with the audience but don't become uncritical of any individual source or of general attitudes in your field.
- Use your expertise to capture complexity for your reader as simply and concisely as possible.
- Don't make promises you can't keep – especially to confidential sources.

CRIME AND COURT REPORTING

Courts

Another round of magistrates' courts closures is likely to reduce further one of the mainstays of news content. Local newspapers are less inclined to travel to a central court where many cases will be from outside their circulation area. This may, perversely, accelerate the trend for courts to be covered by specialists, particularly by agencies that can cover a court centre for multiple titles.

Newspapers vary enormously in the stress they place on court coverage. A few local titles may record every conviction in formatted lists; others include very little routine coverage. In between most titles pick and choose. In a small community, names mean a great deal even where the crime is minor. In big cities, the bar is a lot higher.

Very broadly the more serious the crime the greater the chances of the ensuing court case being covered. Some reporters will only ever be drafted in for the high-profile murder trials. Famous names in court will also fill the press benches as will an unusual story twist in a relatively minor case.

Court reporters are part of the tradition of papers of record but, like any journalist, their prime concern is to dig out the best stories. A court specialist has the edge over the one-off reporter partly because a large proportion of the court routine is not particularly newsworthy. Procedure is time-consuming, particularly at the lower, magistrates' court level, with adjournment after adjournment. A reporter could sit for hours in cases involving non-payment of fines, speeding and minor offences and struggle to find anything to warrant a full story. The skill is to find the tiny minority of cases that will engage readers. That is why court reporting is ripe territory for the specialist.

Court reporters learn to spot the exceptional – the animal cruelty case, the licensing application opposed by local residents or the local celebrity being slipped on to the list. They also develop the contacts who will point them in the right direction and they know their way around court sufficiently to ensure they can find all the necessary information on the case, which can be more difficult than it should be.

Court is a very particular arena for reporters, not just because of the various laws controlling media coverage but because behaviour is limited too. Court authorities – particularly judges – have the upper hand and assertive reporters have to know how to work the system both to get the story and to avoid falling foul of the law themselves. The stakes are raised in court coverage because the price paid for a mistake can be particularly high. An innocent man mistakenly labelled guilty is personally wronged but can also sue for defamation; including material barred by statute can lead to a fine or imprisonment and upsetting a judge can even see a reporter detained for contempt.

Some legal training is crucial; indeed many editors insist on it before allowing a reporter to cover court. For our purposes, the legal basics are covered in Chapter 9 so here we focus on basic court craft. For print journalists, the National Council for the Training of Journalists has a specialist court reporting module, linked to its set text, *McNae's Essential Law for Journalists* (see the Recommended Reading in Chapter 9).

Magistrates' courts

All but a handful of criminal cases in England and Wales start in the magistrates' court, which deals with 97 per cent of offences. The key players are:

- Magistrates – they are not professional lawyers although they have some specialist training. They sit in threes (with a few exceptions); one chairs each bench usually sitting in the middle and announces the outcome, etc.
- Legal adviser – magistrates require a legal professional to advise them on questions of law. The legal adviser reads charges to the defendant and takes the plea. Previously known as court clerk, the adviser keeps procedure in order.
- District judge – a one-person bench is likely to be a district judge with the expertise to sit alone. District judges can be productive for a reporter as they rattle through business. Unlike magistrates, they don't need to retire to take legal advice.

- Prosecution – the prosecuting solicitor is usually a representative of the Crown Prosecution Service (CPS). A helpful CPS prosecutor is a court reporter's dream. A prosecutor tends to stay in the same court all day with all the necessary files. Broadly it is in their interests to aid media reporting but they are under pressure. The appearance of a local authority, Environment Agency or other non-CPS prosecutor suggests something different and potentially newsworthy.
- Defence – at a magistrates' court local legal aid solicitors will be much in evidence and they will change from case to case. It is not necessarily in their interests to facilitate coverage, especially if their client is convicted. Get to know regulars, especially those who like to see their name in print.
- Defendant – the accused stands in the dock and those who have been held in custody before the hearing will be flanked by security guards.
- Witnesses – wait outside and are called as needed into the witness box.
- Ushers – a helpful usher will tell you where the newsiest cases are. Some will have a copy of the full court list, which includes details of charges. Ushers will also give you names of chairmen/women of each bench who makes announcements.
- Press – a press bench may be provided for reporters in the body of the court. The usher will point you to the spot in an unfamiliar court. This usually puts you closer to the action and makes officials aware that the media are present.
- Public – seating is provided for friends of defendants, victims and any others wanting to follow proceedings. Beware of making comments they may overhear.
- Probation officers and others with a professional interest in proceedings may also be in court. Generally they will sit on benches behind the solicitors to observe and/or answer questions. Most reports are provided in writing rather than in person.

Court reporters need to establish contacts with many of these sources for tip-offs on the newsiest cases and to fill gaps in information on the day. There are often lulls in court proceedings, particularly in magistrates' courts, so reporters can use the breaks to clarify details. Some old pros with excellent contacts manage to report on more than one case at a time and do it safely but it is not advisable for a relative beginner.

Crown courts

The crown court handles more serious cases and is more formal than magistrates' courts – very much as a court would be portrayed in the movies. The formality among the bewigged players can make it harder to access key people but it does make it easier to follow proceedings than at the 'messier' magistrates' level.

Key players are:

- the judge – what they say goes – do not risk being in contempt;
- the barrister (counsel) – appears for the prosecution;
- the barrister/solicitor – appears for the defence;
- the clerk – reads charges to the defendant;
- the ushers – again can be make or break, so cultivate them;
- the defendant – stands in the dock, and is likely to be brought up from custody so will have guards;
- witnesses – give evidence from a witness box close to judge and jury;
- the jury – has 12 members – do not report anything said in court in their absence.

It is best not to speak to jury members at all; in the toilet or anywhere. The law is very sensitive about any interference with the jury and it is contempt to report anything about their deliberations. Suspicion alone could cause the trial to collapse, so play safe.

Often a crown court reporter will be looking for a particular case that has been tracked through from the magistrates' court. A specialist will have sources to highlight emerging cases of interest. The backroom staff in court can be particularly helpful – security guards, victim support officers or tea room operators are vital contacts in the mix to ensure a good story isn't missed. If all else fails, a reporter can sit in on the most serious case or in a court where the usher is known to be helpful.

remember

- To be legally safe, court copy must be fair, accurate and contemporaneous. Fairness means balanced, giving both sides, even the mitigation where someone has pleaded guilty. Accuracy refers not just to correct details; an accurate report must not exaggerate or be ambiguous. Contemporaneous means the reports must be used in the first available edition so court copy needs to be submitted and published promptly.
- Double check the basics – be sure of the identity of the defendant including name, age and address; details of the charge, plea – guilty/not guilty; and in case of trial, the verdict.
- Know the outcome – these are many and varied. A defendant may be dealt with and sentenced, fined up to £5,000 by magistrates, jailed, given a suspended or community sentence and/or ordered to pay compensation and costs or may be acquitted. The case may be continuing with the defendant committed for trial, sent for trial, committed for sentence, or adjourned to a particular date and time with the defendant remanded on bail or in custody in the meantime.
- Behaviour – what officials, especially judges, say goes. Do not put yourself in contempt. Turn off mobile phones and be as unobtrusive as possible. Be respectful especially when it is necessary to challenge procedure. When the usher says stand, that includes you – notably when magistrates and judges enter and leave court. Seek permission if you hope to microblog from court.
- Know the law – be confident you can tell the best story that is legally safe. (See Chapter 9 including its Recommended Reading section.)
- Establish reliable sources of information – court lists, ushers, helpful prosecution/defence solicitors/counsel are all vital.

Crime

Reporting crime well is about a great deal more than making regular calls to the police. Crime and anti-social behaviour are issues of great concern to most readers and many say they feel powerless to do anything about it. A good crime specialist will pursue their concerns but also help them understand the myriad ways in which they could actually play a part.

Source for reporting crime

Crime reporters in some areas can still talk directly to a police control room and/or CID; others are limited to police press officers or even web updates. A daily newspaper would call every couple of hours to get updates on the latest individual incidents.

Police services are also obliged to make a great deal of statistical material available and this provides a rich seam of stories. Data-driven articles are now much easier to make engaging courtesy of graphics and mapping software, which can really help to highlight issues over patterns and trends in crime and crime fighting. The Freedom of Information Act is being used gradually to persuade police authorities routinely to place more information in the public domain and can be used effectively to chase up the recalcitrant services.

Grassroots organisations abound in this field, through formal Neighbourhood Watch schemes, the Crimestoppers tip-off line and Police and Community Teams (PACT). Many other agencies are also involved, sometimes through formal Community Safety Partnerships. Councils are major players but are joined by representatives from businesses, schools, health workers, churches and a host of voluntary organisations, particularly those working with the elderly.

Issues in reporting crime

The power structure within policing is a hot topic of debate with the coalition government introducing directly elected police supremos, which is likely to stir great controversy over the boundaries between politics and practical policing as it did in the riots of summer 2011.

The role of victims, particularly in categories such as domestic violence and people trafficking, is also much to the fore and there are plenty of potential source organisations working with them in more or less formal capacities. The coalition government appointed Louise Casey as a commissioner for victims and witnesses. Find out more at **http://www.justice.gov.uk**, a key source of information on the justice system in England and Wales.

Drug and alcohol abuse are major factors in this field too, so a crime specialist should be very well versed in debates over, for example, legalising drugs such as heroin. Patterns of re-offending are key too, pointing the specialist in the direction of the role of the judicial and penal system, which leads to another realm of sources, including ex-offenders and their representative bodies. Prisons are fascinating places and prison governors can be excellent sources as can the staff Prison Officers Association. Similarly there are story ideas galore in the expansion of community-based sentences, anti-graffiti projects or whatever.

Individual crimes are just the starting point to a whole world of story ideas and this is an area renowned for 'initiatives'. With so much in flux, this is a subject that provokes strong opinions, not always as well informed as they might be – which is where a good crime specialist can clean up!

PUTTING IT INTO PRACTICE

When a fragile elderly woman is attacked in her home, the photograph of her black eye and broken nose has a shock value used to highlight her plight and hopefully help to catch the culprit. But for a specialist – indeed any reporter worth their salt – the story does not end there.

A specialist crime reporter can explain how rare such an event is; look at the related pattern of crime statistics; write a background feature on how victims are supported through such an ordeal; follow the police investigation for a day, maybe. The options are limitless. Ideally that specialist tracks the case all the way – through to the conviction of the attacker and further follow-ups on sentencing policy, OAPs' home security and more.

Activity: Sketch out angles for three follow-up stories and identify a variety of sources, images and weblinks for each.

- Crime and community safety matter to most people. A crime reporter might also take on coverage of prisons and judicial changes such as sentencing policy.
- Regular calls to police control rooms and CID can provide news of the latest crimes but many police services now insist on journalists working through the press office.
- Monitor the work of key bodies such as the Crown Prosecution Service, the Association of Chief Police Officers and the Ministry of Justice.
- But don't let police, politicians and other establishment bodies drown out the voices of victims and other members of the public.

BUSINESS, POLITICS, ENVIRONMENT, HEALTH AND EDUCATION

Coverage by issue rather than geography is growing in popularity. Niche and business-to-business (B2B) magazines have always provided jobs for specialist journalists and targeted coverage for an enthusiastic readership. Business is a boom area on all text-based outlets as its audience is more willing to pay for information. Politics is ever present, although it needs to be approached imaginatively to appeal to a mainstream audience. In this section we also offer a few thoughts on some of the other common mainstays of specialist coverage – education, environment and health.

Business

One of the mantras for journalists at global financial agency Bloomberg is: follow the money. Bloomberg operates in every country with a stock exchange so many of its reporters are taking the message very literally by covering direct financial news of share prices, bond markets and the like. Its most lucrative customers are in the money business (its agency services to mainstream media are a secondary service). But even when its reporters are covering natural disasters, politics or sport, the focus is on the impact that news has on the markets. Why does it matter, money wise?

Such a strong financial focus deters some journalists but business reporting is where the jobs are. In an internet age of, currently, predominantly free content, providers of business news can still charge because the information is directly valuable to the audience. Being in the know is not an optional extra for city traders or financial gurus. The *Wall Street Journal* and the *Financial Times* are two print titles that successfully operate a pay wall – making a significant charge for content online.

Many a senior journalist or editor has benefited from spending some time in a business specialism, particularly in the broader reporting of industry, commerce and economics. The best journalists challenge the stereotype of business sections as pro-management ghettoes regurgitating company press releases. The business tag may conjure up images of bosses and banks but the specialism can encompass the whole world of work. Most readers of text-based editorial coverage are economically active or wanting to be, so a wider remit has potential to build audiences.

The old 'industrial correspondent' job title suffered too. It became all about strikes and broader industrial disputes and a specialist could just be caught up in the stalemate of tit-for-tat posturing of the bosses and workers. A conflict makes for an obvious story but here too a specialist should be digging deeper and moving beyond the 'us v them' rhetoric. A non-partisan specialist business reporter needs to challenge the assertions of both management and unions; and subject both to the most thorough reality check possible. A specialist doesn't sit in an ivory tower pontificating but is there seeing how many people go to work, how many trains are running or how many letters are delivered during a strike.

A good specialist doesn't lose interest once the strike or other crisis is over. A company may hit the headlines – say in a row over redundancies – but a specialist keeps in touch for more routine reports, on new products, new contracts, exports, key appointments and more. Tracking the fate of redundant workers can also generate strong copy. Some fascinating tales emerged from the experiences of staff who lost their jobs when Woolworths collapsed, for instance. Be imaginative and consider all those affected by any development.

PUTTING IT INTO PRACTICE

MindMaps are claimed by author Tony Buzan but they are one of several variants on the brainstorming theme. His are as useful as any and have software available to generate the diagrams. They are useful devices for capturing ideas and helping to provide structure to a stream of consciousness. They can also be very useful for a specialist building up a network of contacts and to help generate and shape story ideas.

If you don't take to MindMaps, try another way of logging your ideas. Some people use diagrams more akin to a family tree or are happy to make simple lists. A MindMap can be more dynamic and it's at least worth a try (see Weblinks at the end of this chapter).

Below is the beginning of a MindMap for a business specialist based on the players involved. A parallel sheet could be produced for issues and story ideas.

Activity: Generate your own MindMap(s) for a chosen specialism.

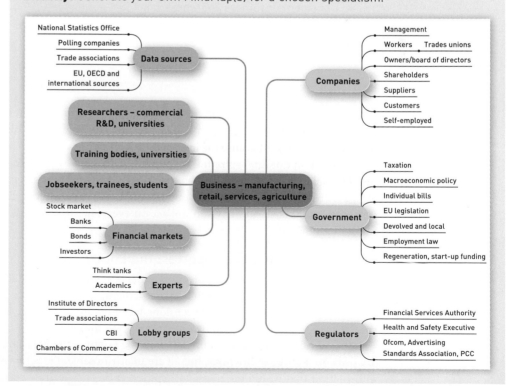

The ethics of business reporting has come under considerable scrutiny not only because of questions over the role of business journalists in the banking collapse but also due to previous concerns over share dealing. Two *Daily Mirror* journalists who ran the City Slickers column were sacked and then convicted in 2005 of insider dealing for profiting from tipping shares in their own newspaper.

The Press Complaints Commission Editors' Code of Practice states in clause 13 Financial Journalism:

(i) **Even where the law does not prohibit it, journalists must not use for their own profit financial information they receive in advance of its general publication, nor should they pass such information to others.**

(ii) **They must not write about shares or securities in whose performance they know that they or their close families have a significant financial interest without disclosing the interest to the editor or financial editor.**

(iii) **They must not buy or sell, either directly or through nominees or agents, shares or securities about which they have written recently or about which they intend to write in the near future.[5]**

Business journalists may also fall foul, as the City Slickers did, of the Financial Services Act and, like any specialists, need to check for legislation in the field which may restrict journalists as well as others working within it.

remember

- Do your research on business structures, key players and at least the basics of the money markets.
- Be professional, not amateur – your sources will expect it.
- Develop a dynamic network across the whole world of work.
- Consider consumers and workers not just companies.

Politics

Political reporting in the UK is very dominated by Westminster but there is much more to it than that, especially on regional titles that are likely to focus on devolved tiers of government, local government and even parish councils. It's all politics.

Politics can be a dirty word in this country. Readership surveys suggest the tag is a turn-off for the audience. Yet it shouldn't be. The public may not be riveted by the petty politicking all too often featured by reporters, and the political process per se can be fairly dull, but the outcomes are crucial and have an impact on everyone. It takes a good political reporter to make that obvious.

Source for the politics reporter: the Lobby

A major feature of political reporting nationally is the Lobby system that grants privileged access to correspondents accredited by Parliament, technically by its Sergeant at Arms. The Lobby is a classic example of the tensions faced by any specialist. Key sources are offering special access but at a price. In this case the price is anonymity.

Lobby reporters are allowed literally into the Lobby – the MPs' areas of Parliament – and are privy to a range of briefings, but all are unattributable. Does this allow for a freer flow of information that would otherwise be kept secret or does it draw correspondents into a cosy club and open them up to manipulation from sources who cannot be held accountable for what they pass on? The latter is probably easier to argue but there is an element of truth in both.

Senior parliamentary journalists on newspapers and in tv and radio are recommended for membership of the Lobby by their employers. Lobby journalists are also invited to 10 Downing Street for regular briefings at which ministers and the prime minister's press secretary will seek to give journalists an 'off-the-record' spin on the day's main political events. The reliance on this system is arguably reduced by an increase in on-the-record and televised government briefings, for example, but it remains controversial.

Issues for the politics reporter

Another interesting debate continues over how confrontational political journalists should be with their sources. Just as overly dominant 'big name' chat show hosts can overshadow their guests, so interviewers with a reputation for toughness may just force an interviewee on to their guard to such an extent that we reach a stalemate, producing little of value for the audience. These dangers are discussed in detail when applied to the political sphere in John Lloyd's (2004) *What the media are doing to our politics*. Others believe the bigger problem is that the media are too supine. For a flavour of that argument try Radio Four veteran John Humphrys's (2000) *Devil's Advocate*.

Political coverage is also criticised for focusing too much on personality at the expense of policy; here as in many areas we seem to be moving inexorably into the cult of personality.

Political reporters will also need some expertise in media law related to their field, most notably regarding the coverage of elections (see Recommended Reading in Chapter 9).

remember

- Cultivate contacts across the political spectrum.
- Do not reveal your own political views if your job is to report objectively.
- Characters can engage the audience but don't allow personalities to squeeze out all policy analysis and impact.
- Don't be too caught up in the politicians' world. Politics reporters can spend too much time in Parliament or City Hall.
- Politics is people – track the impact of proposals in the real world.

Education

Education is a great common denominator, particularly for publications with a strong family readership, notably local newspapers.

Sources for an education specialist

Again a specialist must be sure to build a network of contacts in all relevant sectors. Working through by age can help here from nurseries, through school to further education, higher education and lifelong learning. A good education specialist will be keeping tabs on it all.

Within any one school there will be a head, teaching and other staff; the pupils and parents; the board of governors; the Parent Teacher Association; teaching unions; probably an education authority; Ofsted and other inspectors.

In terms of learning about the power structures of education, set texts such as the NCTJ-recommended *Essential Public Affairs for Journalists* (Morrison, 2011) are a must and will also identify plenty of potential sources.

Issues for an education specialist

Even readers without children have close links, if only from personal experience, to education provision. Education also absorbs a great deal of public spending. Readers remember exam results day, school dinners and their favourite teacher. That familiarity bodes well for the education specialist who can tap into shared and changing experiences across generations.

Within any school there are academic issues of curriculum and achievement. There are physical issues over the building and always funding challenges to update provision, kit and activities. There is huge story potential too in the school's relationship with the community – facilities such as sports centres may be shared; the pupils probably go out volunteering and undertake work experience; their lunch break behaviour may be an issue; and their extra-curricular activities will generate a host of wonderful stories of individual and group endeavour.

Controversies abound in this specialism with funding, social mobility, the public/private split and faith schooling likely to dominate in coming years. The coalition government's free schools policy has created a great deal of coverage, for instance, as has its policy on university tuition fees.

Environment

Environment is clearly a growth area and very much a specialism of the 21st century.

Sources for the environment specialist

Global and local are interwoven in environmental issues more than most. An environment specialist could be dealing with anything from a local Brownie litter pick-up to world climate change talks and the future of the planet as we know it. So the network of sources has to reflect this, looking at key players at all levels. Thankfully many global players, such as Friends of the Earth, operate locally too, which provides journalists with plenty of scope to bring home messages to particular audiences.

Environmental concerns have a strong online profile and this is an area where micro-blogging has also been much used, for instance to co-ordinate environmental protest. Monitoring social media and the blogosphere is likely to be particularly fruitful for an environmental specialist, although it is something all specialists should be doing. A good environment specialist will also become expert on the special provisions of the Environmental Information Regulations 2004, which provide a parallel regime to the more general Freedom of Information Act (see Chapter 2).

Environment is seen to have a 'young' audience profile so is particularly strong in national newspapers such as the *Independent* and *Guardian* that target a more youthful, radical reader-ship. A good environment specialist will reflect this by making a conscious effort to tap into younger and non-establishment sources.

Issues for the environment specialist

The dominant issue of climate change is truly 'glocal', from the global havoc-inducing move-ments of the jet stream to the local kerbside compost collection; from international treaties on carbon emissions to individual decisions to adopt low-energy lightbulbs. This presents a fascinating challenge for a journalist who enjoys the combination of grassroots activity and global concerns; of helping ordinary people conjure with global warming concepts of immense complexity. To make sense of carbon trading requires sound financial knowledge; to report on carbon capture tests scientific understanding. A good environment specialist will have done their homework and take it all in their stride.

Environment specialists may well, as specialists do, consequently find themselves treading on the toes of other specialists focused on business, politics or science as companies re-engineer themselves to cut emissions, subsidies are granted to renewable energy or researchers discover new biofuels. In print an editor may have to decide to which section the story belongs; online multiple tags can be used to ensure the story appears in all relevant sections. Either way a decision may be required on which specialist covers the story in the first place.

As world leaders struggle to find a successor agreement to the Kyoto protocol, the polar ice caps melt and deserts continue to advance, no environment specialist should be short of inspiration.

Health

Health is a fascinating and massive specialism, spanning the most sensitive and personal issues through to the cutting-edge nano technology of emerging medicines.

Sources for the health specialist

The NHS is the UK's largest employer offering a hugely diverse range of services. Decision-making structures tend to be complex. It can be difficult to establish exactly who is responsible for what and the system seems to be in a permanent state of flux. The coalition government is heralding further change with more control, particularly commissioning/purchasing power, being put in the hands of GPs. A good specialist will not only want to know where responsibility for spending public money lies but also how those people exercising power will be held to account.

Health is very much affected by devolution of powers to Scotland, Wales and Northern Ireland that now have their own 'versions' of the NHS. In Scotland, for instance, personal care is free. In Wales prescriptions are free. The media generally have been very slow to catch up with these changes. Most health stories in our London-dominated national media are actually reporting on England alone. At best, they may acknowledge that fact but very rarely will they embrace the contrasting situation in Wales, Scotland or Northern Ireland. Technically this should create huge potential for health specialists outside England but they arguably have yet to exploit it fully.

Issues for the health specialist

This is a massive area of public interest. The NHS alone generates stories galore, be it about waiting lists, availability of medicines, league tables of surgical outcomes or spending at every level. But there is an even richer seam to be tapped outside the institutionally focused coverage. Well-being and healthy lifestyle issues continue to spawn magazine launches and drive enormous online audiences. Diet, drug and alcohol abuse, smoking and fitness are massively popular topics. Alternative medicine is also huge.

One final note of advice. Health specialists have to be suitably inscrutable when it comes to the nitty gritty aspects of their topic. If you can persuade laddish shipyard workers to talk perceptively about why they don't check their testicles for signs of cancer, this could be the job for you.

remember

- Build your networks to involve all key stakeholders.
- Read up on the power structures in your field.
- Remember health in particular accounts for a large slice of public spending.
- Establish the time cycles of your specialism – log the diary dates of union conferences; annual reports; public consultation; budget setting and, for any education specialist, the school holiday weeks.
- Use digital platforms galore to track developments and identify new voices.

SPORT, CELEBRITY AND THE ARTS

Check any news website ranking of hits and sport and celebrity are likely to be right up there – along with the quirky animal stories. Sport and celebrity are both huge drivers of audience figures and, partly because of that, the challenges of covering them have a lot in common. Celebrities loom large in arts coverage too but a good arts specialist will not be overly reliant on the already famous.

Sport and celebrity are competitive areas; they abound in speculation, often completely unattributed, and they are dominated by big names concerned with maintaining a valuable public image and increasingly restricting media access. The more controlling they are, the harder it is even for a specialist to know what is really going on.

Sports clubs and their top players – particularly in football which dominates UK sports coverage – are commercial brands in their own right and want to control their media portrayal. Celebrities are the same, whether movie stars, musicians or the ubiquitous ranks of faces famous for being famous, most likely in a reality TV show.

Whatever the rights and wrongs of a sport and celebrity obsessed culture, we are where we are, which is seeking to satisfy a seemingly insatiable appetite for coverage in two categories where the going is getting increasingly tough for the specialist reporter.

(See 'Spot the fake' in Thinking It Through at the end of this chapter.)

Sport

Sport probably attracts more trainee journalists into the business than any other single specialism. For some it's a poor substitute for a professional sports career but most have a genuine desire to share their obsession with others. It's a very crowded market, especially now every fan, every sports club and every sports personality can tweet, blog and otherwise speak for themselves. A sports specialist has to keep one step ahead – being more up-to-date, knowing more, analysing more, seeing the big picture, provoking debate.

While for many specialists news and comment are still relatively rigorously separated, that division barely exists any more in sport. A huge proportion of coverage – not just match reports – is highly opinionated, even biased and encouraged to be so. All opinion should be well-informed and well-argued. To comment confidently and safely a sports specialist needs a strong grasp of media law. Abuse is common in sport and a specialist needs to know how to avoid the risk of a libel writ. Journalists making a living from punditry are much more likely to be sued than the casual blogger (although they are not immune).

A strong network of contacts will help to beat the competition. Longevity helps as both reporters and players move up the pecking order through a career. Premiership footballers are very picky about who they talk to but a reporter who has covered a player since schoolboy competitions is in with a chance. A good specialist will also look for the untapped areas of their field as well as trying to find a new approach to the routine. They will be able to break out of the highly formulaic weekly cycle that besets particularly football reporting. Not for them the round of team selection, analysis of opposition, manager's fighting talk, match report, post-mortem, injuries and availability doubts, team selection ad infinitum.

Some specialists make full use of their entry-level experience as a general reporter using their extra news-gathering skills to avoid falling into such ruts. The habit-forming nature of sport and tribal loyalties mean some sports fans will soak up repetitive coverage regardless but that shouldn't be a reason to become complacent.

It is also important to remember that there is more to sport than professional football: there is amateur and junior football, which is well worth covering particularly at local level.

There are sports other than football and even sports that are not team games. (This is one instance where stating the obvious can be justified.) A good sports specialist can move beyond soccer. The natural drama of sport should allow for more coverage of minority sports. Women play and follow sport too, albeit not in the same proportions as men but to a greater extent than you would realise from mainstream sports coverage.

PUTTING IT INTO PRACTICE

Commercial pressures and the general tensions of top flight football habitually create tensions between clubs and the media, particularly the local newspaper which will be pushing for saturation coverage, day in day out.

Sometimes clubs want to limit outside coverage for purely financial reasons. They want to strike an exclusive deal or they want to try to make money from media themselves with a TV station, sales of player photographs or whatever. The media becomes a competitor and the club decides it wants to cash in for itself.

Other rows are far more personal, usually triggered by a manager objecting to some coverage or accusing a particular title of being biased in general.

Kevin Keegan fell out with newspapers when he managed Newcastle, Man Utd's Alex Ferguson infamously refused to speak to the BBC for years, and in 2010 it was Southampton's turn to ban all press photographers from its games during the annual spat over coverage rights.

As with celebrities, clubs and their high-profile players want to control how their activity is portrayed. They want to be in the editor's chair for themselves.

Activity: Check out the background of these disputes – **http://www. newsmediacoalition.org** and **http://mu.tv.manutd.com** would be good starting points. Stage a debate between an editor and a chairman of a football club. The editor should put the argument to Manchester United for free access for all journalists. Then take the role of Manchester United putting the case against.

Negotiating access is difficult territory for a specialist especially in sport where clubs expect loyalty from their regular correspondents. It can be rare to reach the goal of mutual respect whereby the club accepts that even a best mate will not always tell you what you want to hear, and wouldn't be a true friend if they did.

Doing deals in secret is always questionable. The readers should know if any compromises have been made – if an interview is granted from a player only if the accompanying picture shows him wearing an endorsed product, for example. If you wouldn't want the readers to know, perhaps it's the wrong deal to make. At very least the arrangement should be spelled out to readers.

Celebrity

This specialism soaks up a lot of talent. While some may question its value, when it comes to giving the audience what they want there is no arguing with the traffic data for both websites and print titles. A celebrity specialist needs to be just as good at the job as any other. Indeed being able to stand out in such a crowded market is a challenge.

It is a gossipy world, tongues may be loosened by the conviviality of many showbiz occasions and there is an acceptance of unattributed material which can be seen to make the celebrity specialist's job easier. But genuine scoops are likely to require the best investigative skills and contacts in the business.

Interviewing celebrities

Prime targets are hard to crack. Bigger names are shielded by agents and PR firms so access is particularly difficult and where an interview is granted it may be reined in by conditions. Limited time is one of the greatest challenges even if a 'name' is relatively forthcoming. It's very difficult to come up with anything meaningful in five minutes so a celebrity specialist has to be particularly well-prepared to make the most of every question.

Every specialist should prepare thoroughly for an interview. There is no point wasting time asking for information that is readily available in the archive. A thorough online search may also point to gaps in previous statements triggering potentially interesting questions.

Celebrities can be awkward about – or just bored by – being repeatedly asked the same questions. David Randall (2007) is particularly useful here in *The Universal Journalist* chapter on Questioning (great title). For celebrities he recommends questions to tease out feelings and personal experiences in the hope of eliciting something new (see Recommended Reading at the end of this chapter).

Others try the ambush technique – asking an entirely unexpected or perhaps impertinent question – in an attempt to wrong-foot the over-prepared interviewee. With luck the mask slips, if only briefly. But this is a high-risk strategy which can offend and lead to early termination of an already brief encounter. Jeremy Paxman infamously asked Blair in an interview about the invasion of Iraq, whether Blair and President Bush prayed together. It clearly ruffled the then Prime Minister but whether it led to a more illuminating interview is open for debate.

Well-known profile writer Lynn 'Demon' Barber is a celebrity interviewer worth tracking. She is renowned for a very direct approach, blunt without being rude, and her technique has yielded many perceptive pieces. She has written for a wide variety of publications, after starting out on *Penthouse* magazine, and some of her collected works can be found in print (see Recommended Reading at the end of this chapter).

remember

- You need to work hard to penetrate the PR shield.
- Sources – and their agents – will fight to protect their PR image.
- Imagination is at a premium to come up with something different.
- Work, work, work those sources.
- Specialisms will overlap. Fight your corner but also consider collaboration.
- Push for on-the-record dealing wherever possible.
- Make access deals transparent.

Arts reporting – music, film, drama, visual arts

Just as celebrity journalists can be fawning, so arts reporters can get carried away by their own personal passions. Arts coverage can easily be driven by the ego of artist or reporter rather than the needs of the reader. Hero worship can blind a reporter to reality, so beware.

Arts specialists are rightly expected to write with enthusiasm, a certain style and creativity but the reports should never be seen primarily as an opportunity to show off. A reporter has to offer the reader something of value – some information or insight – however beautifully written the article is.

Arts coverage tends to be associated with reviewing, which is discussed more fully later in this chapter, but the range is much more varied, including notably profiles, previews and listings. Compiling a user-friendly what's on guide is just as valuable, albeit not as glamorous, as penning perceptive thoughts on a star-studded première.

Having an audience in mind does actually help. An opera preview for a local paper would need to be accessible to the general reader as well as enthusiasts. Previewing the same production for a specialist publication or website such as *Opera* magazine might have a different focus and could comfortably use the language of the aficionado.

For most titles, the aim is to break down the mystique of many art forms not build it up. Arts specialists vary enormously but their passion is usually directed at extending the audience for the arts. They are generally trying to broaden appeal and accessibility not just preach to the converted. Pretentious arts coverage can erect even more barriers to participation. Journalists who want to break them down need to think carefully about how they pitch coverage to their audience while at the same time not patronising them.

So profiles, not just of big names, can draw an audience in. Previews are also particularly important in terms of making potential participants aware of up-coming opportunities. Most venues and art forms have a core audience who may deal direct via a website or membership club; but the arts specialist has the chance to tap into new audiences and open up possibilities for readers. If, courtesy of your coverage, they have a good time then their investment in your publication or website will have been worth it.

If you are serving a local community, ensure amateurs aren't squeezed out entirely by big name one-night stands. Often the local talent relies on the local paper – it may be its only platform. Emerging artists may be taking full advantage of social media but they can easily lose out to the PR-backed big names. Readers like to support local talent and chart their progress. Identify the leading lights – best new bands, amateur theatre companies, best school music, champions at local festivals, youngsters winning scholarships, places on National Youth Theatre programmes etc. Keep tabs too on social media to see what is out there on Facebook, micro-blogs and more. Who is creating a buzz? Who has contracts or tours in the pipeline?

Being an arts specialist gives you plenty of opportunity to celebrate success. A lot of arts coverage is very positive and identifying new/young talent is very rewarding. Here are a few dos and donts for the arts specialist:

- Don't be dazzled by big marketing campaigns. You need to cultivate press officers and publicity specialists, but commercial interests are at play so don't let them determine your priorities. Focus on what is most interesting and useful for readers.
- Don't prioritise your own favourite artists and genres within the overall remit of your publication. Be guided by your audience's enthusiasms more than your own. This is particularly important in the arts where journalists are drawn to the opportunity to work in an environment they love.
- Don't forget community and family events such as matinees for retired people or school trips if you are writing for a general audience.
- Don't forget cost – it's easily done when your tickets are always free. However, perhaps perversely, psychologists reckon that someone who has paid for something, although clearly wanting value for money, is inclined to enjoy themselves and give the event more of a chance than the jaundiced hack in the free seat in front. It can cut both ways. A reviewer can be more demanding than a paying customer.
- Do consider sprinkling some free activities into the mix of your arts coverage.
- Don't forget participation is big too – workshops need a profile not just performances/exhibitions and there is a strong arts dimension to lifelong learning provision.

- Don't forget the money more generally – funding of the arts is a contentious issue, particularly where public money is involved. Story potential is considerable. Think of the coverage generated by Arts Council cuts and the axing of the British Film Council. Try to work out, for example, how much Lady Gaga earns from her tours.

A reporter with an enthusiasm for the arts may land a specialist job from the outset with a magazine, newspaper or website but many will develop their expertise more gradually. Local newspapers in particular may well expect journalists to demonstrate their versatility by contributing the occasional review alongside their reporting. This can be an enjoyable creative outlet to contrast with hard news reporting but, for some, it is a daunting task.

In arts, as in any specialism, you begin by becoming the instant expert, mugging up on as much background as possible on artist, genre, etc. When thrown in at the deep end of a specialism, a journalist must also adopt the standard approach: I may not know the answer but I know someone who does. If expected to cover an art exhibition, ask to visit in advance while it is being hung, interview the artist and, often more usefully, the curator. If all else fails, fall back on the catalogue and other viewers. Every specialist has to start somewhere and even those from a more niche background have gaps in their knowledge and experience. There is always something new to learn.

remember

- Approach any arts genre with enthusiasm and an open mind.
- Do your research.
- Write for your audience – respond to their priorities and enthusiasms not those of PR agents or just your own.

COLUMNISTS, CRITICS AND COMMENTATORS

Columnists

Ask many aspiring journalists where they want to be in five years and they will say: 'I want to have my own column.' Is that good or bad? Journalists tend to benefit from a healthy ego – certainly it helps to have enough self-belief to weather the storms of grumpy sources and their gatekeepers, your editor and audience. Every journalist loves a byline and the opportunity to blog plays straight into that instinct. But ego alone is not enough.

Those same aspiring journalists often have no idea what their column will be about, which triggers this cautionary advice from the columnist Matthew Arnold: 'Have something to say and say it as clearly as you can.'

The best columnists do write sublimely but that doesn't mean their work should be a triumph of style over substance. Only an exceptional columnist can get away with writing about nothing very much: the occasional observation on the vagaries of life in general and witty remark. Even fewer are able to sustain it for long.

Most benefit hugely from having a definite topic – an area of expertise to draw on which allows them to add real value for the audience. A good columnist will investigate the topic before airing their ideas in public. The chances of that happening are greater if we actually reject the idea of columnist as a specialism in its own right. Rather it is a format which a specialist might well adopt to explore a topic in greater depth; to express ideas and arguments triggered by coverage of news events. For an example, read Roy Greenslade's media blog on Guardian Online (**http://www.guardian.co.uk/media/greenslade**).

However, comment is a growth area as many titles, particularly upmarket newspapers, veer away from breaking news to analysis. Heavy marketing of named columnists suggests they are driving readership and that the audience develops a loyalty to a particular pundit who is able to get under the skin of the soundbites on which so much online and broadcast news relies.

See Columnists: The cult of personality in Thinking It Through at the end of this chapter.

Critics

Everyone's a critic – so much so that it's a quip used a great deal online particularly by a leading film review site that takes feedback from movie fans around the world (see Weblinks at the end of this chapter). It is a classic example of readers doing it for themselves and relying on collective wisdom rather than the expertise of a single critic, to assess anything and everything from holidays, to gadgets, to websites.

Some pundits reckon the journalist as critic is an endangered species but, for now, the different approaches seem to be co-existing quite happily. Individual expert critics still command huge followings be it reviewing plays, meals or new cars. Charlie Brooker's television commentaries in the *Guardian* were so popular he got his own TV show; Julie Burchill made her name as a music critic and A.A. Gill is a legendarily caustic television and restaurant reviewer for the *Sunday Times*.

Maybe the contributions will be polarised, with media putting more value on the true specialist reviewer rather than the pool reporter drafted in to do the best they can as a generalist. A general reporter can be marginally better at communicating reactions than most citizen reviewers but a strong specialist can gain a real edge with readers by bringing expert, non-partisan analysis and comparisons to bear.

Many journalists aspire to be critics and most will be involved in reviewing something along the way whether a band, a range of mince pies or a yacht. The more background preparation you can do beforehand and the more imaginative you can be with your responses the better, but remember your role is to help the reader.

It should go without saying that commercial considerations should never enter into your assessment. If they do, any copy should be appropriately labelled as an advertising promotion. When an audience sees anything pitched as editorial they have the right to assume it is a genuine unbiased account. For guidance, consult the Advertising Standards Authority guidelines at **http://asa.org.uk**.

PUTTING IT INTO PRACTICE

When working as a critic:

- Put yourself in the shoes of your readers. For performance-based reviews, this means allowing yourself to be emotionally engaged. The danger of being a professional critic is being too much of an observer rather than a participant. That can cause you to miss out on the real experience of the event. The dialogue going on in your head throughout can be distracting because you are judging as you go, ready to write a review as soon as you leave. Remember an insightful response, particularly to a live event, is emotional as well as intellectual.
- Keep watching/monitoring the audience for their reaction as well as your own. A small audience can indicate poor marketing or a clash of dates rather than a poor performance but an unresponsive audience is a warning sign.

▶ **PUTTING IT INTO PRACTICE**

- Don't try to compare apples and pears. Amateur and professional offerings are of a different standard. Audiences have different expectations – a review needs to gauge whether those expectations were met, not slag something off for not being what it never set out to be. Panto isn't Pinter. A Cohen brothers film is not a Farrelly brothers film.
- Experience is valuable because it means you can make comparisons, for yourself and for the reader. For example, if you liked *A River Runs Through It*, you'll like *Cold Mountain*.
- Reviews can be a hook for a broader discussion. TV review columns are often in that category, particularly a soap opera where so many elements are already familiar. Story lines are more likely to be assessed than performances. What did it have to say? What did it reveal/challenge?
- Paint the word picture. Work hard to share the imagery and atmosphere, with enough detail to bring it alive. Help the reader to see what you saw.
- Be opinionated but back it up with enough evidence so readers can judge for themselves.
- Don't alienate your readers. If you didn't appreciate an arts event or a meal, criticise the artist/performance/chef, not other more enthusiastic consumers.
- Find your own voice.

Activity: Write a 250-word review of the most recent film you saw. Give a star rating out of five. Be opinionated but make every word count so the reader can make an assessment too. (Review a meal, a gadget, or a band if preferred but you have to have experienced it first hand.)

So why do people read a review? At one level, it is a report of the event, a means of sharing an experience both with those who were present and those who missed it. A review captures the moment but it also provides a post-mortem. A positive review might prompt readers to see the show for themselves; it informs audience choice. But remember it is their choice. Your opinion is only useful insofar as it helps them form their own. They aren't intrinsically interested in whether the reviewer had a good time. They want to know: Is this for me? The same applies to restaurant reviews or product tests. You are guiding audience choice, not making it for them.

A review is not an opportunity to parade your personal enthusiasms and prejudices. If a stand-up comedy show has the rest of the audience weeping with laughter but leaves you cold, don't just pan it. Try to identify the nature of the comedy and why there are such different reactions to it. You can be honest about your own response but give an example of a gag – share enough of the experience for readers to decide for themselves.

Strong opinions help to make a review a good read but it is easy to be scathing. Some 'bad' reviews demonstrate a reviewer's ignorance rather than the standard of the work. How does it measure up to the standards expected? Find out enough to judge confidently and have evidence to back up your assessment. That serves the reader best but it is also a requirement of the law. A critical review has to be the honestly held opinion of the reviewer, based on fact. So never review something you haven't seen for yourself. Reviewing is far less of a free for all than many young journalists think so do check out the Fair comment section in Chapter 9 before venting your spleen. (See also the earlier section on Arts reporting in this chapter.)

Comment

A newspaper's own comment column is part of its ethos – it reveals its soul. David Randall in *The Universal Journalist* likens the absence of an opinion column in a newspaper to undergoing a 'personality bypass'.[6] This is where the newspaper speaks.

Editors still refer to it as the leader. It usually appears under a copy of the title's masthead and whoever writes it – a specialist team, an individual reporter or the editor – it is the voice of the newspaper and it is traditionally anonymous. There is no 'I' in leader. The line taken will be decided by the editor and/or key editorial team in keeping with the overall position of the paper.

Whereas reporting is neutral, leaders are comment and readers benefit from a clear distinction between the two. The purpose of the leader is in part to establish what the newspaper stands for. It is a key part of an editor's role in establishing core values. Our UK national newspapers tend to be broadly partisan, sometimes supporting a particular political party or at least broadly of the left or the right. A paper without political allegiance still has values, particularly in championing openness, holding the powers-that-be accountable, challenging racism or whatever. These are reflected in the stances taken over time.

Leaders can be used to:

- create a climate of opinion – challenge received wisdom;
- stimulate thinking – provide insights to contribute to enlightened public opinion;
- provide arguments – offer cogent points for discussion by readers; create a framework for debate, define the issue, what the implications are, what needs to be taken into account, especially voices/interests not being heard;
- put events in context – make connections, relate to history, analyse;
- set an agenda – raise issues;
- establish priorities for a community – highlight hidden aspects;
- campaign – lobby for an area, call for action;
- take a line – leaders nearly always take sides on an issue, more or less emphatically.

The balance between these purposes varies. Campaigning leaders are crusading, occasionally denouncing behaviours or beliefs such as racism; others focus more on general discussion. Some can be tub thumping and more like a case for the prosecution than an unbiased summary of arguments on all sides.

Even a very broad debate needs a conclusion. Leaders are not just about pursuing an academic-style argument; they are not just the logical conclusion of a train of thought. Leaders move the issue on. There needs to be an upshot, even if it just that the issue needs more thought. A leader writer examines the implications of any conclusion – what action should be taken. The editor has to be comfortable with the line taken and stand by whatever is written but the leader is the voice of the newspaper not an individual's personal hobby horse.

A good leader is well-informed and thoroughly researched, like any specialist writing. Editors have access to a unique mix of social/political contacts/information from the broadest spectrum of the community. A good leader writer exploits the paper's vantage point on society to offer special insights for readers. They are like a super-specialist – drawing on the expertise of the whole editorial team to make the connections, piece snippets together and realise the significance of an event or decision which might otherwise go unnoticed.

Topics are driven by what matters most to that title's readers/community. Sometimes the news of the day will touch on a core value or raise issues that cry out to be addressed, such as submarine building in Barrow for the local newspaper or access to information for any title.

A simple structure for a leader would be:

- premise;
- argument – pros and cons – putting one side and/or knocking down other;
- context;
- conclusion;
- **consequences of that conclusion.**

remember

- Have something to say and say it simply – with style but not without substance.
- Separate comment from news so that readers clearly know the difference.
- Be honest.
- Be well-informed.
- Help the readers to judge for themselves.

CHAPTER SUMMARY

Specialisms are a popular option for journalists and can provide marvellous opportunities to combine personal passions and expert knowledge with the intrinsic tensions and challenges of a media career. But that is not an excuse for self-indulgence. It is a fantastic privilege to meet top musicians or powerful politicians – all the main movers and shakers in your field – and it is a privilege that should not be abused. The purpose of undertaking a specialism is to improve the offering to the audience. Readers are your priority – not keeping your sources sweet or yourself entertained.

That said, specialisms do offer an opportunity for a reporter to work regularly off-diary; to generate their own stories, to dig that bit deeper and to work in the best traditions of civic journalism. The potential to break important scoops is immensely satisfying as is the ability to follow through by placing those scoops in context. A specialist sticks with the story and embraces the audience reaction to it.

Remember that as a specialist you should:

- Be worthy of your title – do your homework.
- Familiarise yourself with the issues and power structures of your chosen field.
- Develop an evolving network of contacts making full use of online tools.
- Be deserving of the trust of your sources, editor and audience.
- Don't get sucked into a cosy, protective relationship with your sources.
- Seek out the unheard voices and untold stories.
- Use your imagination.

THINKING IT THROUGH

Is there such a thing as investigative journalism?

This could be answered 'no' by respected hacks bemoaning the demise of so many investigative teams but the challenge here is intended to question the value of considering 'investigative' journalism as a separate category.

Surely all journalism is investigative or at least it should be. If a journalist does not cross-check, chase gaps in information and subject it to a reality check, surely the output does not merit the tag of 'journalism'. It is rightly dismissed as what Nick Davies (2008) in *Flat Earth News* dubbed 'churnalism' – the unquestioning parroting of press releases.

> ## ● THINKING IT THROUGH

Access the manifesto of the US Committee of Concerned Journalists (**www. concernedjournalists.org**). Point 3 states: Its [journalism's] essence is a discipline of verification.

Investigative journalism is in some ways distinctive – it suggests a deeper probing than usual, a gradual build-up of a detailed picture and perhaps undercover work to unearth scandals. The *Sunday Times* Insight team and the World in Action current affairs programme were recognisably 'investigative' when compared with day-to-day reporting. And that intensity of scrutiny is vital in a democratic society. An advantage of recognising its special qualities and demands is that conscious effort must be made to devote resources to it. Reporters, even specialists, are inevitably caught up in a degree of routine 'diary' work. Traditionally an investigative team would be relieved of those responsibilities so they could concentrate on their target areas.

But holding investigative journalism up as some Holy Grail – as something we used to be good at but can no longer afford – risks making many journalists defeatist. It suggests that only investigative journalists can manage a thorough job; that ordinary journalists cannot be expected to question and look beyond the obvious. Yes, resources are tight but no-one who ever worked in the business ever thought they were sufficient. There is never enough time to follow up every conceivable angle of a story but pursuing some is better than not even trying because you are not an 'investigative' reporter.

Investigative reporting has huge kudos and can involve amazing achievements. Advances in computer-assisted reporting have thrown up great potential in data analysis. The scoop over extraordinary rendition of terror suspects by the US emerged from meticulous analysis of flight records. *Private Eye* unearths many of its scandals courtesy of a forensic accountant turned journalist. Technology can't save journalists all the hard slog but it does make a whole range of investigations possible. Check out the Centre for Investigative Journalism (**www.tcij.org**) if you want to know more.

Every reporter can be networked enough to make a difference and need not wait for an 'investigative' label to dig deeper and raise the day-to-day standards of journalism.

Follow up the reading in the recommended list and look for examples in current media that might be labelled 'investigative'.

Ask yourself: What does it mean to be an investigative reporter?

Are obituaries a dying art?

Obituaries are a strange quirk mainly of upmarket UK newspapers. The 21st century challenger could be seen as the online bereavement sites or tribute pages on social networking sites such as Facebook but the formal obituary remains a fascinating format in its own right.

Where a news story reports a death and may include some quotes in tribute, an obituary creates a mini-biography of the deceased to mark their passing. Obituaries record a contribution to a nation or community of someone who made a mark, either famously or behind the scenes. Their subjects tend to be well-known but there are many low-profile significant people – inventors spring to mind – who may have had a major impact on our lives without being a household name.

There is a perversity to obituaries in the UK though. Given our strict libel laws, derogatory comments cannot be made of the living. Yet, although we are legally ●

> ► THINKING IT THROUGH

free to wash the dirty linen of the dead in public, very few obituary writers do. The maxim 'don't speak ill of the dead' tends to hold sway in a remarkable display of restraint.

One classic exception was the *Guardian* obituary of lawyer Peter Carter-Ruck whose specialism in bringing libel actions cost the media millions. Maybe there was an intentional irony in deriding him in no uncertain terms in his own obituary but it was not generally well-received. Few obituaries go that far but they are not as deferential as in the past. Scandals and dark sides are not ignored but perhaps given a softer edge. Like a vicar giving a tribute at a memorial service, the writer of an obituary should ensure the subject remains recognisable, to an extent warts and all. Venting personal prejudices is not encouraged especially if writing the obituary of a politician/ performer who may not be to your taste.

A classic structure for an obituary would be:

- Claim to fame – why they are the subject of an obit. This could be straight or can be a vignette – a phrase or incident that captures their contribution and character.
- Key achievements – landmark moments – edited highlights.
- Character – what was special about them.
- Historical context within their field. A musician, for instance, may not have been famous but is known to have influenced current stars or established a particular style.
- Biography – life story – key achievements – what they are remembered for and some background. Balance according to interest rather than chronology. Some obituaries are very formulaic, plodding through decade by decade. Look for landmarks and the influences on them – parents, mentors, leaders in their field.
- Something we don't know about them – an interest, trait, experience.
- What family they leave – partner, children.
- Style: many use a standard standfirst or sign off with name and dates.

Obituaries are often written in advance. Notes are maintained on the great and the good, often by specialists who maintain the database – known as the morgue. Whole supplements are written and laid out for major royals, celebrities and political leaders ready to print at very short notice, with a quick update. It seems morbid but if you ever have to write an obituary on the hoof you will soon appreciate the benefits of forward planning.

Look up notes on obituaries in the recommended books and read a few examples in the *Times* and *Guardian*, which now include reader-submitted contributions. Check out the tribute sites online such as iAnnounce. Sketch out obituaries for someone you admire and someone who appals you, and examine the moral and journalistic dilemmas of summing up a life.

Ask yourself: What do you think is the best way for the media to mark someone's death?

Columnists: the cult of personality

Bylined columns are seen by some as the salvation of print media and many journalists are being encouraged to blog in an opinionated, chatty style. In sports coverage for instance, the line between news and comment is increasingly blurred. Is the priority to be provocative? That can mean taking sides and being partisan in a way that challenges the notion of a journalist as a neutral investigator.

Robert Peston's blog, for example, as well as being accused of single-handedly threatening to collapse the UK banking system, is pushing punditry into realms that

▶ THINKING IT THROUGH

some consider to be at odds with the BBC's commitment to impartiality. Isn't it a journalist's job to weigh the arguments and opinions of others? Traditional training is at great pains to persuade would-be journalists that their role is to tell other people's stories, not their own. What difference does it make to your sources if they know your personal opinions about them or any other subject? Do readers even care what an individual journalist has to say?

Read a range of blogs by prominent commentators – try the BBC and the *Guardian*'s Comment is Free for starters.

Ask yourself: How does expression of personal opinion fit into the job of a journalist?

Spot the fake

Exposing the truth is an essential part of being a good journalist. The public needs to know what is really going on. Society is ultimately the healthier for it. Yet truth is no longer a complete justification for publishing because the media is obliged to protect individual privacy.

No-one wants their hospital records splashed over the tabloids and there is genuine sympathy for claims to privacy, which is now a human right within UK law. There is a balance to be struck – in the European Convention on Human Rights it emerges as Article 8 (privacy) v Article 10 (freedom of expression) – see Chapter 9.

The quibble is that maintaining privacy can be worth a fortune to celebrities because it protects their image, even where that image is false. Journalists, and their ethical codes, have long held that it is in the public interest to expose the truth about anyone who is peddling a lie, even if that lie concerns their private life. Outing the phoney is OK, and it should be.

The more significant a role someone plays in public life the more likely it is to matter if they are misleading the public. Elected politicians and public servants should not be allowed to mislead the public, even where otherwise private information has to be revealed to prevent it. But should celebrities be allowed to get away with pretending to be something they are not?

And sometimes the print media plays along. The media can be genuine champions of free speech and morality in the public sphere but they can also knowingly misrepresent the situation. There are more grounds for newspapers and magazines being censured for perpetuating myths than for debunking them. Far too many titles collude in the celebrity pretences when it suits agents to raise the profile of their clients and publications to sell copies. The deals struck are far more unethical than occasional intrusive photographs. Journalists and editors who knowingly present false information to the public are the real villains of the piece.

Why should a journalist feel bad about invading the privacy of the great and the good – by revealing that they are neither as great nor as good as they would have us believe? The fabrication that surrounds celebrities in particular leaves them wide open to the media delivering a reality check.

Ask yourself: Should someone have the right to mislead the public about private matters? Does it depend who they are? What if a source asked you to keep a secret in return for an exclusive interview?

NOTES

[1] http://www.societyofeditors.co.uk/page-view.php?pagename=conference2008
[2] http://www.concernedjournalists.org/what-are-elements-journalism
[3] The original checklist appears in Bloy, D. and Hadwin, S. (2011) *Law and the Media*. London: Sweet & Maxwell.
[4] http://www.pcc.org.uk/assets/111/Code_of_Practice_2011_A4.pdf
[5] Ibid.
[6] Randall, David (2007). 696/code-of-practice-2012.A4.pdf

WEBLINKS

http://asa.org.uk   The website of the Advertising Standards Association: the UK's independent regulator of advertising across all media, including TV, internet, sales promotions and direct marketing. Its role is to ensure ads are legal, decent, honest and truthful by applying the Advertising Codes, including those for promotional text as might appear in an advertising feature.

http://www.bbc.co.uk/blogs/thereporters/robertpeston   BBC Business editor Robert Peston's blog gives a running commentary on the business world and provides a good example of the expectations on a multi-media specialist.

http://www.bbc.co.uk/journalism   A positive embarrassment of riches from the BBC's own College of Journalism site for those seeking journalism advice and not just for traditional broadcasters. Discussion strands keep it fresh and it lives up to the BBC tradition of comprehensive coverage. The briefing tab includes specialist tips, including sections on politics and business.

http://www.concernedjournalists.org   Website of the Committee for Concerned Journalists, which follows through on the book by Bill Kovach, its founder, and Tom Rosenstiel.

http://www.everyonesacritic.net   A movie site for non-journalist fans to share their likes and dislikes in film. Such sites have in some ways challenged the role of the professional film reviewer.

http://www.guardian.co.uk/media/greenslade   Roy Greenslade's running commentary on politics, news and the media.

http://www.justice.gov.uk   Covers the workings of the justice system in England and Wales. Very useful for courts and crime reporters but also for those dealing more broadly with social affairs.

http://people-press.org   Interesting data on the audience responses from the Pew Research Centre for the People & The Press.

http://www.tcij.org/   The London-based Centre for Investigative Journalism hosts conferences and events as well as operating a really useful website. It majors on computer assisted reporting with a focus on major investigations.

http://www.thinkbuzan.com   Site of Tony Buzan who originated the MindMap. A software package is now widely available to ease the process and an iMindMap app.

RECOMMENDED READING

Barber, Lynn (1992) *Mostly Men*. London: Penguin Books.
A selection of her profiles, with an illuminating introduction.

Davies, Nick (2008) *Flat Earth News*. London: Chatto & Windus.
Davies expands upon his view that 'churnalism' has taken over the print media.

De Burgh, Hugo (ed.) (2008) *Investigative Journalism: Context and Practice*. London: Routledge.
Thorough context for investigative journalism, including some legal pointers, accompanied by real case studies ranging across print and broadcast. Lots of useful lists for follow-up reading.

Humphrys, John (2000) *Devil's Advocate*. London: Arrow Books.
Robust analysis of media and society which identifies a variety of trends including that of trivialisation of news.

Kovach, Bill and Rosenstiel, Tom (2007) *The Elements of Journalism*. London: Atlantic Books.
Thoughtful offering based on the manifesto of the US Committee of Concerned Journalists. Chapters examine the implications of declarations such as: 'Journalism's first obligation is to the truth'; 'Its essence is a discipline of verification'; and 'It must strive to make the significant interesting and relevant – enter the specialist reporter'. A favourite book for making it all seem worthwhile.

Lloyd, John (2004) *What the media are doing to our politics*. London: Constable.
Sparked a debate on the degeneration of public debate and the degree of responsibility to be laid at the door of journalists.

Morrison, James (2011) *Essential Public Affairs for Journalists*. Oxford: Oxford University Press.
Set text for NCTJ programmes covering local and central UK government. Useful for specialisms related to the public sector.

Phillips, Angela (2007) *Good Writing for Journalists*. London: Sage.
Deconstructs real examples by a fascinating mix of mainly feature writers. Useful chapter on personal and comment columns, including a Boris Johnson motoring column.

Randall, David (2007) *The Universal Journalist*. London: Pluto Press.
Directly useful here for its chapter on comment writing but specialists will find much of value in the news-gathering chapters, particularly 'Handling Sources, Not Them Handling You'.

Tomlinson, Alan and Sugden, John (2008) 'Sports journalism: persistent themes and changing times', in Franklin, Bob (ed.) *Pulling Newspapers Apart*. London: Routledge.

REFERENCES

Davies, Nick (2008) *Flat Earth News*. London: Chatto & Windus.

Humphrys, John (2000) *Devil's Advocate*. London: Arrow Books.

Lloyd, John (2004) *What the media are doing to our politics*. London: Constable.

Morrison, James (2011) *Essential Public Affairs for Journalists*. Oxford: Oxford University Press.

Randall, David (2007) *The Universal Journalist*. London: Pluto Press.

CHAPTER EIGHT
CONVERGENCE

Case study 8.1

FREELANCE broadcast sports journalist Tim Hart was on his way home from work on a sports shifts for Reuters when he returned to his Clapham home to find that rioters were just 200 yards from his front door.

He pulled out his Flip video camera and camera phone and started using Twitter and Facebook to put out updates from the area all through Monday night and into Tuesday morning. The multimedia content he used was put together as a new story and sold to the Reuters agency.

At 5 a.m. on the Tuesday, Tim and a cameraman were sent to Birmingham to cover a cricket test match for Reuters TV and Tim was also being contracted to provide coverage for a sports website.

The next day Tim and his colleague were due to be covering the England v Netherlands game with Tim working as a sports producer for Reuters TV – which was called off due to the London riots. Instead the pair were asked to cover the riots in Birmingham.

His work was used across the media and some of the images of the vigil held for the men killed in Birmingham were provided by Tim. He said:

'I didn't expect to cover the riots, I was very smartly dressed for the cricket and didn't have a spare set of clothes as I wasn't expecting to stay overnight.

When we got to our hotel there were six riot vans outside with police on one side and rioters on the other. We took some shots from our hotel room and then we followed the rioters round but I was also Tweeting. I quickly became a reliable source of information and I was getting people from Australia, Brazil, Angola and the Czech republic (among others) thanking me for the information. It's amazing that these people wanted to know so much about the centre of Birmingham.

My Twitter following virtually trebled overnight.

I ended up doing interviews for the BBC news channel, Radio 4 and an English-language radio station from Holland – BBC Breakfast wanted to [do an interview] but by that time I was asleep as I'd been up for 48 hours covering the events in London and Birmingham.'[1]

His social media and broadcast work didn't just see him get coverage across the media – it also led to an interesting phone call with the police after a friend pointed out that Tim's picture had appeared in London's *Evening Standard* as part of a story about the Metropolitan Police wanting to track down people they believed may have been rioters.

INTRODUCTION

In 2010 the Office for National Statistics (ONS) said that 30.1 million adults in the UK accessed the internet every day – nearly double the figures from 2006.[2] This was partly down to the rise of broadband in homes and businesses – 68 per cent of premises had fixed broadband[3] – and the growth in people using mobile broadband. By September 2011 that had risen to 77 per cent of households connected to the internet and 45 per cent of those surveyed by the ONS used the mobile web.[4]

This power to connect to a high-speed web gives people opportunities to interact with what goes on around them like never before. This gives you the power to find your own news from a variety of sources, rather than being stuck with a local paper and a local radio or TV station and has led to some interesting ideas about what journalism means.

Once media organisations were the conduit for connecting those with a high profile – such as politicians or celebrities – to a mass audience. Now this is no longer the case and these figures can talk directly to their fans: take the popstar Lady Gaga for example. Her predecessors may have had to use the music press, MTV or other outlets to reach fans, but Lady Gaga's Twitter account has (at the time of writing) 12,917,212 followers who actively choose to listen to the latest news and trivia from the musician while she is out and about. A picture of the star surfing, which was posted on her account, got over 360,00 views and almost 1,500 comments from fans.[5] This kind of buy-in from a dedicated community shows levels of engagement that most media organisations would love to have.

Now compare that with newspaper sales. The Audit Bureau of Circulation (ABC) showed that all of the UK national newspapers' market share was down year-on-year. The figures for June 2011 show the average circulation across all of the UK nationals (both daily and Sundays) was 19,493,280.[6]

Obviously these figures alone do not paint a straightforward picture. Take the *Daily Mail* as an example: although the daily paper's circulation for June 2011 was 2,047,206 and the *Mail on Sunday* was 1,927,791,[7] this only shows the number of people buying print editions. The online figures declared as part of the multimedia ABC figures were almost 77 million unique browsers for the month of May (its daily views rose massively to 4,365,716 on average). The company also claims its app is getting 62,000 daily app unique browsers.[8]

And that's looking only at one newspaper organisation. Spread that across magazines, regional and local newspapers and you'll get quite an interesting change in figures that can be interpreted in a number of ways – from the death of newspapers through to the idea of core niche markets or the triumph of new technologies over old ways of working.

What it does show, however, is how many people are getting their news on the web – and not always from the traditional sources, something noted by Cardiff University's Richard Sambrook during his time at the BBC:

'News organisations do not own the news any more. They can validate information, analyse it, explain it, and they can help the public find what they need to know.

But they no longer control or decide what the public know. It is a major restructuring of the relationship between public and media. But it will affect politics and policy as well.

People can now address politicians directly, and politicians can reach the public without going through the media any more. Public discourse is becoming unmediated.'[9]

Whatever this kind of news is, the technologies underpinning it have matured to allow the sharing of insights, photos or videos from people on the ground (citizen media), to journalism as games or interactive graphics. This power to participate (social media) coupled with the power to publish (using simple tools like blog sites) means that journalists have to think carefully about their role.

What is convergence?

Taken literally convergence can mean the coming together of two things, although in the case of journalism it can be described as the coming together of different media platforms – for example tv and online – or the skills of a journalist working across these platforms or even the fact that media companies that traditionally owned newspapers now own broadcasters and even film companies as part of their portfolio, or vice versa.

Peter Williams, former finance director of DGMT (Daily Mail and General Trust, which owns, among other things, Associated Newspapers and the Northcliffe regional newspaper group) said:

'We no longer own regional newspapers, we own regional media businesses, and their objective is to deliver the news, the information, the advertising, to their audience in whatever form both the advertiser and the consumer want to receive it'[10]

Often what people are talking about when they use the term is technological convergence – and specifically the introduction of the World Wide Web, which is able to transmit audio (previously the radio), video (tv) and text (newspapers and magazines) – although text had been carried by the tv stations in the format of Ceefax, Teletext and Oracle, which were essentially a very limited and clunky precursor to the text pages now available via the red button on digital tv sets and boxes.

Most journalists and media companies would now accept we are working in a period that could be defined as a revolution, evolution or transformation of what journalism is about – and one of the words being used to try to describe that way of working and the practices is the term convergence. At its simplest it can be argued that journalism has been defined by the platform the journalists worked for, so many journalists would define themselves as newspaper journalists, magazine journalists and so on. But now journalists are having to learn a range of skills to be able to do their jobs – and some of them are not necessarily things that their predecessors would recognise as being journalism.

Defining convergence

There are many different definitions of what a converged journalist is, and sometimes the term can be used to try to describe the work of an online journalist, a print journalist who also files online or a broadcaster who also blogs. Although no-one can, seemingly, agree on what it means it is worth taking a look at some of the ideas behind what convergence means for journalists.

The discussion about convergence in journalism is nothing new – back in 2003 American journalist Rich Gordon said:

'At a minimum, all journalists will need to develop a basic understanding of the unique capabilities of the different communications media. Increasingly, their employers are going to deliver content to multiple platforms or collaborate with other companies to do so.

[W]e are not necessarily moving into an era when a single journalist needs to do it all – report, write, take pictures, shoot and edit video, and present their stories on the Web. There will always be a need for specialists who do one thing particularly well. But in the converged media organizations of the future, the journalists who best understand the unique capabilities of multiple media will be the ones who are most successful, drive the greatest innovations and become the leaders of tomorrow.'[11]

Moving forward to the 21st century Ed Walker, now a multimedia producer for Trinity Mirror regionals, is one of a number of journalists who could be defined as working in a convergence media setting. Ed ran the hyperlocal site Your Cardiff, which required him to work for print and online in ways that hadn't previously been seen at Media Wales. For Ed a converged journalist is:

'Someone who understands how to tell the story across many media. Can write a 300 word splash, with backgrounder, expanded version for online with embedded multimedia (e.g. map) and edit video package. Sometimes all on one story, other times on many and crucially all within a matter of hours. Maybe that's convergence?'[12]

For some the term convergence creates a false distinction and needn't be used any more. Hannah Waldram, one of the pioneering beatbloggers with the Guardian Local Project, who now works as community co-ordinator on the news team at guardian.co.uk, had this to say to a conference of journalism educators and editors:

'Personally I think we should stop using the term right now – and focus more on how we can use media and online tools to enhance the journalism we do. Talking of "convergence journalism" runs the risk of pigeon-holing a way of working – which could lead to skewed recruitment methods, newsrooms which continue to belittle online practises, and alienation of reporting and news-gathering habits.'[13]

For others like academic Jane Singer convergence will still see journalists doing different jobs. Not everyone will be doing multimedia packages that need to go out in real time – some journalists will be involved in what has been termed 'slow journalism' using techniques based on traditional in-depth print reporting or feature writing to make sense and add context to events rather than just update in realtime, while others will be using a range of tools to publish their reporting process from first tip-off to finished piece – if there can ever be such a thing.[14]

This idea of plurality of roles, rather than everyone being able to do everything, is one that seems to be happening in practice in the newsrooms. Media Wales has been running a converged newsroom for a number of years: by converged it originally meant that all of the papers (*Western Mail*, *South Wales Echo* and *Wales on Sunday*) would operate out of the same newsroom and have a team who were on shift rotas to work on the papers rather than discrete staff.

Alison Gow, former editor of *Wales on Sunday* and Wales Online who now edits the North Wales Daily Post, sees the requirements of the reader actually defining what convergence techniques are required for a story:

'Convergence is one of those phrases that gets whipped out at times of report writing – "We embrace convergence across multiple platforms!" – and yet, when you try to pin it down and define a converged newsroom, it's incredibly difficult (and not especially useful).

To say the Media Wales newsroom is converged would be to claim people were as comfortable designing a page of the *Western Mail* as they were the web page that story gets placed on. They'd be able to shoot and edit a video, then write a 350 word page lead, or run a hyperlocal beat blog and sub the front page splash.

In the real world, that doesn't happen.

But . . . a reporter might run a hyperlocal beat bog and write the front page splash. A videographer might cover a music festival and run a liveblog of the event, and write a review of it. And an advertising rep might sell the front page ad slot to a client along with an online package that includes commercial and editorial partnerships, as seen with Go Green and HealthCheck Wales.

Various subs, designers, newsdesk and writers are able to upload direct to the CMS, but there remains a discrete digital team (with embedded representatives in Sport and Features departments whose roles run from writing and reviewing for print and online, to managing web sections and associated social media, and running online projects).

Equally, a reporter out on a live job might be called on to shoot some video or take a photo on their smartphone and send it back to the digital team or sports writers might run a Q&A liveblog with a team manager. Thinking about it, probably one of the large drivers of convergence in any newsroom is actually, "Who's available to do X?" '.[15]

It's interesting to note that convergence seems to be happening at different speeds around the industry. Keeping with the maxim of cyberpunk author William Gibson 'The future is already here, it's just not very evenly distributed'.[16] A survey by the National Council for the Training of Journalists (NCTJ) in mid-2011 had editors saying they wanted a focus on traditional skills, although some recognised the importance of new digital skills.[17] That may be appropriate for their audience, but for young journalists like Hannah Waldram, Ed Walker and Josh Halliday (the *Guardian*) it is these very digital skills that have got them into some of the new journalism jobs that are emerging.

Although indirectly, the NCTJ survey does make a major point about convergence journalism: the basics of understanding what you are trying to research and communicate to a community are still very much the same as they have always been, but there are significant differences in terms of being able to respond and engage. You may find you have specialisms in certain areas, but it is well worth investigating the tools and techniques available to you.

HISTORY, THEORY AND PRACTICE

Change in journalism is not new. It could be argued that journalism itself came about as a result of the introduction of a revolutionary communications technology – the printing press. The work of Caxton and the other early printers allowed publishers to move away from the costly and labour-intensive process of engraving to a faster and more efficient communication medium. And as printing became cheaper and quicker it led to the early magazines and newspapers. The first English language newspaper was printed around 1620 and by the 1720s there were around 12 newspapers in London alone.

This is an irony not lost on those involved in the current transformation of journalism, as this once-revolutionary means of production is now under threat. Alan Rusbridger of the *Guardian* and John Witherow of the *Sunday Times* both famously told the BBC's Media Show[18] during a radio debate in 2010 that they had bought their last printing presses. Some suggestions are that given the lifespan of a printing press this means that they foresee an end date of about 20–30 years, which would be in accordance with the date of 2043, the time that American journalism commentator Philip Meyer said would be the time of the final newspaper dying out.[19] Notice, though, that the editors were not talking about the end of their brand but rather the last time the papers may be printed on paper in the form we use now

The introduction of desktop publishing and digital plate make-up in the printing of newspapers and magazines led to massive changes in the configuration of newsrooms, which in turn led to the loss of skilled hot metal jobs such as the compositor. This wholesale change in production led to the Wapping strikes[20] and the introduction of the page editor (a sub who could take stories and images that would be placed on a page and sent straight to the printing press, see Chapter 6).

New jobs, roles and skills have developed as a result of digital production, first in print and then onto the web. Journalist Kevin Anderson has been working as a 'converged journalist' since the late 1990s:

'There have always been various forces pushing and pulling in different directions when it comes to newsroom integration and convergence. My experience is that whenever you have a new platform or new role, you always have a convergence of roles. These roles are seen as being experimental, and managers don't want to place a big bet. When I first started online, I was developer, designer and journalist.

We saw this as well as primarily text-based digital journalism added multimedia. This gave rise to the "backpack journalist", the Kevin Siteses[21] of the journalism world. There is a lot of enthusiasm for journalists to do it all, write, shoot pictures, shoot video, record audio and package it all. I have worked like this since the late 1990s first at the BBC and then the *Guardian*. However, I'll be the first to admit that while I can produce multi-platform projects to a high standard, I always appreciate help from a video or audio specialist or an interactive developer. A multi-media, multi-platform superstar is a very hard person to find or even train.

Whenever you have a new role, journalists often end up wearing a lot of hats. For instance, with the rise of data journalism, I've had managers ask me to recommend a person for a role that is really two or three roles. They want a statistician, web developer and data visualisation developer all rolled into one person. Again, just as with multimedia, it's rare to find someone who is a wiz at all of those things. Over time, we'll see specialists emerge.'[22]

These kinds of practices have also seen major changes in how organisations work with their communities.

A CLOSER LOOK

SOCIAL MEDIA AND MAGAZINES

Adam Tinworth was, until recently, editorial development manager for Reed Business Information, Europe's largest B2B publisher, with *New Scientist* and *Farmer's Weekly* as part of its diverse portfolio. Among his responsibilities, Adam was in charge of training staff from across the various magazines in the group and researching industry trends.

'We've certainly shifted from a print-centric model, not least because we've been making more money from online services than print for quite some years now.

And with that has come a shift of purpose for our journalism. In the old model, it was about building a product, pulling together a magazine full of reporting and other content we could sell to two groups: the readers and the ▶

> ▶ **A CLOSER LOOK**
>
> advertisers. On the web, it serves a third purpose – building a community of readers around a topic matter who are then presented with other propositions, including our paid services, through a funnel model. Thus it's much more useful for us to have an on-going dialogue with a wider pool of people interested in our topics, rather than throwing packages of content over the wall once a week/month.
>
> And there are knock-on benefits to this. We're not smothering our free content in ads, which makes it more pleasant to read, and that makes it more likely to build a community. And a community that likes and trusts us is more likely to feed us leads that turn into good stories. Which attracts a bigger community. There's a clear positive feedback loop to doing reporting though social media.
>
> In essence, journalistically we're doing what we always did – reporting on the business activities of a community with the help of that community, for their own benefit. But the tools we have to do this are now considerably better than they've ever been.'[23]

Technology

One of the big changes over the recent past has been the ubiquity of technology – and how easily a particular technology allows people to connect with a way of working that is convenient for them. People used to read the newspaper while commuting on the bus or the train, but a shift in working and commuting patterns saw more driving to work, which in turn saw more people tuning into their favourite radio shows in the morning. The introduction of some of the more compact – or Berliner – formats for national broadsheets can be attributed to ease of use during commuting as well as printing costs, and a number of magazines have adopted compact 'handbag-sized' editions.

The development of the internet and shifts in working patterns have meant that people are able to get their news during their breaks without leaving their desks and don't have to wait until preset publishing slots, be that the 9 a.m. news bulletin, the daily or weekly print slot for the paper or the monthly edition of their magazine. Many media company sites are now becoming round-the-clock organisations that publish web first and use their site to break news while print editions are for longer form, more reflective journalism.

The development of Web 2.0, the so-called interactive web, has allowed people with little technical skills to communicate with each other. They can talk directly to their favourite stars, politicians or footballers without the need for the media in between. But the biggest changes in this area have been the development of mobile technologies, which have seen a rise in what has been termed citizen – or participatory – journalism.

Although community newsletters and fanzines have been around for a long time, it's only in the early part of the 21st century that this term has come to prominence.

Reporting from the frontline – the citizens

One of the seemingly immutable situations created by modern technology is how cost-effective hardware and software become over time. Although broadcast organisations use digital cameras that cost tens of thousands of pounds, anyone is able to capture videos and photographs on smart phones or small hand-held 'blogger cams' like the Kodak ZI series, which will be of decent enough quality to post on the web.

That means that the power to publish and share is no longer the preserve of the professional journalist – since roughly 2000 bloggers have been sharing information and posting pictures, videos and text on the web. So, as Richard Sambrook said in the introduction, if the power to publish is no longer held by the media alone – how do we work with the field as it is now?

'Authority is in the eye of the beholder; it is not innate to the institution itself . . . news and information is clearly no longer the exclusive domain of professionals.'[24]

A CLOSER LOOK

KEY EVENTS IN CITIZEN JOURNALISM

On 26 December 2004, the Indian Ocean tsunami shocked the world when a mountain of water caused devastation. Scenes of the incident and aftermath made their way onto the internet – but it was news that was broken by people with mobile phones rather than the mainstream media organisations

Similarly, on 7 July 2005, London was rocked by a series of terrorist attacks on three underground trains and a bus, which killed 52 people and left over 700 injured. People using cameraphones were quickly posting images and videos that were picked up and used by the mainstream media, including the BBC, and led to a new way of working for the broadcaster (see below).

Another key example of this – defined by some as user-generated content – was when a US airways flight crashed into the Hudson river in 2009. Commuter Janis Krums was on a ferry that was diverted to pick up the passengers of the plane that had crash landed shortly after take-off. He used his mobile phone to take a picture of the crash and then uploaded it via his Twitter account and a Twitter picture service called TwitPic.

His message read: 'There's a plane in the Hudson. I'm on the ferry going to pick up the people. Crazy.'

He beat the mainstream media to the punch with this update, which spread like wildfire over the internet. To date, Janis's picture has been viewed over 779,000 times.

This kind of citizen media can also be part of how journalists work, and has become a major part of the BBC's work since 2005. The Beeb has 23 journalists working at the Hub who verify contributions from members of the public. The team gets around 10,000 contributions per day in the form of social media messages, emails, images, videos and comments, but needs to be rigorous in checking them. The team has a lengthy check process before anything is let through and published by the world-famous media organisation. Its checking procedures include:

- checking geographic locations;
- checking regional accents with local contacts to ensure they are correct for the story context;
- searching for the original material;
- examining weather reports;
- checking military equipment to ensure it is appropriate for the area.

There's a great blogpost by Alex Murray, a member of the UGC hub team at the BBC's College of Journalism blog[25] if you are interested in how the BBC uses these techniques.

Crowdsourcing tools can also be a great boon. These are tools that allow journalists to ask a community for help or information about an event. At its simplest this can be just a Tweet (sometimes tagged #journorequest), but there are much more interactive ways of dealing with community-generated information.

In Egypt a site called **harassmap.org** was set up using a tool called Ushahidi. Although Ushahidi was originally designed to support Kenyan citizen journalists cover post-election violence in 2008, the harassmap team used the web tool to allow Egyptian women to text messages about places where they had been harassed. The site then plotted those messages to show where they were clustered.[26]

These mapping tools have been used to cover a tube strike by the BBC College of Journalism and election coverage by the *Guardian* Local team: just two examples of this kind of participation between journalists and their audience.

remember

- Change is nothing new in the media industry.
- Media organisations and journalists are moving away from print-centric models and adapting to the web.
- The roles and responsibilities of the journalist are changing, but are still rooted in some of the traditional skills.

MULTISKILLING

Andy Dickinson, journalism lecturer at the University of Central Lancashire, has this to say:

'For me convergence is a process. It's looking at all the different things you do and finding common ground. That connection may be enabled by technology but its as much about seeing outside of the strict definition of one medium or another.

It's convergence of process; convergence of content; convergence of audience.

Convergence is realizing that Facebook is not only great for chatting with people but it's also a great digital ear on your community – a great research tool.

That phone in your pocket is a great way to capture a picture for a story.

Convergence is about putting raw data online whilst you research a story.

Convergence is keeping a live blog of an event.

These are all little moments of 'convergence' that work on a number of different levels. Your live blog might mix media but it also gathers in content and audience to take towards the point at which you publish (the traditional convergence point). It's pulling strands together to make sense/content/journalism in a point in time.

In that respect convergence is aspirational and temporal. We will never quite get there because the changing media landscape demands that all these things work on their own. The range of platforms means that the mediums never really converge. But I do think that you can have little moments of convergence that help power a story along and make journalism richer and deeper.'[27]

Getting started

Given the wide range of tools that are available to the digital journalist, this chapter will make some suggestions for tools and ideas that can be used by a convergence journalist. This is not exhaustive but will help you to get to grips with some of the skills that young journalists will be expected to have:

'. . . as news audiences' informational needs and wants changes, and as they seek more choices in getting that information journalists will be expected to adapt . . . Convergence is about being flexible enough to provide news and information to anyone and everyone, anytime and all the time, anywhere and often without abandoning key journalistic values.'[28]

PUTTING IT INTO PRACTICE

As with the research protocols discussed in Chapter 2 and the augmentation techniques of the multimedia sub in Chapter 6, you need to be thinking about what kind of story you are working on and how it will be best set out.

Ask yourself these basic questions:

- Who am I writing for?
- What are the defining features of this story?
- How can I put this across – is this text only, audio, images, images and audio together (soundslides), video or a package of all of the above?
- Does it have a number of locations that would lend themselves to mapping, or are there a number of events that would lend themselves to a timeline?
- When does it need to be ready? (This has serious implications for the amount of interactivity that any package you put together can have.)

These kinds of questions will help you shape the content for your story and ensure you are creating the kind of package that will best support your reader and offer real value to them.

Skills for the multiplatform journalist

As outlined in the introduction to this chapter, the key skills that any convergence journalist will need are very much rooted in those of the traditional print journalist – but with one major difference, the mindset of an experimenter who is prepared to explore new tools and networks.

How to write well

Obviously one of the core skills for young journalists is their written communication – be that in a web article, a tweet or even a script for a podcast. Review the advice in Chapters 2 and 3 and the SEO advice from Chapter 6 to ensure you are on top of your game. The skills of blogging are essentially the same as those of news or feature writing and it is worth bearing in mind the advice in the earlier chapters.

The veracity of your information and the ability to change any mistakes have to be at the forefront of any converged journalist's mind. Although originally used to mock Sky News, the mantra 'Never Wrong For Long' is one to bear in mind on the web. Research properly to ensure you don't make mistakes, but, if you do, correct them as soon as possible. That may mean:

- engaging in the comments on the site;
- responding to Facebook or Twitter messages that point out errors;
- being honest about it and being courteous to the person who alerted you – particularly as you may be able to use them as a source within the story;
- amending or changing the post. (This can cause issues and is well worth looking at in more depth – see the Thinking It Through section on p. 230.)

Research

Research skills have already been covered in Chapter 2 but it is worth reiterating how important having an RSS reader is for journalists. Although there are various readers (including the excellent Netvibes), Google's Reader is a good starting point to allow you to get used to an RSS reader.

PUTTING IT INTO PRACTICE

1 Set up a Google account. If you already have one then you already have Google Reader.
2 Look for the RSS logo on your favourite blogs and websites.
3 Copy the web address and then go back to Reader.
4 Click 'Add a subscription' and paste the link into the box. This will add the web feed for the page.
5 You can also share things publicly on Google Reader, which allows you to show sources for stories you are working on or sites that your readers or community may be interested in.
6 Don't forget the power of perpetual search (see page 48).
7 Remember to be organised. You will quickly build up a lot of links and need to theme them. This is quite easy in most RSS readers as you can create themed folders and then drag your links into the folders as required.
8 Check every day.
9 Credit your sources.

Multimedia journalism

Not all journalists have to be able to produce broadcast audio or video – for most journalists their audio or video is more likely to be actuality, something that is happening in front of them rather than a big documentary-style package. Media organisations may well have professional videographers to help them with that aspect.

Audio

Audio is a very powerful format for journalism, as it allows the audience to get to grips with the interviewee's tone of voice as well as being able to listen to the environment the interview is taking place in. Radio edits are usually quite tight and short to fit in with the schedule but this doesn't have to be the case online.

If you do record your interviews for accuracy purposes, why not think about putting the recording online as part of the package to go with your text piece. Not everyone will want to listen to it in full, but it will also be there to show transparency in your story sourcing.

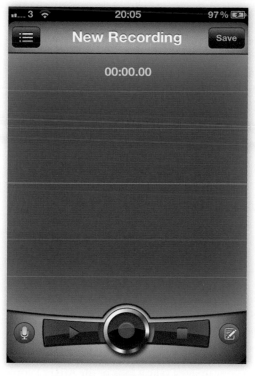

The key thing about audio – whether for broadcast or for online – is quality and that comes in a number of phases:

- quality of preparation – discussed in Chapter 2;
- quality of questioning – discussed in Chapter 2;
- quality of recording.

To achieve a good quality audio recording you need to have decent equipment to capture the noise. Professional level tools like Nagra recorders can cost over £600 but you can capture decent quality audio using a digital dictaphone or even your mobile phone. Even the latest iPod Touch can be used as it has most of the features of a smart phone – apart from 3G connection – so all transfer would have to be over wi-fi. Tools like some of the handheld recorders from Zoom are also decent, low-cost recording options – and there are plenty of similar products out there.

Most mobile phones have the ability to record audio directly, or if you have a smart phone there are low-cost tools like I Said What?[2], an iPhone app that will allow you not only to record, but edit and send audio.

Although recording audio is a skill that requires patience and practice, there are some basics that are worth remembering:

- Learn to use your device – which means reading the manual. Whichever piece of kit you are going to use to record your audio make sure you know how to store audio, and get it back onto a computer.
- Check battery levels – whatever kind of device you are using, make sure you have spare batteries or a charger. There's nothing more embarrassing than having to explain why you can't actually carry out the interview.
- Check audio levels – although you can boost audio slightly in an audio editor this adds noise. Too much audio boosting and you will make your audio unusable.
- Check the sampling level of the file you will be recording with.
- Check what file format you need to send back – will this be a .wav or an .mp3 or other type of audio file?
- Most mobile phones have an adequate microphone and recorder built into them, but consider a plug-in mic if you want to record more often.
- There are also a number of tools for recording phone calls that plug into Skype or paid-for services like Call Trunk, which will allow you to capture the audio from a telephone conversation. But best practice is always to let someone know you are going to record a call.

Once you've got your audio you will then need to edit it. Again there are high-end solutions like Adobe Audition, but there are also free tools you can download to get you started and Audacity is one very popular piece of free software. These editors are very graphical, so you can easily see where to zoom in and make cuts and edits to your audio.

Some websites will not allow you to upload audio directly, so it is worth investigating sites like SoundCloud which allow you to upload a limited amount of audio for free and then embed it in a website.

Video

As with audio, there is a whole range of kit available from the low-cost to the broadcast professional standard that costs thousands of pounds. One of the simplest places to get started is with your mobile phone if it can take videos. Briefly dubbed mojo (mobile journalism) this type of video recording is great for on-the-scene capture.

Most of the advice that is outlined in the section on audio above is appropriate for video capture too – particularly if you are using your phone, as batteries can run out quite quickly. When it comes to editing there is a range of packages available – some that come with your computer (Movie Maker for the PC or iMovie for the Mac), and now several for smartphones including the tablet or phone versions of iMovie that are low cost and easy to use. They might not give you the most professional of edits, but are perfectly adequate for live reporting.

Images

A picture has poetically been seen to be worth 1,000 words – and images really do add value to an online piece. Images or slideshows will add depth to the text and lighten up a grey page. Although photography is an art that takes a lot of practice and understanding, again there are some simple basics that can lift your shots:

- Get to know your camera – so again refer to the manual.
- Learn how to set the white balance.
- Learn the rule of thirds – a way of segmenting pictures to get the best out of them.
- Understand resolution (DPI) differences between print and the web.
- Get a Flickr account – not only will this allow you to upload pictures, the site has a very vibrant community that is a source of images in its own right. However, do be very careful.

For a brilliant look at how not to be creative with your images, take a look at the Angry People in Local Newspapers site at **http://apiln.blogspot.com/**.

Soundslides

Soundslides are a very powerful way of combining audio and images into your story-telling, (sometimes called digital narratives in a slightly different format). Two great examples of this come from the *New York Times*:

- The Assassination of Benazir Bhutto is a combination of photographs from John Moore combined with his experience of being on the scene of the politician's death.[29]
- The second is entitled 'Loss and Healing in Norway'[30] and focuses on the aftermath of the tragic events in Oslo and Utoeya on 22 July 2011.

You've probably got most of the tools you need already on your computer. Some people use video editing software to import the images, set them to an on-screen time and then add an audio track. This has the advantage of being very low cost and easy to do, but can be very time consuming. Great advice on how to create a digital narrative using a video editing package can be found on the website[31] of Daniel Meadows, an award-winning pioneer of digital narratives in the UK.

Some people prefer to use bespoke software packages like Soundslides that allow journalists to import their assets (audio and images) easily and then edit them by drag and drop. This does cost, but isn't going to break the bank.

Curating

American journalism educator and *Guardian* columnist Jeff Jarvis once said: 'Cover what you do best and link to the rest.'[32] He was talking about the way newspapers will rewrite a story or follow it up, when they could actually just show their readers that someone else has covered it. This can be seen as a bit controversial as websites have traditionally sold advertising space on the idea of the number of views that a page gets. So if you are directing your readers to a rival, then how will the business model work?

However, this kind of transparency of showing where news comes from can go a long way to getting rid of the tag 'churnalism' that has been given to news which just recycles content from press releases or other sources. The BBC News website has been very good at doing this, and will include links to the original source of the information on the page. This hasn't been widely adopted, but news bloggers of all types will put in links to where they get the original

story from. A simple way of doing this is to use a bookmarking site like Delicious to create a link bundle that can be added to the end of a story. Delicious is a social bookmarking service that allows users to save interesting articles to the web and then share them with an online community. In this case a simple use of tagging (a unique identifying category or topic word) has been used to collect the links and sources from a story into one virtual folder.

Another way of using links is to actually curate them: in other words gather the information from a variety of sources, which will add background and context for your reader. So instead of just using Tweets or Facebook updates as quotes within the text, you can use a number of different tools to gather information, updates and posts, and put them in one place. There are a number of tools worth looking at, for example Storify, Storyful, Bundlr, Chirpstory and Scoop.it.

A CLOSER LOOK

It's not just the print journalists who need to learn new digital journalism skills. Rory Cellan-Jones, the BBC's technology correspondent, uses a variety of social media tools to help him gather the news, interact with the communities around the specialist communities he covers and publish them.

'Look back even five years and think I was not exclusively a monomedia journalist, but almost all of my attention focused on the mechanics of tv. Today it is all interwoven with my online activity.'[33]

Rory has found that his online activity has allowed him to cover stories that may not have originally made the tv news, using his blog to put reports on.

'Social media makes specialism more possible; blogs allow an outlet for those stories that wouldn't normally be broadcast and a much closer connection with a community that might be the source of those stories and offers the chance to collaborate with them. It's been a sea change for how a lot of us work in broadcasting.'[34]

For Rory, one of the biggest enabling factors in this has been the changes in technology.

'We used to be supplied with all our IT by our employers and that was where we got access to sophisticated IT. Most of us have found our personal IT has been more flexible and powerful than what our employers provide to us.'[35]

Rory now uses his own Mac computer, iPhone and tablet computer as part of his day-to-day equipment.

PUTTING IT INTO PRACTICE   ADVICE FROM THE MAN FROM AUNTIE

- You don't need a very expensive mobile phone; get a cheap Android phone, which will do what you need.
- Experiment, but don't expect to become an expert in every area.
- Try to choose which of those areas – be it photography, videography or social media – will be the one you have the edge in.
- It's vital to use Twitter and Google+ to try to keep abreast of where social media is going by swimming in that pool.

remember

- Manuals may be important, but they are part of the basic drive to ensure you understand your equipment.
- Be prepared to experiment and make mistakes early on, and then learn from them.
- Learn how to set up a blog and use it to build a profile.

INTERACTIVITY

Interactivity in journalism can mean a number of things, from interactive software objects that offer a kinesthetic way to explore a story through to journalists interacting with the audience in real time. This section will look at a number of tools that journalists can use, from the simple through to those that require computer programming or development skills.

Interactivity – Web 2.0 style

Although not every journalist will be involved in developing interactive packages there are other tools that require few technical skills to use and create interactive elements that can be explored. As with much in online journalism, there is a whole range of tools and ideas to consider: this section will look at two interesting ways of working.

Interactive timelines are a simple but effective way of developing another way to allow your readers to engage with a topic. Most are quite simple to use and there is a range of tools on offer – two of the simpler ones to try are Dipity and Time Toast. These have been put to good use in supporting stories and topics. One good example is the knife and gun crime timeline created by Tom Scotney while he was a reporter at the Trinity Mirror group in Birmingham.[36]

Tom was able to plot news stories about gun and knife crimes from the Midlands newspaper group that not only allowed readers to scroll through a time period to look at the reports in an historical order, but the tool also created a map that allows the information to be explored in a different way.

Another way of working that is useful to convergence journalists, but can be very labour intensive, is the liveblog. This is essentially a minute-by-minute update of a site to provide coverage of breaking news. Some organisations, like the *Guardian*, literally update a website on a minute-by-minute basis while others will use tools like Cover It Live or Scribble Live to provide a way of pulling in content from a variety of sources while simultaneously interacting and engaging with a news community. This was put to the test by the *Manchester Evening News* team during the riots in the cities of Manchester and Salford in August 2011.

PUTTING IT INTO PRACTICE   COVERING THE RIOTS WITH THE *MANCHESTER EVENING NEWS'* LEE SWETTENHAM

The *MEN* team had been hearing rumours that something was going to happen during the afternoon, but didn't start live coverage until this was confirmed, at around 5 p.m., as the team didn't want to fan the situation. Around a dozen reporters and six photographers were sent out into the cities of Salford and Manchester.

The reporters' Twitter accounts were added to the Cover It Live blog embedded in one of the web pages, which allows the tool to automatically post any updates from reporters. The team were using Nokia N8 camera phones as they offer images of sufficient quality to be able to use them in print. Team members were also shooting videos on their phones, some of which were uploaded straight to a YouTube account.

Lee and his colleagues at the office were curating and collating web content from the team and the people in the areas at the time.

> 'We were absolutely deluged with comments from readers watching the live blog at the time. We didn't publish anything unless we knew it was happening.'[37]

People were commenting to Lee and the web team about what they had heard, which the *MEN* reporters were able to clarify for them. Cover It Live also allows the page moderators to look through YouTube, Flickr or search Twitter feeds for audio-visual content that can be added into the updates.

Within the first 10 minutes of the liveblog being activated 2,000 people had logged on. This had built to 25,000 live readers by 8 p.m. and this was fairly constant until around 1 a.m. the next morning. The liveblog was kept going for the rest of the week, pulling in messages from those who offered to help with the clean-up of the areas.

The paper had also pledged to cover every one of the court cases as they happened, so these were posted on the liveblog as the magistrates' courts sat throughout the night. This proved to be popular and the liveblog's viewers stayed within the thousands all week.

Lee's final comment:

> 'It was the perfect platform for us to get the story out there, and it proved its worth.'[38]

Open for business – the new transparency

Following the revelations of the *News of the World* phone hacking scandal and the discussion about media access to politicians, both Prime Minister David Cameron and Opposition Leader Ed Milliband said they would be publishing records of meetings with journalists. This opening up of the journalistic process was something noted by media commentator Dan Gillmor who cites the example of the then US Defence Secretary Donald Rumsfeld's department publishing an interview conducted by Bob Woodward and Dan Balz of the *Washington Post* in 2002.

Gillmor, in his excellent book *We The Media* (2006), discusses the implications this kind of transparency – when the interviewee publishes the raw interview – could have on journalism.

> 'It will also make journalists uncomfortable. Our little priesthood, where we essentially have had the final word, is unravelling. But as software people say, that's a feature, not a bug.'[39]

This kind of technique has also been used by the Church of Scientology. It put out a video of its own ahead of a BBC documentary, which showed BBC reporter John Sweeney losing his temper with interviewees to try to show that the broadcaster was being biased.

So if Gillmor is right and the news-makers have the ability to fight back and the old processes are coming to an end, how do we deal with the new news ecology? Some people think the only way is to involve the public from the word go – to open up all of the process of reporting to scrutiny and observation. And maybe as journalists we should think about posting audio versions of any interview that we conduct.

Alison Gow, editor of the *North Wales Post*, is one of the journalists exploring this way of working. In her previous role as executive editor, digital, at Trinity Mirror in Liverpool, Gow set up a liveblog of news conferences and video streamed some of the meeting, allowing the public at large to get involved. This experiment was repeated as the team were invited to become part of an art exhibition at Bluecoats Gallery. Alison then used the ideas learned from these initial forays with the team at *Wales on Sunday*. She set up a Facebook group for her paper to enable staff to be in touch with members of the public; not just to allow staff to post updates from the site, but to actually engage with the public.

The paper opened up a number of its conferences via a liveblog, again asking members of the public to get involved and as part of an attempt to demystify the news process. Another interesting part of this initiative has been the way members of the team have responded. For example, Adam Walker from the paper's design team posted a screen capture of the design work involved in creating front covers of the paper's entertainment section.[40]

This kind of process can protect journalists against charges of manufacturing content but can also lead to other organisations getting in on the story ahead of publication – or can even switch the audience off.

Journalism and coding

For some people interactivity in online journalism means interactive objects, such as Flash-based multimedia packages that allow readers to explore an issue, but interactivity can also be used to describe how readers and audience can actually engage with one another around the research, story-gathering and publication phases of the journalistic process.

Adobe's Flash is an excellent tool for creating packages that can be used to create objects that readers of a web page can use to explore an issue. One example of this is a Flash-based package from the *Guardian* that has combined the work of developers and journalists. The *Guardian* team made the interactive package based around the Twitter messages talking about the UK riots in 2011. In total the team visualised 2.5 million updates to create a timeline leading up to the events and into the clean-up. Readers just drag a slider to look at the chosen time period. One of the issues with tools like Flash is how time-consuming it can be to create these objects – a number of people were bylined for its creation. You may want to explore the tool, which combines drag and drop elements with a coding framework called Actionscript to create the interactive elements.

There is also a range of tools that will allow you to mash-up (combine) information from a variety of sources to help you get answers or create interactive objects. Some of these are what are known as browser-based (you don't have to install them on your computer as they work from a website). Key tools here include Yahoo Pipes, Many Eyes and Many Eyes Wikified. This approach uses very little in the way of coding skills and is a good way to start learning some of the key concepts. The OUseful blog, run by Tony Hirst from the Open University, is a good place to start (see **http://bit.ly/nBCDlQ**).

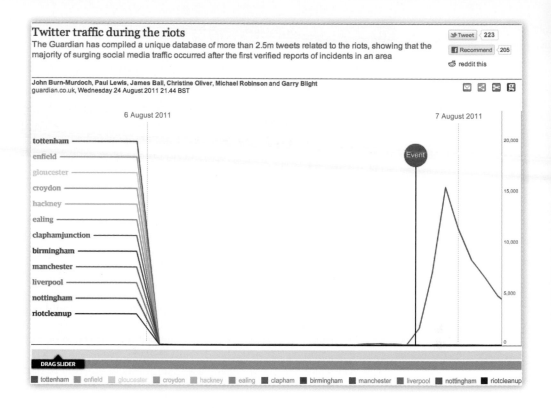

A CLOSER LOOK

GETTING INTERACTIVE WITH ARON PILHOFER OF THE *NEW YORK TIMES*: A Q&A SESSION[41]

How would the NYT define convergence?

Convergence journalism, data-driven journalism – whatever you want to call it – I would define rather broadly. To me, it is the application of new tools and technologies in the service of reporting stories, and new platforms and media in the service of telling them.

Advances in computing power, the availability of broadband, the emergence of high-end open source software all have combined to provide journalists with amazing new tools that can be turned to journalism. That could mean everything from creative application of data mining through a particularly compelling piece of web video.

What are the standout examples of convergence journalism at the NYT?

Our election guide, our Oscars application, a year at war, our wikileaks coverage, and a project we will be soft-launching next week called SchoolBook. All of them brought together bunches of new tools and technologies.

> ▶ **A CLOSER LOOK**
>
> **Regarding convergence of roles (e.g. journo developer) what areas would you suggest young journalists should focus on?**
>
> Generally speaking, the best answer is skills, skills, skills. Young journalists need to be able to do more than just report and write. They are being asked to do audio, shoot video and more. The best way to get ahead is to be conversant in as many forms of journalism as possible, while working to become expert in at least one area. That's the advice I would give.

Obviously these skills take a lot of time and dedication and are beyond the scope of this book – but if you are interested in exploring further then see the Recommended Reading section at the end of this chapter.

remember

- Interactivity doesn't have to be about code, but you could end up as part of a team developing interactive objects.
- Be prepared to learn new skills and see how they can be applied to what you are doing.
- Sites like Scraperwiki can be a helpful way of starting to understand coding by building small programs.

EMERGING TECHNOLOGIES

Futurology in journalism is always a tricky game – Prestel, an interactive text system set up by the Post Office in the 1970s, never really took off in the UK although the French version Minitel did well. Some people will think about media organisation content systems as some of the more important technologies – after all they are the tools that will help a journalist put out information. But it's not necessarily how things pan out.

Take Twitter as an example. It was originally created as a way to allow a group of friends to text message each other and allow conversation, as texting normally ends up in fractured responses that aren't threaded. It was the users who started to define how it changed by adding the @username to show who was being addressed and by building link shorteners to make sure all the space of a message wasn't taken up. Twitter now has in the region of 95 million updates a day going across its network.[42]

This section will look at some of the interesting technologies that are being explored by journalists and that may become part of the mainstream in years to come.

Playing at journalism

Gaming and simulation have long been an accepted part of education and training – think about flight simulators for pilots as a way of testing skills before taking to the air. In fact, Channel 5's *Gadget Show* had one of the team training purely on computer games versions of flight simulators to see if a complete novice could take to the air and fly a light aircraft without the expensive simulators – and it worked.

So, are computer games an element of the classic journalist's adage: to entertain, inform and educate? This could work in a similar way to a tv experiment run by the BBC. *The Street That Cut Everything* forced residents of a Preston street to learn about where their council tax money went and how it was spent by putting them in a setting where they were responsible for the decisions.

A CLOSER LOOK

GETTING INTERACTIVE WITH INTERACTIVE PRODUCER PHIL TRIPPENBACH: A Q&A SESSION[43]

How mainstream do you think a convergence between gaming and journalism will be?

As mainstream as video and text news is now. In their time, radio and television news were both considered frivolous and incapable of serious journalistic content, when each was first introduced. That changed as people grew accustomed to them and began exploring their potential. Games are a powerful medium capable of great sophistication, only now in its infancy. As the medium matures, its place in our society will adjust accordingly. We've already seen great changes in this just in the past 10 years. Besides, text, audio and video each have their place but there are times when frankly a game is the only way of really communicating the truth about an issue.

What are the key examples that have struck you as pointing the way forward?

Budget Hero (NPR), *Six Days in Fallujah* (Atomic, unreleased), and *Energyville* (though that's half advertising as it's sponsored by Chevron). Also *America's Army* (factual but not journalism per se), *Insurgency* (that one is particularly interesting as it's made by veterans). Then there's satire like *September 12th*, most of the stuff made by Ian Bogost, *Oiligarchy* and other *Molleindustria* games (the excellent *McDonald's Game* comes to mind). Particularly interesting right now is *1979*, an upcoming game by one of the producers of *Grand Theft Auto*. I've got separate blog posts going into more detail on all of these on my blog.

If you're looking for an academic exploration of this I'd recommend *Newsgames* by Ian Bogost.

What tips would you offer for student journalists who may be interested in newsgaming?

First of all, I'd say be interested in newsgaming to every student. I think if you're not interested in newsgaming, you should get back to the 20th century because you won't find interesting work in the 21st. Don't want to do interactive news? How charmingly naïve. Go study film or creative writing. Journalism is interactive now.

Harsh, but true. Most editors these days won't hire a journalist who doesn't tweet. Those who will are editors of a publication that will soon sue for bankruptcy. Same goes for newsgaming. It's not quite as mainstream or legit – yet – but the principles that inform it are the foundation of all interactive news production. Principles like compelling interactivity. Procedural rhetoric. Accurate modelling. Experience design. The ability to talk and work with the tech geniuses and create something. These are key features of successful 21st century journalism and they grow like powerful ▶

> ### ▶ A CLOSER LOOK
>
> vines from the seed of newsgaming. Even if you never make a newsgame yourself, you need to know these things so your interactive journalism is good and compelling.
>
> Anyone who wants to write good text journalism needs to read great books, to learn about craft and style. Ditto with interactive journalism and games. Only – surprise! – all journalism exists in an interactive context now. So if you don't study gaming as a journalist, you're essentially choosing your future boss: you'll be working for your schoolmates who did.
>
> #### How to study gaming?
>
> First, game. Game a lot. But game critically. Just as text journalists need to be good writers, a journalist in the 21st century needs to know what innovations there are in gaming. And not just video games. Play innovative board games too – they'll open your eyes.
>
> Second, read. Books by Raph Koster and Jesse Schell are the place to start.
>
> Third, game more, and see the game mechanics underneath the pretty visuals.
>
> Fourth, design your own games. Start thinking about how to explain systems through interactivity.

Location-aware devices

We've already seen news adapting to become viewable on different platforms – from print to web, mobile device and tablet computers as well as internet television. But what about when your phone knows what is happening around you?

Geolocation services such as FourSquare – a social network based around logging in and updating your friends about where you are – have been used by journalists to give people access to information happening around them. The *Wall Street Journal* used the service to tell its subscribers that parts of Times Square had been cordoned off after reports of a suspicious package. The Journal used the service again in August 2011 to show its FourSquare followers where the hurricane shelters were around New York. This could go a step further with the introduction of other technologies into mobile phones such as near field communication – a technology already built into some phones that allows them to react to objects around them or be used as a mobile wallet.

This in turn could be used in the way that some companies are currently using QR codes – smart barcodes – to allow people to explore their surroundings. Augmented reality is another related area that is already being explored both inside journalism and in business. Interesting examples to look out for outside journalism are Layar and the Yell Labs application for the iPhone, which uses a combination of the camera, phone and GPS to work out what is in the local area.

Robots make the news

Another area being explored at present is the use of 'robot' or software journalists that can deal with huge amounts of information. Reuters has a system called NewsScope that monitors news to provide an information service to financial instituions. At its simplest it looks at news flows to determine whether the news is good or bad (sentiment tracking) for a particular company. In 2009 the system also started carrying news stories that were written by the system itself.

The Northwestern University in the USA has been running a project between its computing and journalism departments called Stats Monkey.[44] It essentially employs uses the commonly used phrases found in American sports journalism and applies them to game statistics – and then produces a report. Whether this kind of stats driven journalism will be appropriate for UK sports reporting remains to be seen – but these projects are interesting indicators about the use of artificial intelligence and journalism.

remember

- Technologies are a key part of the research and dissemination process so need to be researched.
- New technologies and trends become part of mainstream journalism quite quickly.
- Be wary of technological determinism – in other words, get the purpose and project sorted before the tool.

CHAPTER SUMMARY

- Convergence is just the latest in a series of ongoing changes in media, admittedly one that is having a major impact on the industry.
- Journalists need to learn new skills given the changing media environment, and a big part of that is learning to work more closely with the people in your online and offline communities.
- Research into new tools and ways of working is a vital attribute of any journalist, and something that will help keep you ahead of the game.
- Be prepared to experiment, but put the story before the tool.

THINKING IT THROUGH

Making changes on the web

The power to constantly publish, amend or update has led to some interesting discussions about accuracy in journalism online. In the past, a magazine or newspaper would have to wait until the next available edition to correct an error – often after a complaint had come in about it. The apology would be relatively small and positioned in the publication following the PCC guidelines.

Online we can amend something straight away – but this brings its own interesting questions. If we make a mistake do we delete the changes and repost the page, take it down and post a new story or just strikethrough the incorrect text and make it very obvious what has happened?

Bloggers will often strike through the text and make a note about what has happened but one of the key issues for media organisations is that mistakes can sometimes come with expensive legal bills. And what about when proceedings are active (see Chapter 9)? How far back in the archives do we need to go to find stories relevant to a case, and should these be taken down completely? After all, a juror is not supposed to be researching a case while a trial is happening – although this does sometimes happen.

> ▶ **THINKING IT THROUGH**
>
> This is an important issue to think about but one that will require very careful application.
>
> _____
>
> **Ask yourself:** What is the best online corrections policy for the type of stories you are working on? How would you deal with a case where you or a colleague completely misinterpreted the information?
>
> ## Transparency
>
> Although opening up the process allows readers access to the whole exercise of putting together a newspaper, magazine or site, is it a good thing? Without doubt it will add depth to stories, giving access to experts and contacts that have never been available before. But what about exclusive content? If you publish your information online as you work things out you could have someone else beat you to the punch with their story. This kind of opening up is not without risk. One Cardiff University student used What Do They Know, the Freedom of Information website, to get data and information that were subsequently used by someone else to get a story. But the student was able to work with a regional newspaper to do his own version of the story. This was public data, so hardly likely to be an exclusive anyway. And both he and the paper were happy with the outcome of the collaboration that came from this data being in the public domain.
>
> The key question here is not whether to engage with the public, but how much of your content should be built in this way? Which of the stories you are working on should be opened up? Or is it the bigger process that concerns us; showing the news values that need to be shown to prove that journalists are not gatekeepers who control the flow of information but are actually working for their communities?
>
> For now, transparency has to be on a case-by-case approach, depending on the rules and regulations of the organisation you are working for but look at the *Guardian*'s Open News project as a sample of things to come.
>
> _____
>
> **Ask yourself:** How open should your journalism process be and who decides what you get to put in the public domain?

NOTES

[1] Interview with the author.
[2] http://www.statistics.gov.uk/cci/nugget.asp?id=8
[3] http://www.culture.gov.uk/news/news_stories/8273.aspx
[4] See note 2.
[5] http://twitpic.com/683mgs
[6] http://www.pressgazette.co.uk/story.asp?section.code=1&storycode=47519&c=1
[7] Ibid.
[8] Ibid.
[9] http://news.bbc.co.uk/1/hi/technology/4630890.stm
[10] Lee-Wright, P., Phillips, A. and Witschge, T., (2011) *Changing journalism*. New York, NY: Routledge.
[11] Gordon, Rich (2003) *The Definitions and Meanings of Convergence*, in K. Kawamoto (ed.) *Digital Journalism: Emerging Media and the Changing Horizons of Journalism*. Oxford: Rowman and Littlefield Publishers.

[12] http://www.edwalker.net/blog/2010/12/22/converged-journalism-and-building-online-communities/

[13] http://hrwaldram.wordpress.com/2010/12/03/what-is-a-fully-converged-journalist-%E2%80%93-nctj-journalism-skills-conference-2010/

[14] Singer, Jane (2009) 'Convergence and divergence', *Journalism*, 10(3), pp. 375–7.

[15] Interview with the author.

[16] http://www.npr.org/templates/story/story.php?storyId=1067220

[17] http://www.nctj.com/news-and events/news/evolution-not-revolution-for-nce

[18] http://www.bbc.co.uk/programmes/b00scxbn

[19] Meyer, Peter (2004) *The vanishing newspaper saving journalism in the information age.* Columbia: University of Missouri Press.

[20] http://news.bbc.co.uk/onthisday/hi/dates/stories/february/15/newsid_3455000/3455083.stm

[21] http://www.kevinsitesreports.com/

[22] Communication with the author, August 2011.

[23] Interview with the author.

[24] Anderson, C. (2007) *The long tail: how endless choice is creating unlimited demand.* London: Random House Business, p.188.

[25] http://www.bbc.co.uk/journalism/blog/2011/05/bbcsms-bbc-procedures-for-veri.shtml

[26] http://washable.com.2011/07/18/harassmap-egypt-sexual.abuse

[27] Communication with the author.

[28] Kolodzy, J. (2006) *Convergence journalism : writing and reporting across the news media.* Lanham, MD: Rowman & Littlefield.

[29] http://nyti.ms/ndc3l5

[30] http://nyti.ms/oSsM5X

[31] http://www.photobus.co.uk/?id=534

[32] http://www.buzzmachine.com/2007/02/22/new-rule-cover-what-you-do-best-link-to-the-rest/

[33] Interview with the author.

[34] Ibid.

[35] Ibid.

[36] http://www.dipity.com/TomScotney/Gun_and_knife_crime_in_Brum/

[37] Interview with the author.

[38] Ibid.

[39] Gillmor, Dan (2006) *We the media: grassroots journalists by the people, for the people.* Sebastopol, CA: O'Reilly.

[40] http://www.youtube.com/user/renduh#p/u/21/iD3_WbXmYmA and http://www.youtube.com/user/renduh#p/u/22/u93Krxae2wY

[41] Interview with the author.

[42] http://www.searchenginejournal.com/the-growth-of-social-media-an-infographic/32788/

[43] Interview with the author.

[44] http://infolab.northwestern.edu/projects/stats-monkey/

RECOMMENDED READING

Bogost, Ian; Ferrari, Simon and Schweizer, Bobby (2010) *Newsgames*. Cambridge, MA: MIT Press.
An academic exploration of this area, as recommended by Phil Trippenbach.

Bradshaw, Paul and Rohumaa, Liisa (2011) *The Online Journalism Handbook: Skills to* survive and thrive in the digital age. Harlow: Pearson.
A good all-round read to help you get to grips with the mindsets and skills behind convergence journalism.

Gillmor, Dan (2006) *We the media: grassroots journalism by the people, for the people.* Sebastopol, CA: O'Reilly Media.
One of the first media commentators to really look at the power to publish that bloggers and other social media users have and offers some interesting thoughts on participatory journalism. While published in 2006 it is still worth a read.

Kolodzy, Janet (2006) *Convergence journalism: writing and reporting across the news media*. Lanham, MD: Rowman & Littlefield.
Although written with the American market in sight, Kolodzy offers some interesting points around convergence and the range of skills required to do it effectively.

Lee-Wright, Peter, Phillips, Angela and Witschge, Tamara (2011) *Changing Journalism (Communication and society)*. New York, NY: Routledge.
An academic look at journalism, this book is the culmination of a whole series of interviews with journalists, editors and publishers looking at what the changes in the industry mean to them.

Shirky, Clay (2009) *Here comes everybody: How change happens when people come together*. London: Penguin.
Clay Shirky is see as one of the leading thinkers around social media and changes in working. This is one of his best-known books and offers an interesting look at the power of social media. His essay and other works are also worth a read (for example, 'Newspapers and Thinking the Unthinkable' available at **http://www.shirky.com/weblog/2009/03/newspapers-and-thinking-the-unthinkable/**).

WEBLINKS

http://www.poynter.org   A website run by the Poynter Institute that offers tips, ideas and case studies from around the world.

http://www.journalism.co.uk   A great site for tips, tools and examples of implementation from across the UK market. Also includes job listings.

http://www.joannageary.com   A great source of links and thoughts from this digital journalist and strategist from the *Guardian*.

http://www.alisongow.com   Insights from the North Wales Post editor.

http://www.andydickinson.net   Thoughts and insights from the University of Central Lancashire's own digital guru.

http://www.onlinejournalismblog.com   Posts from Paul Bradshaw (Birmingham City University and City University London) and his contributors.

http://www.charman-anderson.com/   A site run by Kevin Anderson and Suw Charman-Anderson looking at both the technologies and emerging digital business models on the web.

http://thenextweb.com   Not a journalism site per se, but a great source of information on trends in technology and web businesses.

https://scraperwiki.com   This is a site that allows you to start learning how to get content or information from a site to build mashups (combinations of information from different places). It works in Python, Ruby or PHP so will require you to learn coding, but there are tutorials to get you started.

ACTIVITIES

One of the big issues for any convergence journalist is building an online presence and joining communities. These activities will get you started.

1 Go to Wordpress.com (or Blogger) and set up a blog for yourself. Think carefully about the name as it will be the base for your professional portfolio. And make sure to update it on a regular basis.

2 Set up a Twitter account and make sure your biography has an avatar (picture) and a link to your blog site. Then search for some of the journalists mentioned in this chapter and see who they are talking to – and follow them.

3 Look for journalism groups on Facebook and LinkedIn and join them. LinkedIn also gives you the bonus of having an online CV.

4 Set up your RSS reader and ensure you add feeds that are relevant to you and your topic area.

5 Look at the BBC UGC team's verification process (which can be found at **http://bbc.in/ugchub**). Then look at links or images being shared on a social media site and see which techniques you could apply to verify this information.

CHAPTER NINE
LAW, REGULATION AND ETHICS

This chapter will cover:

- Freedom of Expression and the Human Rights Act
- Reporting crime and the courts
- Defamation, privacy and copyright
- Regulation
- Journalism ethics

Case study 9.1

A male worker in the entertainment industry has an affair with a female colleague, which is an 'open secret' at work. His wife gets to know; the extramarital affair ends and he tells his employer he'd rather not work with the colleague any more although both continue in their jobs for a while. A few months later the woman worker is dismissed. The *News of the World* thinks it knows why and wants to run the story. The man who keeps his job seeks and is granted an injunction – a court order banning the media from telling the tale of the affair. He is back with his wife and children and says the injunction is to protect them.

The injunction is granted by the Court of Appeal, which significantly considers his children's privacy rights when weighing up whether disclosure is warranted.

This much we know from the judgment in *ETK v News Group Newspapers* [2011]. The man is ETK; his co-workers known only as X.

Followers of Twitter and a host of blogs have been told who ETK and X are. We don't know if that information is correct and, even if we did, we couldn't tell you as the media in England and Wales are subject to the injunction. Breaking it would be a contempt of court for which we could face unlimited fines and/or imprisonment.

ETK is one of a host of high-profile litigants – mainly well-known and pretty well-off men – granted injunctions to protect their privacy. Many bans on publication are sought to stop what is known in the media world as a 'kiss-and-tell'. Injunctions can be granted if the court believes there is not enough public interest in the story to warrant the intrusion into privacy and if the secret is not already widely known. Often there is a blackmail element whereby one party is threatening to reveal all in the media unless the errant married actor/footballer/popstar pays 'hush' money, which allows the court to consider the claimant as a blackmail victim.

Commonly now where the parties to the action are well known, the two sides are given anonymity. A judgment is made public but the injunction is anonymised using random initials as in ETK. Super-injunctions involve a further rung of secrecy whereby the media is not even allowed to report that the case exists, let alone who it involves.

An example of a super-injunction was when oil-trading company Trafigura successfully banned the *Guardian* from referring to a report on its activities. Wikileaks and the Twitterati got wind of it but it was only after the controversy reached Parliament that the company backed down. The story did get out (see the *Guardian* editor Alan Rusbridger's response at http://www.guardian.co.uk/media/2009/oct/20/trafigura-anatomy-super-injunction).

Where privacy is at stake, those with secrets to keep are likely to seek an injunction to prevent publication. But, in the absence of an injunction, if the story does run, an individual can claim damages for breach of privacy rights, as Formula One boss Max Mosley did successfully after the *News of the World* exposed his sex life. He received £60,000.

The public express disapproval of the paparazzi but they still put celebrity gossip at the top of all the web rankings. More than a million people had in 24 hours viewed the video of Mosley and five women playing sadomasochistic sex games. Although Mosley won his subsequent privacy action he was not granted an injunction because the material was already in the public domain and it would have been futile – there was no secret left to keep.

Actress Sienna Miller negotiated a £100,000 settlement from the Murdoch-owned *News of the World* for breach of privacy as part of a wide-ranging inquiry into phone hacking which began with the jailing of its Royal editor Clive Goodman in 2007. The newspaper ceased publication in July 2011 amid further accusations of hacking – including into the phone messages of murdered schoolgirl Milly Dowler. The scandal also prompted a wide-ranging inquiry under the auspices of Lord Leveson into press regulation and the relationships between politicians and media owners, particularly the Murdochs. Its recommendations are expected to be far reaching for print online media.

INTRODUCTION

The ETK case is a classic example of the quest to balance privacy rights with freedom of expression within our courts, our regulatory bodies and for ourselves as individual journalists. The move to embrace the rights of a claimant's children is evidence of how the legal framework for journalists changes over time, driven by case law as well as legislation.

These legal requirements have always evolved but the pace of change has stepped up considerably in the face of convergence, burgeoning legislation and the UK's adoption of the European Convention of Human Rights enshrined in the Human Rights Act 1998, which came into force in 2000. Together these trends have created a significant shift in the legal and regulatory framework for 21st century journalists.

Media law in the 20th century tended to focus on rote learning of a lengthening list of legislation and the specific limits each new Act imposed on the work of journalists. In the 21st century the Human Rights Act has effectively superseded all others. A journalist relies every day on the right to freedom of expression and the right to impart information. But this is limited where it impinges on other freedoms. Media law and regulators must decide where the line is drawn when rights collide.

Cases are now judged in terms of balancing rights as defined in the Convention. In practice this is most likely to involve pitting the journalist's right to freedom of expression under Article 10 of the Convention against the Article 8 rights of individuals to protect their privacy and reputation, or their Article 6 rights to a fair trial.

Law, regulation and ethics are also key to the role journalists play in a democratic society. The limits they set and the expectations they create effectively define the arena in which a journalist can operate. A journalist instinctively wants to put as much information as possible into the public domain – sometimes to expose wrongdoing, often to help people understand what is happening in their world and be able to respond to its opportunities and threats.

Multi-platform journalism

Twentieth century regulation tended to be platform specific. So the challenge to regulation from convergence is particularly acute. Even though media law is essentially platform neutral, there are many online circumstances where it is far from easy to draw parallels from earlier case law. The distinctive elements of web and mobile platforms – immediacy, depth and interactivity – all raise significant questions about how the rules apply and who is responsible if they are breached.

Where legal precedent was previously a reasonably reliable guide to what was and was not allowed, 21st century journalists must operate in an even more uncertain legal and regulatory framework. So what are the new rules and how are they applied in practice?

What media law is not

Media law is:

- not fixed – new legislation and case law move the goalposts;
- not black and white – in practice there are many 'grey' areas;
- not always a bar to publishing – it can be an enabler as it is not just about what we can't publish but about knowing what we can publish safely;
- not just about what we publish but about how investigations are conducted;
- not confined to court reporting or 'investigative' exposés – it covers everything we publish;
- not just applicable to journalists – most applies to anyone making material public including microbloggers.

Any legislation has to be interpreted by the courts and so the judiciary has always been remarkably influential when determining the grey areas of meaning, say of the defences under the Defamation Act 1996. But now the scope of the UK Human Rights Act is immense and transcends individual statutes by providing the essential framework for any claim brought against the media that judges must determine on its individual merits.

Where a judgment is taken on appeal to a higher court, the outcome becomes the legal authority on the matter until contradicted by a still higher court, by a more recent case or by new legislation. The highest court in the UK since 2009 is the Supreme Court but its decisions can be appealed to the European Court of Human Rights.

All legislation and related judicial rulings are required to be convention-compliant, give or take each member state's 'margin of appreciation'. This margin allows some leeway for signatories to the Convention where their statute and/or common law have established a particular way of achieving the balancing of rights. The European Court of Human Rights ultimately decides how wide that margin can be in any individual case.

FREEDOM OF EXPRESSION

Journalists are primarily concerned with Article 10 of the European Convention of Human Rights that states:

1 'Everyone has the right to freedom of expression. This right shall include freedom to hold opinions and to receive and impart information and ideas without interference by public authority and regardless of frontiers . . .

2 The exercise of these freedoms, since it carries with it duties and responsibilities, may be subject to such formalities, conditions, restrictions or penalties as are prescribed by law and are necessary in a democratic society, in the interest of national security, territorial integrity or public safety, for the prevention of disorder or crime, for the protection of health or morals, for the protection of the reputation or rights of others, for preventing the disclosure of information received in confidence, or for maintaining the authority and impartiality of the judiciary.'[1]

The more often the world lives up to the maxim attributed to Lord Northcliffe – *news is what someone, somewhere wants you to suppress* – the more a journalist will be pushing the boundaries imposed by law and regulation. Journalists will almost always be on the side of disclosure, often having to challenge claims by others to their rights to privacy, reputation or a fair trial. There are times when the balance will go against them and sometimes reasonably so. If such information would really prevent someone having a fair trial, a society might justifiably restrict its airing to a degree established by legislation and by judicial interpretation.

The right to freedom of expression draws on three broad rationales describing its value to the individual and to the people. The reference to the right to 'impart' information embraces the concept of a public 'right to know'. A journalist defending Article 10 rights may be technically upholding an individual right yet the argument for exercising it most often revolves around the public interest, a much more collective sense. So if a journalist loses the right to put material in the public domain, the public lose out not just in principle but materially by not being privy to that information. This sense of 'public interest' is the most common justification journalists use to uphold the right to freedom of expression but the law does recognise two others. One can be described as self-realisation; the other argues that it is only by the expression of conflicting opinions that the truth can emerge.

The right also embraces the freedom to offend, as discussed by the European Court in *Handyside v UK* back in 1976. It stated:

'Freedom of expression constitutes one of the essential foundations of society, one of the basic conditions for its progress and for the development of every man. Subject to paragraph 2 of Article 10, it is applicable not only to 'information and ideas' that are favourably received or regarded as inoffensive but also to those that offend, shock or disturb the state or any sector of the population. Such are the demands of pluralism, tolerance and broad mindedness without which there is no "democratic society".'

That helps to explain why, for instance, the British National Party has been able to rely on its leaders' Article 10 rights to defend its political pronouncements. Far right politicians have faced challenges from those trying to uphold Convention rights such as those under Article 17 offering protection against 'hate' speech, notably Holocaust denial.

In a case where the courts have to consider competing rights – say a journalist's freedom of speech against a celebrity's right to privacy – the judges must engage in 'parallel analysis' as defined by Sir Mark Potter, the President of the Family Division of the High Court, in the case of *A Local Authority v W [2005]*, reflecting the approach of the House of Lords in *Re S (A Child) [2005]*.

> '**The starting point is presumptive parity, in that neither Article has precedence over or "trumps" the other. The exercise of parallel analysis requires the court to examine the justification for interfering with each right and the issue of proportionality is to be considered in respect of each. It is not a mechanical exercise to be decided upon the basis of rival generalities. An intense focus upon the comparative importance of the specific rights being claimed in the individual case is necessary before the ultimate balancing test in terms of proportionality is carried out.**'

The European Court of Human Rights has a strong record of upholding Article 10 rights when under attack by the State. A classic case is *Goodwin v United Kingdom* [1996] ECHR where journalist Bill Goodwin won the right not to reveal a source in defiance of a UK court order. The court also protected a newspaper threatened with closure by Moldovan authorities (see *Kommersant Moldovy v Moldova* [2007] ECHR.)

Freedom of expression is key territory for journalists and the Recommended Reading at the end of this chapter includes many more specialist texts relating to freedom of speech that merit further investigation.

See also 'Freedom of expression: When should it be curbed?' in Thinking It Through at the end of this chapter.

remember

- Freedom of expression is at the heart of the work of a journalist.
- Article 10 of the European Convention on Human Rights defines a UK journalist's right to freedom of expression and to impart information.
- More broadly, the right relies on its vital role in democratic discourse, self-realisation and the emergence of truth through competition of ideas.

REPORTING CRIME AND THE COURTS

A journalist's Article 10 rights to freedom of expression are most likely to clash with the Article 6 rights of others to a fair trial when reporting crime and the courts. Various statutes curbing the work of journalists are very broadly based on the desire to prevent trial by media. Those most likely to affect journalists, such as the Contempt of Court Act 1981 and the Magistrates' Court Act 1980, are covered in this section but we cannot include them all in one chapter. (See the Recommended Reading at the end of this chapter.)

The 21st century emergence of online and mobile news sources and delivery platforms has thrown up a raft of new challenges to a legal system designed to uphold rights to a fair trial, from concerns over jurors' easy access to potentially prejudicial online archives about a defendant to whether it is acceptable for journalists to microblog from court.

Article 6 of the European Convention on Human Rights establishes that everyone is entitled to a fair and public hearing within a reasonable time by an independent and impartial tribunal, established by law, if deemed to have contravened the criminal law. It goes on to state:

'Judgment shall be pronounced publicly but the press and public may be excluded from all or part of the trial in the interests of morals, public order or national security in a democratic society, where the interests of juveniles or the protection of the private life of the parties so require, or to the extent strictly necessary in the opinion of the court in special circumstances where publicity would prejudice the interests of justice.'

Article 6(2) confirms the principle: everyone charged with a criminal offence shall be presumed innocent until proved guilty according to law.

Contempt of Court Act 1981

The main statute serving to uphold Article 6 rights to a fair trial is the Contempt of Court Act 1981 which again, contrary to the impression given by its title, applies to much more than just court reporting. Almost every section of the Contempt of Court Act has direct relevance to journalists.

The strict liability rule of the Contempt of Court Act states:

1 Conduct may be treated as a contempt of court as tending to interfere with the course of justice in particular legal proceedings *regardless of intent* to do so.
2 The strict liability rule applies to publication which includes any speech, writing, or other communication in whatever form, which is addressed to the public at large or any section of the public.

The strict liability rule applies only to a publication which creates *a substantial risk that the course of justice in the proceedings in question will be seriously impeded or prejudiced.*

The strict liability rule applies to a publication only if the proceedings in question are active at the time of the publication. (Our emphasis in italics.)

When it applies

A journalist must be aware of the contempt risk whenever a situation is 'active', which is from the start of criminal proceedings. The initial steps of criminal proceedings are:

- the issue of a warrant for arrest;
- arrest without warrant;
- the issue of a summons to appear in court;
- the service of an indictment or other document specifying the charge; or
- an oral charge.

In civil cases the risk begins when a case is set down for trial or when a date is fixed for the case to be heard. An inquest is active for contempt when opened, even if adjourned. The risk lasts until proceedings are concluded:

- by acquittal or, as the case may be, by sentence;
- by any other verdict, finding, order or decision that puts an end to the proceedings;
- by discontinuance or by operation of law.

Proceedings become active again if an appeal is lodged. Often at the end of the trial, counsel may state an intention to appeal. This in itself does not make the case active again but it does alert a reporter that there may be only a brief window to run any otherwise risky background articles about how the criminals were caught and accounts of their often dubious past. Checks must also be made to see if the appeal materialises and to track its progress.

Technically a case is active until sentence despite the fact that the jury's role ends with the verdict. Sentences are decided by judges who are considered to be impervious to media coverage so they could hardly argue that press exposure between trial and sentence had prejudiced the outcome. Thus action against the media for contempt would be unlikely once a verdict is reached but it remains risky.

Crime reporters have to be particularly alert to the demands of the Contempt of Court Act. A journalist must not only assess and avoid the risk of serious prejudice but make rigorous attempts to determine if any case is active. So in practice:

- Do not pre-empt the judicial process by presenting anyone questioned, arrested or charged as guilty in advance of a trial. Judges (and coroners) are particularly sensitive to being usurped in this way and they can be unwelcome adversaries even if the Attorney General does not ultimately sanction proceedings under the Act.
- Reports of culprits being caught 'red-handed' are particularly fraught as any account should allow for the possibility that the person apprehended is not the actual offender.
- Take care when reporting on a crime for which someone has already been arrested. The Contempt of Court Act allows for news of the crime to be put in the public domain but, because the arrest makes the case active, care must be taken to separate reports of the incident and the victim from any information on the alleged perpetrator.
- Pictures and descriptions are particularly risky. Many cases hinge on questions of identity and journalists can rarely be sure identity will not be an issue at trial. Publishing a photograph could prejudice potential jurors and be seen to influence witness evidence, possibly invalidating any identity parade, for instance.
- Previous convictions are also a 'no-go' area. Jurors are not generally made aware of a defendant's criminal record during the trial as this was seen as crucial to the principle of being innocent unless proven guilty. Judges can now allow such evidence but remain adamant that it is not for the media to pre-empt that decision.

Apparent contraventions of the Contempt of Court Act arise from publicity given to police 'wanted' appeals. It is common to see a photograph or e-fit plastered across the media of a suspect wanted in connection with a murder and even described as armed and dangerous. Evidently this creates a substantial risk of serious prejudice to any subsequent trial and proceedings are active.

Here journalists have some protection, albeit not in the Act itself. When the associated Bill was being debated prior to enactment, the then Attorney General speaking in Parliament assured the media it had 'nothing whatever to fear from publishing in reasoned terms anything which may assist in the apprehension of a wanted man' (presumably woman too). This has been honoured but is not to be abused. The protection extends only to official police statements, not to exaggerated interpretations of them or to additional prejudicial background information. This exception acknowledges the public interest in suspects being apprehended but the logic dictates that normal rules apply once an arrest is made.

If accused of contempt, publications can also argue that by the time a case comes to trial any jurors will have forgotten the coverage from the time the crime was committed or a suspect arrested. This is known as the 'fade factor'. Months or even years can pass between arrest and trial so it is an effective, and indeed realistic, argument. Even fairly damning coverage early on is not actually creating a 'substantial risk of serious prejudice' to the trial.

Prosecutions of journalists under the Act have been rare. Only the Attorney General can authorise an action and, given that successful contempt action will make it difficult to continue with a prosecution, weighing situations in the public interest can favour the journalist. So a blind eye is turned to all but the most outrageous coverage around the time of arrest and sometimes even clear accusations of guilt as in the arrest of men suspected of the London 7/7 bombing. But in the wake of saturation coverage of the Joanna Yeates murder inquiry around Christmas 2010 two newspapers were prosecuted and fined heavily for contempt for background reporting on an initial suspect (later cleared). His own defamation claims against several titles were also settled in his favour out of court.

Action is also far more likely during or immediately prior to trial as discussed in the next section.

- Is the case active for contempt? A journalist is expected to keep checking.
- Does your coverage create a substantial risk of serious prejudice to a trial?
- Do not assume guilt; do not include photographs, descriptions or previous convictions.
- Could you rely on the fade factor?

Contempt: challenges of convergence

Judges have gradually come to adopt much more media-friendly assessments about how jurors are, or are not, influenced by journalistic material. Arguably they have had little choice given the explosion of material, old and new, which jurors can find online. There was a time when pre-trial coverage could be blocked by curbs on a limited number of controllable, accountable mainstream media outlets. Attempting to apply those limits to the relatively anarchic digital environment is more daunting.

Judges work on the basis that they can no longer protect jurors from exposure to prejudicial information so they have instead stressed the duty on jurors to ignore any such influences (or indeed any other of their prejudices). However, mainstream media can still be called to account for breaches of the Contempt of Court Act, particularly during a trial. A national news organisation is still much more likely to be accused of influencing the jury than an amateur website. The *Daily Mail* and the *Sun* were both fined for contempt for publishing the photograph of a defendant on their websites during his trial. In *Attorney General v Associated Newspapers & Another* [2011] the court ruled that there was a substantial risk of serious prejudice to the proceedings from pictures posted of the accused carrying a gun, particularly as he was claiming he had killed a man in self-defence.

The growth of online news has also changed the contempt landscape as regards archives. The fade factor, for instance, was plausible when today's newspaper was tomorrow's fish and chip wrapper; it is much less convincing when those vivid remarks from the time of arrest are still sitting in an easily searchable online archive during trial. The main reaction has been for judges to order jurors not to seek out such material but newspapers may decide to pre-empt any complaint by suppressing such material during trial and should certainly not link background material to live trial reporting.

This is one of several areas where the courts are still struggling to apply long-established legislation to the 21st century online news environment, leaving considerable uncertainty for mainstream media organisations.

Innocent publication

Other protections are more explicit in the Contempt of Court Act. Section 3 offers a defence for innocent publication or distribution as follows:

'(1) A person is not guilty of contempt of court under the strict liability rule if at the time of publication (*having taken all reasonable care*) *he does not know and has no reason to suspect* that relevant proceedings are active.'

The same applies to a distributor of the material but section 3 puts the burden of proof on the journalist/distributor.

This style of protection, which has a parallel in the Defamation Act, mainly assists distributors rather than originators and is relied upon by internet service providers and by many individuals or organisations that host unmoderated public discussion boards. Once any host is alerted to a contempt risk, the material should be made inaccessible to the public, at least until the case ceases to be active.

A crime reporter having to demonstrate that 'all reasonable care' was taken will have to prove checks to see if the case had become active were made with police right up to deadline.

Discussion of public affairs

A further defence against prosecution for contempt is provided for media coverage of issues that happen to relate to a trial. Section 5 of the Contempt of Court Act, with regard to discussion of public affairs, states:

> 'A publication made as or as part of a discussion in good faith of public affairs or other matters of general public interest is not to be treated as a contempt of court under the strict liability rule if the **risk of impediment or prejudice** to particular legal proceedings is **merely incidental** to the discussion.'

This is a valuable defence. At any time trials are likely to be taking place regarding many of the issues journalists wish to air. For example, a feature on people trafficking may well coincide with the trial somewhere within the circulation area of operators of a brothel using trafficked women. Section 5 allows for the feature to run as long as there is no direct danger of its influencing the trial. The key word from the section is 'incidental'. If the idea for the feature was triggered by the trial then it risks losing the defence as the link will be too evident. Certainly the temptation must be resisted to 'hook' readers with a reference to the trial in headlines or copy. It is never wise to be disingenuous if you want to rely on a legal defence.

The classic example here relates to election coverage. Lord Diplock in *Attorney General v English* [1982] accepted the defence from the *Daily Mail* which ran a piece by Malcolm Muggeridge supporting a pro-life byelection candidate during the trial of Dr Leonard Arthur who was accused of murdering a baby with Down's syndrome. Clearly the relation to an election helped in establishing the need for a proper discussion of public affairs but the fact that there was no explicit reference to the trial was also key.

remember

- Don't mention the trial in your piece if you need to rely on an s5 contempt defence.
- Don't link related discussion boards to reports of 'active' cases and especially not during a trial.

Protection of sources

Section 10 of the Contempt of Court Act is central to protection of journalistic sources. It states:

> '**No court may require a person to disclose**, nor is any person guilty of contempt of court for refusing to disclose, **the source of information** contained in a publication for which

he is responsible, unless it be established to the satisfaction of the court that disclosure is *necessary in the interests of justice or national security or for the prevention of disorder or crime.*'

These are uncomfortably broad exemptions and this remains a difficult area for journalists. It is one of the realms where a journalist is honour-bound to protect a source, whatever a court decides. As this could involve a jail term, no journalist should be cavalier about assurances made to sources. The European Court of Human Rights has tended to rule favourably for journalists in this area. It held, for instance, that action taken to force a Dutch magazine to hand over footage of illegal car racing breached its Article 10 rights to protect its source (see *Sanoma Uitgevers BV v The Netherlands* [2010]).

For advice on handling confidential sources see Chapter 7 and for more on the regulatory position see the section on Regulation later in this chapter, notably the Press Complaints Commission Editors' Code of Practice, which insists that all journalists have a moral duty to protect their confidential sources, without exception.

Postponement and prohibition orders

Postponement and prohibition orders are two further specific restrictions that can be imposed on the media under the Contempt of Court Act 1981. Postponement orders are outlined in Section 4(2), which states:

'. . . the court may, where it appears to be necessary for avoiding a substantial risk of prejudice to the administration of justice in those proceedings, or in any other proceedings pending or imminent, order that the publication of any report of the proceedings, or any part of the proceedings, be postponed for such period as the court thinks necessary for that purpose.'

This power is most often used where a series of linked trials is taking place such that reports of one would prejudice a subsequent hearing. A postponement order was one of the curbs in the infamous trial over the death of Baby P in 2008 to protect a separate forthcoming trial, although the identities were widely leaked on websites. An order can be remarkably frustrating but it is still worth covering the case as the report can be held until the order expires, then published safely as it will be treated as contemporaneous. (See Asbolute privilege for court reports later in this chapter.)

Prohibition orders can be made under section 11, which states:

'In any case where a court (having power to do so) allows a name or other matter to be withheld from the public in proceedings before the court, the court may give such directions prohibiting the publication of that name or matter in connection with the proceedings as appear to the court to be necessary for the purpose for which it was so withheld.'

An s11 order can be imposed where the administration of justice would be frustrated or otherwise rendered impracticable. These orders were devised primarily to protect vulnerable witnesses who would refuse to give evidence if identified to the court and public in the normal way. Members of the security services are likely to be put in this category. That in itself challenges principles of open justice but the restriction becomes disproportionate where an s11 is improperly issued to make a defendant anonymous, say because publicity might make life difficult at work. Any journalist faced with a court attempting to make such an order should cite Lord Justice Watkins, from *R v Evesham Justices, ex p McDonagh* [1988], where he said s11 was not enacted for the benefit of the comfort and feelings of defendants. Any threat has to be serious and real before the court will take it into account in considering an s11.

- Court reports can be postponed under section 4(2).
- Details can be withheld from reports under section 11 only if withheld from the start of the proceedings.
- Departures from the principle of open justice have to be justified.
- Learn the detailed requirements so you can challenge any order that appears not to be valid.
- Always seek written confirmation of the scope of any order.

Juries

Section 8 of the Contempt of Court Act regarding the confidentiality of jury deliberations states:

> '(1) it is a contempt of court to obtain, disclose or solicit any particulars of statements made, opinions expressed, arguments advanced or votes cast by members of a jury in the course of their deliberations in any legal proceedings.'

This is one of the strictest clauses of the Act in terms of the consistency with which it is enforced. The jury is treated as sacrosanct despite arguments that the judicial system would benefit from greater transparency with regard to how jurors reach a verdict.

Reporters need to take great care. Just bumping into a juror in the ladies or gents can cause difficulties. An anxious juror could easily interpret chat as 'soliciting' information and report the journalist to the judge. *The Times* newspaper was found guilty of contempt in May 2009 for breaching s8 in an article interviewing a jury foreman who was unhappy with the verdict reached in the case on which he sat. It was fined £15,000.

See also 'Can juries deliver justice?' in Thinking It Through at the end of this chapter.

- Do not report jury deliberations.
- Avoid all contact with jurors during a trial.

Recording court proceedings

The Contempt of Court Act 1981 extends to specific behaviour of journalists in court. Section 9 bans recording equipment from courts so that it is an offence either to make the recording or publish it without the court's permission. Some judges do allow recording but only in lieu of a shorthand note; not for airing directly.

Separate legislation, the Criminal Justice Act 1925, already banned photography or sketching in the court or its precincts. The 'precincts' are not precisely defined although officials at any individual court will probably advise on their interpretation. Generally any snatched photographs of defendants entering or leaving court should be taken away from any court steps, say, and at least on the public highway. Sketches used in print or on screen have to be drawn by artists from memory.

Filming is also generally banned in UK courts. The US experience has made UK judges wary that parties to proceedings would play to the cameras and/or that others would be intimidated. A concession has been made by the UK Supreme Court, which exempted itself from the ban, and for the sentencing by a judge in serious cases.

The restrictive approach in the lower courts has created an issue over whether it is permissible to microblog reports from court. This can be really valuable for a journalist wanting to spread news of the verdict in a high-profile case but mobile phones are generally banned. It has been a matter for individual judges to grant or deny permission and a consultation exercise was conducted during 2011 with a view to creating more general guidelines on use of mobile media for court reporting.

remember

- Audio recording is banned except with the permission of the court.
- Photography and sketching are banned in the court and its precincts.
- Filming is banned except in the Supreme Court and for some sentencing.
- Microblogging may be allowed at the judge's discretion. A more consistent approach may be adopted.

Magistrates' Courts Act 1980

The Magistrates' Courts Act poses significant limits on reporting for the purpose of protecting trial by jury. Criminal cases start out at magistrates' court before the more serious charges are sent to the crown court for trial by jury. Reporting of these preliminary hearings before magistrates of any offence which could ultimately be tried by a jury are restricted by section 8 of the Act to the following 10 points:

- the name of the court and the names of the magistrates;
- names, addresses, occupations of parties and witnesses, ages of the accused and witnesses;
- the offence(s) or a summary of them, with which the accused is charged;
- names of counsel and solicitors in the proceedings;
- any decision of the court to commit the accused, or any of the accused for trial, and any decision on the disposal of the case of any accused not committed;
- where the court commits the accused, the charge or charges, or a summary of them, on which the accused is committed and the court to which they are committed;
- where proceedings are adjourned, the date and place to which they are adjourned;
- any bail arrangements (which is taken to include any bail conditions, but not any reason for opposing or refusing it);
- whether legal aid was granted;
- any decision of the court to lift or not lift reporting restrictions.

The purpose is to prevent any consideration of the evidence at this early stage. Consequently reports can end up being very brief. But it can be of considerable public interest to publish the basic facts of the proceedings. Full details of the alleged offence with which the defendant is charged are included in the above 10 points and this can allow the story to be fleshed out a little. So rather than referring simply to a charge of murder, the full charge will usually include the identity of the victim, the time, place and other newsworthy information. Note that the list does not include the defendant's plea.

Reports often do go further than the 10 points strictly allow, say by including detail of what the defendant was wearing. Action is unlikely to be taken where such additional information clearly has no bearing on the guilt or innocence of the defendant, but technically any information not covered by the 10 points above is a breach of the Act. Any journalist following a publication's habit of being somewhat lax in this area should still routinely alert the newsdesk if any information outside the list has been included.

Sexual offences

Lifetime anonymity is granted to the alleged victims of sexual offences in the general interests of justice on the basis that, without it, victims would not be prepared to pursue charges and alleged attackers would not be prosecuted. Even with anonymity, many rape allegations do not lead to a prosecution, partly because they often rely on one person's word against another, which can make the chances of conviction slim.

The conditions are set out in a series of Sexual Offences Acts that list the offences covered, including voyeurism; establish the right to lifetime anonymity; and specifically exclude use of the alleged victim's name, address, school or other educational establishment, place of work and any still or moving picture of the person.

In February 2006 the *Daily Express* and the *Daily Telegraph* were ordered to pay a total of £15,000 compensation and fined £4,700 after publishing photographs of the victim of an alleged sexual assault. The photographs had been taken from behind. The woman was a member of the military and in uniform when attending court and it was held that she could easily be recognised.

Lifetime anonymity is significant for the period before and after any trial, so affects any follow-up feature or general reporting with rape victims. Anyone who has made a formal allegation of rape is automatically protected. A victim over the age of 16 may consent to be identified in the media but this must be in writing and clearly not under duress. Anonymity is lost if an alleged victim is later accused of making false accusations.

remember

- Alleged victims of sexual offences are granted lifetime anonymity.
- A victim aged 16 or over can waive anonymity in writing and of their own free will.

Children

Children are also offered special protection under the law, notably via the Children and Young Persons Act of 1933, mainly covering their involvement in criminal actions.

Section 49 of the Act prevents the press from reporting anything that would reveal the identity of a young person appearing before a youth court where it is an offence to publish or broadcast:

- the name, address or school or any particular leading to the identification of any child or young person involved in the proceedings as a defendant or a witness;
- any still or moving image of, or including, any such person.

Care must be taken with other details of a report that might inadvertently identify the juvenile. So an adult witness can be identified but a reporter often has to omit the connection with the child so as to avoid identification, particularly if they are related.

Anonymity can be lifted:

- by the court or the Home Secretary, to avoid injustice to the juvenile;
- by the court, after conviction, if deemed to be in the public interest (a journalist can request a lifting of the order but the court must allow parties to proceedings to have their say before making a decision);
- by the court on application to the Director of Public Prosecutions, to trace a juvenile in connection with certain serious offences.

Protection of the public can be a persuasive argument. The court may accept that a community should be aware of a young person in their midst especially if they are a persistent offender, have been found guilty of a serious crime and/or are at the older end of the age range, say 16 or 17. Anonymity was challenged, for instance, for older juveniles convicted of involvement in the riots and looting of summer 2011.

The anonymity rule does not apply to a defendant who reaches the age of 18 during proceedings.

Section 39 orders

A child appearing in the adult courts, for example as a defendant on a serious charge such as murder or manslaughter, has no automatic right to anonymity. However the child's lawyers are likely to ask the court to issue an s39 order, particularly for child witnesses. The making of such an order is at the discretion of the judge taking account of all the relevant circumstances. Section 39 reads:

> 'In relation to any proceedings in any court the court may direct that –
> (a) no newspaper report of the proceedings shall reveal the *name, address or school, or include any particulars calculated to lead to the identification, of any child or young person concerned in the proceedings* (as either defendant or witness)
> (b) *no picture* shall be published in any newspaper as being or including a picture of any child or young person so concerned in the proceedings except insofar as permitted by the court . . .'

Section 39 applies only to those concerned in the proceedings. Courts are occasionally sympathetic to the plight of family members and may seek to impose an s39 order on adults or on children who are not party to proceedings. Journalists should be vigilant and determine exactly why, and for whose benefit, the reporting restriction has been imposed.

The judge should not order directly that an adult defendant must not be named to protect a child. It is an editorial decision to decide how to protect the identity of the child made subject of the order. Classically, in the case of an adult defendant and a child victim, the adult is named in the interests of open justice but the relationship with the child is omitted together with sufficient other detail to protect the victim's identity as required by the order.

Judges thwarted in an attempt to order anonymity for an adult defendant under section 39 may resort to other legislation, most notably section 11 of the Contempt of Court Act, which is likely to be similarly inappropriate.

PUTTING IT INTO PRACTICE

Simon Brown LJ sitting in the Queen's Bench Divisional Court in *R v Winchester Crown Court ex parte B* [2000] set out the following principles for considering whether a child defendant should be granted anonymity:

- 'Are there good reasons for naming the defendant?
- Considerable weight must be given to the age of the offender and the potential damage to any young person of public identification as a criminal before the offender has the benefit or burden of adulthood.
- Regard must be had to the welfare of the child.
- The court should consider the deterrent effect on others of any publicity as a legitimate objective to be achieved.

▶ PUTTING IT INTO PRACTICE

- There is strong public interest in knowing what has occurred in court and that includes the identity of the defendant.
- The weight attributed to these factors may vary at different stages in the proceedings. After a guilty plea or a finding of guilt the public interest in knowing the identity of the criminal may be the determining factor particularly if the crime is "serious or detestable".
- There may be notice of an appeal. That may be a material factor in deciding to impose an s39 order.'

After considering all the factors relevant to the case, the court must indicate the reasons why an order is imposed or lifted.

Read also the guidance on s39 orders in the Judicial Studies Board guidelines on court reporting available at **http://www.judiciary.gov.uk**.

Activity: A father of two charged with downloading child pornography seeks an s39 order to protect the identity of his own children, and the court orders that his name will also have to be withheld. Would you challenge this order and, if so, on what grounds?

remember

- Only a child can be the subject of an s39 order; it cannot be made on an adult.
- An s39 order cannot be made on a dead child.
- An s39 order cannot be made regarding a child who is not party to the proceedings.
- Always ensure an order is properly made and insist on a written copy.
- Check out how orders are applied in practice in the Judicial Studies Board guidelines on court reporting at **http://www.judiciary.gov.uk**.

For more on the practicalities of court reporting see the Court section of Chapter 7.

DEFAMATION

Defamation laws exist as a counterbalance to freedom of expression offering legal protection to individuals from any unwarranted attack on their reputation. The law also protects the reputation of companies but not councils, so a business can sue for defamation but not a local authority, although its individual officers could.

A new Defamation Act was in the pipeline in 2011 which would bring legislation into line with 21st century case law in this area as well as introducing a single publication rule and some other adjustments. Many of its intended changes are discussed in this chapter but this provides another example of the need for media law students to keep abreast of developments. A check at **http://www.legislation.gov.uk** will establish if a new Act has come into force or whether the 1996 Act remains current.

Broadly a statement is defamatory if it tends to:

- lower a person in the estimation of right-thinking members of society;
- injure (disparage) a person in a job/calling;

- cause a person to be shunned or avoided;
- expose a person to hatred, ridicule or contempt.

Defamation encompasses any attack on reputation. Where it appears in permanent form, in print, online and also broadcast media, it is *libel*; where it is in transient, spoken form it is *slander*. Journalists rarely face slander action but do need to be alert to its risks. This is an area where it is important to remember that the law applies to how we go about our business as well as what we publish. So, a journalist investigating allegations about someone with a third party should take care to word questions carefully and not to make defamatory assertions along the way.

The claimant doesn't have to prove that what you have written is untrue. In legal terms the burden of proof is on the publisher. The standard of proof is on the balance of probabilities. Every person is presumed to have a reputation and that reputation is deemed to have a value. The claimant doesn't need to prove damage has actually been caused but the proposed new Defamation Act would require the potential or real harm to be 'substantial'.

The claimant must show that:

- the 'sting' or thrust of the material was defamatory;
- the complainant was identified (not necessarily named);
- the material was published to a third person.

Defamatory meaning

The words 'complained of' must be capable of being regarded as defamatory. In the absence of agreement to that effect between the parties a judge will have to decide this issue. This creates one of several significant difficulties for journalists in defamation actions. Articles are often open to interpretation and the meaning attributed by the judge may not coincide with the journalist's intention. So a journalist goes into a case not knowing what meaning of the words will have to be defended.

If the judge agrees that the words are capable of being defamatory then the final decision in the case will rest with the jury. A jury can be dispensed with because the judge decides the case is too complex for them. Libel cases have traditionally been decided by a jury but judges have been opting to rule alone and the Defamation Bill 2011 proposes to dispose of juries entirely. (See also 'Can juries deliver justice?' in Thinking It Through at the end of this chapter.)

It is rarely one single word to which a claimant takes exception but the meaning of a paragraph or of the piece as a whole. Precedent does provide some guidance on how the matters are weighed, as described in *Gillick v BBC* [1996]. The focus is on the 'hypothetical reader or viewer' to make that important decision. The Court of Appeal expressed it in these terms:

- **'The courts must give to the material complained of the natural and ordinary meaning that it would have conveyed to the ordinary reasonable reader.**
- **The *hypothetical reasonable reader* is not naïve but he is not unduly suspicious. He can read between the lines.**
- **In determining the meaning of the material complained of the Court is not limited by the meanings which either the claimant or the defendant seeks to place upon the words.'**

Determination of meaning embraces any innuendo in the statements complained of so journalists cannot get away with snide digs. An implied meaning can be defamatory as well as an explicit one. The court decides the meaning of the words published.

Innuendo is discussed in detail in *Baturina v Times Newspapers* [2011]. The *Sunday Times* reported that Baturina, described as Russia's wealthiest woman, had bought a £50 million

London mansion. There would be nothing defamatory about that but for the fact that, had it been true, it should have been listed in the interests of her husband, then Mayor of Moscow. In the context it acquired a defamatory meaning which the *Sunday Times* had to defend even though it had not been aware of that background. Because of such complexities in defending a defamation action, judges are often asked to make an initial ruling on elements such as meaning so that parties can decide whether to settle rather than go to a full hearing.

Also, the 'sting' cannot be removed entirely simply by using the word 'allegedly' when revealing information that undermines the reputation of an individual. The legal authority for that proposition is *Lewis v Daily Telegraph* [1964].

Identity

A claimant can only sue if identified by the publication but it should not be assumed that withholding the name makes the report legally safe. The crucial question is whether or not, from the information published, the 'hypothetical reader' will understand that the 'sting' relates to or includes the claimant.

You do not need to name the members of a premiership soccer team for some people to conclude that your story is about any one of those players who regularly appears in the first team. So not naming can be more risky than naming. If you have evidence against one player you may succeed with a justification defence, but you will have no defence against the others who might successfully claim people took the derogatory statement to apply to them.

Publication

A claimant will need to prove that the material about which they complain has been published. This means that the communication has been seen, as lawyers say, by a 'third party'. Technically one person is enough but the courts are reluctant to proceed on that basis. In *Jameel v Dow Jones & Co Inc.* only five people were known to have accessed a website containing alleged defamatory material and the court ruled it would be an abuse of process to allow the case to continue because it was most unlikely that the complainant's reputation would have been affected. The 'substantial harm' test in the Defamation Bill would potentially raise the threshold in this regard. Some website audiences would be too small to threaten reputation significantly but mainstream print titles would reach too large an audience to rely on this.

Defamation action cannot be taken:

- If a claimant dies.
- If the claimant signed an advance statement agreeing to the publication. It is not enough to have put the offending words to the claimant with the opportunity of rebuttal. A 'no comment' is certainly not consent.
- If publication was more than one year ago. This offers little protection now stories are routinely published and archived online as every time an article is accessed counts as a fresh publication. This effectively meant that the time limit never kicked in. The Defamation Bill 2011 would create a 'single publication rule' to start the clock from first publication, which would be a relief to publishers.
- Where publication of a correction and apology has been formally accepted by a claimant in settlement, known as accord and satisfaction.

In addition, the same complaint cannot be brought twice against the same defendant but a claimant can sue multiple defendants for publishing the same material in different outlets or platforms.

The law may be platform-blind but in reality there are websites galore publishing defamatory material all the time. Unless they belong to a mainstream news organisation they have generally been action-proof. This is because any individual blogger is unlikely to have the assets to make it worth suing as there is little prospect of enforcing any damages award. But more actions are being taken against material on digital platforms and some people will sue on a point of principle.

remember

A defamation action can be brought if the material published:
- bore a defamatory meaning;
- identified the claimant either explicitly or implicitly;
- was published.

Defamation defences

Several defences are available but contesting a defamation action can be very difficult, unpredictable and hugely expensive.

The risk of damages used to be the main fear, particularly when juries were awarding millions of pounds in some cases. Damages were later informally capped at around £225,000. In the 21st century the main concern has been over costs, fuelled by conditional fee arrangements. These 'no win, no fee' deals were supposed to allow poorer complainants to bring actions for defamation, which do not qualify for legal aid. However the risk taken by lawyers is now built into a fee structure. If a media organisation loses an action, it must pay its own costs plus the inflated costs of the claimant and a 'success' fee, which can double the bill. Costs of fighting an action can run into millions of pounds; far greater than any damages. Even if an organisation wins, it may well not be able to reclaim its costs from the loser.

These arrangements are considered to be having a 'chilling effect' on the media by deterring them from running stories of genuine public concern because of the cost of defending themselves against any ensuing defamation writ. The coalition government is committed to abolishing the conditional fee arrangements, probably lowering costs in return for higher damages. This would apply to conditional fee arrangements in all civil actions not just those affecting the media.

For those with the courage and finances to proceed, the defences are:

- absolute privilege;
- qualified privilege – statutory and common law – to include in the Defamation Bill responsible publication on a matter of public interest;
- fair comment – renamed honest opinion in the Defamation Bill;
- justification – renamed truth in the Defamation Bill;
- 'innocent' publication.

Absolute privilege

Absolute privilege is afforded to *fair, accurate, contemporaneous* reports of judicial proceedings in UK in public (and other courts specified in section 14 of the Defamation Act 1996 including the European Court of Human Rights). Provided the conditions are met, this offers a complete defence against defamation for derogatory information reported from court. Contemporaneous means as soon as possible after the case has finished or even while it is proceeding. Online updates, during a break in a trial for instance, can be reported before a final outcome is known as long as they make clear that the case is proceeding and stress that charges are contested. There should also be sufficient coverage of the remainder of the proceedings to provide a balanced account for readers, including the ultimate outcome. It would not be fair to report all the prosecution evidence in a criminal trial, for example, but not make the public aware of the defendant's subsequent acquittal.

The defence only protects proceedings. It does not protect interruptions from the public gallery or corridor conversations with any of the parties or their representatives.

remember

> Absolute privilege protects fair, accurate and contemporaneous reports of court proceedings in public from actions for defamation.

Qualified privilege

The Defamation Act 1996 provides a statutory qualified privilege defence for a wide range of reports, linked to particular public occasions such as tribunals and local authority meetings. These are immensely valuable for journalists and remain a core protection for the reporting of contentious matters which would otherwise be legally fraught. The protection is offered providing the publication can be shown to be fair and accurate, made without malice and of public concern.

The occasions are outlined in Schedule 1 to the Act. Part 1 protects fair and accurate reports of legislatures anywhere in the world, courts anywhere in the world, public inquiries and so on. The Act can be found at **http://www.legislation.gov.uk** under 'legislation'. Part II of the Schedule offers protection for fair and accurate reports of proceedings at any meeting in the UK of a local authority and a wide range of public bodies. It includes reports of a *London Gazette* announcement that a bankruptcy order has been made; but not rumours of insolvency and not company liquidations.

The defence in Part II situations, which includes press conferences and press releases, has a further condition in that it is subject to publication, if requested, of a statement or letter by way of explanation or contradiction. This is not a formal right of reply but it does mean that any journalist relying on a statutory qualified privilege defence from a Part II situation must allow anyone maligned to put their case otherwise the defence is lost.

A specific ruling in the House of Lords (*McCarten, Turkington & Breen v Times Newspapers* [2000]) extended the protection to press releases, which was a major expansion of the scope of the Schedule. Further extensions to its reach were signalled in the Defamation Bill 2011.

Statutory qualified privilege can also protect a journalist who unwittingly publishes incorrect information. If an official body directs an accusation against the wrong person and this is published in good faith, the media is protected from defamation action as long as it puts the record straight when asked. So if a council press release accuses the wrong pub, say, of noise nuisance, the pub cannot sue a publication which reports the incorrect information, as long as a correction is subsequently run.

As ever, a journalist needs to maintain a clear evidence trail to demonstrate the source of material. If relying on the police as a Part II source, for instance, a media lawyer would want to see the reporter's copy of an email from a senior officer, shorthand notes dated and timed or a recording of a press conference, not a vague, undocumented recollection of a chat with a community bobby in the pub.

Statutory qualified privilege protects reports that are fair, accurate, without malice/in good faith, in the public interest. In many cases this is subject to rebuttal.

Responsible journalism and privilege

Statutory qualified privilege is a robust defence where it is available but, if not, a journalist has to fall back on the more general public interest defence of responsible journalism, which has gone some way to increasing the protection offered.

The law provides a 'defence' for journalists who have defamed someone while delivering a public interest story. That defence can be referred to as common law qualified privilege or *Reynolds* privilege after the House of Lords case in 1999 that developed a new framework for applying the common law principles. The Defamation Bill refers to it as 'responsible publication on matters of public interest'.

The House of Lords decision in *Reynolds* is a landmark ruling. It emphasised the protection for freedom of expression but made it dependent upon the report and reporter meeting certain criteria. The information, even if it cannot be shown to be true, must be clearly a matter of public interest as distinct from being of interest to the public. The story may concern corruption in high places, misinformation of a public nature, politicians abusing power or conflicts of interest. Celebrity gossip will not cut it.

The next condition relates directly to journalistic conduct. The question is whether the journalism that went into creating the story was 'responsible'. Ten 'non-exhaustive' factors were set out to help judges to decide whether the journalism was worthy of protection. The common law, said Lord Nicholls:

'. . . does not seek to set a higher standard than that of responsible journalism, a standard the media themselves espouse. An incursion into press freedom which goes no further than this would not seem to be excessive or disproportionate. The investigative journalist has adequate protection.'

It became the practice of judges to take into account all 10 factors when deciding the issue of responsible journalism. The so-called Reynolds factors are now considered more broadly. However, journalists should be familiar with the 10 factors because their professionalism is still likely to be judged by reference to them.

The factors are:

- 'The seriousness of the allegation. The more serious the charge, the more the public is misinformed and the individual harmed, if the allegation is not true.
- The nature of the information, and the extent to which the subject matter is of public concern.
- The source of the information. Some informants have no direct knowledge of the events. Some have their own axes to grind, or are being paid for their stories.
- The steps taken to verify the allegation.
- The status of the information. The allegation may have already been the subject of an investigation which commands respect.
- The urgency of the matter. News is often a perishable commodity.
- Whether comment was sought from the claimant. He may have information others do not possess or have not disclosed. An approach to the claimant will not always be necessary.

- Whether the material contained the gist of the claimant's side of the story.
- The tone can raise queries or call for an investigation. It need not adopt allegations as statement of fact.
- The circumstances of the publication, including its timing.'

If the journalism is palpably 'responsible', a defamation claim is unlikely to be pursued. Although the media has lost several high-profile 'responsible journalism' cases, media lawyers stress that many threatened actions fade away when confronted with a robust, well-documented riposte demonstrating that the factors are broadly met.

PUTTING IT INTO PRACTICE

In *GKR Karate v The Yorkshire Post* [2000] the responsible journalism defence was used successfully by the defendants in respect of articles in its Leeds 'freesheet' that alleged the karate club was 'ripping off' its members.

However, the defence was lost in *Galloway v Telegraph Group Ltd* [2004]. The claimant was a Member of Parliament and had been accused by the *Daily Telegraph* of being in the pay of Saddam Hussein's regime. Galloway was awarded £150,000 in damages.

Activity: Read the judgments in the two cases and establish why the defence succeeded in one case and not in the other. What could the *Telegraph* journalists have done differently to avoid losing the case? You can find these and other cases on the British and Irish Legal Information Institute website at **http://www.bailii.org**.

In *Loutchansky v Times Newspapers* [2001] the *Times* had published an article that suggested the claimant was involved in criminal activities. The newspaper relied on the Reynolds privilege arguing the story was in the public interest. This was accepted for the print edition but not for the online archive. The Court of Appeal took the view that this was 'stale news' and could not therefore enjoy the same protection as contemporary news material. So publications are at risk when archiving legally contentious material if they are relying on the Reynolds privilege.

A CLOSER LOOK

In *Jameel v Wall Street Journal Europe Ltd* [2006] the WSJ pleaded the Reynolds defence in response to the claimant's allegation that he had been named and therefore defamed as a result of an article entitled 'Saudi Officials Monitor Certain Bank Accounts. Focus Is On Those With Potential Terrorist Ties'.

In the High Court the defence failed and this was confirmed by the Court of Appeal. Both questioned the reliability of the sources and the fact that Jameel had not been given sufficient opportunity to comment on the allegations. The WSJ appealed to the House of Lords. (Then the highest court in the land, before the creation of the Supreme Court in 2009.)

There the Reynolds privilege was described as 'a defence of publication in the public interest'. As Baroness Hale commented '. . . the most vapid tittle-tattle about the activities of footballers' wives and girlfriends . . .' might interest the public but '. . . no-one would claim there is any real public interest in being told all about it'.

> ▶ **A CLOSER LOOK**
>
> But this story was different, relating as it did to the so-called war on terror and to US–Saudi relations.
>
> With the public interest test passed the court moved on to question whether the journalism underpinning the story was responsible, which was divided into three topics:
>
> - the steps taken to verify the story;
> - the opportunity given to the claimant to comment;
> - the propriety of the publication at that particular time.
>
> The *Jameel* judgment swung the balance back in favour of freedom of expression and reinforced the defence sufficiently to dissuade many potential litigants since. However, the threshold remains high for demonstrating public interest in the story combined with impeccable journalistic processes of verification. Find the judgment at **http://www.bailii.org**.
>
> See also 'What is responsible journalism and what is in the public interest?' in Thinking It Through at the end of this chapter.

remember

- To claim a defence of responsible journalism the article as a whole must concern a matter of public interest; and the reporter must have behaved as a responsible journalist.
- Keep a paper trail, record conversations, have a file to support any contentious article.
- Target elements of the story with a clear public interest defence; don't embroil characters/angles you can't defend.

Fair comment/honest opinion

Journalists are permitted to exercise their right to comment on matters of public interest and if in so doing they defame someone then a defence of fair comment is available. The current judicial view is that the defence is better described as honest comment and the Defamation Bill 2011 suggests calling it honest opinion.

Whatever its label, it is not just heavyweight political and investigative journalists who rely on this defence. Few gig reviews, restaurant crits or beauty product ratings could escape defamation action without the protection of the fair comment defence. And the onus is on the journalist to demonstrate that the comment was fair.

As Lord Nicholls said in the leading case of *Tse Wai Chun Paul v Albert Cheng* [2001]:

'The purpose for which the defence of fair comment exists is to facilitate freedom of expression by commenting upon matters of public interest. This accords with the constitutional guarantee of freedom of expression.'

The basic ground rules for running a defence of fair comment are contained in this judgment. They are:

- The comment must be on a matter of public interest. Public interest is not to be confined within 'narrow limits'.

- The comment must be recognisable as comment as distinct from imputations of fact. Clearly the context will be central to determining whether the reasonable reader or viewer would regard the information as comment.
- Any comment must be based upon facts which can either be shown to be true or have the protection of privilege.
- The reader or viewer should be able to glean the facts from what has been published. In other words, the reader or hearer will be able to establish a causal connection between the facts and the comment upon which they can base a conclusion. (*This has been eased by the Supreme Court.*)
- The comment must be one which an 'honest person' could hold however 'prejudiced he might be and however exaggerated or obstinate his views'.

Lord Nicholls emphasised: 'Dislike of an artist's style would not justify an attack upon his morals or manners. But a critic need not be mealy mouthed in denouncing what he disagrees with. He is entitled to dip his pen in gall for the purposes of legitimate criticism.'

If the facts on which the opinion is based are not true or privileged the defence fails. And those facts must be known at the time of writing. Supporting evidence that emerges after publication cannot be used in the defence. Nor can a critic rely on hearsay; there is no honest opinion defence for attacking a performance that was, for example, not witnessed, nor in passing on rumours.

The *Cheng* principles were made more demanding in *Lowe v Associated Newspapers Ltd* [2006], loosened in *British Chiropractor Association v Singh* [2010] and clarified by the Supreme Court in *Spiller & Anor v Joseph & Ors* [2010], leaving us – as of 2011 – with a slight easing of the original Nicholls principles outlined above.

One of the influences on the Supreme Court decision in *Spiller* was the barrage of potentially defamatory comment in the blogosphere. The rigorous demands of constructing an argument backed by explicit evidence were unrealistic when applied to, say, a television viewer who just wanted to be critical of a particular programme on their blog. Now 'everyone's a critic' the law couldn't cope without granting a reasonable licence for the expression of honest opinion.

Further changes to this defence, broadly in line with *Spiller*, were proposed in the Defamation Bill 2011.

remember

- The defence of fair comment protects honestly held opinion, based on fact or privileged information known to the author at the time of writing, which is in the public interest and reported without malice.
- A fair comment defence cannot succeed if the facts are wrong or the material on which it is based is not privileged.
- Track any changes to the requirements of the defence if the new Defamation Act materialises.

Justification

A defence of justification or 'truth' demands that what has been written or broadcast is *substantially* true. The burden of proof rests upon the defendants on the balance of probabilities. In practice that can be difficult to establish to a court's satisfaction.

The ability to succeed with a justification defence can depend heavily on the availability and credibility of witnesses. Sworn affidavits are needed from key witnesses before publication and great care needs to be taken over the wording of any article. Meticulous records should be kept to back up any claims.

Even then a witness may fail to appear many months down the line or may not be believed by the court. Infamously in the Tommy Sheridan case, heard by a jury in 2006, the evidence of 18 witnesses was not enough to convince the jury he had attended 'swinger' parties. The *News of the World* had to pay £200,000 damages. Sheridan, a former Member of the Scottish Parliament, was eventually jailed for perjury in 2010 over the denials but many media companies could not have afforded to fight on after such a heavy loss.

The 'quality' of the evidence needed will depend on the nature and gravity of the 'sting'. The law generally seeks to put the publication into one of three categories known as the Chase 'levels' after a case of that name, *Elaine Chase v News Group Newspapers* [2002]:

> 'The sting of a libel may be capable of meaning that a claimant has in fact committed some serious act, such as murder. Alternatively it may be suggested that the words mean that there are reasonable grounds to suspect that he/she has committed such an act. A third possibility is that they may mean that there are grounds for investigating whether he/she has been responsible for such an act.' (per Brooke LJ)

When composing a story, a good journalist will assess any allegations as level one, two or three. The higher the 'level', with one being the highest, the stronger the evidence needed to support the journalist's case for publishing it.

For level one the attack on reputation is being stated as definitely true. Is the story stating as fact that A is compt? Can it be proved? What evidence is there for making that allegation? A level two story suggests there are reasonable grounds to suspect that what is stated is true. Level three is where a report states there are grounds for investigating allegations relating to the claimant. The journalist is reporting that there is enough evidence to suspect the claimant has been involved in certain dubious activities and is calling upon the relevant authorities to investigate.

The levels provide helpful distinctions for how to pitch stories and can help journalists mitigate the chances of being sued but even a level three 'sting' needs to be supported by the best available evidence.

remember

- The journalist running a justification defence must prove the 'sting' of the article is true.
- The court decides the meaning of the 'sting' to be defended.
- Defences are hampered by the availability and reliability of witnesses.
- If a defence fails, damages will be higher.
- Costs can be prohibitive.

Innocent publication

This defence relies on a party being a passive medium of communication and being unaware of the defamatory nature of the material put into the public domain. As the creators of material, journalists would not normally be in a position to employ it. However in the world of online aggregation, blogs, bulletin boards and more, the defence has come to the fore, particularly for internet service providers (ISPs).

The law does not generally treat ISPs as active distributors of the material on their sites. So, for example, in *Bunt v Tilley and others* [2006] AOL, Tiscali and BT were struck out as defendants in a chatroom complaint. But hosts cannot wash their hands entirely of responsibility.

A site that is actively moderated may well make the editor liable, which raises issues over what level of intervention a title should make in its readers' message boards, for instance. Significantly, even where a host does not actively moderate material, where it is made aware of potentially defamatory material, the material should be amended or removed at least until the complaint is investigated.

ISPs do become liable if they ignore such warnings. In *Godfrey v Demon Internet Ltd* [2001] the defence was lost because material had been left on a website for 10 days after a complaint. In this area it is also worth tracking arguments over defamatory material on sites such as Wikipedia which to date has protected itself from defamation actions by removing material in the face of complaints rather than vetting it before inclusion.

remember

- The innocent publication defence applies to passive hosts/publishers of material, not to journalists.
- Once the publisher is alerted to potentially defamatory material, it must be removed swiftly or the defence is lost.

Offer of amends

Where a newspaper defames someone by mistake, it can follow an established resolution mechanism known as offer of amends. This can be employed only where a defendant did not know and had no reason to believe that the statement complained of referred to the claimant and was false and defamatory of the claimant.

The defendant must:

- offer in writing to make a suitable correction and apology;
- publish the agreed material in a reasonable manner;
- pay the aggrieved party any agreed damages and costs.

This is a popular way to bring defamation proceedings to a reasonably speedy conclusion. It can be worth a media organisation going ahead with an offer even where the complainant takes the matter further. The fact that a publication has owned up to a mistake and rectified it will mitigate any ultimate damages if the case reaches court. An offer of amends can be expected to halve what would otherwise be imposed, which also helps to open the door to out-of-court settlements, thus reducing the financial risk for both parties.

Malicious falsehood

This action is rarely used but can be brought over statements that are false even when they are not defamatory. A claimant must prove information is:

- false;
- published with malice (includes recklessness); and
- likely to cause financial damage.

For example, printing an unverified, untrue report that a trader was ceasing business could be actionable because it would be false, malicious (used carelessly without checking) and very likely to lose the claimant money.

PRIVACY

There is no specific privacy law in England and Wales and common law did not recognise breach of privacy as a 'tort' – or wrong – in its own right. Those who claim their privacy has been invaded found a remedy via breach of confidence, which has evolved under the influence of Article 8 of the European Convention on Human Rights into misuse of private information.

Article 8 of the European Convention on Human Rights states:

> '1. Everyone has the right to respect for his private and family life, his home and his correspondence.
>
> 2. There shall be no interference by a public authority with the exercise of this right except such as in accordance with the law and is necessary in a democratic society in the interests of national security, public safety or the economic well-being of the country, for the prevention of disorder or crime, for the protection of health or morals, or for the protection of the rights and freedoms of others.'[2]

The rise of privacy complaints has increased scrutiny of media use of photographs, particularly of children. Injunctions become much more significant too as those striving to keep matters secret will be at particular pains to seek prior restraint. In defamation, a false derogatory statement can subsequently be corrected. Whereas, once a secret is out, it cannot be retracted although damages for the breach can still be claimed.

Reasonable expectation of privacy

Judges in any privacy action decide whether a claimant has a reasonable expectation of privacy. This will depend both on the nature of the information and the circumstances under which it was obtained.

One of the most sensitive areas relates to coverage of the children of famous people. Harry Potter author 'JK Rowling' claimed photographs taken of her son in a pushchair were an unwarranted invasion of his privacy. The case, brought on his behalf, recognised his right not to have his picture published in millions of magazines and newspapers without parental consent even though they were in a public street. See *Murray v Express Newspapers & Another* [2007] and *Murray v Big Pictures (UK) Ltd* [2008].

Sexual relationships are also afforded much greater protection than previously, which has scuppered many a potential 'kiss and tell' exposé. Much to the dismay of *Daily Mail* editor Paul Dacre and others, exposing 'immorality' such as adultery is no longer considered to be of sufficient intrinsic public interest to warrant intrusion into such particularly intimate areas of private life.[3]

Twentieth century rulings relied on establishing that the information had the necessary quality of confidentiality. Some 21st century rulings are still 'classic' confidentiality cases such as that to protect the privacy of Prince Charles's diaries. Although the diaries were shared with his circle, the employee who leaked them to the *Daily Mail* was deemed to be in breach of a contractual duty to protect the Prince's privacy (see *Prince of Wales v Associated Newspapers* [2006]).

In the 21st century these actions have broadened to embrace misuse of private information and there is no longer a need to establish an initial confidential relationship between the parties. Justice Eady in *McKennitt v Ash* [2005] said:

> 'It is clear that there is a significant shift taking place as between, on the one hand, freedom of expression for the media and the corresponding interest of the public to receive information, and on the other hand, the legitimate expectation of citizens to

have their private lives protected . . . even where there is a genuine public interest, alongside a commercial interest in the media in publishing articles or photographs, sometimes such interests would have to yield to the individual citizen's right to the effective protection of private life.'

Privacy in public places

Journalists, and particularly photographers, are having to accept the apparent contradiction in terms of someone being private when in public although they remain far from comfortable with it. The attentions of the paparazzi have largely spurred efforts by celebrities to seek a legal remedy so they can get on with their daily lives without being trailed by photographers.

As well as arguments of principle, this creates further practical difficulties over what is acceptable and what is not. A 20th century journalist or photographer would have considered anything within the public gaze to be fair game. A 21st century journalist has to assess which public places and occasions are public and which might be considered private.

A CLOSER LOOK

The European Court of Human Rights in *Von Hannover v Germany* [2004] set the benchmark for the concept of privacy in a public place. Princess Caroline of Monaco, the wife of Prince Ernst Von Hannover, objected to appearing repeatedly in German 'celebrity' magazines and specifically to pictures of her and her children going about their daily lives. She wanted to establish a right not to be photographed other than when attending public functions.

The court ruled that her Article 8 rights were engaged, i.e. she had a reasonable expectation of privacy even in a public place because the photography created a climate of 'continual harassment leaving a strong sense of intrusion into private life or even a feeling of persecution'.

The photographs did not contribute to 'a debate of general interest'. There was no public interest justification for the intrusion into her private life.

This is a key judgment so do read it[4] and contrast it with the outcome in *Campbell* (see opposite).

Public interest

Where a claimant is deemed to have a reasonable expectation of privacy, the media has to establish public interest grounds for the intrusion or argue that the information is already in the public domain. For a public interest argument to 'win', a breach of public trust is usually required so the case is much stronger if the subject holds elected or other public office. Revelation of a relationship between then Home Secretary David Blunkett and a married woman, for instance, was argued to be in the public interest not because of the affair per se but because it was alleged he had abused his position by intervening in her nanny's visa application and claiming expenses for her train travel.

However, only details that make the story of public interest are covered. Unrelated secrets cannot be divulged along the way. Elements of the revelations against BP boss Lord Browne's male lover were allowed in the public interest insofar as they related to abuse of his duty to shareholders but much of the information the *Daily Mail* wanted to run was ruled out even though Lord Browne weakened his own position by lying to the court (see *Browne v Associated Newspapers* [2007]).

Putting the record straight

The court will also consider whether the public have in any way been misled by the applicant in such a way as to permit the defendants to invoke the public interest defence of 'putting the record straight'. Model Naomi Campbell had publicly denied taking drugs. Why then, asked the *Daily Mirror*, did she need to visit Narcotics Anonymous? Despite supporting her claim for breach of privacy in relation to the photograph, all five Law Lords upheld the *Mirror*'s right to tell the story on the basis it was putting the record straight. See *Campbell v MGN Ltd* [2004][5] which is slightly more generous to the media than *Von Hannover*.

A similar approach was taken in 2005 when David and Victoria Beckham failed to secure an injunction to prevent the *News of the World* revealing information from the couple's former nanny that seemed to involve a clear breach of trust. But publication was allowed to give her an opportunity to challenge the Beckhams' portrayal of themselves as a 'golden couple'.

Public domain proviso

A public figure is likely to be the subject of a whole back catalogue of media coverage, archived online or stored away on paper. This can be used to argue that the material a celebrity wants to keep secret is effectively in the public domain – either this affair, say, or one of several others in the past. The track record of the privacy claimant does have some significance. Any injunction should therefore include what has become known as a public domain proviso. As Justice Eady said in *A v B & Others* [2005]:

> 'An important consideration when assessing the background. . . . is that the claimant has himself made public through the media a great deal of information that might usually be considered as falling within the protection afforded to private or personal information . . .'

Someone in the public eye does not lose entitlement to privacy but if similar information is already in the public domain the judge can decide there has been a 'genuine waiver' of privacy.

The judiciary tends to be somewhat dismissive of online activity and microblogging. Information can enjoy pretty wide circulation outside mainstream media channels without that information being judged to be in the public domain. But even the courts had to accept that the million-plus hits on the Mosley video meant its content could no longer be considered private.

Injunctions

In respect of breach of privacy, injunctions are more likely to be sought to ban publication rather than to seek a remedy afterwards when the cat is out of the bag. But this involves 'prior restraint', which the UK system is traditionally reluctant to apply. This is reflected in section 12 of the Human Rights Act which was designed to make it difficult to ban publication. Instead, the tradition to maintain free speech is to allow the media to publish and face the consequences – the old 'publish and be damned'. However, this is being controversially outweighed by the value attached to individual privacy rights, particularly as regards sexual conduct.

The courts, when dealing with an application for a privacy injunction, have three main considerations:

- Is Article 8 engaged? Does the applicant have a reasonable expectation of privacy?
- Is Article 10 engaged? Is there a public interest in the release of the information?
- Has the applicant satisfied the court that if the case went to trial the applicant is likely to establish that publication should not be allowed?

The questions must be applied to each piece of information the claimant regards as confidential. Each element must be decided on its own facts and circumstances and from these a decision reached as to whether there is a reasonable expectation of privacy.

For example, business information imparted to another because of a relationship or via a domestic situation can be regarded as private. The Court of Appeal in dealing with the Lord Browne injunction accepted that the expression of views to his partner about colleagues should be regarded as private because they had the quality of 'gossip'. However, the court was not prepared to accept that stories about the alleged misuse of BP resources that Browne's former lover wished to put into the public domain should be regarded as private. That approach is consistent with the recognition of the important role of the press under Article 10 in acting as public watchdog. This information, whether true or false, should be communicated to the shareholders and board members to consider.

PUTTING IT INTO PRACTICE

Controversy raged during 2011 over the granting of injunctions to celebrities, often anonymised. This means that, as well as the media being banned from publishing the secret information, they cannot say whose secret it is. This is a serious departure from the principles of open justice compounded in the rare cases of super-injunctions where the media cannot even say an order exists. The Master of the Rolls Lord Neuberger's report, published in May 2011,[6] urged more restraint in the use of super-injunctions and better channels of communication to ensure that proceedings could be as transparent as possible. However, this did not suggest any change in the central balancing of rights to privacy with rights to freedom of expression.

MPs and Lords muddied the waters by revealing information in Parliament such as in the *Trafigura* case and that of former Royal Bank of Scotland boss Sir Fred Goodwin. The courts cannot directly restrain Parliamentary debate but they can make it difficult to report it. The Neuberger report suggested the media may lose their normal privilege when reporting from Parliament because reporting a breach of a court order would not be in 'good faith'. The report also suggested the Speaker of the House might declare some questions 'sub judice'. The judiciary, politicians and media are caught in a three-way battle over what should be private and what the public has a right to know.

Not all applications for injunctions are successful, however. An infamous 'failure' was Chelsea footballer John Terry who tried in vain to stop the media publishing the story of his affair. He sacrificed the England captaincy for a period as a result. But others succeed without our even knowing who they are let alone what their secrets are. Another footballer succeeded in his injunction to prevent his being identified as an adulterer.

Activity: Read the two judgments referred to above and explain why one injunction was granted and the other was not. The judgments in *Terry v Persons Unknown (Rev1)* [2010] and *CTB v News Group Newspapers Ltd and Imogen Thomas* [2011] can be found at **http://www.bailii.org**.

See also: 'What is responsible journalism and what is in the public interest?' in Thinking It Through at the end of this chapter.

Before publishing any story which could be regarded as intrusive, ask yourself:
- Is the information private?
- Does the claimant have a reasonable expectation of privacy?
- Were there expectations of any pre-existing relationship?
- Is the information already in the public domain?
- What is the claimant's history of prior revelations?
- If it is private, is there a public interest in revealing it? Is there a need to prevent the public from being misled or does it contribute to a debate of general interest?

Protection from harassment

Actress Sienna Miller and pop star Lily Allen head a growing list of celebrities who have turned to harassment law to ward off unsolicited media attention, using legislation originally drafted to protect women from stalkers. Photographers have become the main targets of action under the Protection from Harassment Act 1997 for hounding famous faces in the hope of snapping them in an unguarded moment.

An injunction can be granted against any person engaged in a course of conduct which amounts to harassment, and which he knows or ought to know amounts to harassment. So reporters could be included. Breach of any such injunction could lead to a jail sentence of up to five years. Photographers or reporters spotted lurking near a celebrity's home can also be removed. Police can arrest on the spot anyone reasonably suspected of the offence or require them to leave and not return for up to three months. (See also the Hotline operations of the Press Complaints Commission in the Regulation section later in this chapter.)

COPYRIGHT

Copyright has come to the fore in the 21st century mainly because of the extent to which it is breached. The flood of material online has posed a massive challenge to the ability of the creators of original work – be it artistic or journalistic – to protect their copyright.

Copyright exists to defend the right to the benefits of the time, skill and/or ingenuity involved in producing the material. There is no copyright in facts, news, ideas or information itself. The copyright lies in a particular form of words or particular image. Copyright operates on the basis that it is unfair to cash in on the efforts of others. As journalists, we often want to defend copyright in our own work so that a money-making magazine, say, cannot just print an article we have laboured over without paying for it. But journalists can also be remarkably cavalier about purloining material from elsewhere which may be someone else's copyright and which we have no right to reproduce. Sometimes the sticking point is payment. A photographer, for instance, trying to make a living may need and expect commercial outlets to pay to run his images.

In other areas, the owner of copyright may object in principle to the material's being circulated more widely – it may be commercially sensitive or private. A family might, for instance, allow their photograph of a dead relative to appear in a local newspaper but wouldn't then expect to see it in the *Sun*.

Yet many feel existing laws in practice allow entrenched media companies to stifle the creativity of 'insurgents' and squander the potential of digital media to spread knowledge and spur innovation. The influential organisation Creative Commons, for instance, encourages creators to share their output. Its vision involves 'universal access to research, education, full participation in culture, and driving a new era of development, growth, and productivity'.[7]

Others question the viability of laws made redundant and unenforceable by technological advances that make copying and transfer so simple. Existing mechanisms for upholding copyright have failed to keep pace with the proliferation of outlets and the millions of 'culprits', mostly difficult to track and with few assets against which to make a claim. Most print titles, for instance, are happy for their output to be aggregated as it drives traffic to their site; a few have opted out or tried to strike a deal over sharing any resulting revenue. Some, such as the *Times*, operate behind paywalls.

Business models for 20th century print media relied on the ability to generate revenue from audiences – both directly from the audience paying for the content and from advertisers paying for access to that audience. The expectation to date of free content has reduced scope for online payment direct from the audience. If the journalistic material created at considerable expense cannot be contained within a branded portal, the ability to 'monetise eyeballs' through advertising is severely curtailed too and the advertising spend that is generated goes predominantly to the aggregator, notably Google.

In the 20th century the accent on study of copyright was to instruct a journalist how to avoid breaching the copyright of others, in terms of how much of other people's work could be reproduced. In the 21st century those responsibilities remain but the accent is on the widespread challenge to journalists' ability to prevent others reaping the rewards of their efforts: to protect their own copyright. Here again, older case law provides little guidance. Digital platforms that link content and audiences from a multitude of sources challenge old interpretations of where the line should fairly be drawn; or where it can practicably be drawn.

Intellectual property rights

Copyright is a huge area, spilling over more broadly into intellectual property and image rights. The coalition government responded by commissioning Professor Ian Hargreaves, of Cardiff University, to give copyright laws a 'digital makeover'. His 2011 report[8] recommended removing some copying for personal use out of the reach of copyright. As the law stands, format shifting – copying a CD or DVD to a computer or other digital device – is technically illegal even though the original copy was paid for. The report recommended making it legal.

The parodies so beloved of YouTube audiences would also gain protection. A recent example would be Newport State of Mind, a Welsh rap duo's reworking of the Jay Z hit about New York, which was removed after a copyright claim from EMI.

This follows the Gowers review of intellectual property in 2006 which was never implemented, but the pressure for change is now much greater so changes to copyright law can be expected. There is certainly a move away from criminalising those making personal use of material rather than exploiting it for commercial gain.

Copyright enforcement

Copyright is controlled in the UK under the Copyright, Designs and Patents Act 1988, which covers work produced since 31 July 1989. Although this was probably before many of you were born, the date is worth remembering as pictures used by journalists to accompany local history, nostalgia or obituaries, for instance, may well pre-date 1989 when copyright usually belonged to whoever commissioned the work.

The 1988 Act gave more rights to the originators which, in theory, benefited journalists, particularly freelancers. However, the commissioner retains moral rights, notably the right not to have copies made public without permission. So, for instance, a commercial photographer might offer to sell you a client's wedding picture. Although you wouldn't have to pay whoever commissioned it any money, you would need their permission to publish it. An employer owns copyright of work produced by staff unless an individual contract stipulates otherwise. Freelancers own the copyright of their original work, even if it has been commissioned. When the material is sold, a specific deal is made agreeing when and where it can be used.

Platforms operated by mainstream media companies are more likely to face claims for breach of copyright because the audience is larger and because the organisation is easily identified, is a commercial concern and is in a position to pay up if at fault.

Some owners of copyright will send a request to desist rather than launch a formal legal action particularly if the outlet appears not to be deriving a direct commercial benefit from the breach. For example, misuse of a tradename – using hoover/biro instead of Hoover/Biro – in a newspaper is likely to prompt a polite but firm letter from the company reminding the editor of the brand status.

The status of social media and user-generated content can be difficult to determine and not everyone reads the small print – journalists included. Do you know the copyright status of your Twitter account? Does a journalist need permission to access and reproduce your tweets?

If as a journalist you want to reproduce material from other sources you must check its copyright status before use and seek the necessary permissions. You need an explicit, written agreement as to the usage permitted over time and across different distribution platforms. Any platforms you operate soliciting responses should similarly make contributors aware of the terms under which they are submitting material and what other use you may make of it.

Readers' letters involve an implied licence to publish only once, which made sense for print editions but causes confusion once archived online. Formal schedules, such as TV listings and sporting fixtures, are subject to copyright and are usually provided under a licence agreement that imposes restrictions on use and may or may not require payment of a fee. Negotiations, particularly over football information, can be particularly fraught.

Fair dealing

News journalists are given some leeway to use copyright material courtesy of the defence of fair dealing. Extracts from copyright material can be used to report breaking news as long as the source is acknowledged.

Photographs are generally excluded from fair dealing except where they are used, with appropriate acknowledgment, to illustrate a review of work. Copyright is waived on BBC publicity photographs, for instance, as long as they are illustrating coverage of the relevant programme. Any other usage has to be agreed separately and may be denied or incur a charge.

There is also a limited public interest defence against breach of copyright.

Remedies

The owner of copyright can seek an injunction to prevent publication of a work or damages if the work is used without consent. Breach of copyright can also lead to a court fine as it is a criminal offence under the 1988 Act.

remember

- Copyright belongs to the originator, except in employment.
- Consider who owns the copyright of any submitted material and seek necessary permissions for its use.
- Journalists often rely on a fair dealing defence.
- Watch out for changes in copyright laws in the wake of the Hargreaves report.
- Don't be blasé about copyright. Just because material can be copied and reproduced does not make it legal.

REGULATION

Regulatory bodies exist within the media industry so that members of the public can hold editors to account for what their journalists publish and how they go about their business. In the UK, non-broadcast journalists answer to the Press Complaints Commission (PCC), created in 1991 to replace the Press Council, and to its Editors' Code of Practice that covers the vast majority of newspapers and magazines, and their related websites.

Major reforms of press regulation are pending the outcome of the government's Leveson inquiry set up in 2011 in the wake of continuing phone-hacking allegations which resulted in the closure of the *News of the World*. A successor regulator to the PCC will have to be seen to be more independent of the industry, with greater sanctions, probably financial, and a more pro-active approach to setting and securing standards of journalism. Creating a statutory framework for text-based media would be both heavy-handed and logistically fraught given the difficulty of defining its reach in a digital age. An independent regulator is likely to emerge with powers to fine publications but offering incentives to sign up as a means of avoiding more expensive legal actions. This is a particularly dynamic issue so check for latest developments using the weblinks at the end of this chapter.

The print media have operated under a regime of self-regulation in contrast to the statutory controls exercised by the Office of Communications (Ofcom) for broadcasters. Ofcom's powers are derived from the Communications Act 2003. It can fine a channel in breach of its Codes and *in extremis* withdraw its licence to broadcast. The PCC has relied on shaming editors by forcing them to print hostile adjudications and the threat of dismissal for those who have adherence to the Code written into their contracts. But the PCC cannot 'disbar' individual journalists or titles. Journalism is not a profession and the PCC is not a professional association. A journalist cannot be struck off and thus prevented from working by any of the UK's regulatory bodies.

The challenge of multi-platform content

Convergence has created philosophical and logistical challenges to our system of regulation by blurring the boundaries between print and broadcast media that have, to date, operated very distinct regimes. Pragmatically, websites have been viewed as an adjunct to the host brand. The PCC claimed authority over newspaper and magazine websites, even where they include broadcast format audio and video clips.

However, trying to regulate platforms that mainstream media shares with millions of bloggers and so-called citizen journalists may simply become unsustainable and arguably already has. The Leveson inquiry may recommend an extension of statutory regulation but how would we define who it applies to? Broadcasters historically had to sign up to rigid controls in return for access to limited channels and/or public funding. Why would a privately owned website submit itself to such restraint?

See 'Why regulate?' in Thinking It Through at the end of this chapter.

PCC Editors' Code of Practice

For most working journalists, the most significant aspect of the PCC is its Code of Practice, which is likely to be written in to any employment contract. A journalist whose work is found to be in breach of the Code can be sacked. The Code of Practice was created and is updated from time to time by the Editors' Code of Practice Committee made up of 14 editors from national and regional newspapers and magazines. Creditcard-sized versions of it are printed to encourage journalists to keep a copy handy in purse or wallet.

Adherence to the Code is used as a shorthand for responsible journalism, mirroring the expectations of the courts, such as in Reynolds privilege in defamation. When seeking to call upon Article 10 rights or defending defamation actions, compliance is a helpful way to demonstrate that what was run was the product of thorough processes of verification with an ethical underpinning. In the UK the judges have looked to the codes of regulatory bodies such as the PCC to set the standard.

Although any regulatory framework imposes certain curbs that may seem to frustrate investigation, the PCC Code can also be seen as an aid for journalists, offering advice on how a responsible journalist operates (see **http://www.pcc.org.uk**). Something similar is likely to survive Leveson.

Public interest

A particularly influential element of the code is its working definition of the public interest, which is a developing and increasingly significant issue for a journalist seeking to justify running stories that threaten the reputation or privacy of others. The Code states:

> 'Public interest includes but is not confined to:
> - detecting or exposing crime or serious impropriety;
> - protecting public health and safety;
> - preventing the public from being misled by an action or statement of an individual or organization.
>
> There is a public interest in freedom of expression itself.'[9]

Any working journalist should be familiar with every word of the Code and keep up-to-date with amendments. Every clause has a significance but the most contentious tend to be those that allow exceptions where there is an overriding public interest. These clauses, which are asterisked in copies of the Code, cover invasions of privacy, harassment, reporting suicide, children (school), children (sex cases), hospitals, reporting of crime, use of clandestine devices and subterfuge, aspects of reporting trials and payments to criminals.

It is a long list so the PCC is at pains to ensure this is not interpreted as grounds effectively to opt out of those clauses. The public interest hurdle has been raised over time and the Code goes on to state:

- 'Whenever the public interest is invoked the PCC will require editors to demonstrate fully that they reasonably believed the publication, or journalistic activity undertaken with a view to publication, would be in the public interest and how, and with whom, that was established at the time.
- The PCC will consider the extent to which material is already in the public domain or will become so.

- In cases involving children under 16, editors must demonstrate an exceptional public interest to override the normally paramount interest of the child.'[10]

In some instances the Code goes beyond demands of the law. The prime example regards identifying children. Clause 7 (1) states:

> 'the press must not, even if legally free to do so, identify children under 16 who are victims or witnesses in cases involving sex offences.'[11]

Complaint handling

Members of the public can complain to the regulator about non-broadcast coverage that refers to them personally. The service is free to users with publishers, as a feature of a system of self-regulation, funding the organisation as a whole.

A secretariat is employed to process complaints and pursue resolution.

The Commission oversees the system and adjudicates complaints. Adjudication panels have a majority of lay members. Increasing that proportion, or removing editors completely, are options under discussion to make regulation more independent of the industry.

The editor always represents the publication in the process. The secretariat acts as a go-between and attempts to broker a remedy acceptable to both parties. In 2010 the PCC settled more than 540 complaints 'amicably'. If conciliation fails, or is inappropriate, or if the case involves a major policy issue, the Commission will publish an adjudication. Where a complaint is upheld the publication must publish the adverse finding word for word and with 'due prominence'.

Adjudications, in common with court judgments, must weigh competing claims to protect both the rights of the individual and the public's right to know. The PCC aims to create channels for conflict resolution which are faster, cheaper and more accessible than those of the legal system.

A CLOSER LOOK

The PCC has produced an Editor's Codebook (Beales, 2009) to provide further guidance on its operation. The Codebook includes a useful list of its various means of resolving complaints without adjudication. These are:

- 'Clarification. A clarification might be appropriate where something has been omitted from the original article or if it is ambiguous or arguably misleading. It stops short of an admission by the editor that the article was wrong.
- Corrections and apologies. Straightforward factual errors are usually dealt with most cleanly and simply by the publication of a correction. In the case of serious errors, this might include an apology. The Code states that an apology should be published where appropriate.
- Letter for publication. An editor's offer to publish a complainant's letter can be appropriate when: the complainant has an alternative point of view but no substantive factual objections to the piece; where there are a number of minor inaccuracies; where the newspaper has an anonymous and reliable source but no other corroborative material; or where a complainant might for reasons of privacy wish to make anonymous objections to a piece.

> **▶ A CLOSER LOOK**
>
> - Follow-up article. An editor might offer to publish an interview with, or article by, a complainant, if there are sufficient points to be made in response to a previous story.
> - Tagging newspaper records. This is an increasingly popular way of resolving complaints and is offered in conjunction with the above remedies or on its own. The publication's electronic database and cuttings library is tagged with the complainant's objection to ensure the mistake is not repeated.
> - Taking down online material. Many complaints about material on newspaper or magazine websites are resolved by the editor removing it on receiving a complaint. This applies especially to user-generated material that has not been edited.
> - Private letter of apology. Further publicity is often not an attractive option for the complainant, particularly in privacy cases or intrusion into grief. A private apology, often drafted with the help of a complaints officer, and perhaps tagged to the file as outlined above, is sometimes a more suitable remedy.
> - Private undertaking. Similarly, undertakings by the editor about the future conduct of the newspaper and its staff might also give a complainant some peace of mind. Complaints have been resolved on this basis.' (Ibid. p. 8)
>
> Many titles use similar options internally to resolve reader complaints without recourse to the PCC, let alone legal action. *Guardian* readers will be familiar with its regular Corrections and Clarifications column. The paper employs a Readers' Editor as a first tier of recourse for aggrieved readers.

Some opponents of self-regulation believe that with newspapers only money talks – that they will flout any regulations unless the penalty exceeds the potential benefit. Yet one of the reasons complainants dismiss the PCC route is not because it is all about money for the newspaper but because it is all about money for them.

The PCC is often consulted by editors before publication to discuss the pros and cons of a story and how any particular wording or photograph might be treated within the Code. It also offers protection from potential harassment – and not just for royals and celebrities. Anyone caught up in a 'big' story can call its hotline for advice on how to handle the situation and to trigger an alert to publications to back off. Advance notice can also be circulated that approaches by the media will not be welcome. Its 2010 report[12] said it acted 'to prevent media harassment' 100 times and 'made proactive contact with those at the centre of media storms' 25 times.

The regulatory body to emerge from Leveson will not be called the PCC but it is expected to replicate much of its work on complaint handling.

Privacy within the Code

The PCC issues general guidance on privacy as well as adjudicating individual complaints. The number is growing although they remain a small proportion of the total, which predominantly concern accuracy.

The Editors' Codebook, in a section headlined tellingly *Privacy, not invisibility*, states:

- 'Privacy is not an absolute right – it can be compromised by conduct or consent.
- Privacy is not a commodity which can be sold on one person's terms – the Code is not designed to protect commercial deals.

- **Privacy does not mean invisibility – pictures taken in genuinely public places and information already in the public domain can be legitimate.**
- **Privacy may be against the public interest – such as when used to keep secret conduct that might reflect on a public figure or role model.' (Beales, 2009: 24)**

The Editors' Codebook also highlights a range of adjudications, some upheld, some rejected, to help editors and journalists to anticipate where the line would be drawn in similar stories (see Recommended Reading at the end of this chapter).

- A complaint to the regulator is the most common recourse for ordinary members of the public who feel they have had a raw deal from journalists. For many, legal avenues are effectively closed because of cost. The regulator's service is free.
- An editor must publish any hostile adjudication.
- Journalists must comply with the Code and can be sacked if they don't.
- Public interest and how we define it is key to regulation.
- The government's Leveson inquiry will replace the PCC, probably with a more robust independent regulator with power to impose fines. Use Weblinks at the end of the chapter to check for developments.

ETHICS

Many ethical codes exist to guide the individual journalist, predominantly the Editors' Code of Practice discussed in the previous section. But no code can absolve an individual journalist of the responsibility to establish a personal ethical framework: a way of working with a clear conscience. At the individual level, the question of ethics involves deciding what sort of journalist each of us wants to be.

The phone-hacking scandal cast doubt over journalists' behaviour more generally, not just at the *News of the World*. Ethical journalists need to convince themselves and their audience, as well as any court, that the stories run and the actions taken in pursuit of them are justified. Various codes have been written by numerous bodies, including trades unions. Common issues include a commitment to readers; to accuracy; to verifying information; to honesty; and to the public right to know.

Protection of sources is another must for any reputable journalist. This is expressed in the PCC Code as: 'A journalist has a moral responsibility to protect confidential sources of information.'[13] There are no exceptions, even if it entails breaking a court order.

In our digital age, adherence to such codes is also part of what makes someone a journalist as distinct from a casual microblogger.

A CLOSER LOOK

In America the Committee of Concerned Journalists attempted to define journalism and this is developed in Kovach and Rosenstiel's (2007) *The Elements of Journalism*. The committee's idealistic Statement of Shared Purpose reads:

▶ A CLOSER LOOK

'The central purpose of journalism is to provide citizens with accurate and reliable information they need to function in a free society.

This encompasses myriad roles – helping define community, creating common language and common knowledge, identifying a community's goals, heroes and villains, and pushing people beyond complacency. This purpose also involves other requirements, such as being entertaining, serving as watchdog and offering voice to the voiceless.

Over time journalists have developed nine core principles to meet the task. They comprise what might be described as the theory of journalism:

- Journalism's first obligation is to the truth.
- Its first loyalty is to citizens.
- Its essence is a discipline of verification.
- Its practitioners must maintain an independence from those they cover.
- It must serve as an independent monitor of power.
- It must provide a forum for public criticism and compromise.
- It must strive to make the significant interesting and relevant.
- It must keep the news comprehensive and proportional.
- Its practitioners must be allowed to exercise their personal conscience.'[14]

The UK's National Union of Journalists (NUJ) has its own Code of Conduct, which is similar to the PCC's but adds a conscience clause. It states that journalist members have a right to refuse work that would break the letter or spirit of the code. This seeks to protect members if they resist pressure from management to breach it. The flip side is that no individual journalist should succumb to such pressure. A challenge, either individually or with union backing, may cause the employer to back down and see sense but the individual journalist ultimately has to decide whether that employer is worth working for. If, as an individual journalist, you and those in editorial control are poles apart, taking ethical responsibility for your work may demand resignation. Better still, don't take a job with a company whose ethical approach varies significantly from your own.

Style guides are useful indicators of the ethics of an organisation too. *The Economist* and the *Guardian* are two titles that make their style guides public. Although style guides deal with many mundane matters of spelling and punctuation, they also guide issues such as terminology, which can reveal a great deal about attitudes on matters such as race or mental health. Check out the *Guardian*'s at **http://www.guardian.co.uk/styleguide**.

Ethical guidelines on many specific areas of reporting are now emerging, often as a result of a partnership between the media and relevant support groups. The Joseph Rowntree Foundation worked with the Society of Editors and others on a useful booklet: *Reporting Poverty*. There are others on issues such as reporting mental health, reporting diversity and reporting human rights. These do not have the rigour of a code, and media organisations do not formally 'sign' up to them but they are thought-provoking and very useful for raising awareness (see Weblinks at the end of this chapter).

Unethical behaviour can be lucrative and cowboy operators often get away with it even in the long term. But that is true in any walk of life. There are elements of carrot and stick in any code. Ultimately the ethical journalist chooses to be ethical because it is the right thing to do.

See also: 'Journalistic ethics: a contradiction in terms?' in Thinking It Through at the end of this chapter.

remember

- Every journalist needs a personal moral compass.
- A journalist has a moral responsibility to protect a confidential source.
- Take personal responsibility for all your actions as a journalist.
- Be prepared to justify your investigations and your output ethically as well as legally.
- Decide what sort of journalist you want to be and what sort of publication you want to work for.

CHAPTER SUMMARY

Media law, regulation and ethics combine to provide the essential framework guiding the work of the journalist. On a practical level, a journalist has to know and understand the law and codes of practice to function safely without ending up in court and/or being sacked. But, although they can be seen as shackles, their combined effect generally enhances journalism and forces journalists to reflect on their work and role in society, which has to be a good thing.

Knowing more about media law, regulation and ethics will increase your chances of:

- keeping your job and liberty;
- being a responsible journalist;
- working in the public interest;
- making informed judgements about how to investigate stories;
- avoiding or at least reducing legal risks so that stories can be run that would otherwise be dropped;
- becoming a 'thinking' journalist who understands the consequences of their actions and the reasons for them;
- sleeping at night.

THINKING IT THROUGH

Freedom of expression. When should it be curbed?

Many media challenges to the right to privacy or reputation are derided these days as motivated simply by commercial considerations. Few people seem prepared to believe that decent journalists can be driven not primarily by money nor even by individual rights. Journalists believe in the value of information to citizens within a democratic society so that the powers-that-be can be called to account and an enlightened public opinion emerge.

As Lord Steyn said in *R v Secretary of State for the Home Department, ex p Simms* [2000]:

> 'Freedom of expression is, of course, intrinsically important: it is valued for its own sake. But it is well recognised that it is also instrumentally important. It serves a number of broad objectives. First, it promotes the self-fulfilment of individuals in society. Secondly, in the famous words of Holmes J (echoing John Stuart Mill) "the best test of truth is the power of the thought to get itself accepted in the competition of the market". Thirdly, freedom of speech is the lifeblood of

> ### ▶ THINKING IT THROUGH
>
> democracy. The free flow of information and ideas informs political debate.
> It is a safety valve: people are more ready to accept decisions that go against
> them if they can in principle seek to influence them. It acts as a brake on the
> abuse of power by public officials. It facilitates the exposures of errors in the
> governance and administration of justice of the country.'
>
> As J.S. Mill, the British philosopher, also said: 'Truth should never be denied a
> platform' but neither should even half-baked ideas. The concept of a free trade in
> ideas logically embraces the right to be wrong; to make claims that further debate
> exposes as erroneous.
>
> Freedom of expression seems to be afforded more value when the defendant is a
> state. The European Court of Human Rights has stepped in frequently to protect an
> individual citizen, journalist or publication from the heavy-handed actions of their
> government, including the UK's.
>
> But the judiciary, especially in our courts, becomes less sympathetic when the media
> is the defendant. There the claimant tends to be underdog and the media too easily
> cast as the villain of the piece.
>
> ---
>
> **Ask yourself:** Having read this chapter and the relevant Recommended Reading, what
> value do you believe society and our courts should place on freedom of expression?
> What curbs, if any, should or can reasonably be placed upon it?
>
> ## Can juries deliver justice?
>
> The right to a fair trial in England and Wales in more serious cases is reliant on 12
> jurors being able to decide on the evidence before them whether the defendant is guilty
> or not. Our judicial system needs to believe that jurors are capable of this. Because it
> is felt jurors may be prejudiced by what they read in print or online, media coverage
> of criminal proceedings is restricted, most notably through the Contempt of Court Act
> 1981. In the USA there is no such protection, which made it legal to publish all the
> unflattering background information, for instance, on IMF boss Dominique Strauss-
> Kahn when he was arrested on rape charges in New York in May 2011, which were
> later dropped. Was that fair? Would it have stopped him getting a fair trial or would
> jurors have ignored what they had read? Does nobody then get a fair trial in the USA?
>
> The questions are particularly hard to answer in terms of trials here because only one
> significant study has been allowed into the workings of juries. Is the judiciary scared of
> what researchers would find? Is our reliance on jury trial all smoke and mirrors? The
> one recent official research commissioned by the Ministry of Justice in 2010 from
> Professor Cheryl Thomas[15] found juries to be fair, effective and efficient.
>
> Yet the gradual reduction in the use of juries – in complicated criminal fraud trials or
> as proposed in civil defamation actions – is unnerving too. We have traditionally trusted
> our peers – 12 good men (and women) and true – to decide who is telling the truth,
> who should win or lose. We traditionally trust the jury's ability to bring common sense
> as well as fine legal judgment to bear. But who delivers justice better – judges or juries?
>
> ---
>
> **Ask yourself:** If you were a juror, could you put pre-conceived notions aside to decide
> the case on its merits? Would it matter if you had read about the defendant online?
> If you were a defendant in a defamation action would you prefer a judge or a jury to
> decide your fate? ▶

▶ THINKING IT THROUGH

What is responsible journalism and what is in the public interest?

The concepts of 'responsible journalism' and 'public interest' are central to many media law judgments. The courts are tending to be more demanding of how journalists behave as well as what they publish. The Supreme Court decision in an appeal against *Flood v Times Newspapers Ltd* [2010] set the bar of a responsible journalism defence in defamation. The reporting of allegations against a Metropolitan Police officer was considered by the Court of Appeal to be irresponsible although it appeared to be written with the *Jameel* judgment in mind. Check the Supreme Court Ruling at http://www.bailii.org.

The definition of 'public interest' is also rather fluid. In the *Spiller* case, where the defendant relied on a fair comment defence, remarks about the reliability of a band were deemed to be in the public interest; yet the sexual conduct of high-profile public figures is not; nor, in *Trafigura*, was a report into the activities of a company subsequently fined for dumping toxic waste. Oh, that more heed might be paid beyond the realms of fair comment to the exhortation of Lord Nicholls in *Cheng*: 'Public interest is not to be confined within "narrow limits".'

Parliament took up the cudgels too with Lord Stoneham of Droxford objecting in May 2011 to the injunction granted to bank boss Sir Fred Goodwin on the basis that the public had a right to know about his private life as part of the events leading to the collapse of the bank and its bailout from the public purse. There is a gulf too between the courts and the print media over the exposure of 'serious impropriety', which for journalists has included immoral and/or adulterous behaviour.

Clearly the courts' view of what constitutes a 'debate of general interest' is more highbrow and narrow than that of journalists, some politicians and possibly the public.

Ask yourself: What are the features of 'responsible' journalism? Are the courts defining public interest too narrowly?

Why regulate the media?

Journalists, in exercising their own freedom of speech, provide a catalyst and a hub for the whole of society to express itself. So why would we want to regulate them?

Journalists need to hold authority to account so what authority, voluntary let alone statutory, could reasonably regulate them?

In the 20th century when media entry costs were high, only a relatively limited number of outlets were able to communicate with the masses. Regulation, whether desirable or not, was at least logistically possible. In the 21st century when anyone with access to the right phone or computer can instigate a mass global conversation, the issue of regulation becomes more fraught in principle and practice.

Who says what is and is not OK? Why isn't the law of the land enough? The challenges of digital media have made us question the whole future of media regulation. If expectations are too high and sanctions too severe, providers will just opt out wherever they can. Why face fines from Ofcom and jump through all the regulatory hoops when you can run an online station under the radar? Why sign up to the Press Complaints Commission successor body if it can impose fines on your publication? Shouldn't obeying the law be enough?

▶ THINKING IT THROUGH

But many of those who appreciate the BBC's reputation as a source of reliable and credible information on which the public can depend argue that strict regulation is a necessary condition for safeguarding its impressive standards. Would the public gain or lose from a free-for-all?

The contents of this chapter will provide you with some possible response but there are no right and wrong answers here. The situation is dynamic so use the Weblinks at the end of the chapter to check for the latest developments, particularly on the Leveson inquiry. Regulation is up for grabs and there are many different views on where it could and should go from here.

Ask yourself: Is regulation of text-based journalism necessary and, if so, how might it be best be achieved? Should standards be encouraged or enforced?

Journalistic ethics: a contradiction in terms?

The continuing fall-out from the phone hacking admitted by the *News of the World* and alleged at one other newspaper at least has confirmed the worst suspicions of those who believe journalists are the lowest of the low. Public trust ratings consistently rank journalists down with used car salesmen and estate agents, although the BBC and local newspaper reporters fare a little better in more detailed surveys.

Journalists' watchdog role and duty to challenge the powers-that-be makes it unlikely that they will ever be universally loved and admired. Some still joke that journalists know they are being objective if they are derided equally by everyone. Others hark back to some golden age of high moral purpose that almost certainly never existed. But is there a crisis of trust in our journalists? If so, is it deserved and what might be done about it? Can a more ethical approach restore faith in the fourth estate?

Ask yourself: What sort of journalist do I want to be? What's my role? What's my ethical code?

NOTES

[1] http://www.echr.coe.int
[2] Ibid.
[3] See his speech to the Society of Editors, Bristol, November 2008 at: http://www.societyofeditors.org
[4] http://www.bailii.org
[5] Ibid.
[6] http://www.judiciary.gov.uk/media/media-releases/2011/committee-reports-findings-super-injunctions-20052011
[7] http://www.creativecommous.org
[8] Digital Opportunity: A Review of Intellectual Property and Growth at: http://www.ipo.gov.uk/preview-finalreport.pdf
[9] http://www.pcc.org.uk
[10] Ibid.
[11] Ibid.

[12] PCC Annual Review 2010 at: http://www.pcc.org.uk/review10/statistics-and-key-rulings/complaints-statistics/key-numbers.php
[13] http://www.pcc.org.uk
[14] http://www.concernedjournalists.org
[15] http://www.justice.gov.uk

RECOMMENDED READING

Barendt, Eric (2007) *Freedom of Speech*. Oxford: Oxford University Press.
This is a core and influential text examining the concept of freedom of expression.

Beales, Ian (2009) *The Editors' Codebook: the handbook to the Editors' Code of Practice*. London: Newspaper Association *et al*.
The Editors' Code of Practice, which regulates the behaviour of print journalists in the UK, is succinct and helps to reinforce the basics. But alone it cannot provide all the answers to what is and what is not acceptable under the Code. This Codebook provides essential guidance on where the PCC draws the line as it conducts a balancing act very similar to that of the courts to determine if an editor, in pursuit of freedom of expression, has overstepped the mark.

Bloy, Duncan (2006) *Media Law*. London: Sage.
This is a useful nuts and bolts guide, geared more to law students, but offering a helpful framework for journalists.

Brooke, Heather (2007) *Your Right to Know: How to use the Freedom of Information Act and other access laws*. London: Pluto Press.
American journalist Heather Brooke is a high-profile user of the UK's Freedom of Information Act, becoming something of an expert on how best to take advantage of it. Her role in the ultimate disclosure of MPs' expenses was the subject of a Channel 4 documentary. Check out her other publications too.

Dodd, Mike and Hanna, Mark (2012) *McNae's Essential Law for Journalists,* 21st edition. Oxford: Oxford University Press.
The set text for media law courses accredited by the National Council for the Training of Journalists, which covers a lot of ground.

Hadwin, Sara and Bloy, Duncan (2011) *Law and the Media*. London: Sweet and Maxwell.
This offers more in-depth analysis of the impact of the Human Rights Act on media law with up-to-date case studies including Mosley and super-injunctions, viewing developments from a legal and journalistic perspective.

Kovach, Bill and Rosenstiel, Tom (2007) *The Elements of Journalism: What newspeople should know and the public should expect*. London: Atlantic Books.
Thoughtful offering based on the manifesto of the US Committee of Concerned Journalists embracing matters of ethics and conscience as well as journalistic purpose.

Quinn, Frances (2011) *Law for Journalists*. Harlow: Pearson Education.
This is a well-regarded text packed with practical advice for journalists that would make excellent follow-up reading. This chapter has introduced the main elements of media law but working journalists need to know more and this builds on the material covered here.

Randall, David (2007) *The Universal Journalist*. London: Pluto Press.
This book is like having a mentor through the maze of all things journalistic, including a valuable chapter on ethics.

Rozenberg, Joshua (2004) *Privacy and the Press*. Oxford: Oxford University Press.
The BBC specialist reporter examines one of the key areas of media law.

WEBLINKS

http://www.5rb.co.uk   Details of significant judgments are provided by 5 Raymond Buildings, a legal practice specialising in media law.

http://www.creativecommons.org   The organisation Creative Commons, as part of its campaign for greater information sharing, promotes licences that 'provide a flexible range of protections and freedoms for authors, artists, and educators'.

http://www.concernedjournalists.org   This is the site of the American Committee of Concerned Journalists whose Code is examined in the chapter.

http://www.bailii.org   Really useful website where you can track down all the cases discussed in the chapter and others you may hear of.

http://www.judiciary.gov.uk   The Judicial Studies Board guidelines for court coverage can be found here as can useful background information and updates from the judiciary of England and Wales.

http://www.legislation.gov.uk   Here you can find copies of all the Acts cited in this chapter and any others you want to read.

http://www.levesonenquiry.org.uk   Check the latest developments from the Leveson Inquiry.

http://www.ofcom.org.uk   Check out Ofcom's broadcasting code to contrast it with that of the PCC and also compare its procedures and sanctions.

http://www.pcc.org.uk   The PCC provides a wealth of information including the hotline for the public, full details of adjudications, its reports and guidance on application of the Editors' Code. This should also link to its successor body.

http://www.holdthefrontpage.co.uk   The Hold The Front Page website for regional journalists offers commentary and regular media updates from media lawyers Foot Anstey and others.

http://www.societyofeditors.org   The Society of Editors has endorsed a range of reporting guides covering ethical and practical aspects of reporting on issues such as mental health, ethnic minorities and poverty.

http://www.guardian.co.uk/styleguide   This establishes the basics for consistency's sake but embraces the ethical dimensions of use of language, for example regarding minorities.

REFERENCES

Beales, Ian (2009) *The Editors' Codebook: the handbook to the Editors' Code of Practice.* London: Newspaper Publishers Association *et al.*

Kovach, Bill and Rosenstiel, Tom (2007) *The Elements of Journalism: What news people should know and the public should expect.* London: Atlantic Books.

CHAPTER TEN
WORKING AS A
JOURNALIST

This chapter will cover:

- Starting out – training and work experience
- Getting in – job hunting, CVs and interviews
- Moving on up – building a reputation and career development
- Making it pay – entrepreneurial spirit and freelancing

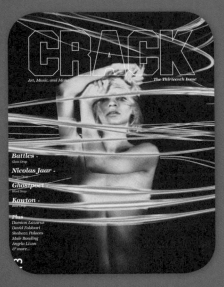

Case study 10.1

CRACK magazine is a 21st century phenomenon. It's certainly a product of its age. To marketing types, it's an emerging music-cum-lifestyle brand. From a journalist's perspective, it's a print and digital offering with lots of fringe benefits spanning the real and virtual worlds of its audience. Even calling it a magazine is something of a misnomer as its high-end style is delivered on tabloid newsprint; it's free and it is much more than a magazine.

Music nights and merchandising are all part of the mix feeding off a smart website. Digital know-how means the *Crack* name also exploits all kinds of social media. There are Crackcasts, mixes, downloads, a videoblog, lots of YouTube links, Facebook Likes, Twitter, Spotify, issuu and more under the banner of '*Crack* – art, music, and hype'. Find it at http://youlovecrack.com. And it's homegrown, literally. Launch editor Tom Frost took his postgraduate diploma from Cardiff University back to Bristol and began to work out how to make a living from his combination of passion and talent for writing about the music industry.

In a potentially crowded market, Tom, with mate and artistic director Jake Applebee, has carved a niche for *Crack* by tapping into the particular vibe, or what one online fan called 'the cultural spirit', of his coolly alternative home town.

A business plan secured initial set-up funding – at least for computer kit, website design and printing of the first editions in 2009. The initial issues were produced at home but *Crack* now has its own premises and has expanded its reach to include Cardiff. A free model meant the distribution network was crucial to success. *Crack* needed to be seen in the right places and picked up by the right people. Local knowledge meant Tom knew which outlets were crucial and enough advertisers were convinced by the package in print and online.

Tom's laid-back savvy has combined with the kind of hard graft usually only those working for themselves understand and can sustain especially when, certainly initially, it didn't generate big bucks. But creating a viable entity and generating enough cash to sustain it is a massive achievement particularly as it launched in difficult economic times. Keeping your own publishing operation afloat is immensely satisfying in a masochistic kind of way.

Journalists setting up on their own is nothing new. Many of us have tried it in our time. Results are unpredictable and patchy. Some self-start businesses come and go very quickly. Others survive independently or are snapped up by bigger enterprises. Being brave enough to step away from the monthly pay cheque hasn't always paid off in the short run – at least not financially. But many big names of mainstream media have had a spell as their own boss, on an independent title or at least as a freelance.[1]

The short-lived *Sunday Correspondent*, 1989–90, with Peter Cole as launch editor, gave a leg up to, among others, Robert Peston, the BBC's business editor featured in Chapter 7, and to trainees Jonathan Freedland and Ian Katz, now of the *Guardian*. Simon Kelner was its sports editor before moving on to be a long-serving editor of the *Independent*. Many of its staff benefited enormously from the experiment in terms of career progression although it is painful to experience the failure of a treasured project.

Digital media has made it even easier to launch new titles because entry costs are so low, especially online but in print too. Yet gaining purchase on an audience in the digital world is tough. A website or app has to be more than a nine-day wonder to have much hope of paying off. Sustained success is hard to achieve but is necessary for those wanting their journalism to be more than a hobby.

The ways of making a living as a journalist have never been so varied – the challenges are greater than ever but so are the opportunities. How you view the prospects will depend on your aptitude and drive but also on whether you are an optimist or pessimist. Similarly, what sort of role you take as a journalist will be determined by your strengths and passions but also by your attitude to risk-taking.

As print media profit margins fall from the dizzy heights of 30 and 40 per cent, the competition for mainstream journalism jobs becomes even greater. Yet for independent operators who can get by on much slimmer margins, the potential is enormous.

INTRODUCTION

Journalism is a fantastic occupation and its widespread appeal adds a particularly competitive edge to entry which is disproportionate to the salaries generally on offer. Referring to it as a vocation can reflect the enthusiasm and sense of purpose the best journalists exude but more often it applies because its practitioners choose to pursue it even though they could earn more money elsewhere.

For some journalists, their role as the Fourth Estate in a democratic system is paramount. They are driven by journalism as a public good, by the people's right to know and by the vital need to contribute to the exchange of information and ideas so that an informed, enlightened public opinion might emerge. Not every journalist shares those lofty ideals but, to the extent that information is power, verifying it, making sense of it and projecting it into the public domain can make an immense contribution to society even when the subject matter is local people's day-to-day lives rather than great affairs of state. Similarly a journalist can open up opportunities, stoke passions and stimulate debate in any and every area of human interest and endeavour – from international politics to knitting.

One of the qualities working journalists share is a focus on audience. However fulfilling the job is for us personally, our raison d'être is the reader. Audience comes first. It is about what they care about far more than what we care about. Being able to turn a personal enthusiasm into a career is certainly one of the attractions of journalism but there is a concomitant danger of self-indulgence. Journalism is predominantly about telling other people's stories, not your own.

STARTING OUT

Journalism has seen a dramatic shift away from on-the-job apprenticeships towards formal pre-entry qualifications and post-graduate training programmes. The changes have been gradual and mirror a general expansion in university education, which has raised the educational entry requirements in many fields.

Now the typical entrant will have at least a university degree and most likely a post-graduate vocational qualification. Arguably, at a time when around 50 per cent of youngsters go on to higher education, it is likely that someone bright enough to handle the challenges of journalism will have a degree whereas in most of the 20th century many able candidates were excluded from university. The introduction in 2012 of annual fees of up to £9,000 may see a shift back towards strong candidates seeking direct entry with publications rather than accumulating a four-year debt.

This has broader implications for the socio-economic profile of journalists. See 'The rights and wrongs of work experience' in Thinking It Through at the end of this chapter.

Journalism training

Those wanting to become journalists need to understand employer expectations and, in practice, it remains the case that a good vocational post-graduate qualification will significantly increase your chances of employment, particularly in the mainstream UK print-origin media. Readers of this book may already be embarked on some form of journalism training but it is still worthwhile considering the different options and how they set you up for the future.

'Where journalism careers begin . . .' is the tag line for the MA/PgDip Journalism programmes at Cardiff University where the three authors of this textbook all teach. The vocational orientation is clear as it is on a range of equivalent post-graduate courses, especially those accredited by the relevant training bodies.

The key bodies for print/online journalists are the National Council for the Training of Journalists (NCTJ), which was traditionally newspaper-focused, and the Periodicals Training Council (PTC). Although both are accrediting bodies, they are different sorts of organisations. Both 'accredit' training programmes in terms of quality assurance and are close enough to the industry to establish the scope and standards expected from vocational courses. However, the NCTJ additionally awards its own qualifications that now span multimedia output.

So a trainee specialising in newspaper/online on an NCTJ-accredited programme will take NCTJ exams, possibly in addition to in-house assessment. These cover shorthand, media law and public administration, as well as practical reporting tests and a portfolio. Specialist options are also available, for example in sports reporting and subbing (production). Would-be journalists emerging from accredited courses tend to have better employment records. Many regional and local newspaper editors want to recruit trainees with the first round of NCTJ qualifications – known as prelims.

Regional newspapers, despite suffering financially, continue to employ many trainees, partly because there are simply many more local than national titles and because the tradition of developing as a journalist on a local paper remains. Relatively few trainees are taken on at national titles that tend to seek and can attract more experienced recruits.

Journalism training, even on accredited programmes, varies enormously which is perhaps a healthy aspect of the sector. Journalism demands variety. There is an inherent tension between standard-setting and the plurality required for the exercise of genuine freedom of speech.

Some editors may reasonably be criticised for being anti-intellectual and even now still anti-graduate but there is some justifiable concern over the concentration of recruitment from a pool of predominantly middle-class white trainees. No editor wants a newsroom full of 'clones' – all the product of very similar training programmes and social backgrounds. Nor do readers. There is a real dilemma between wanting to employ trainees who can be trusted to function effectively based on a clear vocational grounding and wanting diversity in a newsroom – journalists who think differently as well as those from varied class and ethnic backgrounds.

However, journalism training does not have to involve university. There are accredited programmes at further education colleges and a growing range of commercial providers (although some only recruit graduates). There is also a choice to be made between training at under-graduate or post-graduate level. The latter led the way more than 40 years ago on the basis that under-graduate programmes should maintain an academic focus and that the vocational element would kick in at the later stage.

This retains many advantages. Would-be journalists can read whatever subject they want at under-graduate level and commit to the spirit of education for education's sake. It also, in theory, means the post-grad courses can draw from a very diverse pool. In particular it opens up journalism training to science graduates. Journalism needs more recruits from non-humanities backgrounds and, at the very least, it means these trainees have some sort of wider subject hinterland to bring to their work.

The challenge of the post-graduate model, about to become acute, is that it demands four years of fees. Under-graduate programmes, which combine early academic phases with a third year, say, of (accredited) vocational training, are likely to gain in popularity as financial pressures mount.

There are also arguments over how this preparation phase should be balanced. Are post-graduate programmes providing an education or training? Some academics believe journalism training lacks sufficient intellectual content to sit easily within a university environment. Academic content has been increased in some instances for courses to qualify as education rather than just skills-based training, which does not always square with the requirements of accrediting bodies.

Most institutions resolve this by adopting some form of the reflective practitioner approach. Programmes at both under-grad and post-grad level do tend to have some element of self-examination, of ethics, of the role of journalism in society and of what constitutes great journalism. 'Thinking' journalists needs to understand the nature of their craft and its potential contribution to society and to the economy. See 'What makes a great journalist?' in Thinking It Through at the end of this chapter.

So, once you have thought through what sort of balance of academic/vocational preparation you want, the question will be which programme to choose. In journalism training terms, many roads lead to Rome. If you have the talent, many of the courses will set you up reasonably well for a journalistic career. But it is worth checking out the centres with the best track record in the areas that matter most to you.

See your choice of training as a test of your journalistic skill. You need to investigate thoroughly and ask lots of questions until the options begin to become clear. Research your target; seek out a range of views from different perspectives such as editors and new recruits. The career trajectory of alumni is one obvious area to examine. Universities will soon be required to provide more information in this area but in the meantime find as much as you can from websites. Look up the career paths of journalists you admire and track back to where they started. Big names on the alumni list are encouraging but make sure you have more recent examples too. Find out the mix of first jobs of alumni; how they move up the ladder and how fast.

Other questions to ask of any training programme include:

- How 'hands-on' is it? How much contact time do students have? How much 'real' journalistic output is produced?
- What is the industry experience of the tutors and how recent is it? Which tutors will actually be working with you? How available are they?
- Is the course accredited by the relevant training body?
- Does it include shorthand, media law and public administration?
- How much multimedia content is there? If you are taking a print specialism, is there scope for video training, for instance?
- How much work experience or exposure to audience is there?

Find out what your target employers want. Check out any of the job adverts for those titles and see what is expected at entry level. What are the priorities?

Look for programmes that are trying to strike a balance between core basic skills, around idea generation, information gathering and story-telling, and up-to-date digital sourcing and content delivery. In a 2011 survey of 100 regional newspaper editors for the NCTJ[2] the top four most important skills cited were writing, finding news stories, interviewing and legal knowledge – while at the bottom of the list came social media, web skills and interaction with readers. But that doesn't mean the skills at the bottom of the ranking aren't important. Another element of the challenge for would-be entrants and their trainers is that editors want it all.

Editors want trainees who can hit the ground running and who may be expected to take on a similar workload to a senior with little extra in-house support and on significantly less pay. That means graduate trainees aren't left champing at the bit on a diet of weather reports and golden weddings but it can push them to the other extreme where they feel weighed down by the pressure of expectation and the need to shoulder considerable responsibility very early on.

PUTTING IT INTO PRACTICE

Select a target title where you'd like to work. It could be *Cosmopolitan* or *The Times*; it could be your local newspaper or a business-to-business publication. Find out what you can about the backgrounds of the editorial staff. Who and how does your target employer recruit? If that doesn't include raw recruits, identify an entry-level publication that could be the stepping stone to your dream job a few years down the line.

Then work backwards. How would you develop the profile needed to match its expectations? What sort of training would put you in the strongest position to make an application? Run through the questions suggested above then compare and contrast at least half a dozen options. The websites of accrediting bodies would be a good start but you need to do some thorough digging. (See also Weblinks and Recommended Reading at the end of this chapter.)

If you are already on a training programme, set yourself clear goals to develop the skills and profile expected by your target employer(s). Aim to fill gaps and take on projects that will provide strong evidence that you have what they are looking for.

A journalist needs a fascination with people as well as more broadly with current affairs and politics. It's great to have a passion, such as sport, but many titles, and hence training programmes, want a broader outlook at entry level so do mug up more widely even if you have a specialism in mind.

Journalists have to combine creativity with great attention to detail. Accuracy is key so take great care, particularly in your course application. The more competitive programmes are likely to call you for interview and may well test your spelling and punctuation alongside general knowledge and news sense. Bear in mind:

- Trips to Cambodia are great – but only if you can talk perceptively about your visit.
- As journalists ourselves we are trained to weed out the phoney.
- Under-graduate degree subject barely matters. Transferable skills arguably come from degrees such as politics, history, economics or psychology as much as from English.
- Don't confuse being a journalist with being a writer. We aren't training novelists.
- Be prepared for constructive criticism. You've a lot to learn.

Applicants need to convince us they can develop into promising journalists. We need to be sure journalism is the career for them and be confident that an editor somewhere will want to employ them at the end of the course or that they will have the talent to make it on their own.

Work experience

First be sure journalism is where you want to be. How can any applicant who has never worked in a newsroom know that world is for them? Convince yourself and it will be much easier to convince your target admissions tutors.

At Cardiff we look for much more than a one-term stint on a student newspaper undertaken as a CV panic measure. Even applicants with more sustained or senior student involvement look stronger on paper if they have real-world experience to back it up. Running your own blog is great but on its own it's unlikely to be enough, particularly if it's more personal than journalistic.

Work experience is immensely valuable. If a stint on your target publication doesn't fire you up, then you need to find a new target. There is no point being a journalist if you don't love your job. It doesn't have to be every minute of every day but the sense of satisfaction needs to be there. Otherwise you'd be better off financially and emotionally doing something else. On the other hand, one bad experience at an inhospitable publication doesn't necessarily mean you have to write off the whole idea of being a journalist. Every title is different in its organisation and ethos. Often the tone of the working environment and the employees will match the title, but they don't always.

Some journalists are much more at home in one format than another. News may be the driver for some; more contemplative feature writing will suit others. Some will want the opportunity to do both but that's another story.

Undertaking a variety of work experience placements certainly makes sense. If you are serious about a journalistic career, start as soon as you can, spending one or two weeks volunteering at a variety of titles over at least a year in the run-up to applying for a training programme. Your reaction to the experience also creates a much more credible story at interview. A few bylined cuttings and interesting anecdotes give you something to talk about and give recruiters confidence that you can handle a demanding media environment.

In the UK, a short-term work experience placement is more common than a more formal internship although the terms aren't always used consistently. An internship tends to indicate a longer and more-structured engagement, which can effectively become an extended trial period. This can be particularly valuable if there is some payment, even the minimum wage, and if there is a genuine prospect of at least casual employment with the title at the end of it. But beware volunteering for more than a couple of weeks without being paid. See 'The rights and wrongs of work experience' in Thinking It Through at the end of this chapter.

The dreaded tea-making or coffee runs may well be part of your duties but most newsrooms will give you some scope to make a real journalistic contribution. Generally, the more prestigious the publication the less likely you are to win bylines but online strands have scope to be more generous with volunteers.

Try to read the situation. As a journalist you need strong antennae for picking up a vibe from people so start to develop it on work experience. You need to be assertive without being thoroughly annoying. Don't, for instance, bother a news editor right on edition deadline with a feature idea for next week. Only interrupt with a message that the front page splash has fallen through or that something more earth-shattering has just happened. Get that balance right and you are likely to have a productive time and be remembered fondly.

If you are really reined in, soak up as much as you can from observing the more experienced journalists around you. Ask to accompany them on a job or at very least learn from their telephone technique. What questions do they ask? How do they respond when the person on the other end clearly isn't giving them a straight answer? Some cajole; some are more aggressive. See which approaches seem most fruitful.

Try to set up an interview towards the end of your stint with whoever is responsible for recruiting – the title's editor if possible but it could be a managing, associate or deputy editor or even a news editor. Ask for feedback on your contribution and about what they look for in their entry-level recruits. Ask about how and when they take on trainees. Many titles will have work-experience students in most weeks of the year so aim to leaving a lasting – and positive – impression on the key decision-makers and check if there is scope to return or to contribute in some way during your subsequent training course.

Keep good records of your placements too. Obviously copies of any material published need to be kept for a portfolio but make notes too about the organisation. What is the hierarchy? What different roles are there? How does it make its money? And, very importantly, what is its audience and how does that drive the agenda and style of working? That gives you the opportunity to talk with insight about the publication at interview to demonstrate reader and industry awareness. It should also make you think through the sort of title you would be proud to work for and what management style and working environment might suit you best. From an ethical perspective too, is this the sort of operation you would be comfortable with?

remember

- Ask yourself what you need from your journalism training.
- What combination do you want of academic and vocational study?
- How important is accreditation among your target employers? Check their job adverts.
- Identify your potential early on so training courses will want to offer you a place.
- Adopt a questioning journalistic approach from the start.
- Set up several work experience placements and make the most of them.

GETTING IN – JOB HUNTING, CVs AND APPLICATIONS, INTERVIEWS

Securing a first job in journalism can seem the most daunting challenge of all. Some entry-level posts will certainly open more doors than others but, again, the potential career paths to the top in journalism are many and varied. Hardly anyone makes it in one bound and, despite the raised educational requirements, it is still a business in which most people start at the bottom. So one of the challenges is to find a job that will be satisfying in the short term but also be a springboard to a sharp and swift rise through the ranks.

Experiences and skills developed during your training course will probably have provided a fairly clear steer to a range of target publications but some entrants will be keeping an open mind. This is where advice can appear contradictory. Being able to isolate a specialist strength which would appeal to a limited number of employers – say international business agencies – helps to focus your job search efforts and hopefully set you out from the crowd. It is worth indentifying where there is the best possible match between your profile and what an employer is seeking.

But that may be too limiting. Your target title(s) may not be recruiting. In the late 20th century many publications took on a number of trainees every year on top of their main staffing numbers. In the 21st century most will only recruit where there is a vacancy and perhaps not even then. Others may be able to take on a trainee to replace a senior rather than not recruit at all. So it also makes sense to keep an open mind about what entry level jobs are of interest.

Geography can be a big issue here. Students appear to be less adventurous about relocating to an unknown part of the UK. That could be because they need to bite the bullet and live at home so as to avoid getting into even more debt while they survive on entry-level wages for a couple of years. For local papers that can be an appealing prospect. In the early days of graduate recruitment, editors tended to alternate between the local lad/lass familiar with the patch and a bright young thing from university. An applicant who combines top-class training with local knowledge should be able to offer the best of both worlds and thus be eminently employable.

But again the vacancies might just not be there. So it is best not to rule out starting out in pastures new. Getting to know any community as a journalist is a fascinating process and often fresh eyes will yield stories that a jaded local might miss. Most journalists are quick to create a social circle, both within and outside work.

journalist with multimedia publishing skills.' This could be tweaked to achieve the best match by stressing contact building, feature writing or a special area of interest.

CVs are written in reverse chronological order, generally because your most pertinent experience is usually the most recent. So again your vocational journalism course is more relevant than GCSEs.

PUTTING IT INTO PRACTICE

Put a basic CV together on one side of A4 to support applications for journalism jobs.

Think about your achievements. Make sure you can answer questions about whatever you include and have evidence/examples to back up. Pretend you are an editor receiving the CV – what questions would you ask such an applicant? What would make you stand out?

Pick a vacancy notice in your area of interest. Read it very carefully, mug up on the publication, its company, its editor, its latest developments, its online offering. Find out as much as you can. Tailor your CV to tempt the editor to invite you for interview.

Now take a second advert for a different job at a different title. If the ad wants a self-starter, pop in a couple of bullet points about stories you initiated. Sift through your cuttings and achievements to find evidence to match the stated requirements. Adjust your CV to suit and see what a difference it can make.

Keep all the examples to create a bank of evidence for future CVs or to use at interview.

Go online to check out advice sites such as **http://www.workthing.co.uk** and see how your CV compares with the samples given.

Once you have a CV bank together writing a covering letter should be fairly straightforward. This allows you to emphasise even more explicitly the key areas that match your profile to the employer's needs. By all means praise the publication and make it clear how much you would love the job but remember the editor isn't there to do you a favour. She wants to know what you have to offer. Focus on your value to the title not vice versa.

Maximise the relevance of the content, then double and triple check the facts and spelling in every application letter, form and CV before submission. Take particular care with the editor's name and don't rely on the top mention of a Google search. Use the title's own site and be absolutely sure you are accurate. Ideally ask a trusted friend or tutor to read all the material too. It's much easier for a third party to spot errors. And guard against cut and paste. Keeping different versions of your application letter and CV is good practice. But be sure to make every application individual. You wouldn't be the first to mention Reuters in an application to Bloomberg or vice versa but that's not how you want to be remembered by their recruiters.

Interviews

Interviews are the next hurdle – if you are lucky. There is no shortage of general interview advice so here we'll focus on a few specific journalistic pointers.

Never be tempted to busk an interview by relying on your natural brilliance and obvious talent. Once in a blue moon it might wow your interviewers but it's not worth wasting all the other opportunities along the way.

Find out as much as you can about the interview process. Check the details in advance with whoever is setting up the interview – possibly the editor's secretary. Many invitations to interview are rather vague. Who will actually be conducting the interview? What format will it take? Will there be tests? How long is it likely to last? Don't be afraid to ask such key questions as they could give you the edge. Knowing what to expect can help to ease nerves and make it easier to maintain the necessary poise on the day.

Use contacts with any recent recruits for useful tips on what to expect but don't bank on the procedure being identical every time. As in journalism, preparation is hugely valuable but not if it creates fixed expectations. Really good planning should enhance your ability to respond to the unpredictable. And update your research on the publication. Read the latest issues and online activity. Have an opinion and be prepared to suggest improvements. An element of criticism can be fine as long as it is constructive. Focus on identifying gaps in the offering; extras that would suit its target readers. That way you can demonstrate both confidence and industry knowledge.

Again keep the focus on the benefits you would bring to the title. Have examples to back up your claims. That is where a well-organised portfolio can support your cause. It makes sense to include your 'big' stories, which might look impressive in themselves but their added value is the evidence they provide of your talents. So work out in advance what each cutting says about you. Did it come from a really good contact? Did you turn it round particularly quickly? Did you use inventive means of persuading the source to give you an exclusive angle? So when you are asked a stock interview question about your favourite/biggest/trickiest assignment your portfolio will contain the answer and the back story to go with it.

remember

- Build up your network of contacts and exploit it for general jobs advice as well as for tip-offs about specific openings.
- Match yourself to the specific vacancy or, with a speculative application, to the needs of your target title.
- Put yourself in the editor's shoes. Why are you the right person for the job?
- Structure a portfolio both online and in hard copy form which really showcases what you have to offer.
- Be prepared from the point you apply to be put on the spot and prove you have what it takes.

MOVING ON UP

Within a couple of years of landing your first journalism job, you will be wondering what to do next. And it might be sooner than that. Traditional newspaper training via the NCTJ, for instance, sustains a model which combines pre- and post-entry training. Most journalists on a local paper, say, join as a trainee/junior from a self-funded training scheme but then spend about another 18 months developing as a reporter before taking the second stage of the NCTJ qualification, the National Certificate Exam (NCE), and becoming a 'senior' reporter.

Success in the NCE is one of the most obvious triggers for any journalist to ask: what next? Some will want to be a specialist news reporter or perhaps look to move into features, sport or production or on to newsdesk. Or it may be the time when they look to move up from a weekly to a daily or from a regional to a national title. Some may switch platforms into regional radio or television or even into a PR career if the hours/pay have begun to pall.

An editor seeking to keep a talented new senior will recognise that a new direction and more responsibility may be required. But how do you become the senior the editor doesn't want to lose; the one they want to fast-track through the organisation?

Building a reputation

Being valued as a journalist is largely about the ideas and content contributed; about the specific expectations of the role. But even notoriously bloody-minded cynical hacks have to be team players to a greater or lesser extent. Just as creativity has to combine with attention to detail, so the writing strengths of the rugged individualist have to be synchronised with the demands of a production team whatever platform you work for. That means more than just meeting deadlines; it means making it easier for colleagues who create the other links in the chain to do their bit towards getting your work in front of the public. Once you have landed your first job, you need to work out how to maximise your contribution and chances of success.

Working effectively

The fixed deadlines of print publications used to create a natural rhythm to the day, week, month or even quarter. There was an obvious time to draw breath, to catch up on routine tasks or invest in some contact-building before the deadline pressure began to bite again. In a 24/7 rolling news environment, there isn't the equivalent sense of 'job done'. So you have to develop your own triggers for knowing when to stop.

Journalists have a tendency to become workaholics and it is easy to succumb especially as the industry rewards those who will go the extra mile. The danger of showing willing as a new journalist is in becoming a workhorse – the mug always bailing out everyone else and spending every waking hour in the newsroom. There are times when working round the clock will be a must but it shouldn't be routine.

Every journalist also needs to be aware of the physical risks of the job. The flash riots of summer 2011 were a prime example of how an everyday local reporter could suddenly be in considerable danger and a potential target of troublemakers. Seek training in this area and ensure adequate risk assessment is being carried out by you and your employers.

Journalists habitually deal with people *in extremis* so should understand not only how their sources may be reacting to trauma but also the potential personal impact of exposure to the tragedy of others. Journalists need to develop the skills and awareness to protect themselves long-term from the various rigours of the job. However you find your work–life balance, your input will be much more productive if you understand how you and your role fit into the process of producing the title you are working on whether in print, online or some combination of the two.

Newsdesk

Start in the editorial department with your immediate team and line manager. The news editor or content editor is likely to be line manager for entry level recruits so your first 'boss'. Newsdesk will assign your work, check it, re-write it if minor changes are enough or return it to you if major re-working is needed. You will feed ideas through the newsdesk, seek advice on content development and volunteer for assignments.

Newsdesk is responsible for story choice; story development, timings and priorities; allocating jobs, often with an expected word count; progress chasing, copy checking and tasting; and often also packaging content page by page. Newsdesk editors need to keep staff busy, make the most of each story and keep copy flowing to production with the necessary images or graphics. Theirs is a massive juggling act of chasing possibilities and grappling with the deadline realities. Newsdesk may be split by geography, say with a deputy who looks after district editions for outlying areas, or it may be split by subject area. There may be different shifts responsible for different editions, or focused mainly by platform.

Wherever you work there will be a procedure which will be more or less obvious. Find out what it is and stick to it. You are a link in a chain – don't be the weak one. Learn the routines of job allocation, recording contacts and general internal communications. Stick rigidly to any instructions about how file names are to be used on your work and exactly how to submit it. Production flow is crucial and you need to ensure your precious material is in the right place at the right time.

Ask what is expected. If you are told 300 words by 10.30 give them 300 words by 10.30. Or you may be told to 'give it what it is worth' which is a tricky equation for a beginner to calculate. Initially aim to match the prevailing style and tone of your publication before developing a more individual style. Well-organised and/or large editorial teams may provide a style guide as discussed in Chapter 3. Otherwise check out similar stories in the archives.

Understand how your line manager operates. Give newsdesk reason to have confidence in you. Meet its deadlines. Submit error-free copy. There are ways to be canny too. If newsdesk is repeatedly short of nibs (news in briefs) make it your habit to file a few every day. News editors appreciate reporters who solve more problems than they cause.

Have sympathy for newsdesk editors who are generally up to their necks. In most organisations, the newsdesk is the engine room of the publication. Also, although staff do not have the seniority or responsibility of the ultimate editor, theirs is likely to be the most hassled role in editorial. They may struggle to be your buddy too.

The editorial team

Find out who else in the editorial team may have more time for you – an established senior or a sympathetic sub for instance. When new to a newsroom, try to identify the driving forces other than the obvious newsdesk executives. Watch them and learn from them, feed ideas and questions to them when you get the chance. Who is important enough to attend planning meetings and news conferences? Who is earning the most bylines?

Also, be warned that your more senior colleagues will tend to judge you by your worst work rather than your best. Individual flair is great but consistency is highly valued too.

Production

Journalists work in the 'creative industries' but print titles are also part of a manufacturing production process which needs to churn out copies to deadline. This can create one of the classic splits within editorial teams. The content creators generally want to push deadlines as late as possible so as to include the latest updates and the juiciest quotes. But the production team needs to get pages away to hit deadlines on presses where time is money and hold-ups are costly in terms of print charges and lost copy sales further down the line.

The content team is where you are most likely to start out but the two may be merged. This is more common on magazines and in specialist newspaper departments such as features and sport. Where material is less time-sensitive, it is easier to multi-task by reporting first and then laying out pages.

Newsroom structures vary greatly for a host of reasons – some historical, some because of the nature of the title, some because of an editor's preference or the mix of talent available. Digital production has tended to telescope roles by removing several stages of the production process so the mix of roles expected has become even more varied. See 'The multi-platform journalist' in Thinking It Through at the end of this chapter.

Understanding how the editorial content is projected for maximum impact is important, even it is not directly your job. If you have specialist designers or sub-editors, they will be enthused by imaginative images and graphics as much as by your immaculate prose (and it had better be immaculate if you want to keep production on side). Your success relies heavily on achieving a reputation for quality and reliability with other team members who can sink one of your features or help it to fly. There are journalists in far too many organisations whose name on a file of copy is the kiss of death, eliciting groans from subs who have re-written and corrected similarly inadequate contributions too many times before. If they tell you, at least you have the chance to improve but they won't necessarily take the time, so don't just assume all is well. Seek feedback, particularly if your work is being extensively reworked.

You need to find out about these other players who may be at one remove from your immediate working circle. What do they do? What are their requirements/demands? People at different points in the process have different pressures and priorities.

If you are fortunate enough to have specialist photographers, cultivate them. Think about how your work could be illustrated and share ideas but respect their expertise. Aim to include them at an early stage. Don't wait until your story is written before suggesting a photo opportunity.

The editor

However the editorial staff of your title is structured and however many layers of hierarchy exist, at the top of it sits the editor. In common with other executives, those occupying the title work in very different ways. Some may be a strong newsroom presence clearly involved with the main stories of the day. Others tend to work behind the scenes. That does not necessarily mean their impact is any less. One way or another, establish a constructive working relationship with the editor if you possibly can.

PUTTING IT INTO PRACTICE

The word 'editor' is part of many job titles but only one person can be *the* editor of a publication. There may be managing editors, associate editors, editors-in-chief and more. The distribution of power may be blurred. But whoever is responsible for the publication content, legally, to regulators and to the audience – whoever has power to hire and fire the journalists – is effectively the editor of that title. Muddying those waters can cause significant difficulties both internally and externally as many senior editorial figures have learnt the hard way.

As journalists are promoted they classically gain responsibility for areas of content: maybe just a weekly specialist page but perhaps a whole section or ultimately as editor of all the publication's content. Often a team of people comes with the responsibility yet there may be little training provided in the necessary leadership, organisational and motivational skills. Getting the best from people may not be a skill a good journalist automatically possesses and journalists certainly aren't trained in the detail, say, of employment law, which is a vital for those involved in appointing and managing staff.

At editor level, a further raft of responsibility for legal matters, budgets and strategy adds to the mix.

Think about the elements of an editor's job. Read the relevant chapter by Sara Hadwin in the Bob Franklin book listed in Recommended Reading at the end of this chapter, on the work of a local newspaper editor.

Activity: Write a job description and person specification for the editor of a specialist magazine. What functions does the editor fulfil? What knowledge, skills and experience would the editor need?

The virtual newsroom?

One 21st century twist to the newsroom environment is the trend towards remote working. At its extreme a few titles have created an entirely virtual newsroom with all communication conducted digitally by staff working from wherever suits them – the reporters out on the road, the production staff putting pages together from anywhere in the world.

Like many trends this isn't an entirely new phenomenon but it is accelerated by technology. Freelancers have always worked apart. Central subbing hubs are not entirely new. Outsourcing parts of the production process has been going on for years in areas such as colour reproduction when it became technically possible and much cheaper to have the work done in Hong Kong. Physical proximity is no longer a technological requirement.

There are at least two major drawbacks to this. One matters particularly to community-based publications where reader interaction is high and the regulars still prefer a face-to-face approach. There was much to be said for the High Street newspaper office into which anyone could walk with a story (or to place an advert). A journalist being there in real human form still counts for a lot in UK communities.

But much is lost for the journalist too. The vibrancy of newsroom working is part of what makes the job so rewarding; what gets the adrenalin flowing. Working remotely threatens that sense of collective endeavour: the easy pooling of ideas; the keeping it real. Team members can easily become emotionally as well as physically remote from each other. Perhaps 21st century journalists will feel the distinction between the real and the virtual less acutely but not everyone is suited to working alone.

Non-editorial departments

An entry-level journalist will also need a grasp of how editorial interacts with other departments such as advertising, production, distribution, copy sales and marketing.

Understanding the roles of other departments does not – and must not – necessitate compromising editorial integrity. But colleagues who, for instance, spend their careers tempting new readers to your title develop massively helpful insights into the strengths and weaknesses of the publication. They can be a source of many well-informed ideas for improvement. Some may clash with editorial ethics or standards and can be rejected, but most will not.

A publication sold mainly on subscription, for instance, appeals to its audience in rather different ways from one predominantly competing directly on the newsstands. Subscriptions also help to build up a very clear audience profile and knowing who your readers are is crucial to the success of any title.

As editorial you also want to know what your audience responds to. Which magazine cover generated the highest sales in particular outlets? Which newspaper billboards boosted circulation in the city centre?

Your sales outlets of shops and newsagents generally want reliability, especially on delivery times. Buying print titles is a habit. A newspaper, for instance, may be bought on a lunchbreak or picking up children from school. If it isn't there the sale is lost.

Staff in other departments can be great sources too. They are out and about meeting people and, particularly for newspapers, they are likely to live in your circulation area and share many of the experiences and concerns of your audience. Van drivers can be particularly good at picking up snippets. Advertising reps can help too. They will often be driven primarily by trying to get publicity for their clients. This can produce friction although the battles may be fought out higher up the company. If in doubt, check with your line manager but generally treat their information like any other. A journalist must always be aware of the agenda of any source and judge the information supplied on its merits. Advertisers shouldn't get preferential treatment but they should not be ignored either.

Career development

A good employer will take responsibility for your career development. You may be lucky enough to be groomed actively within a company good at developing and rewarding talent. Big companies, for instance, put considerable effort into succession planning and some take full advantage of their internal access to a flexible pool of proven talent. Others leave you to fend for yourself and may even resist your attempts at self-improvement.

Ultimately, with or without the support of your boss, you have to take responsibility for your own career development. Before accepting even an entry-level job you should assess and ask about the potential. The word 'promotion' is often avoided these days either because of a recognition that opportunities can arise within a flattened hierarchy that aren't technically more senior but may still be worthwhile, or because companies want to avoid a salary increase.

You will have to negotiate some of those equations for yourself at various stages of your career. But, as any business expert and/or psychologist will tell you, there is a great deal more to job satisfaction than financial remuneration. Sometimes a sideways move is needed to flesh out a range of skills. Traditionally newspaper editors were expected to have at least some subbing experience so many completed a stint on production so as to tick all the boxes. Others were talented or persuasive enough to be promoted anyway. There are very few hard and fast rules in the business of journalism.

Another crucial skill in career development is to recognise what matters to you. The external hierarchy of success is just that. A role perceived as a 'top' job won't necessarily deliver job satisfaction – although for many ego-driven journalists it most certainly will! That is where the typically generalist entry-level jobs in UK journalism can pay off by offering a 'taster' for you and your employer as you establish where your strengths lie and which elements of the job you most want to focus on. The options are endless, which is both encouraging and daunting. Certainly a journalist could be driven mad by 'what ifs': what if they had made the leap to the nationals, specialised in music journalism or stuck it out as a freelance?

Journalism careers are more fluid than ever which makes them both more risky but potentially more rewarding. None of us need get stuck in a rut given the pace of change in the industry, both of our audience and of our means of reaching them. Journalists need to be comfortable with change while remaining clear about core beliefs and what matters most about the job. All of us have to navigate the possibilities for ourselves.

Most companies have some sort of formal appraisal system, which provides at least one opportunity a year to ask formally for support with skills development or refresher courses. Newspaper editors rank knowledge of media law highly for instance. But, like many aspects of the job, it can't be learnt once and for all at pre-entry stage. Media law is dynamic so follow-up training is a must.

But don't rely just on formal training. Much can be learnt informally on the job, through e-learning or simply by careful and regular analysis of industry developments. Monitoring media news is valuable not just for possible job opportunities but for inspiration. Keep a close eye on direct UK competitors but look abroad as well.

remember

- Journalists are strong individuals but most rely on a team to reach their audience.
- Aim to be a good colleague and understand your part in the bigger picture.
- Learn skills of self-preservation to protect yourself from the physical risks, stress and potential long hours.
- Be adaptable and open to new ways of working.
- Seek out responsibility and join in experiments.
- Keep learning and developing your skills through formal or informal training.

MAKING IT PAY

The digital developments of the 21st century have thrown the funding models for journalism into a state of flux to a greater extent than possibly ever before. On the down side, paid staff jobs are being lost as established titles downsize and work feverishly to find new online and other revenues to replace lost print advertising.

In the 20th century print model, readers of editorial content paid for the privilege by buying their favoured newspaper or magazine either over the counter or on delivery/subscription through their letterbox. There were enough of them to attract advertisers who secured enough business to keep coming back. The cover price/circulation revenue and the advertising revenues combined paid to print and distribute the titles and significantly paid the wages of the journalists and others employed to create them.

The balance of those revenues varies enormously from title to title. Generally a mass circulation newspaper such as the *Sun* would make proportionately more of its revenue from the cover price than from advertising, whereas on a small weekly, for instance, the majority of revenue would come from advertising.

As attention switched to digital platforms, audiences and advertising for many titles dwindled, with advertising usually falling faster. Titles have felt the pain to different degrees depending on their revenue mix and also on their relative success at leveraging new revenue streams from associated digital platforms. In the UK the *Guardian* (owned by a not-for-profit trust) has led the way, moving to a web-first policy and experimenting with a host of potential money-making digital offerings. But it has not been easy – or so far possible – even for the most ambitious to make the money add up. The expectation of free content online means that most titles have gone for audience numbers and sacrificed the revenue readers used to pay for content. (However, customers have been prepared to pay something for mobile apps and some, mainly niche business titles, operate 'pay walls'.)

The resulting digital advertising revenue has not kept up, even to replace lost print advertising let alone compensate for lost cover price money. The market has developed such that digital advertising 'rates' are a fraction, perhaps only one hundredth, of those in print. Advertisers pay to reach potential customers – the bigger the audience, the more they will pay. Charging works very broadly on a price per thousand. For a given audience, for every £1 paid for print, advertisers pay a penny online.

Thankfully individual deals can be rather more complicated than that. The web can match customers to products more cleverly, which can tempt advertisers to pay premium rates, but the search engines, particularly Google, have tended to be the ones to cash in there rather than the content providers. There is still money in the process but much of it has slipped through the fingers of mainstream media into the hands of the aggregators and delivery platforms.

Entrepreneurial spirit

There are, naturally, optimists and pessimists when it comes to the prospects of journalism-based businesses. There are certainly enough winners and losers to argue either way. Some think news organisations will find a way to make enough money between a mix of print and digital to sustain a reduced, but still dynamic, editorial team whether locally or nationally. The *Guardian*, for instance, is pushing hard on e-tailing and the creation of bespoke (paid-for) offerings within its broadly free content model. Some local papers are turning weekly instead of daily, which is a huge regret. Yet survival as a weekly is better than closure from both community and commercial perspectives.

The other glass-half-full approach is the view that while mainstream media jobs may dwindle, digital platforms, or some print/digital combination, offer massive opportunities for inventive entrants to show the print dinosaurs how it can be done. The opening case study of *Crack* magazine is just one of many new permutations that span the media choices of the 20th and 21st centuries. Entry costs are lower than ever and young imaginative journalists are creating new paths to making it pay. We evolve; we find a way.

Many regional newspapers and magazines are still profitable, even through recession. Without major corporate investors to keep happy and debts to repay, much lower returns are viable for independently owned titles. Many journalists are doing it for themselves – setting up their own community titles in print and online. There are regular reports of local launches on websites such as Holdthefrontpage. It has been done before, but a new phase could be under way as the big companies perhaps lose interest.

There is also the question of whether newspapers should receive public funding. Should we have public service print titles in parallel with the BBC? If we focus on journalism as a public good, on its contribution to a dynamic public sphere, then why not? See 'Public service publications' in Thinking It Through at the end of this chapter.

A piecemeal approach is perhaps more likely but there is potential to secure some public funding for editorially led community titles. Journalists emerging from training courses may be eligible for start-up grants through their local authority or university.

There is also scope for philanthropy. Charitable funding for public-interest journalism is more established in the USA but there are examples in the UK, notably the London-based Bureau of Investigative Journalism. The not-for-profit organisation based at City University, London, was established in April 2010 with a £2 million donation from the David & Elaine Potter Foundation. It has already established a healthy track record of collaborations with mainstream print and broadcast media on significant investigations. Find out more about its work at **http://www.thebureauinvestigates.com**. Also in late 2011 the Russian owners of the Independent newspaper set up the Journalism Foundation to support journalism around the world.

Some websites already operate with funding coming from supporters. Crowd-funding can be generated for commercial operation but more often finance is raised through a subscription pitched as a form of charitable giving – a sense of supporting a cause rather than paying for content. Permutations of a not-for-profit model could work at a local level as they do with trusts set up to run community shops or pubs, for instance.

PUTTING IT INTO PRACTICE

Imagine being your own boss and making a living from your journalism. Think about what sort of mix of income sources would be open to you. If you were to launch an online or print title, what local or specialist knowledge could you draw on to attract an audience and generate revenue?

A journalist may well benefit from a lively blog primarily as a profile-raising showcase to leverage freelance commissions from mainstream commercial publications, but trying to generate some revenue from it makes sense even if that alone won't pay the bills.

Where might there be a gap in the market? What added value could you provide? Could you generate transactional streams by linking to commercial sites? Would you explore the potential for e-tailing?

Activity: Sketch out a business plan for the format of your title, in print, digitally or both. Who would be your target audience and how would you reach them? What content would you provide and how? How would you make it pay?

Freelancing

Freelancing offers a long-established means of making a living from journalism, particularly in magazines. So it perhaps sounds rather 20th century in comparison with news of online start-ups and digital revenues. But this is another area expected to flourish in the 21st century with more journalists trying it and more frequently.

Some journalists work in a freelance capacity throughout their careers. Others may use freelancing to establish a name for themselves until they can secure a full-time job. Real high fliers find it can have tax advantages over a standard staff contract. Or simply when times are tough it sounds better than 'unemployed'.

Freelancing as part of a portfolio career could also cover a transition, say from a staff job on a regional newspaper to casual shifts on a national; or between print and broadcast jobs. The difference now is that freelancing is more likely to combine with an entrepreneurial element and/or related work in training or media advice.

Freelancing fits with the concept of the journalist as a brand with a reputation built up in various fields and being less reliant on one mainstream title. More journalists are likely to be multi-tasking in terms of generating income too, working for more than one employer and probably on their own account simultaneously. A columnist, for instance, may have a regular slot in one title to pay the bills but can supplement that in their own right, particularly by building an online profile. Expertise in an area as demonstrated on a well-run blog can generate commercial commissions but also digital revenues, not just from direct advertising but through transactional streams as readers click through into related sites.

Freelancing has always required some skills of self-promotion and marketing to secure work but the 21st century freelancer is likely to find an even greater accent on entrepreneurial ability. (See also the chapter by Ros Bew on Freelancing in the Bob Franklin book listed in the Recommended Reading at the end of this chapter.)

Many of those who have gained a headstart on generating digital revenues via a website, and particularly those with most success at exploiting social networking sites for business purposes, are making additional money from sharing the secrets of their learning curve with those attempting to emulate them. Such opportunities might be short-lived as digital entrepreneurs catch on fast but money can be made by being one step ahead.

remember

- Journalism-based businesses are easier to launch than ever.
- Entry-level entrepreneurs can experiment with new business models particularly in the digital domain.
- A combination of creativity and business acumen can pay off.
- Think through whether you are suited to be your own boss.
- New dimensions are being added to freelancing.
- Making a living as a journalist can take many forms and involve many, simultaneous sources of income.

CHAPTER SUMMARY

- Do you really want to be a journalist? Unless you are sure you could probably earn more money with much less effort doing something else. Once you have convinced yourself, it will be much easier to convince a training provider and ultimately an editor.
- Be a journalist. Build initial skills and confidence by work shadowing, blogging, contributing to student media or creating a hyperlocal news site. Showcase your talents.
- Apply journalistic skills to your search for training, work experience, a first job and career development. Develop contacts, exploit networking opportunities, research your target courses/employers, be enthusiastic and dogged.
- Having it all – that's what editors want from a prospective journalist. Individual talent combined with strong team-working skills. Creative flair and obsessive attention to detail. Expert in the chosen field but with a massive hinterland of multimedia skills, enthusiasms and ideas.
- Keep learning and developing. Journalists need to keep abreast of world events but also changes in their own industry. Be prepared to experiment.
- Do it yourself. Media business models are at best in a state of flux. Making it pay is a huge challenge but a generation at home in the digital age should be best placed to work out how to secure great journalism for the future.

THINKING IT THROUGH

The rights and wrongs of work experience

Contacts are the holy grail of journalists yet they are also at the root of one of the industry's weaknesses. Networking is important in every walk of life and very obviously so in journalism. So aspiring reporters who are born well-connected can hardly be expected not to attempt to exploit their in-built advantage. But where does that leave those without ready-made contacts? Employers who passively accept those who make the approaches risk drawing from a very narrow privileged band of potential recruits.

Relying on informal networking is not only prejudicial, it deprives the industry of recruits from the range of backgrounds needed to ensure the breadth of outlook required.

Good journalists are aware of the baggage of upbringing and become acutely aware that they are not typical even of their readership let alone society at large. But it is very easy for people from relatively comfortable backgrounds to make sub-conscious assumptions about the lives of others; about what constitutes good/bad news and very broadly what matters. Consider, for instance, the minimal coverage given to the cut in post-16 education grants that support youngsters from low-income families compared with the hike in university fees that affects mainly middle-class households.

You don't have to be from a working class background to understand poverty and you don't have to be Asian to report on ethnic minority issues. But if a newsroom is staffed by exclusively white middle-class journalists other perspectives can all too easily remain marginalised. Beyond that it is simply not fair effectively to restrict entry to those who can afford four years of higher education followed by six months of unpaid work as a magazine's editorial assistant before being considered for a staff job, or even paid shifts.

▶ THINKING IT THROUGH

Efforts are being made in some quarters to regulate the use of 'voluntary' placements. See the campaigns by the National Union of Journalists and Skillset, for instance. The most exploitative work placements are effectively slave labour and some may be in breach of minimum wage legislation. Reputable employers will be examining their work experience arrangements not just to comply with the law and best practice but also to consider how they can be used to reach a broader mix of potential recruits.

Would-be journalists need to weigh up the pros and cons of the deal. A couple of weeks' experience without pay might be a reasonable trade-off for the CV but too many youngsters are encouraged to stay longer just to fill gaps in the newsroom.

Think about what duration of work experience would be beneficial for you. Should you be paid for any work that is published? Is the deal fair to you and to other potential recruits?

What makes a great journalist?

Journalists take more brick bats than bouquets. That suggests an essential requirement is an ultra thick skin. Yet perversely journalists actually require a great deal of sensitivity: to empathise with others; to understand what makes people tick; and to sense when they are being misled.

Ask editors to list the recipe for a great journalist and most would have curiosity and determination as key ingredients, perhaps with a twist of Nicholas Tomalin's infamous 'rat-like cunning'.

Journalism is, as we have observed, both an individual and a team game. There are many massive egos in the business. Journalists love a byline but it makes us very exposed as individuals. Our triumphs and disasters are out there for all to see and readers, especially with the facility of digital communication, are increasingly able to call us to account. The fall from grace of the *Independent*'s Johann Hari in September 2011 is one classic example that saw a journalist forced to apologise for misleading readers by exaggeration, invention and a frequent sleight of hand to suggest a proximity to sources that did not exist. (See also the phone-hacking inquiry in Chapter 9.)

Check out the websites of your favourite print titles and see how they describe what they are looking for. Titles such as the *Guardian* run masterclasses that include advice from specialists on how to get your foot on the ladder.

David Randall, who has written a whole book on great reporters (2007), is a useful source and many journalists' autobiographical accounts explicitly or implicitly cover the issues of what makes them good at their job. Internationally, Woodward and Bernstein, of Watergate fame, must be two of the most famous and inspirational reporters of the 20th century but there are many more. From a global perspective, journalists with major reputations include the late Anna Politkovskaya and Seymour Hersh.

Look too at the journalism that wins awards nationally and internationally. The judges' comments will help to explain what makes it great but the decisions can be controversial.

The multi-platform journalist

Trainers, editors and individual journalists have all had to adjust to changes in roles triggered by the digital dominance of the 21st century. Dyed-in-the-wool newspaper hacks have had to adapt to create online content. Many have become bloggers, micro-bloggers and their own photographers, sound recordists and camera operators. ▶

▶ THINKING IT THROUGH

A single journalist can attend an event and capture multimedia content but there are limits to what can be achieved with one pair of hands. Raw material mainly requires a skilled edit to have mass audience appeal and that takes time. News-gathering often requires a reporter to be physically present to witness an occasion, to interview a particular source, to track others down. As the final whistle blows do you file a personal post-mortem on the match or chase the manager down the tunnel? Not every story can be covered adequately by one person however multi-skilled.

Technology has tended to telescope tasks and reduce the number of links in the chain. Editorial content passes through far fewer stages than it did in the days of hot metal production and, of course, a single journalist can publish direct to the public via a host of electronic devices.

News organisations with multiple titles and a whole portfolio of platforms are gradually getting to grips with the permutations. Most newsrooms have kept space for the specialists – for some of the reasons outlined in Chapter 7 arising from the demands of the job but also because some journalists are so skilled in one particular area of the job it seems wasteful to spread them into areas where they struggle.

There isn't a one-size-fits-all solution, which on the whole makes life more interesting for the journalist. Many newsrooms operate very flexible combinations of roles, as they always have. Sports departments traditionally worked as self-contained units generating and producing all their own pages. For some titles that has become the norm with the removal of barriers between content and production teams.

Many entry-level reporters will be expected to absorb more elements of other editorial and production roles. Rather than just providing raw text, they may be taking their own photographs, generating their own graphics, writing headlines for print and online editions, and providing links, running blog commentaries and Tweeting breaking news.

For some, being able to control the whole package is a huge bonus; for others they find themselves struggling to do justice to most of the elements or dispirited by the preponderance of pre-ordained formats. Journalists are filling spaces, be it on websites or print pages, to order like never before. To some, that's the equivalent of replacing true artistry with a painting-by-numbers kit.

So how much multi-tasking makes sense? Stephen Quinn (2005) is worth reading on this topic (see Recommended Reading at the end of this chapter). He identifies a phased approach to media convergence, moving through ownership convergence (which has been limited in the UK by competition rules), through tactical convergence and structural convergence to information-gathering convergence, which can, as intimated above, put quality at risk. He envisaged a further phase of story-telling and presentation convergence where a central team decides the treatment appropriate for each story – some just for print, others all platforms – and allocates the appropriate resource – sometimes a multi-tasking lone ranger, at others a mixed team of talents to do justice to all the elements and platforms. Similarly roles would vary in the degree to which they were multi-skilled or multi-platform to allow journalists to play to their strengths.

Some editors believe computer programming skills should be more to the fore so that journalists can use and develop digital offerings more flexibly and intuitively rather than relying on a separate technical team. Others want more scientists than English majors to help the audience make sense of what is going on in the world. Check out, for instance, *Guardian* editor Alan Rusbridger's 2010 Hugh Cudlipp lecture

> ▶ THINKING IT THROUGH

(at **http://www.guardian.co.uk/media**). Its title *Does journalism exist?* does more than hint at the challenges facing serious journalism as the 21st century gets into its stride.

But how does the contribution of the literary genius compare with that of the computer nerd? Is it all about numbers or all about people? Is it about substance or presentation? What exactly is a journalist's job in the 21st century?

Public service publications?

The concept of journalism as a public good is much to the fore across the world as digital developments challenge the business model for mainstream media, especially in print. In the UK there are question marks over the future public funding of the BBC via the licence fee and potential experiments with some direct public funding of local television and perhaps even local newspapers. However, at the same time as the government is contemplating funding from the national purse, it is curbing local government forays into council newspapers by restricting their advertising take to help protect existing privately owned newspapers.

There are certainly concerns about how quality journalism will be paid for. Niche and very upmarket publications such as the *Financial Times* are having some success by charging for digital content. Some Murdoch titles have followed suit. Others put some content behind pay walls but keep most of it free to access so as to drive up audience figures. The *Guardian* is resolutely committed to predominantly free online content and its editor Alan Rusbridger believes the audience will determine the platform delivery. Its digital offerings are superb but the operation is heavily subsidised by its owners, the Scott Trust, to a level that is not sustainable. The efforts to date to generate digital revenue are not covering the costs of its traditional cohort of journalists.

The ease with which material can be placed in the public domain means that most of the information we read on digital platforms is produced by full-time paid journalists. Citizen, community or hobby bloggers who make little or no money from the content they publish, abound. But will they make it impossible to make a living from journalism? They certainly don't remove the need for journalists who live up to the kinds of ideals of the Committee for Concerned Journalists, whose co-ordinated, comprehensive and prime purpose is to 'provide citizens with accurate and reliable information they need to function in a free society'.[3]

Society needs journalists, so is it reasonable then for society as a whole to pay for their services? That's the principle behind the existence of the BBC. Would more of the same in print enhance citizens' ability to understand our world, contribute to it and thrive within it? Would they want to pay for it?

BBC journalism mainly deserves its reputation for quality and reliability but its public service remit comes with constraints which may or may not be reasonable.

Given the myriad alternatives to the BBC, we can live with its shortcomings and the adverse impact of political pressures in certain areas because there are many alternatives. What would the constraints be on a publicly funded newspaper?

Digging out news, finding out what people need to know takes time and effort. Turning it into meaningful information that engages an audience takes skill. Can we really rely entirely on the piecemeal, erratic efforts of well-meaning individuals running a blog as a sideline? They certainly enhance the overall insights into the world around us but they don't replace the work of journalists. How can we, or should we, pay for journalism?

NOTES

[1] See, for instance, Penny Vincenzi's tale of a 1970s magazine launch, The *Observer*, 11 September, 2011.

[2] Review of the NCE at: http://www.nctj.com/assets/library/document/n/original/nce_report_by_paul_watson-way_2011, pdf

[3] http://www.concernedjournalists.org

WEBLINKS

http://www.holdthefrontpage.co.uk; http://www.journalism.co.uk; http://www.guardian.co.uk/media; http://www.pressgazette.co.uk   All four sites are worth following for industry news and developments as well as specific job vacancy and training advice.

http://www.nctj.com   The National Council for the Training of Journalists runs its own journalism qualifications as well as accrediting individual courses.

http://www.ppa.co.uk/training   The Periodicals Training Council accredits magazine-orientated courses and provides the training framework for the PPA – the voice of professional publishers. Digital support and advice includes the Magscene app offering free advice for careers in magazines.

http://www.workthing.com   Lots of advice on job search as well as vacancies

http://www.opendemocracy.net   An interesting example of a not-for-profit site with philanthropic funding. Check out its business model and list of donors.

RECOMMENDED READING

Alden, Chris (2005) *In Print: a career in journalism*. London: Guardian Books.
Half-guide, half-directory focused on getting in but also where it might take you. Supported by a second half listing potential employers on every paid newspaper, national and local plus TV and radio stations.

Anderson, Chris (2006) *The Long Tail: how endless choice is creating unlimited demand*. London: Random House Business Books.
His original contribution to 'the new economics of culture and commerce', which takes an optimistic view of the opportunities in a digital world. He has written more since so check out his follow-up publications.

Beckett, Charlie (2008) *Super Media: Saving journalism so it can save the world*. Oxford: Wiley-Blackwell.
A really good read conveying the 21st century benefits of the 'networked' journalist.

Bull, Andy (2007) *The NCTJ Essential Guide to Careers in Journalism*. London: Sage.
Books of specific careers advice date rapidly but there is much still of value here with snapshots of individual career paths as well as entry-level guidance. More up-to-date information on individual accredited training programmes is available directly from the NCTJ.

Conboy, Martin (2011) *Journalism in Britain: a historical introduction*. London: Sage.
The curse of living in 'interesting times' is nothing new although the pace of change has arguably accelerated. Conboy's book provides thought-provoking historical contexts to our 21st century dilemmas over what it means to be a journalist and how we reach our audiences.

Franklin, Bob (ed.) (2006) *Local Journalism and Local Media – making the local news*. Oxford: Routledge.
Wide-ranging contributions on the challenges of regional UK media. Of particular relevance here are Peter Cole's chapter on educating and training local journalists; Sara Hadwin on the work of a local newspaper editor; and Ros Bew on freelancing.

Franklin, Bob and Mensing, Donica (ed.) (2011) *Journalism Education, Training and Employment*. Oxford: Routledge.
Interesting collection with a global dimension and notable contributions on internships, the 'long tail' applied to training and the impact of editors' preference for recruiting post-grads.

Hargreaves, Ian (2003) *Journalism: Truth of Dare?* Oxford: Oxford University Press.
A good general read for any aspiring journalist but check out in particular the chapter entitled 'Matt's Modem: Tomorrow's Journalist'.

Quinn, Stephen (2005) *Convergent Journalism an Introduction: writing and producing across the media*. London: Focal Press.

Randall, David (2007) *The Universal Journalist*. London: Pluto.
An in-print mentor for the thinking journalist with special reference here to the chapters on 'What makes a good reporter?' and 'How to be a great reporter'.

REFERENCES

Quinn, Stephen (2005) *Convergent Journalism an Introduction: writing and producing across the media*. London: Focal Press.

Randall, David (2007) *The Universal Journalist*. London: Pluto.

The Longman Practical Journalism Series

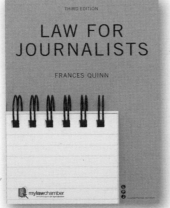

THIRD EDITION

LAW FOR JOURNALISTS

FRANCES QUINN

2011 | ISBN 13: 9781408254141

THE ONLINE JOURNALISM HANDBOOK

SKILLS TO SURVIVE AND THRIVE IN THE DIGITAL AGE

PAUL BRADSHAW & LIISA ROHUMAA

2011 | ISBN 13: 9781405873406

Di Hand & Steve Middleditch

DESiGN FOR MEDIA

A handbook for students and professionals in journalism, PR and advertising

PEARSON

2012 | ISBN 13: 9781405873666

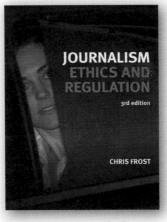

JOURNALISM ETHICS AND REGULATION

3rd edition

CHRIS FROST

2011 | ISBN 13: 9781408244685

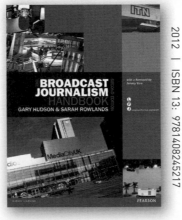

BROADCAST JOURNALISM HANDBOOK

GARY HUDSON & SARAH ROWLANDS

with a foreword by Jeremy Vine

MediaCityUK

PEARSON

2012 | ISBN 13: 9781408245217